ROCK ART OF THE AMERICAN INDIAN

ROCK AMERICAN

Written and illustrated by

CAMPBELL GRANT

ART OF THE INDIAN

For Lou, Gordon, Roxanne, Sheila, and Douglas

Since this book was first published, there has been a great increase of interest in American Indian rock art. Many new articles and books have been written, including *Canyon de Chelly: its people and rock art* by Campbell Grant in 1978. At least two organizations specializing in rock art have also come into being — American Rock Art Research Associates and Canadian Rock Art Research Associates. Both these groups have yearly seminars in different parts of the country, and their subject now has a large following. *Rock Art of the American Indian,* however, remains a classic work in the study of prehistoric American rock art, and so this facsimile of the original printing retains its important role in the literature. Copies may be ordered from the present publisher, address below:

a publishing and
distributing company
Since 1972

OUTBOOKS
217 Kimball Ave.
Golden, CO 80401

ISBN 0-89646-060-6

FOREWORD

With the proliferation of writings on primitive art, it is remarkable to note that this book by Campbell Grant is the first general study of rock art in North America. While rock art has always occupied a paramount position in studies of European and African prehistory, it has been almost totally absent from similar studies of North America. In fact, even recent general histories of primitive or prehistoric art convey the impression that the only significant contribution of this continent lies in the sculpture of the Northwest Coast and the pottery of the Southwest. Campbell Grant has done much to dispel this limited view. His numerous articles and above all his recent book, *The Rock Paintings of the Chumash*, are notable contributions to the study of primitive art.

The author combines in his approach to his subject the seriousness and objectivity of the anthropologist with the sensitivity and perceptiveness of the artist. This present study well illustrates the advantages to be gained by looking at primitive art from the points of view of both the art historian and the anthropologist. This is especially apparent in any attempt to discern broad stylistic patterns in time and space. It is the formal aspects of an art form, not its subject matter or technique, that make it possible to distinguish one style from another. The different stylistic modes of rendering an individual form basically establish and distinguish one style from another.

One myth dispelled by this study of North American rock art is that the primitive artist approaches his work with a high regard for the nature of his medium and for the surface upon which it is placed. In every instance in North America where a single style is represented in both painted and engraved examples, the artist's major concern has been to render the form in as identical a fashion as possible, and to minimize or to gloss over differences in technique. Thus technique was a means for the artist to realize subject matter through form; it did not form an essential element of the expressive language of the painting or engraving.

Another theoretical problem that the author has touched upon is the fundamental question of the place of art-as-art in prehistoric societies. The argument that "art for art's sake" did not exist within prehistoric societies is in reality meaningless. From ethnological studies of primitive cultures, it is obvious that all groups shared a basic aesthetic sensibility. A vast majority (perhaps all) of the material objects manufactured by man contain an aesthetic element to one degree or another. This is especially true in primitive cultures. In some instances the aesthetic element appears as a conscious addition, something added to the primary function of the object; in other cases it is so completely interwoven that the primary function and the aesthetic element are essentially one.

The question to be asked then is not whether "art for art's sake" existed in primitive society, but rather what form the art assumed and what the function of art was within a given society. Using the term religious in its broadest sense, there can be little doubt, as Campbell Grant points out, that the prime function of most North American rock art was ritualistic. At the same time, though, one should not overlook the fact that through its use of a visual form, each painting or engraving also acquired an aesthetic content. Thus one can readily see how closely interwoven are the inquiries of the anthropologist and the art historian into primitive art. If one is to look into the function of art in a primitive or prehistoric society, as the anthropologist does, he must first understand the basic nature of man's aesthetic sensibility, and then he must understand the form, i.e., the style, through which this sensibility has been expressed. It is the task of the art historian to provide an understanding of this aesthetic sensibility and of how it has been realized in form.

It also is hoped that this book will provoke other anthropologists and art historians to devote more serious study to this neglected aspect of North American primitive art. As Campbell Grant has indicated, there are really few areas in North America that have been thoroughly recorded, let alone thoroughly studied. Nor have there been any penetrating studies of the movements and extreme intermixing of styles that occurred in North America. There is as well the fascinating subject of sources, especially the diffusion of many basic elements northward from Mexico.

This study by Campbell Grant of the rock art of North America is then an excellent and perceptive example of how the disciplines of anthropology and art history may be combined to produce a meaningful picture of an extremely significant aspect of man's prehistoric past.

DAVID GEBHARD

University of California, Santa Barbara

PREFACE

In 1960, I saw my first rock painting in the rugged San Rafael Mountains near Santa Barbara, California. With the support of the Santa Barbara Museum of Natural History, I undertook the job of recording all such sites in the region. In three years of intensive field work, the number of known rock-art sites was raised from 17 to over 80. Later the study was expanded to include all of California and some adjoining states. This work was supported by grants from the National Science Foundation and resulted in a number of articles on the subject.

In the fall of 1964, I was asked by the editors of Thomas Y. Crowell Company if I would consider doing a book on the rock art of North America. My immediate reaction was to turn down the idea. The information necessary to put together such a project was simply not available. However, with considerable misgivings, I agreed to explore the literature and to see if it would be possible to obtain the many photographs that would be required. My two prime needs were information on site locations and picture material. Hundreds of letters were sent off to universities, museums, historical and archaeological societies, national parks and monuments, and many individuals, some of whom had written articles and others of whom had collections of photographs. The response was overwhelming. Armed with the information I received, I took a 12,000-mile trek through the country visiting sites, photographing and taking notes. But even such a trip was not nearly enough to cover the subject. I still had to depend in great part on the firsthand information and photographs of others who had done work in the field.

Before I was through, I had become deeply indebted to a great many people. Without their help, this book would not have been possible.

I am very grateful to the following people who took the time to answer my questions, lend books, give articles and reprints, and supply me with the all-important photographs: Donald N. Abbott, C. Melvin Aikens, Robert Babcock, Eric Barney, Roland E. Beschel, Clark W. Brott, William J. Buckles, H. Thomas Cain, Carl H. Chapman, David L. Cole, Carl Compton, Stuart W. Conner, Harold Cundy, Joseph Doctor, Frank Fryman, Jr., Robert E. Greengo, Gutorm Gjessing, Henry Hadlock, Roderick Haig-Brown, W. N. Irving, Frank M. Jones, Tim Jones, Frederica de Laguna, Sherman P. Lawton, Douglas Leechman, R. S. MacNeish, Charles R. McGimsey, Carling Malouf, Irving M. Peithman, William J. Schaldach, Carl Schuster, Agnes Sims, Ivar Skarland, James L. Swauger, Raymond H. Thompson, Spencer A. Waters, Henry Weldon, Joe Ben Wheat, Warren Wittry, and H. M. Wormington.

In addition, I am indebted to the following people who furnished photographic material: Mrs. Heber Bennion, Jr., Dean R. Brimhall, Carl Browall, Joan Colbrook, Katherine Capes, Harold S. Colton, John E. Cook, Dorothy Dancker, Edward B. Danson, Alfred E. Dittert, Jr., Henry During, Erle Stanley Gardner, James C. Garner, Jeanne B. Hillis, Howard Hughes, Carl E. Jepsen, Merritt S. Johnston, Thomas F. Kehoe, Edward L. Keithahn, Olive Kelsall, Kenneth E. Kidd, Monroe P. Killy, Paul W. Klammer, Clement W. Meighan, Franklin V. Montford, Thomas Mulhern, Dorris L. Olds, Choral Pepper, Jean M. Pinkley, Velma Pontoni, Annie Sanders, Polly Schaafsma, Earl M. Semingsen, James Sleznick, Jr., Dean Snow, Christy G. Turner, Ronald Wauer, Merle W. Wells, Harry Wills, and Thomas A. Witty.

I am especially grateful to Frank Magre for making available his unpublished work on the rock drawings of Missouri; to Selwyn Dewdney, whose Canadian studies made the Northern Woodland section possible; and to Robert F. Heizer of the University of California, who has patiently answered endless questions over a period of years. John J. Cawley, Donald Martin, and Dale Ritter were especially helpful in furnishing me with site records and many fine photographs. Throughout the project, I was aided by the National Park Service, the U.S. Geological Survey, and the National Museum of Canada.

I am particularly indebted to the late Dr. Donald Scott of the Peabody Museum and David Gebhard of the University of California, Santa Barbara, leading authorities on prehistoric rock drawings, for their reading and checking the manuscript and for their many suggestions.

Finally, I am very much obliged to Barbara Lawrence, who typed and checked the various drafts of the manuscript from my almost illegible originals.

All text drawings and photographs without credit lines are by the author.

CONTENTS

PART I: THE ARTISTS AND THEIR ART   1

   1 Background   3
   2 Techniques   12
   3 Styles   18
   4 Interpretation   28
   5 Rock Art as Art   40
   6 Dating   43
   7 Important Design Motifs   54
   8 Methods of Recording   68
   9 Preservation of Sites   74

PART II: ROCK ART AREAS   79

   10 The Far North   81
   11 The Northwest   83
   12 The Columbia-Fraser Plateau   92
   13 The Great Basin   100
   14 California   106
   15 The Southwest   115
   16 The Great Plains   130
   17 The Eastern Woodland   136
   18 The Northern Woodland   145

   Conclusions   151
   Notes   153
   Suggested Reading   155
   Bibliography   156
   Index   171

PHOTOGRAPHS AND DRAWINGS

Red, white, and black painting, California   3

Pecked drawing, southeastern California   5

Black and red painting, Texas   6

Scratched drawings of moose, Nova Scotia   7

Red Eskimo painting, Alaska   8

Red painting, Durango   10

Incised animals, southern Wyoming   11

Red painting, California   12

Pecked animal, Arizona   13

Abstract paintings in black, California   14

Abstract pecking, Arizona   18

Red painting, Texas   19

Red painting, Sonora   20

Red painting of cow moose and calf, Ontario   21

Red painting of killer whale, Alaska   23

Linear patterns in red, California   24

Pecked drawing of horse, Utah   24

Stylized pecked figures, Utah   24

Abstract curvilinear pecked designs, California   25

Pecked abstract rectilinear anthropomorphs, California   26

Incised drawings of horsemen and shields, South Dakota   26

Pit-and-groove markings, west-central Nevada   26

Pecked figure, Wyoming   28

Puberty rites painting in red, California   30

Pecked figures, New Mexico   31

Pecked drawing of sea monster, Alaska   32

Design suggesting kachina *mask, Utah*   33

Incised drawing of medicine animal, northeastern Nebraska   35

Incised battle scene, Alberta   36

Red painting of Mishipizhiw, Lake Superior Provincial Park   37

Red painting of crescent and round shapes, Arizona   38

Pecked Hopi clan symbols, Arizona   39

Pecked figure, Utah   40

Black painting of animals, Baja California   42

Red painting of man with gun, Texas   43

Horsemen and sheep, Utah   44

Pecked figure, California   45

Incised drawing of cranes, Wisconsin   46

Pecked spear throwers, eastern California   50
Hunters with atlatls and mountain sheep, California   51
Horsemen and buffalo in red, Texas   52
Dated Indian painting in red and black, British Columbia 53
Red painting of thunderbird, Texas   54
Red hand painting, northern Arizona   55
Hand and footprints, Utah   56
Scratched palm design, Nova Scotia   56
Pecked, incised, and painted bear tracks   57
Pecked serpent, New Mexico   58
Red painting of tattooed serpent, Texas   58
Pecked thunderbird, Iowa   58
Pecked drawing of thunderbird motif, Missouri   59
Pecked mountain sheep, Arizona   60
Hohokam pottery design of humped-back flute player   61
Portrait of Kokopelli, the humped-backed flute player,
    New Mexico   61
Black painting from rock shelter, Sonora   62
Pecked shield figure, southern Nevada   63
Incised, pecked, and painted shield figures   63
Detail of Pawnee buffalo robe painting   63
Pecked shield figure on basalt, New Mexico   64
Maze design near Hopi town, northern Arizona   65
Irish, Cretan, and Indian drawings of Minoan maze   66
Incised drawings of animals, West Virginia   67
Pecked bear prints, Idaho   68
Pecked drawings on boulder, West Virginia   70
Author photographing paintings in Sonora   71
Incised drawings being chalked for photography   71
Sample form for recording field notes   72
White painting near Coyote, Coahuila   74
Polychrome painting, California, as it appeared in 1894 75
Detail of same site after vandalism by gunfire   75
Elaborate vandalism, New Mexico   76
Pecked drawings, Maine   77
Pecked scroll, Alaska   81
Eskimo pictographs in red, Alaska   81
Pecked human faces, Alaska   82
Pecked mask designs, Alaska   82
Red painting, British Columbia   83
Pecked mythological creatures, southeastern Alaska   84

ILLUSTRATIONS
XII

Pecked sea monster on boulder, southeastern Alaska	85
Stylized head painting with coppers, British Columbia	85
Stylized figures pecked on bedrock, British Columbia	86
Beach boulders with masklike designs, British Columbia	87
Pecked drawings of sea monsters, Vancouver Island	88
Fish shapes on boulder, Vancouver Island	88
Killer whales and masks on granite, Olympic National Park	89
Head of mythical woman ruler, Oregon	90
Red painting, Washington	92
Bear tracks and stylized figures, British Columbia	93
Red paintings near Lytton, British Columbia	94
Red painting, northeastern Washington	94
Stylized and abstract drawings, Washington	95
Elk and mountain sheep, Washington	96
Mountain sheep panel salvaged before flooding, Washington	96
Bear tracks, game animals, and humans, Idaho	97
Pecked animal, California	100
Concentric circles with traces of red paint, Oregon	101
Polychrome designs inside a lava tube, northeastern California	102
Pecked figures on basalt, California	102
Mountain sheep, California	103
Abstract pecked designs, west-central Nevada	103
Red painting, California	104
Brown and white painting, California	106
Red and white painting, California	107
Hands on smoke-blackened wall, California	108
The Painted Cave, near Santa Barbara, California	109
Polychrome panel at Carrizo Plains, California, in 1894	110
Red Chumash painting, California	110
Red, white, and black painting, California	111
Maze pecked on granite, California	112
Red, black, and white Yokuts painting, California	112
Fret and mazelike painting in red, California	113
Red painting, California	114
White painting, Cave Valley, Utah	115
Ceremonial figures on sandstone cliffs, Utah	116
Life-sized figures pecked on sandstone, Utah	117
Brown and white anthropomorph, Utah	118
Mummylike figures in red-brown, Utah	119

Pecked mastodon, Utah 119
Pueblo-type figures, northeastern New Mexico 120
Navajo drawing, northwestern New Mexico 120
Corn plant and Navajo yei pecked on sandstone,
     New Mexico 121
Navajo yei painting, New Mexico 121
Shield motifs, New Mexico 122
Abstract pecked design, Texas 123
Pecked design, Arizona 124
Fabric or pottery designs, Arizona 125
Great Basin–type drawings, Arizona 125
Red and white anthropomorphs, Sonora 127
Large polychrome figures, Baja California 127
Pecked drawing, Sinaloa 128
Deeply pecked design, Coahuila 128
Pecked designs, Durango 129
Incised warrior on horse, Alberta 130
Red painting along buffalo migration route, Alberta 131
Pit-and-groove carvings, southern Alberta 131
Pecked supernatural beings, northwestern Wyoming 132
Pecked anthropomorphs, Wyoming 133
Naturalistic horses and riders, Kansas 134
Stylized incised figures, Kansas 135
Pecked footprints and abstract designs, South Dakota 135
Bird with speech symbol, eastern Missouri 136
Pecked footprints, Ohio 137
Pecked figures, Minnesota 138
Designs on limestone boulder, northeastern Missouri 138
Painting of bilobed arrow, Missouri 138
Pecked fertility symbols, Missouri 138
Figures on limestone bedrock, northeastern Missouri 138
Drawings of fish and deer, northeastern Missouri 139
Meandering patterns on steatite, North Carolina 139
Incised stone tablet, Tennessee 141
Animals, tracks, and anthropomorphs, Pennsylvania 142
Pecked designs on Dighton Rock, Massachusetts 142
Algonquin thunderbird and other figures, Pennsylvania 143
Red and yellow painting, Alabama 143
Red painting of caribou, Saskatchewan 145
Buffalo transmitting power to man, Saskatchewan 147
Female figure, possibly shaman, northern Saskatchewan 148
Design by Mimac Indians, Nova Scotia 149
Pecked mythical fish, Vancouver Island 156

MAPS

Rock art sites in North America (upper section) 16
Rock art sites in North America (lower section) 17
North American rock art styles 22
Rock art areas of North America 80
Distribution of rock paintings in the Canadian Shield
  area 146

Part I

THE ARTISTS AND
THEIR ART

1 BACKGROUND

In the summer of 1879, Marcelino de Sautuola, an amateur archaeologist, was excavating at the entrance to the cave of Altamira in northern Spain. His five-year-old daughter, playing inside, looked up at the roof of the cavern and discovered the now celebrated paintings of bison made during the last ice age by Paleolithic cave-dwelling hunters.

This discovery led to many others in southern France and northern Spain and the study of rock drawings began. The paintings and engravings were almost invariably of long-extinct animals like the mammoth and woolly rhinoceros, and the earliest may be nearly 30,000 years old.

The published descriptions of these finds by the pioneer investigator Henri Breuil created a worldwide interest in the subject of rock art and spectacular new discoveries have been made in many lands—the great Tassili complex of drawings in the Sahara Desert, the beautiful animal paintings in central and south Africa, and the weird *wondjina* and X-ray pictures from Australia. All these have been described in handsomely illustrated books.

It is curious that North American rock art is practically unknown to the general reading public. The existence of innumerable rock drawings in the western states was often noted in the writings of the early explorers and actually many articles and a few books have been written on the subject. Unfortunately, however, most of these are buried in obscure scientific publications, available only to the researcher, or are in local newspaper articles or back issues of a few magazines, particularly *Arizona Highways* and *Desert Magazine*.

This book is an attempt to synthesize present knowledge on the subject. The study has entailed a thorough search of the literature, many personal communications with investigators, and considerable field work.

Red, white, and black painting, Caliente Range, California.

3

Unfortunately a single volume on such a complex subject can serve only as an introduction to a much neglected part of our country's heritage.

Many of the points covered in this book, particularly those dealing with age and interpretation, are debatable and as new evidence is turned up, present views will change to fit such evidence.

Scattered through the rocky section of North America are great numbers of curious paintings and carvings. Many of the pictures are done with great care and skill—others are mere scrawls. In some regions the drawings are highly abstract while in others the dominant style is realistic. The working surface is usually granite, sandstone, or basalt, though rock art has been found on almost every kind of stone in the country.

The existence of rock art in North America was noticed by many of the early explorers. Father Jacques Marquette, exploring down the Mississippi in 1673, described several painted monsters on a cliff near the present site of Alton, Illinois. Dighton Rock in Massachusetts, covered with strange designs, has been studied and argued over since the first drawings were made of it in 1680. Father Eusebio Kino described and mapped the "Painted Rocks" (actually engravings) near Gila Bend, Arizona, in 1711, and in 1776 the explorer Father Silvestre de Escalante, attempting to find a land route from Mexico to Monterey, saw carved rock figures in western Colorado. As settlers traveled through the mountains of the Southwest in the early nineteenth century, great numbers of drawings on rocks were noted.

The first serious scientific study of American rock art was made by Colonel Garrick Mallery in 1886. This "preliminary paper," *Pictographs of the North American Indians*, ran to 256 pages and discussed picture making by Indians on all sorts of materials—stone, wood, bone, and skin. Seven years later Mallery produced his magnum opus, the monumental *Picture Writing of the American Indian*—822 pages of scholarly research, of which about a quarter was devoted to rock art.

This formidable volume, issued by the Bureau of American Ethnology, became (and still is) the foremost authority on the subject and until the present no further attempt has been made at a broad study. There has been a great deal of work on specific sites and regional complexes but such work, with some notable exceptions, has been confined to scientific literature. A few leading archaeologists, like Robert F. Heizer and Clement Meighan of the University of California, have been actively attacking the subject for a number of years, and *Prehistoric Rock Art of Nevada and Eastern California*, by Robert Heizer and Martin Baumhoff, published in 1962, is a major work on the rock pictures.

Many professional archaeologists in the United States, however, have been avoiding the problems raised by rock-art sites because of the difficulty of correlating the rock art with specific native cultures. Since there has always been more than enough digging to be done at important sites, the consideration of the rock drawings has been continually shelved for the future. The reluctance of professionals to enter the field has brought workers into the vacuum from amateur groups, and valuable local site surveys have been published by many state and county archaeological societies.

Since the publication of Mallery's great work, many thousands of sites have been recorded west of the Mississippi; the number east of the Mississippi has grown little since his time. The recording of sites in Canada has hardly begun, and here again the field work is being conducted by tireless amateurs like Selwyn Dewdney, an artist from Ontario. In Mexico, where investigation of the superb high civilizations has beguiled the time and energies of professionals for generations, the humble rock pictures have been almost completely neglected. Although there must be many thousands of sites in northern Mexico (treated in the present work as part of the Southwest), there are only about a dozen slim articles on the subject.

It is not surprising that most of the rock pictures are found in the West. From the Rocky Mountains to the Pacific, the land mass is folded into innumerable rocky ranges cut by great river systems. Smooth stone surfaces for the artist's brush or stone chisel are to be found almost everywhere. This is the region through which passed the major continental migrations moving down into Mexico and South America and peoples of many culture patterns have been living in this land of rocks for many thousands of years.

The question that comes up most frequently is, Who made these strange and mysterious drawings on stone? Unhappily the long silence on the subject by the archaeologists has brought hordes of eager amateurs into the picture with endless fanciful explanations. All sorts of full-fledged Old World people are seen wandering about and leaving messages on stone—Greeks, Chinese, Romans, Egyptians. Even the long-suffering Lost Tribes of Israel are dragged in. "Lost Continents" such as Mu and Atlantis are related to rock pictures—books and articles are written in defense of the most absurd theories. Some enthusiasts spend their time trying to decipher the "writings," believing that somewhere a key exists that will unlock fabulous secrets usually connected with lost treasures. Many rock drawings are seen as maps to such sites; others are Masonic symbols or zodiac signs. There is almost no pseudoscientific nonsense that has not at some time been staunchly upheld by the incurably imaginative "researchers."

Pecked drawing from Black Canyon, southeastern California. From photograph by John Cawley.

These people all have one thing in common—they conduct their investigations in reverse. They have a pet theory and then look for evidence to support it, discarding anything that seems to disprove the cherished idea. One such person who had spent many years in pursuit of rock drawings and their meaning recently wrote that he had never read any books on the subject as this would have interfered with his research! These amateur experts are loath to accept a simple explanation. The idea that an ordinary Indian would spend considerable time pecking out an intricate design in hard stone to help insure his wife's bearing him a healthy man-child is too humdrum. No consideration is given by these people to the fact that the American Indian did not think as we are trained to and he did not interpret his ideas as we do. His world was largely a world of the supernatural and he often pictured unseen beings and forces on stone.

The rock pictures in North America were the creations of the American Indian and no one else. As any understanding of American rock art must be based on some knowledge of its creators, it will be well to start at the beginning.

The North America of 20,000 years ago was a hunter's paradise. The familiar big-game animals, such as moose, caribou, mountain sheep, buffalo, musk-ox, and elk, were here in countless numbers and with them were many animals now extinct, such as the giant ground sloth, the woolly mammoth, the mastodon, a giant buffalo, the horse, and the camel. The only thing missing was the hunter. Man had not appeared in the New World.

The Pleistocene or Ice Age was drawing to a close but the Wisconsin ice sheet still covered most of the northern half of the continent, extending as far south as central Iowa. About 15,000 years ago, the ice sheet began its final retreat, opening up an ice-free route through the Mac-Kenzie River valley. The great masses of water withdrawn from the oceans to build the glaciers had lowered the sea level several hundreds of feet and where Alaska and Siberia nearly meet at the Bering Strait, a broad land bridge connected the continents. The stage was set in North America to receive visitors. Let us see what was happening in Siberia.

The greater part of Siberia remained unglaciated during the Wisconsin and here we must look for the first people to enter the New World. Doubtless they were small bands of hunters, following the big game as it moved seeking forage. Some time before 10,000 B.C., some such group of fur-clad hunters went farther east than ever before and so began the population of North America. The American "Indian" had arrived.

The earliest archaeological finds of man in the New World show definite Australoid characteristics—low brow ridges, protruding jaws, and long, narrow head—certainly a far cry from the hawk-nosed Mongoloid of the Western Plains. Down through the centuries, small groups of hunters straggled over from Siberia and many diverse strains have been

Black and red painting, Concho County, Texas. Redrawn from A. T. Jackson.

Scratched drawings of moose, Kedgemakooge Lake, Nova Scotia. Redrawn from Garrick Mallery, 1893.

identified. Harold Gladwin, in *Men Out of Asia*, identifies five migrations —Australoid, Negroid, Algonquian, Eskimo, and finally Mongoloid, the type that was to blend with and dominate all others. Though other writers are far less explicit than Gladwin, it is certain that the present-day Indian is a composite, ranging from tall and thin to short and stout, with a skin coloring from dark brown to nearly white. But, from the Arctic Ocean to Tierra del Fuego, Indians all share one dominant Mongoloid characteristic—straight black hair.

There were several routes open to the first migrants. Most of Alaska, surprisingly, was unglaciated and the hunting parties could have followed the game up the Yukon River to the MacKenzie drainage then south to the Western Plains. Another possibility was to follow the Alaskan coastline north, travel east along the Brooks Range to the mouth of the MacKenzie, then south to the plains. A third route would skirt the ice shelf along the Pacific coast (human remains on Santa Rosa Island off the southern California coast have been dated at over 10,000 years old).

The country seen by the first arrivals south of the ice sheets was profoundly different from what we know today. During the latter half of the Wisconsin glaciation, a period of heavy and widespread rains known as the "Great Pluvial" created many huge lakes, particularly in the Great Basin. Only a tiny fraction of ancient Lake Bonneville, at one time the size of Lake Superior, remains—the Great Salt Lake. Forests and immense grasslands covered the Southwest, creating conditions for big game similar to those still found in central Africa.

As the glaciers continued their retreat, the oceans rose and the land bridge connecting the continents was covered by water. But the crossing was still possible by boat or on foot when the winter ice formed, and the migrations continued. Driven by pressure from people to the south or following game, the hunters continued to move into the New World. The major movement was along the slopes of the Rockies, fanning out to east and west, or south along the Sierra Madre Mountains in Mexico,

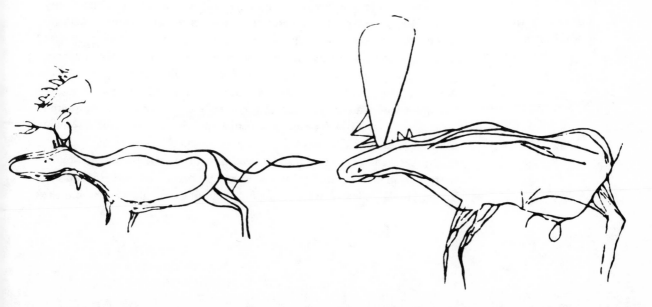

through Central America into South America and finally to Tierra del Fuego.

The first hunters of whom we have definite knowledge made excellent tools and projectile points. Their chief weapon was the spear, hand thrown or cast with a spear thrower or *atlatl*—the bow was a much later introduction. With this puny arsenal, early man hunted and in his camp refuse we find the bones of many extinct animals. Through the radio-carbon-dating method, we know roughly when some of these animals died out. Most—including the native horse and camel—disappeared between 10,000 and 8,000 years ago, with a terminal date of around 6,000 years ago for the mastodon.[1] What caused this great extinction is unknown but changing climate and hunting pressure from man must have played a large part. As the climate in the Southwest grew drier, and the game scarcer, many hunting groups were reduced to deer, mountain sheep, and rabbits. Their diet was augmented by edible seeds and roots and a food-gathering culture began. There is a milling stone from this period dated about 5400 B.C.

According to a recent article by Dr. Richard S. MacNeish, an astonishing thing was taking place about 5000 B.C. in the Valley of Tehuacan, in south-central Mexico—the people had discovered agriculture.[2] Cave remains show that several varieties of beans, chili, squashes, and, most important, corn, had been domesticated. Similar remains of corn have been found in Bat Cave, Arizona, and radiocarbon dating indicated they were between 4,000 and 5,000 years old. With this development village life was first established and it became prevalent throughout most of the Southwest at an early period.

At least four thousand years ago a new group of people began to move into the New World. Eventually these Indians occupied the forested country from Puget Sound to Newfoundland, all sharing a common Algonquian-language stock.[3] Cord-marked pottery, the bow, and the domesticated dog were introduced sometime during this period. These newcomers were hunters, creating a Woodland culture in Canada and the northern United States. Later they augmented this with agriculture in the areas where climate permitted. The country was filling up and groups of people were moving around or being pushed out by stronger groups seeking greener pastures. The Eskimo arrived fully equipped to face life along the bleak Arctic coasts and here they remain today. Other people settled in the Northwest and may have come by sea. They shared some rather extraordinary things with the Maoris of New Zealand—huge sailing canoes, plank houses with gable ends, and feather mantles.[4]

Uto-Aztecan-speaking nomads moved into the Great Basin, the Southwest, and on into Mexico. Prominent in this group were the Shoshone, Paiute, Hopi, Tanoan Pueblo, and Comanche in the United States and the

Red Eskimo painting, Cook Inlet, Alaska. Redrawn from Frederica de Laguna, 1933.

Aztec in Mexico. Tribes sharing the Athabascan language pushed down into northwestern Canada where they are still found. By A.D. 900 two vigorous tribes from this area, the Navajo and Apache, had left the main group and were moving down into the Southwest.

A brief look at the known prehistory of the Southwest is important as this area is one of the major rock-art regions in North America. Through intensive study of the ruins, many of which have been dated by tree-ring counts from building timbers, and identification of cultures through pottery association, building techniques, and artifacts, we know a good deal about the Southwest from about the birth of Christ to the coming of the whites.

At about A.D. 200 small groups of hunters and foragers, and primitive agriculturists raising corn, squash, and cotton, were living in cave shelters from southern Nevada to western Texas. The term Anasazi (Navajo for "the old ones") is usually applied to the people living in the "Four Corners" area, where Utah, Arizona, New Mexico, and Colorado meet. Their early phase, called Basketmaker, later evolved into the Pueblo culture. People with much the same Basketmaker culture were living in the upper Gila drainage and as far east as western Texas. All made baskets but true pottery had not yet appeared. Not long after A.D. 200 new ideas were gradually introduced, possibly by people moving in from the plains to the east. They brought the bow and arrow, pottery, and the rectangular earth lodge.

By A.D. 600 the Anasazi had occupied more territory but were still confined to the general area of the Four Corners. The foragers of southeastern Arizona were in contact with people from Mexico who brought, among other things, beans, a new type of corn, and polished pottery. The movement of people and the assimilation of new ideas continued for many years. By 700 the Hohokam migration from Mexico had introduced a relatively high culture to the Southwest. These people had advanced ideas on canal irrigation, built large ball courts, made excellent decorated pottery, and carved skillfully in stone. By 900 people still lived in small one-family houses and the communal multistoried pueblo had not yet appeared. Various peoples like the Mimbres, Mesa Verde, and Hohokam continued to develop their distinctive cultures. The life was a peaceful agricultural one but pressure was beginning to come from the outside, forcing some of the peripheral settlements to be abandoned. Nomadic Athabascan tribes—the restless, aggressive Navajos and Apaches—were moving down along the Rockies from western Canada.

As the pressure increased, scattered groups began to concentrate toward the north in refuge areas where the first fortresslike pueblos were built, culminating in such great structures as Pueblo Bonito. About 1100, as the Athabascan invasion grew, the southwestern tribes went through an intensive period of pueblo building, although many of them were abandoned after a few years. The greatest effort of the harassed pueblo builders was at Mesa Verde, where the spectacular ruins testify to the need to fortify for survival. Unfortunately the actual attacks must have taken place away from the protection of the pueblos when the people were working their fields in small groups. By 1300 even Mesa Verde had been abandoned and the pueblo people were concentrated in three main areas—the Hopi villages on Antelope Mesa in Arizona, the Zuñi villages in New Mexico, and the Tanoan and Keresan pueblos on the upper Rio Grande. The southern tribes had been destroyed or were moving into the Sierra Madre Mountains of Chihuahua and Sonora. Aside from the fortlike pueblo settlements, the country was solidly in the hands of the Navajos and the Apaches when Coronado came through in 1540.

During the eighteenth century contact between the whites and the Indians had been made almost everywhere and it is possible to draw a broad picture of the Indians from northern Canada to northern Mexico.

The Eskimos along the far northern coasts had a culture tied to the sea and the hunting of large sea mammals, but the caribou was an important big-game animal during its seasonal migrations. The Athabascan and Algonquian tribes of the northern forests and the tundra country were hunters who depended heavily on the large game mammals—the moose, elk, musk-ox, and, above all, the caribou. In the Northwest, the Indians lived in permanent villages on the salmon rivers and their culture was dependent on harvesting this fish.

In California, there were many large, permanent villages where people lived by seed gathering (especially the acorn), augmented by hunting and fishing. The Great Basin Indians lived as nomads, harvesting piñon nuts in the mountains and various seeds in the deserts. They were skillful hunters of deer, antelope, and mountain sheep. The plateau country drained by the mighty Columbia River is harsh and bleak except along the river courses and here the tribes lived in semipermanent villages, hunting most of the year and fishing during the seasonal salmon runs. In the Southwest, from the upper Colorado and Rio Grande rivers down into Mexico, the tribes continued to depend on agriculture, with corn the most important crop. Even the warlike Navajo did some corn raising but their life was being radically changed by two Spanish innovations— the horse and the domestic sheep. By raiding the ranches the Navajo became horsemen and nomadic herdsmen and the enormous flocks of sheep on their reservations today are still their main food source. In the early 1700's the acquisition of the horse had created a new way of life in the high desert and Great Plains. There the Indians evolved a Plains culture based entirely on buffalo hunting. The horse gave many tribes a mobility they had never dreamed possible. In the Eastern Woodland

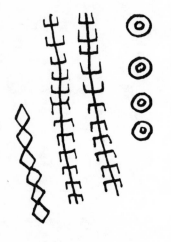

Red painting, Cerro Blanco de Covadonga, Durango. Redrawn from J. Alden Mason, 1961.

Incised animals, Lucerne Valley, southern Wyoming. Redrawn from Russ Grimshaw and Clyde May.

many people left their cornfields and pottery and the beginnings of a sedentary village life to become hunting and fighting nomads on the plains. Wandering hunters from the north and west converged on the grassland with its numberless buffalo now easy to hunt on horseback. Easy access to this inexhaustible food supply made the Plains Indians wealthy and independent.

In the southeastern Woodland where agriculture started about the time of Christ, the growing of corn never assumed the same importance that it had in the Southwest. Forests and streams provided abundant hunting and fishing and the ease of living led to large permanent settlements. Not long before the Spanish encountered them in 1540, these southeastern tribes had acquired some cultural traits that were astonishingly like a watered-down version of those found in the high culture centers of Middle America, including earth pyramids, feather mantles, a well-defined caste system, elaborate carving in stone, and, in certain areas, human sacrifice. Their culture was so far advanced over the northeastern Woodland Indians that they became known as the "Civilized Tribes."

In the northeastern Woodland, agriculture arrived late, about A.D. 1000 in the New England area, and the principal means of sustenance continued to be hunting. By the 14th century, a wedge of Iroquoian-speaking people from the Mississippi Valley had split the great Algonquian bloc as far north as the Saint Lawrence River.

These vigorous newcomers brought some astonishing new ideas. They formed what amounted to an Indian League of Nations, levying tribute from their less organized neighbors and controlling much of the northeastern United States until the coming of the whites. These people practiced agriculture, lived in stockaded villages, and had a social organization reminiscent of the Southeast and Middle America. North of the areas where corn would grow, hunting continued to be the way of life.

This was the picture of the "American Indian" when the white invasions began. These were the complex and varied peoples who painted and engraved the mysterious rock pictures sometime between 10,000 B.C. and the present. In subsequent sections, some partial answers will be given about the creators of rock art in specific areas. Enough data is at hand to make some valid conjectures on the late prehistoric and historic periods, but on the earlier material there is much that can never be known.

2 TECHNIQUES

Red painting, Tulare County, California. From photograph by Robert Luthey.

The terminology of rock art is confusing. In this country, two words—petroglyph (rock engraving) and pictograph (rock painting)—occur frequently in the literature. Some investigators reverse these definitions—others add petrograph and pictoglyph. In Europe the inclusive term is "rock art," with "rock painting" and "rock engraving" the subdivisions. There can be no confusion with this method and several authorities in the United States are now adopting it. In this book, I have mainly followed the European system, using petroglyph and pictograph only where it is more convenient or in reference to published works. Therefore, it will be well to get them straight at the start.

PETROGLYPH—AN ENGRAVING ON STONE

A drawing on stone that is pecked, incised (carved), scratched, or abraded, or a combination of these techniques.

Petroglyphs are the most common form of rock art in North America and they occur by the thousands, especially in the Southwest and the Great Basin area. Most petroglyphs are produced by rock pecking. This can be done in two ways—by striking the surface of the rock with a sharp piece of harder stone or, for more precise control, by chiseling the rock, using a hammer stone to pound on the stone chisel. The design is usually started with a series of dots joined into lines by continued pecking. Flat tones are indicated by close all-over pecking or by abrading the surface (rubbing or scraping with a harder stone).

The three rocks most frequently used are sandstone, volcanic basalt, and granite. All of these, especially in the desert regions, are subject to strong patination, a darkening of the surface caused by oxidization. Over a period of many years, some surfaces become blue-black, an effect

12

known as "desert varnish." When such a patinated surface is broken by the pecking stone, the original much lighter rock color is exposed, giving the design excellent contrast. In rare instances a wall is smoke-blackened and the design is made by removing the blackening over the design areas. In one California site the design is made by cutting through dark lichen to fresh stone.

On some rocks such as the softer sandstones and steatite, designs are incised or carved into the surface and with this technique, the lines are sometimes as deep as an inch or more. Another type of rock art usually listed under gravel petroglyphs is huge figures made on the ground by outlining the shapes with small stones or boulders. In the lower Colorado region of California and Arizona, there are giant animal and human figures made by removing certain stones from areas where all the stones are covered with a dark mahogany-colored desert varnish, thus creating designs in the light sand beneath. These great figures (one is 167 feet long) show up as yellowish-gray figures on a dark brown background. Somewhat similar figures were made in North Dakota, where small rocks were piled up to delineate the design.

PICTOGRAPH—A PAINTING ON STONE

Most of the rock paintings found in North America are painted in various shades of red, ranging from a bright vermilion to a dull brown-red. Sometimes they are in black and rarely in white, while in the regions where polychrome painting was done, a favorite combination was red, black, and white. In a few areas like the Four Corners country of the Southwest, western Texas, and the Chumash territory in southern California, some elaborate polychrome paintings were made with blue, green, and yellow added to the palette.

The enduring pigments used in the rock paintings were earth colors. The red was almost universally made from the iron oxide hematite. Certain tribes, like the Paiute of eastern California, enriched the color by heating the mineral in areas where a naturally brilliant earthy hematite was unavailable. Yellow was made from another iron oxide, limonite, and white from chalky deposits such as diatomaceous earth or minerals like gypsum and kaolin. There were a number of different sources for black, including manganese ore, charcoal, and roasted graphite. The greens and blues were probably derived from one or more of the copper ores so

Pecked animal, possibly a mountain lion, on sandstone, Petrified Forest National Park, Arizona. Photograph by Richard O'Hanlon.

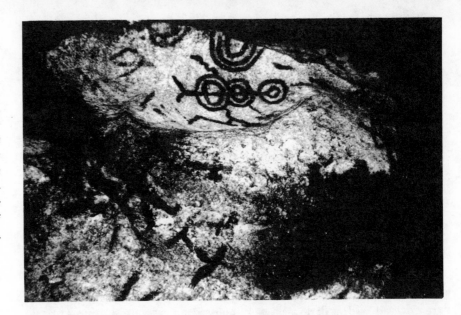

Abstract painting in black, Riverside County, California. This painting is in a cave above a Cahuilla village where Juan Bautista de Anza camped in 1775. A horseman in the same cave probably depicts one of Anza's men.

common in the desert country. In some areas where hematite was unavailable, burned clay was ground for pigment. In British Columbia, one method of producing red paint was by baking yellow ochre. In this process, yellow ochre was ground into powder and kneaded with water into balls about the size of walnuts. These were flattened into discs, and baked on a hot fire which converted the yellow ochre into red ochre.[1]

The earthy ores were ground fine in stone mortars and often molded into cakes for storage, to be available for body painting, rock painting, or any decorative use. For rock painting the pigment was reground and mixed with some sort of oil binder to give it permanence. The type of binder certainly varied from place to place but animal oils, blood, white of egg, and vegetable oils were all readily available and any would serve the purpose. The Yokuts of the San Joaquin Valley in California often used sap from the common milkweed *Asclepias* mixed with oil from the crushed seeds of the Chillicothe *Echinocystis*.

The application of the paint to the rock surface was usually done with brushes, some of which have been found in cave shelters. They were made from frayed ends of yucca, twigs or bound masses of fiber like that of the Amole *Chlorogalum*. Pointed sticks may have been used as applicators, and for some of the cruder paintings it is obvious that finger painting did the job. Occasionally the drawing was made directly on the rock with a piece of hematite or a lump of charcoal.

Small paint mortars, sea shells, and the like were used for palettes, and at the larger sites, small depressions were sometimes ground in the rock below the painting to hold colors, traces of which can still be seen.

DISTRIBUTION OF TECHNIQUES

The maps on pages 16 and 17 show the general location of rock-art sites in North America. There are many blanks, especially below the Rio

Grande, where great numbers of sites doubtless exist but the field work in that region has scarcely begun. In the United States only nine states have no recorded rock drawings—Delaware, Florida, Indiana, Louisiana, Mississippi, New Hampshire, New Jersey, South Carolina, and Vermont.

In areas where careful investigations have failed to locate any rock-art sites, there are two basic reasons for the lack—either no appropriate rock surfaces were available or there was no rock-drawing tradition. In Canada sites have been known in British Columbia for many years; more recently, Douglas Leechman and Selwyn Dewdney have been recording the rock art of Alberta, Saskatchewan, Manitoba, and Ontario. I have been able to verify only four sites in Quebec Province, five in Nova Scotia, and one in New Brunswick. So far, no discoveries have been made in Newfoundland or the Yukon.

The four main concentrations of rock art are in California, the Columbia Plateau, the Great Basin region, and the Southwest. The work of recording, especially in the Southwest, is very far from being complete yet several thousands of sites have been recorded. Robert F. Heizer has estimated that there may be 15,000 or more such sites in the western United States. It is not surprising that rock drawings are rare in the Great Plains area but even here paintings and incised drawings are found on the infrequent rock outcroppings. In contrast to the abundance of sites in the West, fewer than 200 rock art sites have been found east of the Mississippi.

The regions where the two basic techniques occur are remarkably well defined. Starting at the extreme northwest part of Alaska, Eskimo incised and pecked designs are found at the few known sites down to and including Kodiak Island. At the Eskimo sites in Cook Inlet and Prince William Sound, the rock art is painted. In southeastern Alaska and the adjoining coastal strip of British Columbia and Washington, the typical northwestern rock art is almost entirely pecked or incised. Inland sites from the Fraser River south to central Oregon and east in a broad zone to eastern Ontario are chiefly painted. In central North America from the Pacific to the Atlantic, pecked or incised designs predominate, with large concentrations of paintings in southern California and Utah. The last region includes southwestern Texas and northern Mexico, and the known sites are mainly painted.

In most of the areas containing rock art, both techniques occur but one or the other form is always dominant. In later chapters where each region is discussed separately, a more detailed breakdown of the two techniques will be shown. Fairly often both painting and carving occur in the same general locality and even at the same site. Rarely the two techniques are combined in the same design with the pecked or incised lines filled in with paint.

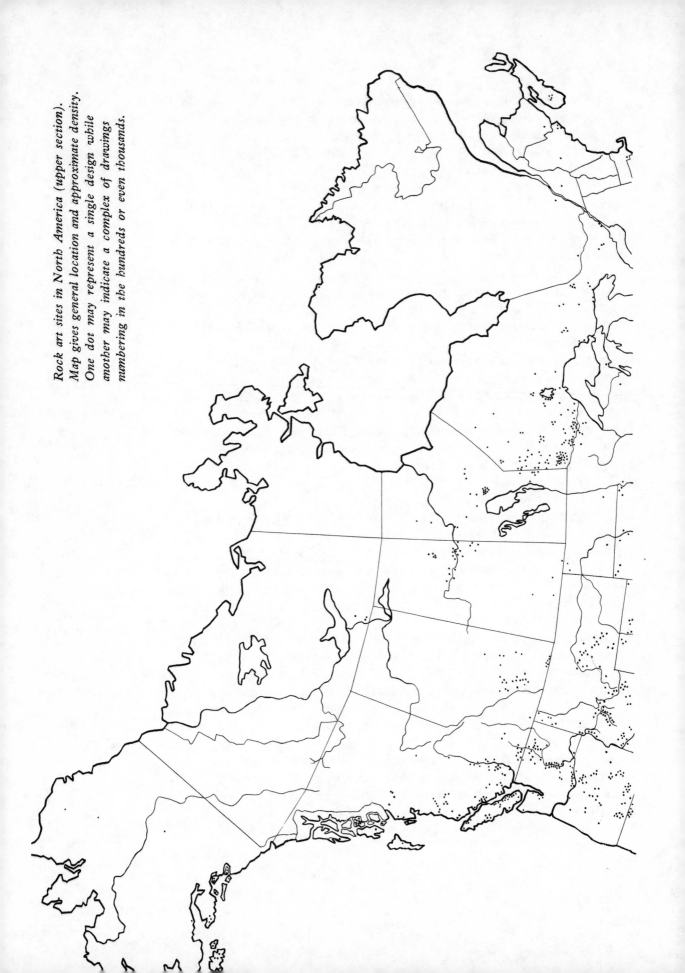

Rock art sites in North America (upper section). Map gives general location and approximate density. One dot may represent a single design while another may indicate a complex of drawings numbering in the hundreds or even thousands.

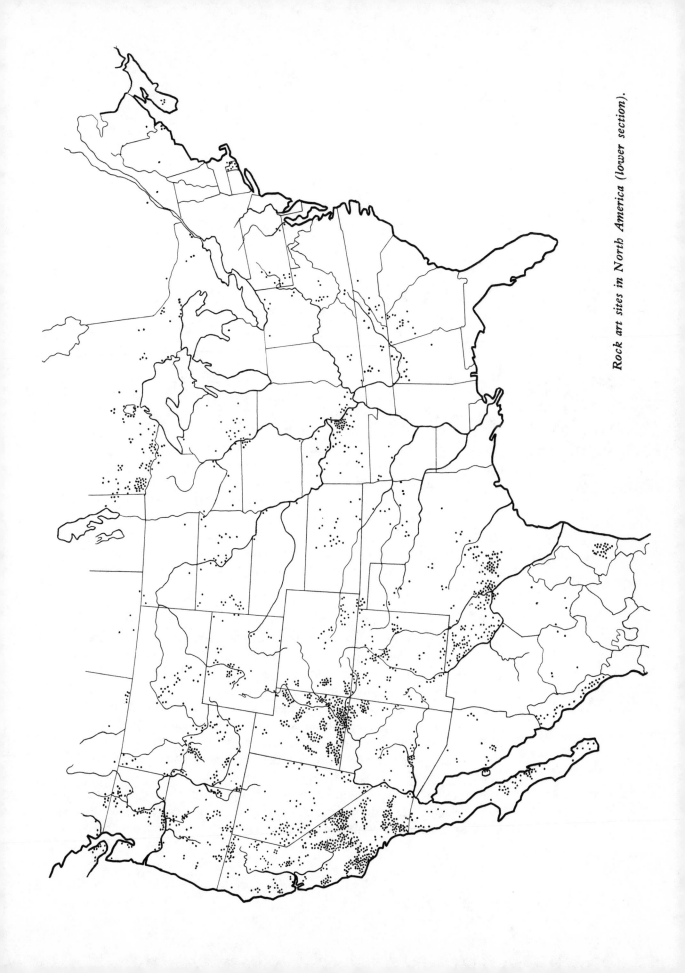

Rock art sites in North America (lower section).

3 STYLES

Abstract pecking, Wupatki National Monument, Arizona.

In the history of art there has been a noticeable tendency for forms to evolve from naturalistic, through stylized, to abstract. Any major deviation from this pattern is usually due to a strong new influence coming from outside. These art developments have occurred many times in different parts of the world and invariably they have occurred where peoples have been leading a sedentary existence in settled villages and cities. The art of the nomadic hunter on the other hand has a tendency to remain static. For countless centuries, the cave art of Paleolithic man continued to depict the major game animals and very little else. Mesolithic man in eastern Spain added the hunter himself to the scene but the beautiful paintings remained highly naturalistic. With the dawn of agriculture in the Near East, true village life began and new art forms appeared.

This generalization seems to work in the New World as well. The oldest examples of rock art are to be found in the petroglyphs of the Great Basin and the Southwest, where there are often as many as three or four designs superimposed one over the other. Of course it would have been ideal if a rock-art-producing people had lived at the same spot for thousands of years in complete isolation, allowing us to make a perfect reconstruction of their style changes and development. Unfortunately this never happened and we are faced with many puzzles that may never be properly explained. It is important to remember that though the Anasazi people of the Southwest remained in the same general area for a very long time, they were exposed to pressures from the outside and there were many migrations and shifts in population going on in the area, bringing not only new ideas but disruption or destruction of old patterns. Between 1958 and 1961, Christy Turner had a unique opportun-

18

ity to study the petroglyphs of the Glen Canyon area of the Colorado River before it was flooded by the waters of Lake Powell. He was able to distinguish five different styles in a chronological sequence through super-imposition, and association with ruins and pottery.[1]

David Gebhard has described four basic styles in his study of the petroglyphs of Wyoming.[2]

Type I	Small realistic animal and human drawings.
Type II	Nonrealistic outlined humanoid forms; animals remain realistic.
Type III	Large panels of highly stylized anthropomorphs; animals remain realistic.
Type IV (Historic)	Typical northern Plains Indian art—realistic humans, animals, especially the horse.

Here is a clear transition from a naturalistic style to an abstract approach, broken in late prehistoric or historic times by encroachment from the east—Plains Indian hunters with their realistic art tradition (although Gebhard has remarked that there is no way to prove that Types I, II, and III were all made by the same people). It is interesting to note that the animal drawings remain realistic through all four periods, reflecting a continuing dependence on hunting and hunting magic.

DISTRIBUTION OF STYLES

PRINCIPAL ROCK-DRAWING STYLES*

The areas in parentheses indicate regions where the style is concentrated. This listing is of necessity a great simplification of the problem. In some areas a number of these styles occur.

Painted	*Pecked or Abraded*	*Incised or Scratched*
Naturalistic (Northern Woodland, Columbia-Fraser Plateau, Southwest)	Naturalistic (Great Basin, Southwest)	Naturalistic (Great Plains)
Naturalistic Polychrome (Southwest, Great Plains)	Stylized (Northwest, Southwest, Great Plains)	
Stylized (California, Southwest)	Abstract Curvilinear (Great Basin)	

Red painting, Meyer Springs, Texas. From photograph by Donald Martin.

* For areas, refer to area map, page 80. The location of styles is shown in greater detail in the chart on page 150.

Painted	Pecked or Abraded	Incised or Scratched
Stylized Polychrome (Southwest)	Abstract Rectilinear (Great Basin, Southwest)	
Abstract Linear (California, Great Basin)	Pit and Groove (California)	
Abstract Polychrome (California)		

Sometimes these terms can be confusing, especially *stylized* and *abstract*. I give my interpretation:

Naturalistic   Done in a realistic or natural manner.

Stylized   Recognizable subjects rendered in a conventionalized or nonrealistic manner.

Abstract   Having little or no reference to the appearance of objects in nature.

At some sites, two or more styles are included in a single panel.

PAINTED (NATURALISTIC)

This style is confined to the regions dominated by a nomadic hunting economy. The paintings are mainly simple, rather crude representations of men and animals. In most areas the drawings are done in red alone, though black and white were sometimes added.

A major concentration is in the lake and river country of the Northern Woodland, where men in canoes, moose, elk, and buffalo are common subjects. There are occasional representations of mythological creatures like the water panther of the Ojibwa and the ubiquitous thunderbird. Some simple abstract elements occur but they are subordinate to the naturalistic style. This style continues westward through the prairies of western Canada to the Columbia-Fraser Plateau. Paintings feature many animals, chiefly deer and mountain sheep, with a few rare fish and buffalo. An abstract element, a semicircle with rays, often occurs with naturalistic forms. Human forms are abundant, especially twin figures, sometimes with linked hands.

An isolated area where naturalistic rock paintings were made is on the Alaskan coast east of Kodiak Island, where the Eskimo painted very simple pictures in red representing killer whales, various land mammals, and humans.[3]

PAINTED (NATURALISTIC POLYCHROME)

The finest examples of this style are found in two small areas in the Southwest. In the Canyon de Chelly, northeastern Arizona, there are

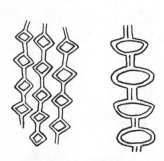

Red painting, Sierra Santa Teressa, Sonora.

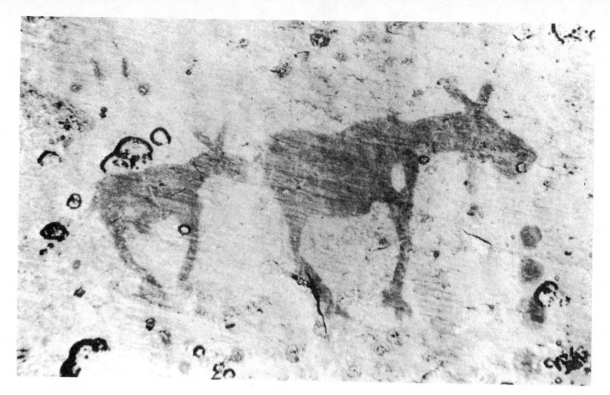

Naturalistic painting in red of cow moose and calf, Darky Lake, Quetico Provincial Park, Ontario. Photograph by Selwyn Dewdney.

many panels featuring horsemen, priests, antelope, and the like. These fine paintings are done by the Navajo and are reminiscent of Plains paintings on buffalo robes. In eastern New Mexico and western Texas there are a few sites with realistic polychrome animals by the Apache.

PAINTED (STYLIZED POLYCHROME)

This handsome style is confined to the Southwest. The best examples are from the Four Corners region, especially northern Arizona and northern New Mexico. The most characteristic figures are the square-shouldered, triangular-bodied *kachina* figures and the textile and pottery designs of the Anasazi. *Kachina* is the Hopi term for supernatural beings impersonated by men wearing masks during tribal ceremonies. The *kachinas* still play an important part in the religious life of these Indians. This style had a wide dispersal in the Southwest and there are examples from southern Nevada to southwest Texas.

Outstanding examples of this style are found in Navajo paintings from Carrizo and Largo canyons in northwestern New Mexico and the Sierra Santa Teressa near Hermosillo, Sonora.

PAINTED (ABSTRACT POLYCHROME)

The only concentration of this style, the finest flowering of rock painting in North America, is in the Santa Barbara-Kern-Tulare regions of

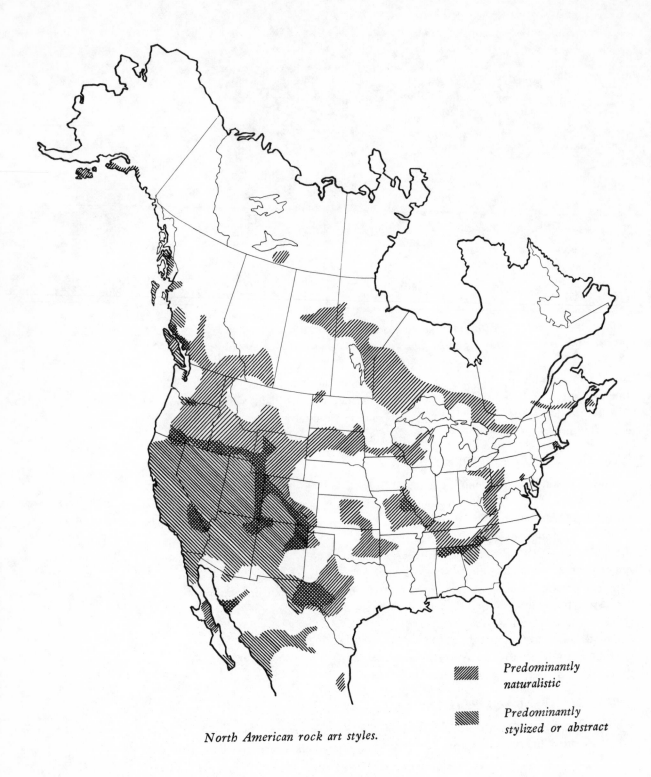

Predominantly
naturalistic

Predominantly
stylized or abstract

North American rock art styles.

California. Basically simple designs like concentric circles are elaborated in the most extraordinary and diverse ways. The main device is to put multiple outlines of contrasting colors around shapes. There is much use of dotted outline both by itself and to add complexity to already complex figures. There are many fanciful anthropomorphic and zoomorphic creatures. The most beautiful paintings are in the coast ranges of the Santa Barbara area but the Kern-Tulare or Sierra Nevada foothill region paintings are so similar in technique that there must have been a considerable exchange of ideas.

Red painting of killer whale, Cook Inlet, Alaska. Redrawn from Frederica de Laguna, 1933.

PAINTED (ABSTRACT LINEAR)

In the coastal ranges south of Los Angeles, there are many isolated boulders and small rock shelters where simple rectilinear red designs occur. There are few design elements, mainly zigzags, chevrons, and diamonds, and occasionally hand impressions. Along the western edge of the Great Basin (western Nevada and eastern California) there are a few sites with curvilinear designs. The elements are simple—concentric circles, rows of short lines, connected circles and bisected circles. The most striking examples of this style are found near Hermosillo, Mexico, where there are many thin-line drawings of great complexity suggesting textile designs.

PECKED (NATURALISTIC)

Of all realistic pecked designs, that of the mountain sheep appears most often and occurs over a very large area. It has been recorded from every mountainous region where the now rare species occurred, from eastern California to Texas and north into Montana. The animal is invariably drawn in profile but often the horns are drawn as if the head were turned to the front. At times just the head is shown front face. Many other animals like the buffalo, deer, coyote, and horse are pecked into sandstone and basaltic rocks. The bear was seldom attempted but was usually represented by the bear track. Human figures are nearly always drawn front view and look rather like gingerbread men. Even when holding a bow and arrow, the figure is rendered front view. On page 24 is a beautiful pecked rendering of a horse. This is probably a late Navajo drawing but is so unlike anything else in the country, it must reflect white-influenced school training. There are naturalistic pecked drawings in the Eastern Woodland featuring men, animals, birds, especially the thunderbird or men in thunderbird costume and many kinds of tracks.

PECKED (STYLIZED)

This type of rock drawing is concentrated in two widely separated regions—the Northwest and the Southwest. The Northwest pecked de-

Abstract linear patterns in red on granite near Poway, California. Photograph from the San Diego Museum of Man.

Pecked naturalistic drawing of a horse, probably Navajo, from the Glen Canyon region of the Colorado River, Utah. Site is now under water. Photograph from the Museum of Northern Arizona.

Stylized pecked figures near Moab, Utah. Photograph by Tom Mulhern.

signs are chiefly of supernatural beings, water monsters, and anthro-pomorphic figures. A characteristic design is the human head, often drawn without an outline and showing only eyebrows, eyes, nose, and mouth. This design tradition has been adopted by some Eskimo tribes in the region around Kodiak Island. Designs are on granite boulders and of necessity are deeply pecked. Many of the rocks are submerged at every high tide and yet the designs are still clearly visible.

In the Southwest, the most typical designs are *kachina* figures and masks, textile and pottery designs, and "shield" figures rather shallowly pecked on sandstone or basalt. The shield decorated with heraldiclike designs is widespread through the Plains, Southwest, and Great Basin. Often head, arms, and legs are added, giving a Humpty Dumpty effect. In the Fremont culture region of eastern Utah, there are extremely well executed, elaborate figures in ceremonial regalia.

PECKED (ABSTRACT CURVILINEAR)

This style (in which curved lines predominate) is found in both west-ern and eastern United States and Mexico but the greatest concentration is in the Great Basin. The most characteristic form is a sort of aimless

Abstract curvilinear pecked designs, Death Valley, California. Photograph by Donald Martin.

Pecked abstract rectilinear anthropomorphs, Petroglyph Canyon, Coso Range, California. Photograph by Donald Martin.

Incised naturalistic drawings of horsemen and shields, Cave Hills, South Dakota. Photograph from the South Dakota Department of Highways.

Pit-and-groove markings, west-central Nevada. Photograph by Donald Martin.

meandering line, but concentric circles, suns, dotted patterns, clusters of circles, and the like are common. Mountain sheep drawings and representations of *atlatls* are often found associated with this style.

PECKED (ABSTRACT RECTILINEAR)

The abstract rectilinear drawings (predominantly straight lines) are usually found in association with the abstract curvilinear style in the Great Basin and in the Southwest, and the straight-line elements are often superimposed on the curved-line designs and are of a later period. Design elements include rake and ladder shapes, textile designs, grids, various geometric shapes, humans, and bows and arrows. It is interesting to note the naturalistic mountain sheep is very often associated with abstract rectilinear petroglyphs as the only realistic element.

INCISED (NATURALISTIC)

This is the common style in the Northern Plains where the few available areas are of soft rocks, chiefly sandstone. Many of the pictures seem to be late prehistoric or historic and feature horsemen, buffalo, animal and bird tracks, shields and shield figures. The shield motif is recurrent in the Northern Plains as far north as Alberta. Many of the incised rock designs are reminiscent of typical late Plains drawings on skin. There are scattered examples in the Eastern Woodland but the style appears to be a late development reaching its peak after 1750 with the introduction of the horse and the creation of a Plains culture. In a small area in Nova Scotia there are drawings in a unique naturalistic style scratched in smooth slate.

PIT AND GROOVE (ABSTRACT)

These markings hardly qualify as rock art as there is rarely any feeling of pattern. They are circular pits, from one to two inches in diameter, seemingly pecked out of the rock at random, with deeply incised lines around and between the pits. They are rarely found in rock shelters but commonly occur on isolated large boulders. The few examples recorded in central Alberta Province are on glacial erratics—large blocks of quartzite carried south more than 800 miles by glacial action.

The largest number of examples of this style are in west-central California where they are the most abundant type of pecked rocks. In a few instances curvilinear meanders occur with the pit-and-groove elements. In northwestern California, there is one site with bear tracks cut into the stone between the pits, and in one Alberta site a bison head has been added.

4 INTERPRETATION

Pecked figure, Dinwoody Lakes, Wyoming. Redrawn from David Gebhard, 1951.

Interpretation is the most difficult and controversial part of any study of rock drawings. Much of our information has come from living Indians who have taken part in ceremonies involving drawing on rocks or who have copied prehistoric designs. In many instances, however, comments on ancient rock pictures by present-day Indians are highly unreliable; they are apt to tell any fanciful tale to make their questioners happy or to get rid of them. When ceremonial objects, such as masks, that are still in use today by the descendants of the rock-art makers are portrayed, we can be reasonably certain of the significance. Of course we can know only in a general way the reasons for the drawings; precise meanings could come only from the original creators.

CEREMONIAL

The American Indian world was filled with symbolism and mysticism. A complete belief in the spirit world was a guiding factor in all things. Each man had to deal with the plant and animal world every day on the closest terms and his identification with nature was complete. As long as he remained a wanderer and hunter, his religious and ceremonial observances were of the simplest sort. But when he became a village dweller, adopting a sedentary life, the pressure of food gathering lessened and he found himself with more leisure time. He invented complex ceremonies, minor gods around the supreme giver of all good things, and elaborate rituals to communicate with them. Rock drawings were often made in conjunction with ceremonies. Still today the Navajo shamans make symbolic sandpaintings on the ground during healing ceremonies. The ceremonial use of painting continues in northwestern Australia, where the *wondjina* paintings of strange anthropomorphic beings are periodically

28

repainted by the chief of the group under the protection of that particular *wondjina* to assure fertility, rain, increase of animals, and good hunting.[1]

It is certain that great numbers of the rock pictures in North America were made ceremonially to aid in getting all good things—health, fertility, rain, prosperity, and the like. Many of these paintings and engravings were made by the shaman or medicine man, or by tribe members under his direction. The shaman has existed in primitive societies from the days of the sorcerers depicted on the walls of the Paleolithic caves of Europe to the present day. The shaman has the power to communicate between the world of the spirits and the world of men. He can conduct ceremonies to exorcise evil spirits or to appeal for the protection of good spirits. He can also be a physician and officiate at healing ceremonies. A shaman acquires his special power through fasting, isolation, petition to supernatural beings, and by dreaming.

In a number of areas, rock paintings were made in connection with puberty rites. James A. Teit has described the meaning of the paintings made by the Thompson River Indians of British Columbia:

Adolescents of both sexes made records of remarkable dreams, pictures of what they desired or what they had seen, and events connected with their training. These records were made with red paint on boulders and cliffs wherever the surface was suitable . . . Rock paintings were also made by adults as records of notable dreams, and more rarely, of incidents in their lives.[2]

Teit married a Salish woman and lived with these Indians for many years. He knew several Indians who had taken part in such ceremonies and his evidence is thoroughly reliable. At puberty, boys were required to go into the hills on a spirit quest and through praying and fasting, they might have a dream or vision of a supernatural being who would be their guardian and helper in later life. A boy's visions naturally reflected his future hopes. A would-be great warrior hoped that his spirit quest would bring a vision of some aggressive being or force, such as thunder, the sun, grizzly bear, hawk, or eagle. Boys who wanted to be mighty fishermen wanted visions of fish, canoes, ducks, fishing gear, and so on. Gamblers wanted to envision valuables for wagering and aspiring athletes, swift animals and birds. On their return from such an experience, they might be sent to some distant, lonely spot to record their visions on rock with paint.

The girls' puberty ceremony was far more elaborate. They were secluded in a special hut and made to perform many symbolic tasks to ensure industry and ability after marriage. They dug long shallow trenches, collected spruce needles, and wove mats and baskets of grass. It was usual for the girls to bury food where two trails crossed and to hang the mats and baskets they had made on bushes. At the end of their period of seclusion the girls painted representations on rock of the offerings they had made and the tasks they had performed. A few of the symbols painted by the Thompson River girls during the puberty rites are an X, meaning the crossing of two trails; cross-hatched lines, indicating matting; and a curvilinear line with short radiating strokes, representing unfinished basketry.

Among the Nez Percé of Idaho, girls during puberty ceremonies made paintings of objects seen in dreams or connected with the rites. The Quinault boys of Puget Sound made rock paintings during puberty ceremonies and the drawings depicted mythical water monsters seen during their dreams. Julian H. Steward, in *Petroglyphs of California and Adjoining States*, described puberty ceremonies as practiced by the Luiseño and Cupeño Indians of southern California:

Among the Luiseño the girls went through an elaborate ceremony at puberty . . . This consisted of placing the girls in a pit with heated rocks for three days. On the morning of the fourth day, they left the pit and their faces were painted black for a month. For the second month, vertical white lines were painted on their faces, and for the third month, wavy red horizontal lines. The last was called the "rattlesnake" design. After further ceremonies in which a ground painting was used, the girls had a race to a certain rock. Here relatives of the girls stood to give them red paint when they arrived, and they painted diamond-shaped designs, representing the rattlesnake, on the rock. Among the Cupeño the ceremony is much the same.

This type of design is common in southern California and is almost the only style found over a large area. Here is an example of a southern California puberty drawing.

Rock pictures played a part in fertility ceremonies, and the design element of the bisected circle, considered a fertility symbol in many parts of the world, is abundant in the West. Phallic drawings are frequently

seen at southwestern sites and a fine example is shown here. This amusing rock pecking seems to show, in the clearest posterlike manner, the wish of the male figure for a man-child. In many parts of the West isolated boulders are covered with the distinctive pit-and-groove markings. Such carved boulders are especially abundant in northern California, and in the Pomo territory were known as "baby rocks" and were used ceremonially by women wanting children.

Certain tribes in North Dakota considered the turtle a symbol of productivity and turtle charms were worn by girls hoping for family life and children. Turtle designs have been found pecked and incised on granite boulders in North Dakota and South Dakota and may have represented fertility figures.

In many parts of North America, the shamans had the power to control the weather—to make it rain or to stop the rain. The ceremonies connected with rainmaking reached their greatest elaboration with the Hopi Snake Dance in Arizona. Among the Tolowa, Karok, Hupa, and Shasta Indians in northwestern California, pit-and-groove rocks were used to control the weather.[3]

At one of their fishing places, the Hupa had a sacred rain rock called *mi*. By this rock lived a spirit who could bring frost, prolong the rainy season, or cause drought if he was displeased. When someone was sick or hard frost came, it was thought that someone mourning the death of a relative had passed near the stone and had offended the *mi*. To placate this touchy deity a feast was given and the food was cooked near the rock. The shaman would pray for warm rains to melt the frost while sprinkling the rock with incense-root water. If the end of a rainy spell was needed, powdered incense-root was sprinkled on the rock. The person who had offended the deity was expected to make public apology for passing by the *mi*'s dwelling in so unholy a condition.

The Shasta of the Klamath River area believed that long straight parallel grooves would make the snow fall, and to stop a snow storm a scratch was made across and at right angles to the groove. The conical pits produced rain and wind, and the rain could be stopped by covering the rock with powdered incense-root.

The ubiquitous thunderbird motif is connected with the belief that these enormous supernatural birds caused thunder by flapping their wings and lightning by opening and closing their eyes. It has been reported that at the Twana reservation in Washington, there was a carved thunderbird on a basaltic rock and that if the rock was shaken, it would cause rain because the thunderbird was angry. Eastern Woodland carved rocks representing men wearing thunderbird costumes have been recorded, but whether these had any connection with rainmaking rites is unknown.

Pecked figures, Navajo Reservoir, New Mexico. Redrawn from Polly Schaafsma, 1963.

Puberty rites painting in red on granite, San Jacinto Mountains, California. University of California photograph.

Wherever naturalistic animal rock pictures are found, it is almost certain they were made as hunting magic or to increase the supply of game. Very often the animals are depicted pierced with arrows or spears. In the Northern Plains of Alberta, there are a few drawings of buffalo and other big-game animals. Some of these have been found on cliffs at buffalo jumps (high cliffs over which the animals were stampeded).

Robert Heizer and Martin Baumhoff in a recent study of the rock art of Nevada and eastern California state their belief that most of the rock art in Nevada was created in connection with communal hunts for deer, antelope, or mountain sheep. They have located many large petroglyph sites on known migration trails and in narrow draws leading to water. The remains of stone blinds and fences used in sheep or deer ambushes are found near some sites. Other sites are on game trails in areas ideal for antelope corrals. They noted the almost total absence of rock pictures in areas unsuitable for taking game. It is known that among recent Great Basin tribes, a hunt-shaman often directed the communal hunt and it seems likely many of the pictures were pecked by the shaman himself or under his direction prior to the hunt.

According to Edward L. Keithahn,[4] the Tlingit petroglyphs on the Northwest coast are usually located on beach boulders near the mouths of sockeye-salmon streams and are placed so that they face the sea and are submerged at high tide. He thinks that they were made to insure or increase the salmon runs by supernatural means. They often depict such deities as the raven, killer whale, and sea monster.

There are many rock paintings of sea and land mammals and hunters in boats in Cook Inlet and Prince William Sound, Alaska. An Eskimo has said that they were made by whale killers on the rocks of secret places to brink luck. Another informant said they were made by persons who wanted to become shamans. The student shamans would speak to the paintings and give them offerings of food and clothing. Shortly thereafter they were ready to become full-fledged shamans.[5] It is a practice among the present-day Ojibwa of Lake-of-the-Woods, Ontario, to leave offerings of clothing, tobacco, and prayer sticks on the rocks below a painted rock.[6]

The use of masks and the impersonation of supernatural beings are common to the ceremonies of aboriginal man in all parts of the world. The Eskimo of northern Quebec Province made rock carvings of masks on steatite boulders and the curious nonoutlined faces from Kodiak Island and the Chugach faces from Prince William Sound may also be masks. According to H. I. Smith, the petroglyphs near the present village of Bella Coola, British Columbia, representing the faces of anthropomorphic beings, were made in connection with winter secret society

Pecked drawing of sea monster, Wrangell Island, Alaska. Redrawn from a photograph by Edward L. Keithahn.

Design suggesting kachina *mask, Glen Canyon region of the Colorado River, Utah. Site now under water. Museum of Northern Arizona photograph.*

ceremonials where members would pound on them while singing. In the Southwest, particularly the Galisteo Basin in New Mexico, there are rock drawings of *kachina* masks similar to those in kiva murals, some of which are used in present-day Pueblo ceremonies. In northern New Mexico there are beautiful polychrome *yei* figures done by the Navajo that closely resemble supernatural beings personated in the Yebitchai ceremony. The masked *yeis* were closely modeled after the *kachinas* of the Hopi. The early Spanish explorers entering the Southwest in the second half of the sixteenth century described elaborate wall paintings in some of the pueblos and remains of these remarkable ceremonial paintings at Awatovi and Kuaua have been recovered in surprisingly good condition. These complex and beautiful polychrome paintings of anthropomorphic and zoomorphic beings were probably created some time between 1300 and 1500, the ultimate flowering of an art tradition that had been developing as rock art over a very long period. As the ceremonial life of the Pueblo Indians came more and more to revolve around the kiva, there was undoubtedly a lessening of the importance of the rock painting or carving.

The extraordinary and complicated rock paintings in the Santa Barbara–Tulare region of California were certainly created for ceremonial use. In the Chumash area, there are caches of ceremonial objects in the immediate vicinity of painted sites, and in the Yokuts territory, Indian informants have said that the paintings were usually made at a place where ceremonies were performed and that ceremonial objects were often hidden near the paintings. At a major site in the Chumash area, a continuous frieze of paintings 200 feet long is located around the base of a huge natural rock amphitheater rising some 75 feet from the plain. Deep trails cut into the stone lead to the summit where hundreds could sit and look down into the painted section below. It takes little imagination to envision the impressive rituals that must have taken place at this great site.

The Indians of certain areas believed in a number of very special supernatural beings who had great power to help bring about hoped-for results. In the Chumash country of southern California, the people prayed to Sup or Chupu, the giver of all good things. We do not know what this powerful deity looked like but the shamans may have personified him in a variety of ways—there are a number of very potent-looking anthropomorphic figures in the region.

The beautiful polychrome Chumash paintings are almost invariably located in remote, mountainous areas, away from the main population centers along the coast. It is possible that these painted sites are connected with dream or vision quests so important to the American Indian, and that some of these paintings represent such visions. Most of the southern California tribes used the hallucinogenic drug *toloache* or jimsonweed in certain ceremonies, particularly puberty and initiation rites. The root of this common plant was ground and boiled making a liquor that was drunk by ceremony participants. Many of the fanciful Chumash designs may have been produced under the influence of this aboriginal LSD.

In the Great Lakes country and the upper Mississippi Valley, several tribes worshiped a curious being known by many names, such as water panther, water monster, water lynx, and medicine animal. This is usually depicted on rocks and birch-bark scrolls as a clawed animal in profile with a horned head turned full face and a serrated tail curving around the body. This fanciful creature was known to the Ojibwa as *Mishipizhiw*. In 1673, Father Marquette described such a figure painted on a cliff near the present city of Alton, Illinois:

While skirting some rocks, which by their height and length inspire awe, we saw upon one of them two painted monsters which at first made us afraid, and upon which the boldest savages dare not long rest their eyes. They are as large as a calf: they have horns on their heads like those of a deer, a horrible look, red eyes, a beard like a tiger's, a face somewhat like a man's, a body covered with scales, and so long a tail that it winds all around the body, passing above the head and going back between the legs, ending in a fish's tail. Green, red, and black are the three colors composing the picture.

Incised Winnebago drawing of medicine animal (chalked), northeastern Nebraska. Nebraska State Historical Society photograph.

This extraordinary picture could not have been very old as another
missionary coming down the Mississippi in 1699 noted that the figures
were almost obliterated. Marquette's description would indicate that what
he saw was exactly like the medicine animal of the Winnebago. In 1838
one of the figures was still visible but in 1847 the whole face was quarried
away. The present painting is the third re-creation of Marquette's creature, each more fanciful than the last. A local sign company is responsible
for the most recent effort. It is 50 feet long and bears no relationship
whatsoever to any Indian painting style.

Much additional material on ceremonial interpretation and the relation
of rock drawings to myths will be found in Part II, on Rock Art Areas.

MNENOMIC

Lacking a written language, aboriginal man has long used pictures as
memory aids. With them he recorded objects, concepts, legends, tallies,
and records of time. In historic times the Dakota Indians had winter
counts as a system of chronology. The record was kept on a buffalo
hide. Each year or winter was indicated by a drawing symbolizing some
outstanding event, such as an outbreak of smallpox, a successful horse
raid, or the death of a chief. In the event of another outbreak of smallpox, the same symbol would be used. Many incised rock drawings in
the Great Plains region are done in the same style as the winter-count
drawings. The Ojibwa kept track of the order of their ceremonial songs

by symbolic pictures on birch-bark scrolls. The illustrations would give the order of the stanzas and the subject matter of each particular stanza, and the subject matter would be a reminder of the words.

Modern Hopi interpret a number of Arizona petroglyphs as records of the four legendary Hopi migrations of the clans. At many rock drawing sites, there are numbers of short straight vertical lines sometimes in association with animal drawings. It has been suggested that these represent tally marks to record how many animals were taken. It is also possible that each actual drawing of the animal might represent a kill, but lacking ethnographical information, this is pure speculation. In the Southwest there are many carefully pecked designs, suitable for blankets, pottery, and sandals, that look like records for future reference.

RECORDS OF IMPORTANT EVENTS

In the Great Plains region and in the Northern and Eastern Woodlands, there was a tradition of making drawings to commemorate important happenings, usually connected with warfare. The Plains records are almost invariably on skin, but occasionally incised or painted on stone. There is an incised rock panel on the Milk River in southern Alberta that looks like a battle scene: 30 men with guns, 45 other figures, 22 tepees, and 9 horses, some harnessed to travois. In 1852, Henry Schoolcraft described how an Ojibwa, Chingwauk, drew on birch bark for him the record of a successful warlike raid across Lake Superior by a south shore shaman-warrior named Myeengum. The drawings showed Myeengum, his clan symbol, the various legendary beings—like the great serpent and the fabulous water panther—that would aid him in his venture, the five canoes carrying his warriors, three suns to indicate that the passage took three days, and various other symbols. Chingwauk told Schoolcraft that the original painting was made on a cliff of the north shore of Lake Superior. In 1958, over 100 years later, Selwyn Dewdney found the paintings at Agawa Rock exactly as indicated on the birch-bark scroll.

Some Tlingit rock drawings seem to have been made as records of property sacrificed at potlatches or as records of other important events.

The potlatch ceremony practiced by all Northwest Indians was an unusual business. The most important aspect of the Northwest Coast culture was the endless preoccupation with social status and the manipulation of wealth. A chief would give an elaborate feast called a potlatch to celebrate the comng of age of a grandchild, the erection of a house or a totem pole, the birth of a son, and so forth. Many guests were invited and they were obliged to bring many gifts. In the course of the celebrations that might last several days and included feasting, dancing, and other entertainment, the chief would give away slaves, blankets, coppers, canoes, and other valuable property to his guests, who could not decline the presents. The receiver of gifts was obligated to return them with interest at a later time. The host would often ruin a rival by presenting him with far more than he could repay or by publicly destroying much valuable property, which put the rival under the obligation of destroying an equal amount to escape humiliation. This prestige madness was carried to the point where a host would destroy coppers valued at ten thousand blankets each, or burn his canoes and house. The coppers were sheets of copper made in the form of a shield about two feet wide by three feet long. These sheets were often painted with a design or the crest of the owner and were the ultimate in visible signs of wealth.

On the Nass River, British Columbia, there is a painted cave featuring 14 coppers and on the Skeena River near Prince Rupert there is a rock face with six coppers, four with crests and a large anthropomorphic head. These two sites are both in Tsimshian territory. On Petley Point, in Kwakiutl territory, there is a painting showing coppers, boats, and animals.

Recorded at two sites in the White Mesa region of northern Arizona are almost identical drawings, one painted and the other pecked, that may be records of an astronomical phenomenon. Each drawing depicts a crescent shape over a round shape and the astronomer Fred Hoyle has raised the possibility that the Pueblo Indians once occupying the area might have witnessed the supernova of A.D. 1054. On July 4 of that year, Japanese and Chinese astronomers saw an extremely bright nova that was easily visible in broad daylight. This famous supernova, believed to be the origin of the Crab Nebula, was about six times as bright as Venus and was probably the brightest starlike object ever recorded. Astronomers have been able to determine that on July 4, 1054, the moon was in crescent phase directly over and close to the supernova, exactly as shown in the rock drawings. Archaeologists have verified an Indian occupation of the area between 900 and 1100. Representations of stars and planets have been noted in northern Arizona and southern California, and at an elaborate site near Los Angeles there are paintings that could have been inspired only by comets or shooting stars.

Red painting of Mishipizhiw, the fabulous night panther, Lake Superior Provincial Park. Redrawn from Selwyn Dewdney, 1962.

Incised battle scene, Milk River, Alberta. Redrawn from Selwyn Dewdney, 1964.

CLAN SYMBOLS

An American Indian clan is an intratribal group, related by blood and organized to promote its social and political welfare. The clan is named for the totem animal or object that is considered its guardian spirit. This is not to be confused with the personal guardian spirit obtained by the individual during puberty dreams and trances. The membership in a clan is usually inherited at birth and the individual is identified during his lifetime as a member of the Bear Clan or the Eagle Clan or the Oak Clan— the possibilities are almost endless. Each clan has one or more symbols to represent the clan.

Many of the often repeated designs found pecked in the rocks, particularly in the Southwest, are clan symbols. At Willow Springs near Tuba City, Arizona, there are sandstone boulders covered with drawings of many different elements. There are repeats of each element, usually neatly arranged in a row. Modern Hopi Indians are able to recognize all but a few of these as clan symbols. Each symbol records that a member of that particular clan passed by that way on a trip from the Hopi villages to collect salt at the springs near the junction of the Colorado and the Little Colorado. The great canyon is regarded with awe by the Hopi—from its depths the ancient Hopi emerged and back to these depths the dead return. From ancient times the Indians have made the journey to get salt from the mysterious and dreaded canyon—only the brave would undertake the trip—and it was natural they would want to commemorate their daring.[7]

Red painting of crescent and round shapes, possibly representing supernova of 1054 A.D., White Mesa, Arizona. From photograph by William C. Miller.

Two typical clan symbols are the bear track, always drawn to show the pads and curved claws of the grizzly, the device of the Bear Clan, and the grotesque humped-back flute player, emblem of the Flute Clan.

Animal and thunderbird figures on birch-bark scrolls of the prehistoric woodland Indians like the Ojibwa and the Menomini closely resemble petroglyphs at several western Wisconsin rock shelters. The principal use of the symbols by some historic tribes was as memory aids for the order of songs and dances in various ceremonies and these were inscribed on birch bark or the mnemonic boards of the shamans. In addition, such symbols, especially the thunderbird, were drawn on early land treaties of the Menomini during the 1790's in place of a signature.

DOODLING AND COPYING ANCIENT DESIGNS

A small number of the rock pictures were doubtless done as a form of amusement and to while away an idle hour. Such aimless rock pictures were certainly confined to pecked or incised designs. The preparation of materials for making a rock painting (see chapter 2) would hardly

Pecked Hopi clan symbols (chalked), Willow Springs, Arizona. Some of the clans represented on this rock are the Cloud, Coyote, Spider, Corn, and Rope. Museum of Northern Arizona photograph.

appeal to the rock doodler but implements to peck a design into the rock—a hammer stone and a flint chisel—were ready at hand almost anywhere.

There is ethnographic evidence that some crude pictures were done by children and others were copies of older examples on the same rock surface "made for fun" by recent Indians with no knowledge of their meaning. In the Great Basin area of California there are obviously old designs, half obscured with patination, next to identical fresh designs.

5 ROCK ART AS ART

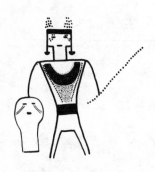

Pecked figure near Vernal, Utah. From photograph by John Cawley.

Since "art for art's sake" was not the main consideration in the mind of the Indian creators and the pictures on the rocks were put there for special purposes, usually ceremonial, to many American archaeologists the art aspect of rock pictures is secondary and to some nonexistent.

The art historian takes exception to this narrow point of view. He notes that nearly all the ancient arts in the world were motivated by religion. The superb ritualistic carvings, paintings, and metal work of Egypt are certainly art. The temple figures of the Greek gods, personifications of supernatural beings, are universally considered art. There are many examples of rock art, such as those featuring crude stick figures or curvilinear meanders, that no one would classify as art; but the moment an aboriginal craftsman bothered to pick out a particularly smooth and colorful piece of rock on which to peck a carefully conceived and decorative figure, you are dealing with an artist. True, he may have been a tribal shaman whose main concern was to put down a visualization of a certain supernatural being for ceremonial use, but if he was concerned in the least with composition, design, or craftsmanship, his work has to be considered art. This has long been recognized in Europe where the study of rock paintings and carvings has been in the hands of art historians as well as archaeologists. In the great mass of European publications on the subject, it is referred to as rock art and the familiar American terms of petroglyph and pictograph are unknown.

Only during periods of prosperity and freedom from want has man had the leisure to develop great art. In North America, rock pictures usually attained the stature of art in those areas where a nomadic hunting culture had been supplanted by a stable sedentary culture nurtured by an abundant food supply near at hand. These qualifications are met in the salmon-economy villages of the Northwest, the fishing and acorn-gathering settlements of the Santa Barbara–Tulare region in California, and the corn-growing villages of the Southwest. In these three areas, North American rock art reaches its highest development.

There seem to be three stages in the development of a rock-art tradition:

1. The primitive hunters and food gatherers. These people have no fixed villages and constantly move about seeking game or seed crops. Their ceremonies consist chiefly of healing rites, taboos, and superstitions, and their rock drawings are mainly crude representations of game animals, hunters, and a few mythological beings. Indians like the Ojibwa never got beyond this stage.

2. The primitive village dwellers. They can be hunters, food gatherers, or primitive agriculturists but their sedentary life has allowed them the leisure to develop regular ceremonial practices and art styles. Typical of this stage are the Chumash of California and the Fremont culture in Utah. The finest rock art was developed by Indians at this culture stage.

3. The highly developed village dwellers. These people have evolved elaborate ceremonies and pantheons of gods, and their best artistic efforts are no longer found on rocks. Better and more convenient surfaces are used with more sophisticated results. Three outstanding examples of this higher culture stage are the superb carvings on wood and stone of the Northwest Indians, the kiva and sand paintings of the Hopi and Navajo in the Southwest, and the Mexicanized art in wood, copper, and shell of the Southeast. In all of these areas, rock drawings had ceased to play a major part by the start of the historic period. Of the three, only the Southwest had a long rock-art tradition.

The great variation in quality of Indian rock pictures is the result of two factors. The most obvious, of course, is that individuals differ enormously in ability. More important is the rare appearance of a forceful person with original ideas and talent who sets a new art style that is accepted and imitated over a wide area.

It is curious that the hunting people of the New World who painted and carved thousands of naturalistic animal forms on rocks across the continent never approached the excellence of the Paleolithic cave painters of southern France and northern Spain. It is not that they were incapable of doing that sort of work, but that they simply did *not* do it. There are several possible explanations for this. The European paintings were made over a very long period of time during the last great ice age. The population above and below the Pyrenees must have been remarkably sparse 30,000 years ago and the small bands of hunters were undoubtedly concentrated in and around the numerous deep caves in the glacier-covered regions. The deposits found in the caves and rock shelters testify to long occupation that allowed ample time in one spot for the development of their distinct high art form. At a very early period, a highly naturalistic painted art tradition was developed, probably sparked by a single highly gifted individual. (Such a person was Giotto, the first great painter of the Italian Renaissance.) The similarity of technique in nearly all the sites has often been remarked on. Down through the years, the older drawings were held up as models and the technique remained unchanged. Paleolithic man was a conservative—his flint tools underwent little change for many thousands of years and the same seems true of his approach to art.

The nomadic hunters of the New World plains and woodlands, unhampered by perpetual snow and ice, pursued the migrant game herds and seldom stayed long in any one place. Theirs was a life of constant change and movement with no hope of acquiring the leisure necessary for the development of a higher art form. Occasionally a site is discovered in the hunting country with a far better than average animal drawing. Given the opportunity, the individual who created it might have been the nucleus of an art tradition.

The Athabascan nomads who infiltrated the Southwest plateau country and came to be known as the Navajo acquired rather rapidly most of the ceremonial and artistic traditions of the Pueblo people. These borrowed ideas flowered under the hands of the clever Navajo into the highly developed art tradition we know today. Their excellent polychrome rock paintings in northern New Mexico seem midway in style between the Pueblo kiva figures and the highly stylized Navajo sandpainting anthropomorphs.

Black painting, Baja California. From photograph by Velma Pontoni.

6 DATING

Determining the age of prehistoric paintings and carvings is difficult and absolute datings are rare. A number of dating methods can give partial answers. Some give relative chronologies so that in a given area it can be determined which drawings are older. Other methods give approximate datings, give or take a hundred years or so. In a very small number of cases the age of the rock art can be exactly stated.

Some North American rock pecked designs are in all likelihood far older than any existing paintings. Rock paintings are made on boulders, on cliff faces, and in shallow rock shelters where most of them are under constant wind and water attack. Under these conditions few could be older than several hundred years. On the other hand, designs pecked into dense basaltic rock could endure for thousands of years. The conditions that protected the Paleolithic paintings in Europe for so many thousands of years in great underground caverns did not exist in this country.

Red painting, Real County, Texas. Redrawn from A. T. Jackson.

BY PATINATION

Most of the rock drawings in the Great Basin and in the Southwest are made by pecking through the dark patina or "desert varnish" to the original lighter rock color. Desert varnish is a blackish or brownish stain of hydrous iron and manganese oxides on rock surfaces. It is most conspicuous in desert regions but is also found in rain forests and at high altitudes. Although the pecked designs are nearly all on the sandstone and basaltic rock so common in the western desert, desert varnish occurs on almost any kind of rock. There are various theories to account for its formation. One attributes it to rain water that has soaked into the rock and then been brought back to the surface through capillary action.

The water brings various chemicals in the rock, such as carbonates, sulphates, and oxides, to the surface. Some of these tend to darken and harden the surface of the stone. In addition to the darkening caused by deposition of soluble chemicals, there seems to be a darkening due to the action of direct sunlight.[1]

Another theory is that ample sunlight and moisture were needed for the formation of the conspicuous deposits of desert varnish on the Colorado plateaus and the principal deposits must have been formed during pluvial periods, making the older varnish perhaps as old as the late Wisconsin glacial, ten to fifteen thousand years ago.[2] According to this theory, desert varnish is being formed at a very slow rate today in the Southwest where rainfall is scanty. The new desert-varnish deposits are restricted to places that are often wet. Boulders along the Colorado River between high- and low-water stages are stained a very dark brown. In California, petroglyphs on granite rocks below high-water mark in the Kern River Gorge have turned an intense black.

Donald Martin of Santa Rosa, California, who has devoted much time to the study of western rock art and particularly to the problem of desert varnish has a different idea. He has taken heavily patinated stones from the Mojave Desert back to Santa Rosa, located in the coastal ranges where the summers are hot, the winters cold, and the yearly rainfall averages over 30 inches. After two years of exposure in this climate, all patina had vanished from the stones. This would indicate that desert varnish could not have formed during periods of unusual rainfall.

If Martin's hypothesis is correct, the Mojave Desert basaltic rocks were patinated during and after the decline of the last great rainy period, the "Little Pluvial" of some 3,000 or 4,000 years ago. Thus no designs pecked on such rocks could be more than 2,000 to 3,000 years old.

For arriving at relative chronologies through a study of patination, it is necessary to have varying degrees of desert varnish on petroglyphs at the same site. The older the carving, the darker the patina. At many sites, some of the pecked areas are identical in patination and weathering to the natural rock surface; others that are known to be at least 150 years old look as fresh as if they had been pecked yesterday. At the present time there is no way to determine the rate of patination, but totally patinated designs may be several thousand years old.

BY SUPERIMPOSITION OF STYLES

Often one design has been pecked over another—the superimposed drawing done later than the partially obliterated underdrawing. Sometimes three or more designs in differing styles are layered in a recognizable sequence. Patination and weathering are useful additional clues to separate these multiple superimpositions. Once the sequence of styles has been established, a yardstick is created to judge relative chronology of styles anywhere in the region, even where no superimposition occurs. For example, in the Great Basin area, the rectilinear abstract style is often found over the curvilinear abstract style and is more recent. The curvilinear abstract drawings are almost invariably found beneath the other styles and can be safely designated the earliest Great Basin style. One of the arguments in favor of a fairly recent dating for the rock paintings in California is the rather rare occurrence of superimposition. Of the 80 sites recorded in the Chumash region, only six show such evidence.

Pecked figure, Petroglyph Canyon, Coso Range, California. From photograph by John Cawley.

Where designs are pecked or painted over designs of a similar style, there is the possibility we are dealing with a single period in time and the superimposition represents deliberate obliteration. The Hopi ceremonial kiva paintings were periodically covered wth plaster and new designs applied. The Kuaua kiva had 87 layers of plaster, 25 of which were painted with elaborate mural designs.[3] The Navajo sand paintings, destroyed after each ceremony, demonstrate ritual obliteration.

BY RADIOCARBON TEST

The radiocarbon method of dating organic materials was developed by Dr. Willard Libby at the Institute of Nuclear Physics, University of Chicago, and has been particularly valuable in dating American Indian remains. Carbon 14 (a radioactive isotope of carbon) is formed in the atmosphere when cosmic rays bombard nitrogen atoms. All living things absorb carbon 14 at a constant rate, but at death, the absorption stops and the carbon 14 atoms start disintegrating at a known and steady rate. After $5,760 \pm 30$ years have elapsed, half the carbon 14 atoms have dis-

Horsemen and sheep, Arches National Monument, Utah. Photograph by Tom Mulhern.

integrated. A sample of the organic material to be dated is purified and processed through apparatus that filters out background radiation. The number of beta particles given off per minute, measured by a Geiger-counter technique, determines the amount of radioactive material left in the sample, and consequently the approximate date at which the sample ceased to be a living organism. The method allows for a margin of error in each direction, and radiocarbon dates are often written like this: 2,700 B.P. (before present) ± 220 years.

This dating method has been applied to rock art but without much success so far. I recently collected some paint samples from a badly eroded site near Santa Barbara, hoping that enough of the original organic paint binder remained for radiocarbon dating. Unfortunately the sample was too small for a conclusive dating but the laboratory report indicated no great age. I then tried dating basketry fragments from a painted cave. The sample proved to be 120 ± 80 years old. Clement Meighan has dated a palm-wood peg from a painted cave in Baja California that proved to be 530 ± 80 years old. The dating of associated artifacts can never give an absolute dating for the rock drawings but it does indicate a period when the site was occupied by people who *might* have made the pictures.

BY OVERGROWTH OF LICHENS

Many petroglyph sites have design areas partially covered with lichens, and various investigators have discussed dating such sites by establishing the age of the extremely slow-growing lichens on the pecked surfaces. The recent studies by Ronald E. Beschel on the growth rates of Arctic lichens have provided the methods for such dating.[4] The growth rate varies greatly depending on the species, type of rock, and climate. The periods when the growth conditions of water, warmth, light, and food are favorable are very short in most areas, and some of the crust lichens grow as little as a fraction of a millimeter in diameter per year.

Growth rates have been arrived at through actual measurements (the longest observed lichen growth covers only about 40 years) and comparisons with lichens of known age. In the latter case, it is necessary to know when a rock was first exposed to the air-borne lichen spores. This is possible with certain volcanic rocks, rocks turned up during old road-building operations, gravestones, rocks emerging from drained lakes, and the like.

Through studying the growth of lichens, maximum ages have been determined for a number of species (around 700 years in several instances). On the basis of present knowledge, lichen growth-rates can be used to date sites later than the approximate 700-year lichen age limit. Beschel has estimated the age of one lichen-encrusted Eskimo site as "at

Incised drawing of cranes, Gullickson Glen, Wisconsin. From photograph by Warren Wittry.

least 500 years" and Gerhard Folmann, using Beschel's methods, has recently given an average age of 430 years to the great rock figures on
Easter Island.[5] It is obvious that this method has great possibilities for
solving dating problems in regions where favorable lichen growth conditions are found.

BY DEPOSITS COVERING DESIGNS

Robert F. Heizer and Martin A. Baumhoff have described three Nevada
sites where rock drawings occur in association with alluvial deposits and
occupation debris that give some dating clues.[6]

In the first instance, the designs are pecked on a cliff above an alluvial
terrace of gravel. Excavation of the terrace disclosed buried petroglyphs
extending to a depth of over twenty feet. The terrace is part of a large
alluvial fan formed by a small intermittent stream and a gradual accumulation of the deposit is indicated by the stratification of the sand and
gravel into thin, even beds. The annual rainfall of the region averages
two and a half inches, indicating a very long time for the building of the
terrace.

At another site, a large red *kachina* figure was buried up to the
shoulders by four or five feet of camp debris. This amount of debris in
a rock shelter would indicate several hundred years of occupation and at
least that age for the painting.

The third instance is somewhat different. Here the pecked designs are
in a large rock shelter and above an accumulation of 20 feet of deposit.
The upper levels of this shelter contained materials of cultures dating
from historic times to around 1000 B.C., while the lowest-level materials
date from about 4000 B.C. As the drawings could not have been made
until the debris reached its present level, they must have been made
within the last 3,000 years.

BY RATE OF EROSION

All rock drawings are exposed to the destructive forces of erosion but
the rate of this erosion can vary enormously. Fine-grained rocks like
basalt and quartzite are highly resistant to erosion while the coarse sandstones are very susceptible to wind and water damage. Rock paintings
are far more apt to be destroyed through erosion than are pecked and
carved designs, and the Indian craftsmen, aware of this problem, almost
invariably did their painting in rock shelters where there was maximum
protection from the scouring effects of wind-blown sand and rock-destroy-
ing moisture. On the other hand, nearly all rock-pecked drawings are on
exposed cliff faces and individual rocks.

There is a site in the Nojoqui Valley, near Santa Barbara, that was pictured in Mallery's book (1893) with five pages of polychrome geometric patterns. Today there is hardly a trace of the painting to be seen. The cave entrance faced the prevailing wind and the paint was literally sand-blasted away. These paintings could not have been over several hundred years old. Mallery also pictured the Painted Cave on nearby San Marcos Pass. This well-known painting is still exactly as it was in 1893. In this instance, the cave opening allowed the wind to strike a six-foot-wide section of the painting. This section has been obliterated, dividing the picture into two parts. The Mallery paintings show that this destruction had already taken place over seventy years ago.

BY ASSOCIATION WITH ARTIFACTS

Indian artifacts found near rocks with pecked designs or painted caves can sometimes be used to indicate approximate dating. In the Sierra Madre back of Santa Barbara, California, many objects of bone, wood, and shell, typical of the late Chumash culture, have been found in rock shelters near painted sites. At a number of these sites, Spanish beads and other postcontact material have been recovered. The evidence would indicate that the paintings are relatively recent and that the practice of rock painting continued in this area at least until the start of the Spanish-mission period.

In the Pueblo areas of northern Arizona and New Mexico, artists sometimes stood on the house roofs in order to paint or carve designs on the rock wall above. Emil Haury has described a site in northeastern Arizona where paintings occur on the wall of an overhanging cliff. Against the cliff are a number of houses built in contact with the rock wall, a practice followed only in late Pueblo times (A.D. 1200–1300). Many paintings were made from these roof tops and the most common design element was the hand (see chapter 7). Since the Pueblo Indians had abandoned the area to the Navajos by 1300, it is reasonable to assume that these designs were made prior to that date. There is one cut timber from the site with a tree-ring date of 1247. The later Navajo drawings are shallow scratchings on the cliff face, mostly of animals and horsemen.

The best correlation of prehistoric artifacts with rock drawings has been made by Christy G. Turner. When the Glen Canyon region of the Colorado was threatened with inundation by the creation of Lake Powell, a salvage program to record several hundred archaeological sites was undertaken. Pecked designs were found at many sites in association with pottery that has been dated and ascribed to specific cultures.[7] Turner's assumption that the rock pictures are contemporaneous with the pottery seems valid. His dates for the drawings are from before A.D. 1050 to late historic times.

Most American Indians deny any knowledge of the rock drawings or their creators. Ute and Southern Paiute Indians have said the pictures were made by supernatural beings or by ancient peoples or by animals when they were men. Some Idaho Indians ascribe the designs to the medicine men, who were the only people who could interpret their meaning. Other Idaho Indians hold that the rock pictures were made by mythical creatures or that they fell from the sky. Modern Pueblo Indians sometimes carve symbols on rocks and some of the clan symbols described in chapter 4 were made not many years ago, according to Hopi informants. Ute Indians admit to copying old designs whose meaning was unknown to them "just for fun," while the Western Yavapai of Arizona sometimes made petroglyphs in imitation of ancient ones.

In chapter 4 on interpretation, there are descriptions of the puberty-rites paintings made by some Salish tribes in British Columbia and the Luiseño in southern California. Women have been interviewed who actually painted such pictures in the late 19th century. These two areas are unique in giving us exact information on how these pictures were made, when, by whom, and why. Near Pueblo sites in Canyon de Chelly, there are naturalistic polychrome paintings that are attributed to a Navajo Indian, Dibe Yazhi. These paintings were made in the 1830's.

Such instances are rare. In most areas, the practice of making rock pictures had died out long before trained investigators entered the field.

BY SUBJECT MATTER

Objects depicted in rock drawings can often be a clue to relative chronology. In some Great Basin sites in California, there are pecked representations of the *atlatl,* the spear thrower that preceded the bow and arrow in this country by many thousands of years. In the Coso Range lying between Death Valley and the Sierra Nevada, there are three narrow basaltic gorges where prehistoric hunters left thousands of drawings connected with the hunting of Bighorn sheep. They show graphically the gradual shift from the spear thrower or *atlatl* to the bow and arrow. There are many representations of the stone-weighted *atlatl* associated with the dimmer and more heavily patinated designs. The figures covered with a moderate coating of desert varnish include a few *atlatls,* hunters holding *atlatls,* and many examples of hunters with bows and arrows. The most recent drawings, with little or no patina, often depict the archer but not *atlatls.*

In another section of the Great Basin several hundred miles to the north (Lovelock Cave, Nevada), this weapon change has been roughly dated. Radiocarbon tests and artifact stratification indicate an occupation

Pecked spear throwers, Little Lake, eastern California. These atlatls *added an extra joint to the arm. The circular shape in the middle of the weapon probably represents a stone weight to give added force to the thrust. Photograph by John Cawley.*

span of nearly 3,000 years. At the lowest level, only *atlatl* fragments have been found. The bow appears here about 500 B.C. and completely supplants the *atlatl* by 1 B.C. The introduction of the bow in the Anasazi region of the Southwest came much later—sometime between A.D. 200 and 400.

With the coming of the white man in the 16th century, the historical period begins and we have an approximate dating guide every time the Indian artist included such subjects as horses, guns, ships, priests, and church buildings on his rock panel.

The best of these is the horse and rider as we know the exact date of many of the early exploring and fur-trapping expeditions into the various Indian regions. The first horses to enter the New World (after the native horses became extinct thousands of years ago) were brought in by Hernando Cortes during the conquest of Mexico in 1519. Later, Coronado on his march to Quivira in 1541 introduced them to the Indians of the Great Plains and it is probable that some of the carved pictures of riders found in the Southwest date from this period.

Juan de Oñate established the colony of New Mexico in 1598, bringing with him horses, cattle, missionaries, and settlers. As trading expeditions went north on both sides of the Rockies, knowledge of the horse traveled

Hunters with atlatls *and mountain sheep, Petroglyph Canyon, Coso Range, California. Photograph by Donald Martin.*

Horsemen and buffalo painted in red, Meyer Springs, Texas. Bullet holes and names have been repainted. Photograph by Dale Ritter.

into the Plains and various tribes began acquiring them (usually by theft) and building up their own herds. The movement of horses from their Spanish point of origin was not a rapid one—the Pawnee on the Central Plains were using horses for hunting early in the 18th century and the Cheyenne to the west had their first horses about 1780. In the Northern Plains, the Blackfeet obtained horses from the Kootenay, Shoshone, and other tribes across the mountains about 1800. When the Lewis and Clark expedition traveled through the Northern Plains in 1803–4, they noted that all tribes seemed supplied with horses. The rock drawings in the Plains region very often show mounted riders; thus none can be dated much before 1750 and most must have been made after 1800. In California, the first horses were brought in by Juan Bautista de Anza in 1775 and there are crude representations of riders in a cave directly above one of his known camp spots in Riverside County. Drawings of horses are rare in southern California and nonexistent in northern California, for with the arrival of the Spanish, the mission system quickly destroyed the major Indian cultures and with them the practice of making rock drawings.

Dated Indian painting in red (left) and black (right) showing animals and a Japanese fishing boat, Kwakiutl Territory, British Columbia. Redrawn from Gutorm Gjessing, 1952.

Cave paintings in southwestern Texas sometimes show mission buildings and priests. These must have been made around 1600, when the Spanish settlements along the Rio Grande were being established.

In the Northwest, the rock carvings along the coast do not show historically datable subjects but paintings occur in the Kwakiutl and Nootka territories that are in the same realistic style as those done by the neighboring Salish tribes and include such subjects as horses, wagons, steam and sailing ships, and coppers. The sailing ships could date from about 1860 to 1900. Coppers, wealth indicators among the Northwest Indians, occur on a rock panel with a Kwakiutl canoe and the date 1921. On the same panel are some animals, a Japanese fishing boat, and the legend SUTSUMA 1927. As the dates are in the same pigments as the rest of the drawing, there is little doubt they are contemporary and unique—a dated Indian painting!

The foregoing dating techniques establish that rock drawings have been made by the American Indian for several thousand years, the practice continuing in certain areas until very recent times. The earliest examples may be in the Great Basin region of eastern California and southern Nevada, with the curvilinear style and the associated *atlatl;* the most recent, the Kwakiutl paintings from British Columbia.

There is at present no evidence that rock paintings or carvings were made during the early millennia of man's wanderings in the New World but someday such evidence may be found.

7 IMPORTANT DESIGN MOTIFS

Red painting, Meyer Springs, Texas. From photograph by Donald Martin.

Though techniques and styles vary tremendously across the country, a number of highly distinctive design elements occur, with local variations, over vast areas. The seven chosen for discussion in this chapter seem of particular interest. The first three—the hand, the bear track, and the thunderbird—are found in almost every major rock drawing area in North America. The others—the mountain sheep, the shield figure, the plumed serpent, and the humped-back flute player—have a more restricted range.

THE HAND

Perhaps the earliest drawings of man are the hand stencils in the caves of southern France and northern Spain. The technique is similar in all these sites—the subject placed his hand flat against the rock wall and the artist blew a diluted pigment around the edge of the hand, giving an effect exactly like modern "air brush" painting. Some of these have been dated in the Upper Paleolithic, possibly 30,000 years ago. Many of these hands show finger amputation and are identical to hands done in the same technique by Australian aborigines. Finger amputation usually connected with mourning ceremonies was practiced by primitive peoples in many parts of the world. It was done by the Tlingit, Tsimshian and Haida in the Northwest and by some of the Plains tribes,[1] but the only instances where mutilation is shown in rock painting are from southwest Texas.

In North America the hand is often the principal motif in a rock panel and in a number of cases in the Four Corners region, the blown-stencil

54

technique is employed, identical with the Paleolithic and Australian examples.

Occasionally a wall surface will be literally covered with hundreds of hand prints. There is such a site in the Santa Lucia Mountains of Monterey County, California. The cave wall is smoke-blackened and some 246 hand prints appear in white. The technique seems to have involved coating the hand with paint, pressing it onto the wall and, when dry, scraping away portions of the impression to give a curious skeletal effect. About 15 per cent of the hand prints were of the left hand, reflecting the usual proportion of left-handedness. There are small children's hand prints at the lower levels and adult hands higher up.

There are many hand prints in Buttress Canyon in northeastern Arizona. They were made by pressing the paint-daubed hand against the cave wall, but most have been retouched by brush. The fingers are elongated and, in some cases, zigzag and voluted patterns have been scratched in the palm areas, giving a decorative effect. The hands here are often paired and seem contemporaneous with the many square-shouldered anthropomorphs painted in the cave. In the newly created Canyonlands National Park in southeastern Utah, the "Cave of 200 Hands" shows the elaborations found in the Santa Lucia and the Buttress Canyon sites in conjunction with realistic animal and human figures.

Red hand painting, northern Arizona. Redrawn from E. W. Haury.

In southern California, small hand prints of adolescents occur with many of the simple diamond and zigzag designs associated with puberty rites. Pecked designs of hands, common through the Southwest and the Great Basin, usually occur singly on panels with masses of other design elements. There is one fine example of realistic incised palm designs done by the Micmacs in Nova Scotia.

The hand prints were probably a form of signature and where great numbers are found together, may have represented some sort of identification with a tribal unit. In certain instances they were made during a ceremony—this is certainly true of the puberty-rite prints.

THE BEAR TRACK

The bear was a most important animal to the North American Indian, the living symbol of strength and courage. To kill a bear, especially the formidable grizzly, was a great feat and no higher badge of courage could be gained by a warrior than a necklace of grizzly claws. The grizzly and the more timid black bear are the most widespread of the North American carnivores and played a major part in tribal ritual and mythology.

In California, certain shamans were known as bear doctors. It was believed that the bear doctor could turn himself into a grizzly and in this

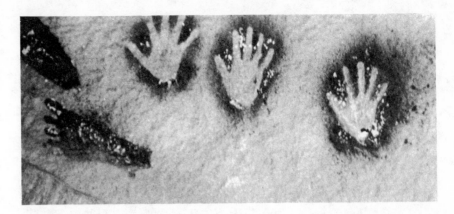

form he would destroy enemies. The ferocity and tenacity to life of the grizzly appealed to the imagination of the Indians and the power of such shamans was thought to derive directly from the animal. In the Chumash region of southern California, there is a cave high on the side of a brush-covered mountain where 49 bear tracks are carved into the smoke-blackened sandstone. This may well have been the scene of bear-doctor activities. The mass use of bear tracks was unusual, but there is another example of it pecked on the rocks at Lake Pend d'Oreille, Idaho.

The usual way for the Indian artist to draw the bear tracks was to show the paw pad as a single squarish unit with five round toe pads lined up above. But often, especially in the plains, the paw pad is divided by a lateral center line and the toe pads are replaced by long curving claws—unmistakably a grizzly track. This grizzly motif was used by some tribes like the Hopi as a clan symbol.

The bear track often occurs associated with shield figures in the manner of a heraldic device and at Castle Gardens, Wyoming, there is a plains-type engraving of a clothed figure whose garment is covered with bear-track designs.

East of the Mississippi the bear track is usually in association with other animal and bird tracks, the most common being the deer and the turkey. It is likely that these tracks were made in connection with hunting magic—to help assure success in the pursuit of that particular game.

THE PLUMED OR HORNED SERPENT

Certain symbols form cultural links between peoples divided by race, religion, and historical background. Such a symbol is the plumed serpent.

The chief deity of the great Toltec civilization of Mexico (A.D. 856–1250) was Quetzalcoatl, god of learning. Legends describe him as a bearded white man who taught the Toltecs the arts, the calendar, writing, and law. Quetzalcoatl is often personified as a feathered rattlesnake and representations of him adorn many ruins of temples. The feathered-serpent cult was carried into the Maya country in Yucatan by the Toltecs where the god was known as Kukulcan. The Aztecs (A.D. 1324–1521) took over the Toltec culture and continued the cult of Quetzalcoatl. In the San Francisco Mountains of central Baja California, there is a spectacular plumed serpent sixteen feet long surrounded by black and red men and six deer. We can only guess that the snake deity in this case was somehow related to hunting magic.

North of Mexico, the symbol appears frequently as a feathered or horned rattlesnake. In the Hopi country, there are rock carvings of both types and they also occur on kiva wall paintings in the ruins of Kuaua near Bernalillo, New Mexico, and at Awatovi on Antelope Mesa, Arizona. The Hopi knew him as Palulukon or Water Serpent, and in Zuñi mythology he was Kolowisi, the Great Horned Serpent, guardian of the springs and streams. Beautiful pecked rock pictures of this deity are plentiful in the Galisteo Basin south of Santa Fe, where there were a number of Tewa pueblos between A.D. 1250 and 1692. To the Tewa, this deity was known as Awanyu. Modern black pottery from San Ildefonso portrays the plumed serpent copied from ancient designs. In southeastern United States, the plumed rattlesnake, drawn in the Mexican style, occurs engraved on stone discs, shell gorgets, and pottery at Spiro, Oklahoma; Moundville, Alabama; and Etowah, Georgia. These finely executed draw-

Bear tracks. 1. Pecked, near Santa Barbara, California. 2. Pecked, northern New Mexico. Redrawn from Polly Schaafsma, 1963. 3. Pecked, North Carolina. Redrawn from J. W. Cambron and S. A. Waters, 1959. 4. Incised, Nebraska. Redrawn from Garrick Mallery, 1893. 5. Pecked, Lake Pend d'Oreille, Idaho. 6. Red painting, British Columbia. Redrawn from Douglas Leechman, 1954.

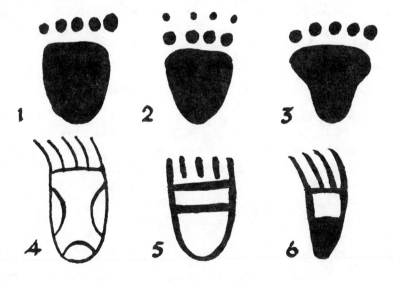

Pecked serpent, Galisteo Basin, New Mexico. Redrawn from E. B. Renaud, 1936.

Red painting of tattooed serpent, near El Paso, Texas. Redrawn from A. T. Jackson.

ings are from the Mississippi culture (1200–1600) in Osage and Creek territory. The best examples date from shortly before the coming of the Spanish and indicate strong Mexican influence. Almost nothing is known of what meaning the plumed serpent had for the southeastern Indians. The Natchez considered the serpent second only to the sun symbol in their ceremonies and "tattooed serpent" was the hereditary title of the war chiefs. The Cherokee who overran the Creek territory in eastern Tennessee and northern Georgia shortly before the arrival of the Spaniards called this serpent Uktena and it figures as an evil being in their legends. There can be little doubt that the design but not the cult spread north and east from Mexico not long before the Spanish Conquest.

The northern limit of the plumed serpent in the United States coincides roughly with the northern limit of Mexican influence on cultures and art forms—northern Arizona and New Mexico in the Southwest and southeastern Oklahoma in the Eastern Woodland.

THE THUNDERBIRD

This supernatural being was well known in many areas of North America. Thunderstorms were believed to be caused by an enormous bird that made thunder by flapping its wings and lightning by opening and closing its eyes. The rock drawings of the thunderbird vary from quite naturalistic in the Southwest to highly stylized in the Northwest and Eastern Woodland; but wherever they are found, the bird is always represented with the head to the side and the wings extended in "spread eagle" position.

Some plains tribes believed that the thunderstorm was due to a contest

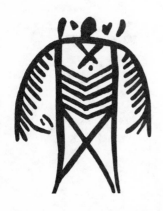

Pecked thunderbird, Alamakee County, Iowa. Redrawn from M. McKusick.

between the thunderbird and a huge rattlesnake or water monster. On the Northwest Coast the thunderbird was supposed to be catching whales during a thunder storm. A Salish tribe in British Columbia thought that the thunderbird used its wings as a great bow to shoot arrows and the noise was caused by the rebound of the wings.

Many tribes used the motif as a clan symbol. With the Hopi, it was the Eagle Clan. The Thunderbird Clan was the most important of the Winnebago Indian clans. This being was their most popular deity and his influence was sought by all. He was a clan ancestor and a guardian spirit bringing success in war and long life. Powerful shamans sometimes claimed to be a reincarnation of this benevolent deity. They pictured the thunderbird on rocks, wood, woven articles, and in effigy mounds.

THE MOUNTAIN SHEEP

The range of the Rocky Mountain sheep and its closely related geographical races covers the mountainous regions of western North America from British Columbia to northern Mexico. Wherever it is found, there are rock drawings of this fine animal.

Pecked drawing of thunderbird motif, Washington State Park, Missouri. From photograph by Frank Magre.

The mountain sheep is rarely painted, but almost invariably occurs as a pecked design in profile, though sometimes there are attempts to show the head alone front view. Styles range from crude scratched drawings on basalt boulders in southeast Oregon to superb life-sized pecked renderings in the Great Basin region of southeastern California. In the Coso Range of the Mojave Desert in Inyo County, California, are two canyons —known as Petroglyph Canyon and Renegade Canyon—where there are miles of well-executed engraving, including thousands of sheep. Sheep still exist in small bands in these barren mountains and are rigidly protected. These drawings were certainly made for hunting-magic rituals and often hunters are shown with *atlatl* or bow and arrow.

The representations of the sheep are mainly naturalistic but within this limitation, there is a wide range of style. Some have square bodies, occasionally patterned; others have curious boat-shaped bodies, flat on top and round below. The legs are usually shown stiffly vertical but in a few instances there has been an attempt at movement, an innovation doubtless frowned on by the solidly conservative community.

There seems reason to believe that the immense concentration of sheep drawings in this region represents a starting or focal point in the tradition of rendering this animal. Giving some credence to this idea, Robert Heizer and Martin Baumhoff, in *Prehistoric Rock Art of Nevada and Eastern California*, state that analysis of Shoshonean (Uto-Aztecan) dialects of the Great Basin indicates that the ancestral home of the Nevada Shoshoneans (Northern Paiute, Southern Paiute, Western Shoshonean) is in southeastern California, possibly in the vicinity of Death Valley. The linguistic evidence also suggests the Shoshoneans migrated from this area north along the eastern flank of the Sierra Nevada until they had occupied the entire Great Basin and Colorado Plateau. Besides the tribes already mentioned, this would include the Bannock, Shoshone, and Ute. It has been postulated on the basis of the slight dialect differences over vast areas and on archaeological evidence that this tremendous migration took place between A.D. 1200 and 1800. By the latter date the Shoshonean people were firmly established in their present territories. It would be strange indeed if these peoples did not take their rock-art traditions with them, and the mountain sheep hunting-ritual picture would be a part of these traditions. There are boat-shaped sheep from Monument Valley in southern Utah that are strikingly similar to the boat-shaped sheep from the Coso Range in the California desert.

The sheep (and other game animals) are always rendered in a naturalistic manner even if the rest of the panel is highly stylized and abstract. An unmistakable portrait of the hoped-for quarry was obviously of great importance.

Pecked mountain sheep, Marsh Pass, Arizona. Redrawn from A. V. Kidder and S. J. Guernsey, 1919.

THE HUMPED-BACK FLUTE PLAYER

This engaging and ubiquitous mythical being is found in the Southwest from the Four Corners area into northern Mexico. The portrait of Kokopelli, the humped-back flute player, appears countless times carved and painted on the rocks and painted on the pottery. That he has been a popular figure for a long time is shown by his appearance at Basketmaker sites 1,200 years or more ago. He appears on Hohokam and Mimbres pottery dated at around A.D. 1000–1150 and in association with pottery from northern New Mexico several hundred years later.

The classic type is of a sticklike figure with bent-over back playing on a flutelike instrument (Hohokam red-on-buff pottery). He varies enormously however. Sometimes he leans on a cane, sometimes he holds bow and arrow, often he is outrageously phallic. His hump varies from large to nonexistent. Occasionally he looks quite like a beetle or turtle. In any guise, Kokopelli is unmistakable.

In the upper Rio Grande villages, Kokopelli was said to wander from village to village with a bag of songs on his back, and as a symbol of fertility he was particularly welcome during the corn-planting season. In modern times, certain medicine men in the Andes travel from village to village with a flute and a sack of corn. It is intriguing to speculate on a connection between this modern custom in South America and the humped-back flute player of the Southwest.

Among the Hopi, the humped-back flute player was the symbol of the

Flute Clan. Kokopelli is widely known as a symbol of fertility and used to figure prominently in Hopi dances. God-impersonators dressed with prominent erotic costume-details as Kokopelli and his wife Kokopellimana charmed and delighted the Hopis with their antics but proved too earthy for the tourists. Today, the gay couple appear rarely and in a thoroughly censored routine.

At the Hopi village of Hano, Kokopelli appears as a black man, Nepokwa'i—even the *kachina* doll of this figure is painted black. The Hano people believe the hump is filled with buckskin for making shirts and moccasins to barter for brides. Nepokwa'i may be based on Esteban, the Negro of Fray Marcos de Niza's ill-fated 1539 expedition to find the famed Seven Cities of Cibola. Esteban was stoned to death by the Zuñis for molesting their women.[2] It is not known how far into Mexico this motif occurs but the humped-back creature shown on page 62 is from a rock shelter in the Sierra Santa Teressa in Sonora. Nearby was a similar archer shooting an antelope.

THE SHIELD FIGURE

This curious motif is identified with the Rocky Mountain region of the Southwest and Northern Great Plains regions. The northernmost record is from southeastern Alberta, south of Calgary. The major concentrations of the so-called classic shield figure are in Montana, northern Wyoming, and eastern Utah, though it occurs occasionally in southern Idaho, South Dakota, northeastern and central New Mexico, Arizona, northern Texas, and southern Nevada. The most common version consists of a circular shape, usually decorated with heraldiclike partitions and devices. Protruding from this circular design are a head and legs, and often a spear, feathered stick, or lance appears obliquely above the circle at two o'clock or ten o'clock. In other versions, there are one or more arms showing, which hold weapons such a spear, stone club, or bow. Wherever they are found, the drawing technique is the same as the prevailing rock-art technique in the region. In the Great Plains area, the shield figures with rare exceptions are crudely incised on soft sandstone. Occasionally, as at the site south of Calgary and at some Montana and Wyoming sites, the motifs are painted. Many sites in the Colorado drainage of eastern Utah have shield figures—both painted and pecked—that show careful workmanship and ingenious design. In this region the shield figures often occur at sites with the typical Fremont culture petroglyphs. There are a few beautifully painted examples from kiva wall paintings at Kawaika-a and Awatovi ruins, northeast of Flagstaff, Arizona, and at Pottery Mound, near Albuquerque, New Mexico.

Determining where this highly distinctive design motif started is diffi-

Hohokam pottery design of humped-back flute player. Redrawn from H. S. Gladwin, 1937.

Pecked portrait of Kokopelli, the humped-back flute player, Cieneguita, New Mexico. Redrawn from E. B. Renaud, 1936.

cult. Did the idea of the shield figure originate in the Great Plains and spread north and south and west? Or was it part of the Fremont culture pattern of eastern Utah adopted later by nomadic tribes from the plains?

Dating is important here. The oldest sites seem to be in the Fremont area. This culture, apparently derived from the Great Basin, was strongly influenced by Basketmaker and Pueblo traits from the south. It came to an end about A.D. 1150 according to H. M. Wormington. The shield figures from the Fremont area are characterized by lack of arms and the use of geometric designs on the shields. There are no historic period objects like horses depicted at any shield sites.

In the Great Plains area, however, there are a number of sites like those at Writing-on-Stone on the Milk River in southern Alberta, where typical shield figures are shown both with horses and mounted. Identical shield figures on horseback were painted on a Pawnee buffalo robe sometime prior to 1800. Thus, the practice of making shield figures continued well into the historic period. These later shield figures usually have one or more arms to hold various weapons such as the lance, bow and arrow, and war club, and are sometimes phallic. The interior designs on the shield often show animals, animal tracks, and humans.

In Arizona and New Mexico, the motif seems late. The shield paintings at the Awatovi kiva can be dated at not later than 1700 (though they may be at least 100 years older) when the pueblo was destroyed, while those at Kawaika-a are somewhat earlier. The shield figures at Comanche Gap in the Galisteo Basin can be dated at somewhere between 1250, the approximate date of the start of Galisteo Pueblo settlements and 1692, by which time the region was abandoned due to Comanche and Apache attacks. The kiva shield figures are painted while the Galisteo Basin figures are pecked, but in both instances they far surpass in execution and design any other examples of the motif.

The shield-figure motif can scarcely have originated with the Plains Indians. Their history as Plains Indians has been a brief one, dating from the introduction of the horse in the 18th century. Their art was chiefly derived from the Eastern Woodland culture, which never produced anything but the most rudimentary rock-art tradition. Far more plausible is the theory that this singular design motif was created at some time and by someone in the Fremont culture region of eastern Utah; that the motif became popular and spread through this area, ultimately diffusing into distant regions by means of the constant migrations and the forcible displacement of aboriginal populations that was still going on at the beginning of the historic period.

I believe that the earliest shield drawings are associated with warfare between the Fremont people and aggressive nomads from the north—probably the Indians later known as Navajo and Apache. The large shield

Black painting from rock shelter, Sierra Santa Teressa, Sonora.

Shield figures. 1. Incised, Writing-on-Stone Park, Alberta. From National Museum of Canada photograph. 2. Incised, Castle Gardens, Wyoming. From photograph by David Gebhard. 3. Red painting, Fergus County, Montana. Redrawn from K. G. Secrist. 4. Pecked, White Canyon, southeastern Utah. Redrawn from Julian H. Steward, 1941.

Detail of Pawnee buffalo robe painting. Redrawn from J. C. Ewers.

Pecked shield figure, Grapevine Canyon, southern Nevada. From photograph by John Cawley.

Maze design near Hopi town of Shipaulovi,
northern Arizona. Photograph by John Cawley.

would be ideal for protecting warriors against arrows during an assault
on a defended position.

A solid bit of evidence was discovered near Torrey, Utah in 1925—
three large buffalo-hide shields decorated in abstract patterns and large
enough to cover the entire torso were found in a cave shelter. These
shields were radiocarbon-dated just before this book went to press. The
tests indicated that they were made between 1650 and 1750 or just prior
to the beginning of the horse-oriented Plains culture. The plains warriors developed a small shield averaging about 20 inches in diameter.

The shield drawings in the Fremont area (abandoned by 1150), at
Pottery Mound (abandoned by 1450), and in the Galisteo Basin (abandoned by 1692) certainly suggest that the peaceful corn-growers were
under considerable pressure from the warlike newcomers.

THE MYSTERY OF THE MINOAN MAZE IN ARIZONA

In the first chapter I stated my belief that the design motifs in North
America originated on this continent though there was much diffusion of
styles and design elements over vast areas as populations were constantly
on the move.

Just south of Oraibi in northeastern Arizona there are five curious
symbols in the form of mazes carved on a rock. Near another Hopi town,
Shipaulovi, the same intricate design occurs. According to modern Hopi
Indians, this design represents the myth of emergence and is called by the
Hopis the Mother Earth symbol, Tápu'at (Mother and Child). The passages in the maze are the paths that man must follow on his Road of Life.
In southern Arizona, an identical design is carved on the inside wall of
the upper story of the ruin of Casa Grande. In 1761 a Spanish traveler in
Pimeria Alta (Arizona and Sonora) noted that the Pima drew this symbol
in the sand. In his manuscript account he drew a picture of the maze
that was exactly like the Hopi versions. A Pima Indian said that the

Stylized shield figures pecked on basalt,
Galisteo Basin, south of Santa Fe.
Photograph by John Cawley.

*Three examples of
Minoan maze. Top—
Pecked, Ireland. After
photograph in* Illustrated
London News. *Middle—
Maze on silver Cretan
coin. Redrawn from
H. S. Colton, 1917.
Bottom—Pima design,
Arizona. Redrawn from
H. S. Colton, 1917.*

symbol was used in a children's game and was called the house of Tcuhu. The design is found today in modern Pima basketry.

This symbol is so intricate and so unusual that the idea that it could be independently devised twice is not credible. Yet this maze symbol, *exactly* the same in every detail, occurs in Europe. The earliest example is on an Etruscan vase dating from the late 7th century B.C. Examples are found carved on glacially scratched rocks in the Camonica Valley of the Italian Alps that have been dated between 500 and 250 B.C. A silver coin from Knossos in Crete (200–67B.C.) features the same maze symbol. A massive block of granite from the Wicklow Mountains in Ireland (the Hollywood Stone) is carved with the identical maze and there are two such designs carved on a ledge in Rocky Valley, Cornwall.

These European mazes appear to be much the same age—several centuries before and after Christ. They are probably Iron Age cult symbols, spreading from Crete through the Etruscan people of northern Italy to the Camunian civilization in the Italian Alps, where culture patterns were affected by the Etruscans to the south and the Celts to the North. The cult symbol might have traveled to Britain and Ireland through the Celtic tribes of mainland Europe or it might have been carried to the islands by the Romans during the Roman occupation, A.D. 43–450.

To explain the appearance of this distinctive symbol in Arizona, Harold S. Colton has listed three possibilities: "First, these symbols may have arisen independently in the new and old world. Secondly, the symbol may have originated in the old world and have been transported to the new in pre-Columbian times. Thirdly that the symbol was introduced into America with the Spanish conquest." [3]

The first possibility can be discarded as a million-to-one shot. Simple basic motifs such as whorls, frets, and crosses will occur to designers anywhere who are working in pottery, basketry, or weaving, but the extraordinary complexity of the Minoan maze would indicate that the design must have spread from a common source. I think the second possibility unlikely as an early introduction would indicate a wider diffusion than the three occurrences in Arizona. It is quite possible that this maze motif in America had a Spanish origin, not earlier than 1600, and that the intriguing design caught the fancy of the Hopi and the Pima.

Carl Schuster, who has been collecting material on this motif for many years, points out the possibility of two additional sites, one in the Galisteo Basin in New Mexico (Tewa Pueblo territory), and the other in the state of Nayarit, Mexico. If this last site could be authenticated, it would greatly extend the range of this extraordinary design in the New World.

There are a number of curious design conventions that appear as details on rock figures. Three of these, the weeping eye, the speech motif, and

Incised drawings, showing heart-line of animal on right, West Virginia. Redrawn from Garrick Mallery, 1893.

the heart-line, are so distinctive that they can be traced from area to area. Such motifs can be transmitted slowly through exchange of cultural ideas with other tribes and rapidly by migration, where the migrating group take many of their old traditions to their new homeland. Some examples may be the result of independent invention.

The weeping eye (usually vertical lines from the outer edges of the eyes) occurs in the Mississippi culture of southeastern United States, in Wyoming, Montana, Utah, and on the middle Columbia River.

The speech motif (a curved design coming from the mouth of animals, birds, and humans) is found in many Mexican murals and bas-reliefs and in incised shell and copper designs from the Mississippi culture. The only rock-drawing examples are birds with speech symbols in eastern Missouri. This symbol undoubtedly spread north from Mexico in late prehistoric times.

Many Indian tribes drew representations of game animals with a "heart-line" running from the mouth of the animal to the vital organ. The Ojibwa called such drawings *muzzin-ne-neen*, and they were used in hunting-magic ceremonies. When an arrow was drawn piercing the heart of the animal it was hoped that equal success would attend the hunter in the field. This motif is found in West Virginia, Minnesota (where the heart-line also occurs in human figures), Montana, Wyoming, Utah, and New Mexico. It seems likely that this convention originated in the Eastern Woodland and moved through the Great Plains to the Southwest.

8 METHODS OF RECORDING

Pecked bear prints, Lake Pend d'Oreille, Idaho.

The field techniques of recording a rock-drawing site have become somewhat standardized during the last thirty years.

Much of the recording of rock pictures has been by freehand drawing. In many ways it is the poorest method. It takes a rather good artist with a keen and observant eye to copy these paintings and engravings accurately. Unskilled attempts are often worse than useless and bear only the vaguest relation to the original when compared to a good photograph. As a means of copying details too faded or eroded to be picked up by photography, however, field sketches—in pencil or ink, water color or pastels (with approximate scale indicated on the margin)—can be extremely useful. Charles la Monk, a California artist, employed a method of oil paint over a sheet of Masonite sprinkled with eroded sand from the actual rock face to simulate the rock surface. This ingenious technique provides a rather exact facsimile of a small section of painted surface but is entirely too laborious to be considered a standard recording procedure.

Probably the best of the freehand-drawing techniques involves attaching string grids to the rock face with tape. The drawings can then be scaled to the original by making the copy on graph paper or drawing paper with grid drawn to suit desired scale. Different colored inks may be used on tracings of rock drawings to record superimpositions.

Many recordings are made by direct tracings. A common method is to fasten sheets of transparent plastic onto the rock surface with masking tape. The designs are then traced with colored pencils. Henri Lhote, in preparing copies of the Tassili rock paintings in the Sahara, took a team

68

of artists directly to the sites where, armed with great sheets of tracing paper and ladders, they made tracings of all major pictured surfaces. These were then transferred to drawing paper and the finished copies made on the spot. Selwyn Dewdney uses a variation on this technique. He soaks rice paper and applies it to the surface to be recorded with a sponge-rubber roller. The damp paper becomes completely transparent and clings to every irregularity of the rock surface. The incised lines are then traced with a sharpened piece of chalk.

In another method of duplicating carved surfaces, a lightweight cloth (or paper) is taped over the design and a printer's roller carrying oil-base printing ink is rolled over the surface producing a direct-image print.

At sites where the designs are deeply cut, reverse molds may be taken with latex, wax, or plaster of Paris, thus recording even the irregularities of the rock surface. These techniques are used only to record small areas or single figures as the procedure is slow and laborious.

By far the most successful method is photography. It is best to take both black-and-white and color shots of the surfaces to be recorded. The black-and-white shots are needed if the photographs are to illustrate an article or to mount in field books for ready reference. The color slide is indispensable for painted surfaces or where the natural color of the rock is an important factor. In addition, slides can be used for illustrated lectures or classroom work and also for projection on paper if line drawings are required. Most of the text figures in this book were traced from such projections. A good color slide will faithfully give not only the details of the designs but the texture and color of the surrounding rock surface. With the camera, large areas can be covered quickly and accurately.

Most carved and pecked sites can be photographed with available light as they usually occur on cliff faces and isolated boulders, but in many areas the paintings are deep in rock shelters where the creator placed them to escape the weathering effects of wind and water. Here the recorder must often resort to time exposures or flash. The light electronic-flash units available today are very handy for this work and will take up to 150 pictures on one charging of the battery.

When taking picture by available light, the best results are often obtained on a gray day or if the subject is in the shade. Sunlight coming at about a 45-degree angle will sometimes give excellent definition to a carved or pecked design if the surrounding rock is smooth, but if the surface is rough the irregularities can mask the design.

Among rock-art students, there is a sharp difference of opinion on the use of "chalking." One school holds that some designs lack contrast and the only way to get a good photograph is to chalk over the design to heighten the contrast. In the case of some rock carvings where there is no patina to contrast with cut surfaces or where the design has weathered to the same color as the rock mass, there may be some justification for chalking. The dissenters have many objections to it: the original appearance of the drawing is ruined by application of chalk; the work is often done without proper observation, so that different chalkers interpret what they see or think they see quite differently; chalking destroys any effect of superimposition; and with proper illumination, chalking is entirely unnecessary. Use of a side- or top-lighted flash will often bring out details that will not show up on a straight front-lighted subject. Chalk should never be applied to rock paintings since there is no way to remove it without harm to the painting. Pecked or incised rock drawings are usually in exposed positions, and the winter rain can be counted on to wash away the chalk. (I have two publications describing the same rock-pecked panel from the Galisteo Basin in New Mexico; each author had carefully chalked in what he saw or thought he saw on the rock surface and the results were just different enough to allow the two writers to come to startlingly different conclusions.)

Emmanuel Anati, the recorder of the great complex of rock engravings

Pecked drawings (chalked) near Wheeling, West Virginia. String grid is for making scale drawings. Note creature with heart-line in foreground. Photograph from Carnegie Museum, Pittsburgh.

Author photographing paintings in the Cara Pintada Gorge, Sierra Santa Teressa, Sonora. Photograph by Dean Blanchard.

Incised drawing being chalked prior to photography. Milwaukee Public Museum photograph.

*Sample form for record-
ing field notes.*

SANTA BARBARA MUSEUM OF NATURAL HISTORY
PICTOGRAPH SURVEY RECORD

1. SITE Horse Canyon   2. NUMBER CGK-4   3. COUNTY Kern

4. MAP Bakersfield T32S/R34E/S15   5. ELEVATION 4000

6. LOCATION Driving from Bakersfield, take first canyon road left
   past Monolith. At 3 miles take road Right - drive 2.1 miles -
   cave is high on left across small dry steam. Two caves - painted
   cave to right...27' wide, 6' high, 16' deep.

7. DIMENSIONS OF PAINTED AREA   About 6'x15'

8. KIND OF ROCK   Andesite

9. POSITION OF ROCK   Facing east

10. COLORS   Red,yellow,white,black,green

11. DESIGN ELEMENTS   Abstract 2,4,21,34,37,40,66,67,68 - also a
    number of unique designs featuring curved parallel
    lines to give rainbow effect

12. SUPERIMPOSITION   None

13. EROSION   slight

14. VANDALISM   none

15. ASSOCIATED FEATURES   Many bedrock mortars in adjoining cave

16. REMARKS   Near a heavily traveled road. Possibility of vandalism
    extreme

17. PREVIOUS DESIGNATIONS FOR SITE   none

18. PUBLISHED REFERENCES   none

19. RECORDED BY   Campbell Grant and J. J. Cawley

20. DATE March 1962   21. PHOTOS   Color

in the Camonica Valley of northern Italy, had a special problem that he solved in a unique way. The picture rocks were covered with earth and moss, and when cleaned, had too little contrast to photograph. The entire design area of the rocks was coated with a thin gouache solution. When the surface was dry, it was wiped over with a damp cloth, leaving a faint tint in the incised areas. This method proved far faster and more accurate than chalking, and the smallest details showed clearly for photography.

It is important to know the scale of the rock pictures and all photographs should include an object of known length, preferably a six- or twelve-inch ruler.

Often paintings are overlaid with a calcareous deposit from water seepage, obscuring the designs and making photography difficult. To overcome this, Henri Lhote in recording the Sahara rock paintings used an application of kerosene, which made the deposit temporarily transparent. A like result can be obtained with water applied with a small pressure sprayer. In both instances, the reds and blacks are intensified but the paler colors like yellow and white tend to lose contrast.

The field notes should be transferred to a form containing all pertinent information that would enable other students to relocate any recorded site. Such forms are in use by a number of institutions, such as the University of California and the Santa Barbara Museum of Natural History. The general location is marked on a topographical map of the area, which will give elevations, and township, range, and section numbers. Later a sketch map is made to scale, showing pertinent terrain features and boulders or rock faces bearing designs.

9 PRESERVATION OF SITES

White painting near Coyote, Coahuila. Redrawn from J. Alden Mason.

Fifty miles northeast of Santa Barbara, California, are the Carrizo Plains, a forbidding, waterless valley between low desert ranges. Every few years, enough rain falls for the ranchers to mature a scanty wheat crop or to feed cattle. The area is well known to birdwatchers; it is a major wintering spot for sandhill cranes, which come every year by the thousands to feed in the stubble fields. In the center of the plains, an enormous sandstone rock, shaped like a horseshoe, rises over 75 feet, forming a natural amphitheater. On its walls the prehistoric inhabitants of the region painted hundreds of complex polychrome designs (a detail of the main panel, photographed at the turn of the century, is shown here).

Today the site is a complete shambles. Beer cans and empty rifle cartridges litter the ground, and the paintings that survived the gunfire are painted over or carved with names and dates. What was the finest rock-painting site in the United States has been completely ruined by senseless vandalism.

The legacy of aboriginal rock art in the United States is being destroyed at an ever accelerating rate. Before the coming of the whites, the only destructive forces were the natural ones of wind and water. Designs pecked in hard rock are highly resistant to both types of erosion but carvings in soft sandstone and all paintings are highly susceptible to water damage and the scouring effect of wind and wind-blown sand. Only paintings located in favorable spots protected from rain by rock shelters and facing away from prevailing winds have survived with the original brilliance of their color intact.

74

Polychrome painting from the Carrizo Plains, California, as it appeared at the turn of the century. Kern County Land Company photograph, 1894.

Detail of the Carrizo site photographed in 1962, showing the results of vandalism by gunfire.

The immediate and constant danger to these prehistoric drawings comes from the enlightened white man. Some people cannot resist the temptation to scrawl their names over the old Indian designs. Some scratch their name and the date; others use oil paint; the latest method is by paint-spray cans. Another variation of this brainless pattern is to shoot at the rock pictures, anything circular being especially attractive to marksmen.

There is one famous instance in New Mexico where the scribblings of the white man at an aboriginal site have genuine historical interest—at Inscription Rock, El Morro National Monument. This towering landmark, site of two ruined Zuñi villages, has long been a favorite camping spot due to a large natural reservoir of water at the base of the rock. There are hundreds of names incised in the soft sandstone, including that of the first colonizer of New Mexico, Governor Oñate, dated 1605. Many subsequent governors left names and messages alongside those of explorers, soldiers, scouts, traders, and immigrants. A particularly elegant signature is shown here.

But the Sunday beer-can-and-rifle vandal is a minor menace compared with destruction in the name of progress. Topping the list of rock-art destroyers is the hydroelectric and flood-control dam. One of the largest concentrations of aboriginal rock drawings in North America was on the basalt cliffs along the Columbia River from The Dalles to the Grand Coulee. Many large dams have been constructed between these points, taming the mighty river beyond recognition and inundating thousands

An example of handsome vandalism, El Morro National Monument, near Zuni, New Mexico. Photograph by John Cawley.

Pecked drawings near Machiasport, Maine. Site now under water at high tide. From Garrick Mallery, 1893.

of rock pictures. When the Glen Canyon region of the Colorado was flooded by the rising waters of Lake Powell, many hundreds of sites were lost. Dams have drowned the West Virginia sites along the Kanawha River and the sites at Safe Harbor on the Susquehanna River in Pennsylvania. Unfortunately aboriginal man, irresistibly attracted to living in the rocky canyons of the great rivers, often made his ceremonial and magical drawings just above high water. With the dams now building and on the drawing boards of the U.S. Army Engineers, a continuing loss of these irreplaceable paintings and carvings can be anticipated. In addition many sites are destroyed each year by road building.

In the last few years, however, the government, though committed to dam construction, has encouraged long-range salvage operations wherever the project threatened extensive archaeological material. Such a salvage operation in the Glen Canyon area is described by Christy Turner in *Petroglyphs of the Glen Canyon Region*. Equally enlightened is the attitude of a few large corporations like the El Paso Natural Gas Company, which has opened up vast areas in archaeologically rich northern New Mexico. Whenever important sites are threatened by road-building or pipe-laying operations, work is held up until the material can be examined and described by experts. The cost of the study and publication costs are met by the company and the projects have come to be known as pipeline archaeology.

The federal government and some state agencies have become increasingly concerned with the destruction of so many of these rock-art sites and a start has been made to save something for future generations. The most successful results have been achieved in the Southwest, where many fine sites are now protected by their inclusion within national parks and monuments, such as Chaco Canyon National Monument, Zion National Park, Canyon de Chelly National Monument, etc. Here trails and roads are created to take the tourists to rock-art sites that are constantly under supervision.

At the state and local levels, a number of excellent attempts to preserve sites have been made. In Massachusetts, Dighton Rock has been moved from its original position, where it was subject to daily inundation by tides, to higher ground. The Ginkgo Petrified Forest Museum at Vantage, Washington, created by the Washington State Parks and Recreation Commission, has on display a number of large blocks of stone covered with rock carvings salvaged before flooding by the Wanapum Dam below Vantage. Farther down the river, the Winquatt Museum at The Dalles has a large collection of such salvaged carved stones. The Arizona State Parks Administration is protecting the Piedras Pintadas near Gila Bend, the site described by Father Kino in 1711.

Many property owners, especially ranchers who have examples of rock art on their property, are very protective, either out of regard for the engravings or paintings themselves or to insure their privacy by keeping the location of such sites secret. The well-known Painted Cave near Santa Barbara has been in private hands for a great many years and the last two owners have maintained a locked iron gate at the entrance. As a result, this fine example of aboriginal art is in good condition, though periodically the lock is smashed and a few names scratched on the painting.

Any and all efforts to save these irreplaceable treasures should be encouraged but much more needs to be done. In the state of California, where the most spectacular North American paintings are found, there is only one rock art site under official protection. This is the vast complex of pecked designs in Renegade and Petroglyph canyons, inside the Naval Ordnance Test Station in the Coso Range of Inyo County. These sites have recently been designated a national landmark and can be visited under Navy supervision.

Part II

ROCK ART AREAS

For convenience in discussing the rock-art zones, I have arbitrarily divided the continent from the Arctic Ocean down to the 23rd parallel in Mexico into nine geographical areas. These areas coincide in the most general sort of way with the natural and cultural regions and rock-drawing stylistic areas. To maintain continuity I have started with the northern section of each rock-art area and worked south.

Most of the rock art in North America occurs on smooth basaltic rock or sandstone, both of which are abundant in or adjacent to the western mountain ranges. In the eastern United States, the majority of the designs are found on the horizontal surfaces of bedrock, usually limestone.

The type of rock to a large extent dictates the technique of applying the drawings. On exposed basalt, sandstone, and limestone, pecking or incising is favored. Both paintings and pecked designs are found on granite. Wherever possible, the paintings are on undersurfaces or areas protected by a rock overhang. The pecked designs are usually cut deeply to bring out patterns, as granite does not give the sharp contrast of patinated basalt or sandstone. In areas where the sandstone forms rock shelters, painting predominates, but in the Southwest, especially in Utah where there are an infinite number of sandstone cliffs covered with dark desert-varnish patina, pecking is the preferred technique.

In areas where ample rock surfaces are present without rock drawings of any kind, the only explanation is that the occupying Indians simply lacked a rock-drawing tradition.

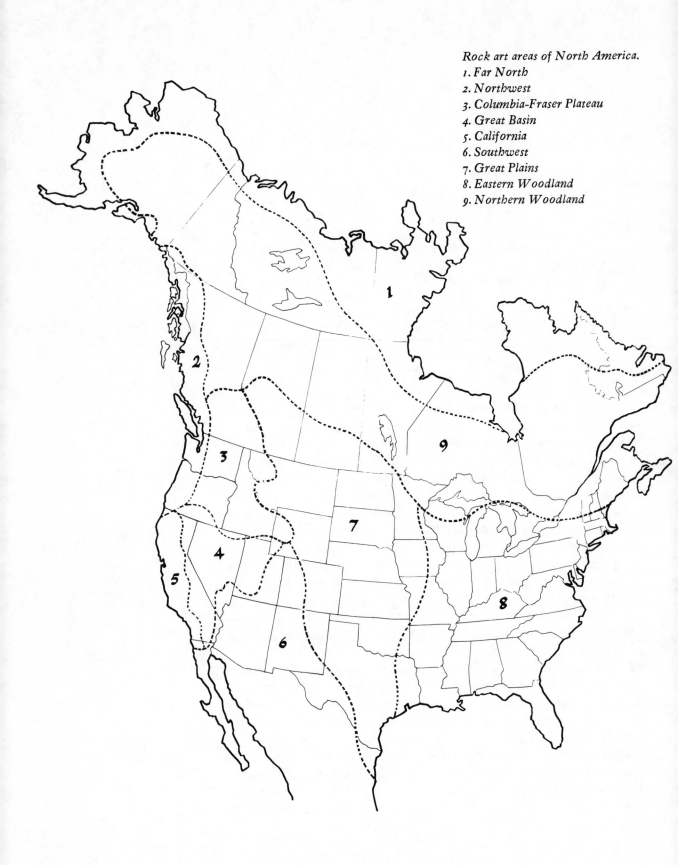

Rock art areas of North America.
1. Far North
2. Northwest
3. Columbia-Fraser Plateau
4. Great Basin
5. California
6. Southwest
7. Great Plains
8. Eastern Woodland
9. Northern Woodland

10 THE FAR NORTH

Pecked scroll, Wrangell Island, Alaska. From photograph by Edward L. Keithahn.

This forbidding region stretches along the northern edges of the continent from Prince William Sound in Alaska to Labrador in eastern Canada. With the exception of the coniferous forests of the Kodiak Island-Prince William Sound region, it is a land of tundra—wastelands of moss and lichen; a land of bitter cold—short summers and long winters. The Eskimos and the Aleuts sharing a common Eskimo culture live on the coasts of this vast region, seldom venturing far inland.

Modern Eskimos have a rather highly developed art in the form of carved ivory and stone but few of their rock drawings have been recorded. The northernmost site on the continent was found in 1950 by a party of geologists in the foothills of the Brooks Range in northern Alaska. Designs resembling corncobs and deeply incised lines arranged in a rather haphazard manner suggesting tool sharpening occurred on a single sandstone slab. It is quite possible this is doodling by an Eskimo hunting party waiting for game.

Another site in the Brooks Range occurs in a now-empty village that was occupied until the late 19th century, where there are incised boulders in the *kadigi* or men's house. On the Seward Peninsula there are some crude paintings in red and black of human figures. These three sites are the only ones known in northern Alaska.

The next rock drawings are found far to the south on the southwest tip of Kodiak Island—two sites on cliffs and granite boulders at Cape Alitak. The petroglyphs are made by pecking and are from a quarter to three-quarters of an inch in depth. The subjects are human faces of which only the features are drawn, and whales, land animals, and some simple nonrepresentational figures, like spirals and lines of dots. The nonoutlined faces are not unlike those found in the Puget Sound-Strait of Georgia region. Eskimos on Kodiak Island and nearby Afognak Island

Eskimo pictographs in red, Prince William Sound, Alaska. Redrawn from Frederica de Laguna, 1956.

Pecked mask designs (chalked), Alitak Point, Kodiak Island, Alaska. U. S. Geological Survey photograph.

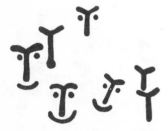

Pecked human faces, Kodiak Island, Alaska. After Heizer, 1947.

have reported numerous paintings in red on these islands similar to those on the mainland to the east. According to the Eskimos, the pictures were made for hunting magic and to record game killed.

Frederica de Laguna has recorded many Eskimo paintings in red from Cook Inlet and Prince William Sound, northeast of Kodiak Island. Here again are nonoutlined faces, human figures, game animals, particularly whales and canoes. Eskimo informants said that these pictures were associated with whaling rituals and hunting magic. The nonoutlined face that is first encountered on Kodiak Island is a widespread design motif throughout the Northwest Coast, perhaps the most characteristic of the area.

These Alaskan drawings are all rather crudely conceived and executed. Those from southern Alaska show a strong influence from the Northwest Coast.

The only other Eskimo rock-art site is on the other side of the continent, in northern Quebec. It is located in an old steatite quarry on an island near Wakeham Bay. Saladin d'Anglure, carrying out a social anthropology study in 1961, was taken to the site by Eskimos who were making the trip to get steatite for their carvings. The designs, numbering over 50, were all of masks, some human, others animal. The Eskimos made extensive use of masks, which, among the Chugach and Aleut, were supposed to represent the familiar spirits of shamans. Such masks were worn during ceremonies and are often found with mummies in burial caves. The Eskimo rock drawings appear to be chiefly game animals and ceremonial masks. The masks may represent a cultural trait acquired from the Northwest Coast Indians, who wore elaborate masks in dances to represent supernatural beings. The age of the Eskimo designs is unknown but there are a few clues; they do not appear to have been made by living Indians and there are no articles portrayed of white manufacture. On the other hand, there is no evidence that they are very old. It is possible that most of them are late prehistoric.

11 THE NORTHWEST

Along the heavily timbered northwest coast of North America, from Yakutat Bay in southeastern Alaska to Trinidad Bay in California, a unique and complex culture was shared by a number of tribes. The principal groups are the Tlingit, Tsimshian, Haida, Bella Coola, Kwakiutl, Nootka, and Coast Salish. It has often been noted that the higher cultures of America grew out of a settled agricultural economy, but here the leisure time to develop elaborate social and ceremonial patterns was provided by the inexhaustible supply of natural resources along the shores and rivers.

Red painting near Tyee, British Columbia. Redrawn from National Museum of Canada photograph.

The two major resources of the region were the western red cedar or canoe cedar and the Pacific salmon. Mollusks of all kinds and many large game animals, both land and marine, were important, but it can be said that the culture was essentially a cedar and salmon culture. Although the coastal region had many fine trees like the Douglas fir, the soft, straight-grained cedar was preferred. The magnificent tree gave them canoes, huge communal houses, bark cloth for clothing, and utensils of all kinds, while the immense runs of five species of salmon provided fresh fish for part of the year and smoked salmon for the remainder.

The art forms from the Northwest are widely known and admired; the intricate stylized animal forms that occur everywhere, spectacular totem poles, carved vessels in cedar and argillite, figureheads for the large dugout canoes, and fantastic carved and painted ceremonial masks. It is not surprising that this art tradition dominated their rock carvings too, though with few exceptions their finest work was confined to carving on wood or the easily worked argillite (a slatelike stone without cleavage).

There is no reason to believe that much of the rock art of the Northwest is very old or for that matter that many of their most spectacular achievements, such as the prowed sailing canoe and the gabled communal

83

house, with totemic carvings on the front, were not imported ideas. Such canoes and communal houses were long established in Polynesia and a number of writers have remarked on the possibility that these famous voyagers brought new ideas and tools to the Northwest. The totem pole, so characteristic of the Northwest Coast, appears to be a recent development. Many European and American vessels visited the area between 1774 and 1794 and these ships brought iron tools to the Indians. The first totem pole was described in 1791.[1]

From the rock paintings of the Chugach Eskimo of Prince William Sound to the next known examples in southeastern Alaska near Sitka, there is a distance of approximately 450 air miles. Doubtless there are more examples between these points that may be recorded in the future but much of the intervening country is covered with glaciers and heavy forest where inconspicuous rock carvings might well go unnoticed. This is Tlingit territory and the carvings occur on Wrangell and several adjacent islands.

A complex arrangement of figures carved on a boulder near Sitka was interpreted by an elderly Tlingit as a representation of the creation myth. This legend is common to all Northwest Coast tribes and indeed in various forms is found throughout North America.

According to this legend, in the beginning the world was a confused mass of rock and ocean, enveloped in darkness and controlled by powerful spirits who possessed the elements necessary to human life. Yehlh, a benign spirit, who could assume any shape but particularly that of a raven, created man. Over the strenuous objections of the other spirits, he was able to give his children light, fresh water, fire, air, and other good things. After all was done, he disappeared.[2]

On Etolin Island, at about high-tide level, there are many smooth dark rocks, seldom over three feet in diameter, with single figures carved on them. The designs are chiefly animal motifs and represent totemic or clan symbols of the Stikine tribe. There are highly stylized drawings of the wolf, bear, raven, shark, killer whale, eagle, and human head, both outlined and without outline. On Wrangell Island to the east, there are similar carved beach boulders, some with fantastic marine beings referred to by the local Indians as sea monsters.

In the section of British Columbia adjoining Alaska, the Tsimshian territory begins and here all the sites are on the mainland. Several are painted and most of them are on the banks of the Skeena and Nass rivers. Some painted sites feature coppers, the distinctive status symbols discussed in chapter 4 on interpretation. These wealth indicators might have been recorded on stone to commemorate a potlatch or they might have been drawn by someone who hoped to acquire such riches.

South of the Tsimshian territory are numerous carved sites in the terri-

Pecked mythological creatures from Tlingit area, southeastern Alaska. Redrawn from G. T. Emmons.

Stylized head painting with coppers near Tyee, British Columbia. National Museum of Canada photograph.

Pecked sea monster on granite beach boulder (chalked), southeastern Alaska. Photograph by Edward L. Keithahn.

Stylized figures pecked on bedrock, Bella Coola Valley, British Columbia. National Museum of Canada photograph.

tory of the Bella Coola Indians. Here the typical rock picture is deeply incised on isolated boulders. The ubiquitous human face, both outlined and nonoutlined, occurs frequently with anthropomorphs often featuring large eyes and omitting the nose. These are often near river mouths and subject to tidal action and heavy erosion. Drawings in many cases are made on rather small boulders, as in the case of the Wrangell Island carvings.

Farther south are the Kwakiutl, occupying the northwest third of Vancouver Island and adjoining land along the coast to the north. Here there are both painted and carved drawings. The paintings are certainly later than the carvings, some having been made in the last forty years, and show strong influence from the Coast and Inland Salish, with realistic figures quite unlike those in the typical stylized Northwest tradition.

The Coast Salish occupied the circumference of the Gulf of Georgia, Puget Sound, and most of western Washington down to the Chinook territory along the lower Columbia. These people, closely related to the Inland Salish of the Fraser-Columbia Plateau, seem to be late-comers to

Beach boulders with masklike designs, Bella Coola River, British Columbia.
National Museum of Canada photograph.

*Fish shapes on boulder,
Nanaimo, Vancouver
Island. National Museum
of Canada photograph.*

*Pecked drawings of sea monsters, Nanaimo, Vancouver Island. National Museum of
Canada photograph.*

Killer whales and masks pecked on granite (chalked), Cape Alava, Olympic National Park. Note weeping eye. Photograph by Dale Ritter.

Head of Tsagaglalal, mythical woman ruler, pecked on basalt with traces of red paint, near The Dalles Dam, Oregon. Photograph by Jean Hillis.

the coast, having pushed down the Fraser and spilled over the Cascades into western Washington. Many rock-art sites are known from this region, both painted and carved. The carved sites are older than the painted and are in the tradition of the Northwest petroglyphs farther north. At Sproat Lake and at Nanaimo on Vancouver Island, there are outstanding examples of carved mythological beings not unlike the sea monsters from Wrangell Island. On the shores of the Strait of Georgia and in Puget Sound there are carved beach boulders with outlined and nonoutlined heads, like those in the Bella Coola territory and farther north.

The painted sites, almost invariably done in red, are quite naturalistic, featuring canoes, salmon, cetaceans, deer, a double-headed animal with snakelike body, humans, ladderlike designs that might represent salmon weirs, and the classic type of thunderbird. Occasionally painted heads are reminiscent of the carved heads. A good clue to the age lies in the fact that the drawings closely resemble those painted on the power boards used in the great winter ceremony of the Indians around Puget Sound— power boards that were made up until quite recent times. For the most part, the Coast Salish paintings are done in the same manner as those made by the Inland Salish tribes along the Okanogan and Fraser rivers.

The warlike Nootka, who occupied southeastern Vancouver Island, made both painted and carved designs. A number of painted areas in Nootka Sound depict horses and other postcontact motifs, and are in the realistic style of the nearby Coast Salish. South of Puget Sound there are a few carved sites on the lower Columbia that reflect the classic Northwest style. A noteworthy example is the carved and painted head of Tsagaglalal, a legendary woman ruler who was turned to stone by Coyote. It is very skillfully pecked into basaltic rock high above the Columbia River at the present site of The Dalles Dam. Remains of red paint on the rock suggest that the lines of many of the Northwest carvings were originally filled in with paint that has eroded away.

12 THE COLUMBIA-
FRASER PLATEAU

*Red painting, Okanogan
River, Washington.
Redrawn from
H. Thomas Cain.*

This region embraces the middle Fraser River watershed and the Columbia drainage above The Dalles. In British Columbia, it is mainly a hilly country with many long river and lake valleys enjoying a mild and dry climate. In the United States, the middle Columbia country to the east of the Cascades is hot and dry. Some of the tributaries are very large rivers such as the Deschutes, Salmon, and Snake rivers cutting through deep gorges and semidesert country. Bordering the plateau country are the heavily timbered Cascade Mountains to the west and the Rocky Mountains to the east.

The Inland Salish tribes, closely related to the Coast Salish on the west of the Cascades, occupied a territory from the middle Fraser River, British Columbia, to the Columbia River near Vantage, Washington. There are many rock-art sites and the techniques and styles are remarkably similar over the whole region. The northernmost sites are in Shushwap country above Lillooet. They are mainly carvings on flat rock surfaces and boulders along the Fraser Canyon. A few paintings on limestone are quite realistic, showing men with bows, bighorn sheep, bear paws, salmon, thunderbirds, and a motif that is very often seen to the south in the Columbia drainage—a semicircular shape with attached rays. Additional designs here are canoes, beaver, and cranes. These paintings are all rather crudely done, suggesting the use of the finger as paintbrush, and are in red with occasional black or yellow.

To the east, similar paintings are found in the territory of the Okanogan Indians and include horsemen, additional evidence that most, if not

all, of the existing Salish paintings are recent—late prehistoric and historic.
Many of the sites are located on cliff faces overlooking the confluence of
two streams.

Along the lower Okanogan and upper Columbia rivers in Washington,
the paintings become more sophisticated, the execution is more careful,
and new design elements are encountered. It is obvious that in this region,
brushes of several sizes were used, allowing for better workmanship. The
rayed semicircle (sometimes referred to as "sunburst") appears with increasing frequency, sometimes alone but more often forming a halo above
single anthropomorphic figures and twinned anthropomorphic forms. The
"twinned" brothers is a common motif as far down the Columbia as
Vantage and represents characters from a widespread Indian myth. Other
new elements include patterns made with a series of dots and animals
enclosed in circles.

The Columbia River from the Okanogan to The Dalles had innumerable
rock-drawing sites prior to 1941, when the Grand Coulee Dam went into

*Red paintings of bear tracks and stylized figures, Pavilion Lake, British Columbia.
National Museum of Canada photograph.*

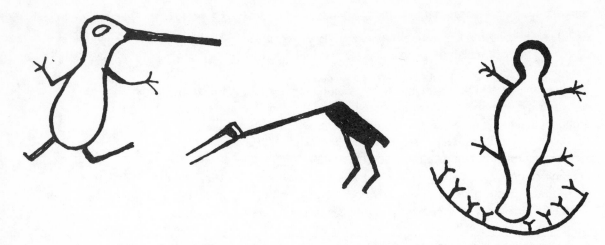

Red paintings near Lytton, British Columbia. Redrawn from N. Hallisey.

operation. There are now ten major dams between Grand Coulee and Bonneville dams. Most of the rock-art sites are inundated and we have only drawings and photographs of many of them.

From Wenatchee and on south, rock carvings occur in association with paintings. The subject matter is identical to what has been described on the lower Okanogan and the shift to carving reflects the type of rock available. Through much of the Salish territory, the "country" rock is granite, which is excellent for paint but a poor surface for pecking or incising, while the basalt cliffs of the Columbia Gorge below Wenatchee, with their dark desert-varnish patina, make an ideal surface for pecked petroglyphs.

Drawings of animals, especially the deer and the mountain sheep, are common along the river gorge and there is one site with a good painting of a buffalo. Occasionally the animals are pierced with a spear or arrow. The rayed arc becomes highly elaborate, with double arcs and radiating dots, and the twins appear with horned and feathered headdresses and sometimes as fish. Fish are rare, although this is the great salmon river south of Alaska. The best site on the river was near Vantage, with over 300 figures, but the pictures are all under water today. Near Yakima, the rayed arc becomes a headdress surrounding a nonoutlined face of eyes and nose. This is the most characteristic motif from the middle Fraser River in British Columbia to The Dalles in Washington.

Red painting, Omak Lake, northeastern Washington. Redrawn from H. Thomas Cain.

The main travel route along the Columbia was by water and the canoe traffic has been vividly described by Lewis and Clark. The concentrations of rock pictures were at village sites, fishing centers, and trail crossings. The middle Columbia was a meeting ground of cultural influences, from the Great Plains to the east and from the Northwest. The arrow-impaled animals in the gorge are in the tradition of the Plains, where such drawings are plentiful. There are no examples in the middle Columbia of

Stylized and abstract drawings on the Columbia River near Beverly, Washington. Site is now destroyed. Wenatchee Museum photograph.

Elk and mountain sheep near Vantage, Washington. Wenatchee Museum photograph.

Mountain sheep panel salvaged before flooding by Wanapam Dam, Columbia River, Washington. Now at Ginkgo State Park, Vantage, Washington.

Bear tracks, game animals, and humans painted in red and black, Salmon River drainage, Idaho. Photograph by Donald Martin.

Caucasian objects or horses; either the drawings predate the coming of the whites or there simply was no contact between the whites and the Indian rock artists.

At Big Eddy above The Dalles Dam, a typical Northwest carving of Tsagaglalal occurs on the same rock face with characteristic middle Columbia rayed arcs painted in red and white. There were famous fishing grounds at the Long Narrows near The Dalles before the building of the dam, and the great river for several miles was compressed to a several-hundred-foot-wide channel of boiling white water. At the fishing camps near the falls and rapids, the Chinook and various Sahaptin tribes carved and painted their designs. Characteristic motifs from this area include the four-pointed star and an owl symbol known locally as the Spedis owl. Mountain sheep drawings are plentiful but again there are few pictures of salmon. It seems certain that the deer and sheep were always drawn in connection with hunting magic to aid in the securing of these wary animals—the easily taken salmon, on the other hand, needed no fishing magic to be brought to the nets or harpoon. In addition, the rock pictures of this region include many strange anthropomorphic beings reminiscent of Northwest mythological creatures.

The rock paintings and carvings on the Columbia tributaries in Idaho bear little resemblance to those in Washington. The sites in northern Idaho are all on or near big lakes. A ledge of schist on Lake Pend d'Oreille is decorated with 28 bear tracks done in the northern plains style and on Lake Coeur d'Alene to the south there is a pecked site with abstract designs. The Salmon River of central Idaho flows through heavily forested country and on granite cliffs and in caves there are many paintings. These are crudely done in red and closely resemble in style and subject the paintings found in western and central Montana. The paintings are representations of humans, large game animals, arrows, tepees, and horsemen—suggesting a strong northern plains influence from the eastern side of the Rockies, and dating many of them as post-1750, when the Indians of the region were beginning to acquire horses.

To the south, the environment and the rock art are very different. The Snake River plain is high sagebrush desert country with the river cutting through the lava bedrock. Rock-pecked designs are found along the lava cliffs—the Indian artists took advantage of the patina-blackened rocks and paintings become rare. The designs from this area differ greatly from the paintings of central Idaho. They are stylized and abstract in typical Great Basin style, though occasionally Plains motifs occur, like the curved-claw bear tracks and shield figures near Gooding. The Great Basin elements are mainly in the rectilinear abstract style and include grids, concentric circles and arcs, dot patterns, triangles, stylized humans, and realistic mountain sheep with horns drawn in side view. The Shoshone Indians, holding the southern watershed of the Snake, were in close contact with the Great Basin and undoubtedly migrated north from that area taking their rock-pecking technique with them.

The principal tributaries of the Columbia in Oregon east of the Cascades are the Deschutes and the John Day, and there are many red-painted sites along both streams. The style is naturalistic with some abstract or indeterminate elements, and is reminiscent of the paintings in central Idaho. Subject matter includes humans, snakes, mountain sheep, deer, hands, zigzags, and rayed circles. The execution of the paintings is quite poor and suggests that the paint was applied by finger. This region was occupied by various Sahaptin people like the Tenino and the John Day tribes.

13 THE GREAT BASIN

Pecked sheep, Coso Range, California. From photograph by Donald Martin.

As the name implies, the Great Basin is a vast region with no outlets to either ocean—all the streams empty into marshy sinks or saline desert lakes like the Great Salt Lake in Utah and Mono Lake in California. The Basin includes most of Nevada and sizable sections of Oregon, Utah, and California.

Bounded on the west by the Cascades, the Sierra Nevada, and the California coastal ranges, and on the east by the Wasatch Mountains of Utah, much of the Basin is true desert, with intermittent streams and springs the only source of water.

Unsurprisingly in such a harsh environment the cultural level of the Indians was extremely low. These were the Indians the early trappers and explorers saw grubbing for roots with digging sticks and hence dubbed "Diggers." Zenas Leonard, a fur trapper with the Walker expedition of 1833, describes the Indians (probably Paiutes) he saw near Humboldt Lake:

These Indians are totally naked—both male and female—with the exception of a shield of grass which they wear around their loins. They are generally small and weak, and some of them are very hairy. They subsist upon grass-seed, frogs, fish, etc. . . . Their habitations are formed of a round hole dug in the ground, over which sticks are placed, giving it the shape of a potato hole—this is covered with grass and earth—the door on one side and the fire at the other. They cook in a pot made of stiff mud which they lay on the fire and burn; but from the sandy nature of the mud, after cooking a few times, it falls to pieces. . . .[1]

The culture of the Great Basin Indians is an excellent example of the effects of environment and lack of contact with higher cultures. Most of the Basin people are of the Shoshonean branch of the Uto-Aztecan language family, the same people that in more favorable environments

100

produced the Hopi and the Aztec cultures. The Shoshoneans who migrated northeastward looking for greener pastures acquired the horse and a Plains culture.

The nomadic existence forced on the Great Basin Indians, constantly moving from camp to camp in small hunting and food-gathering bands, precluded the establishment of elaborate ceremonies such as those created by the corn-growing Hopi. It is not surprising that most of the Great Basin rock pictures are very simple and in many instances rather crudely done. What ceremonies existed were doubtless simple rites connected with hunting magic, rainmaking, and fertility.

The rock art of the Klamath and Modoc Indians in southern Oregon and northern California is so typical of the Great Basin that it has been included in this section though that area drains into the Pacific Ocean and the cultures of these Indians are more closely tied to California and the Northwest. Many of the designs are crudely scratched on basaltic boulders; others are painted where slanting rocks afforded some weather protection. The designs are of the simplest type—concentric circles, meandering lines, zigzags, stick men occasionally phallic, elk, deer, sheep, and lizards.

The only site I know where there are paintings in a true cave is near Tule Lake. The entrance is a hole in the ground near tumbled masses of lava rocks, and it was necessary to enter the cave with a rope because of

Concentric circles pecked on basalt with traces of red paint, near Bly, southern Oregon.

Polychrome designs inside a lava tube, Lava Beds National Monument, northeastern California. University of California photograph.

Figures pecked on basalt, Petroglyph Canyon, Coso Range, California. Photograph by Donald Martin.

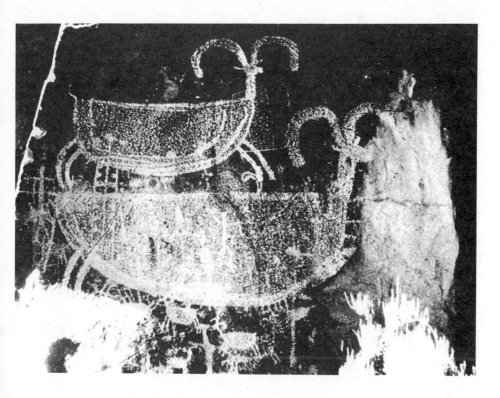

Mountain sheep, nearly life size, Petroglyph Canyon, Coso Range, California. Photograph by Donald Martin.

Abstract pecked designs (chalked), west-central Nevada. University of California Archaeological Survey photograph.

a 12-foot drop to the ground inside. The cave is a lava tube formed during ancient volcanic action, several hundred feet long and about 30 feet in diameter. Many paintings in black, white, and red occur in the areas free from water seepage.

In Nevada the majority of the many recorded sites are concentrated in the Sierra foothills and near springs and desert lakes. This is the country of the Northern Paiute and the Western Shoshone and there is little doubt that many of the pictures were pecked, painted, or scratched by these Shoshonean people.

Through most of this country the pecked drawings are of the crudest type with meanders, connected circles, grids, and concentric circles predominating, but in southern Nevada and southeastern California something new appears. The sheep that occurred in crude scratched drawings near the Oregon border appear here by the thousands in pecked form and often very well done. Hunters are shown using the *atlatl* as well as the bow, and a few sites depict horsemen, indicating a very long timespan for the rock-art tradition of the region. There are frequent stylized anthropomorphs wearing figured garments and many designs suggesting fabric and basketry motifs. The great numbers of sheep drawings indicate that hunting magic was the basic reason for the rock art of the region. The greatest concentrations are in the California desert regions from Death Valley west to the lower Sierra Nevada. There are some paintings in the desert ranges here, chiefly of naturalistic game animals, but geometric patterns also occur, particularly in the Joshua Tree National Monument.

The southeastern California and southern Nevada region is all Shoshonean territory and the principal tribes are the Western Shoshone, Chemehuevi, and Serrano. The tremendous numbers of rock pictures concentrated in the area suggest that the tradition of rock drawing there was a very long one. As noted earlier in chapter 7, this small area might have been the starting point of the widespread Shoshonean migrations that went west, north, and east in search of a better life, taking with them their rock-drawing tradition.

Studies are only just beginning on the rock drawings of western Utah but from evidence at hand, the drawings are in the typical Great Basin styles with Basketmaker and Puebloid influences at the eastern edge, where anthropomorphs with triangular bodies, *kachina* figures, and humans with Pueblo-type side-locked hair occur. This same type of subject is found at many painted sites in southeastern Nevada.

Robert F. Heizer and Martin A. Baumhoff have described seven styles from Nevada: [2]

Red painting, Joshua Tree National Monument, California.

Style	Method	Characteristic Elements
Great Basin Representational	Pecking	Mountain sheep, quadruped, foot, hand, horned human, *kachina*
Great Basin Curvilinear Abstract	Pecking	Circle, concentric circles, chain of circles, sun disc, curvilinear meander, star, snake
Great Basin Rectilinear Abstract	Pecking	Dots, grids, rakes, cross-hatching
Great Basin Painted	Painting	Circles, parallel lines
Great Basin Scratched	Scratching	Sun disc, parallel lines, cross-hatching
Puebloan Painted	Painting	*Kachina*
Pit and Groove	Pecking	Pits and grooves

14 CALIFORNIA

Brown and white painting,
Tulare County, California.

California is an extraordinary state—it offers every type of climate and environment. The Great Valley, actually two valleys, the Sacramento and the San Joaquin, is bounded on the west by the coastal ranges and on the east by the Sierra Nevada. To the north is the Cascade Range, and to the south the Tehachapi Range separates the Great Valley from southern California. The rainy northern coast, home of the giant redwoods, extends as far south as Monterey. Below Monterey, the coast ranges become progressively drier until they are semidesert in southern California. Northeastern and southeastern California are included in the Great Basin section.

Of the six language families in America north of Mexico, all but the Eskimo occur in California. In no other part of the country is there anything like this diversity of peoples in so small an area. In contrast, the Algonquian-speaking tribes are found in unbroken sequence from Puget Sound to Nova Scotia. A possible explanation is that California west of the Sierra was on a migration route from the earliest times and groups were continually splitting up as they passed through this region, some liking what they saw and settling there, others continuing onward. With this diversity of topography and peoples, it is not surprising that almost every type of rock art is found in the state.

The rock-art sites in northern California are chiefly of the pit-and-groove type. Almost invariably they occur on isolated boulders in the foothills of the coast ranges and the Sierra Nevada. Ethnographic information indicates that these were used in rainmaking and fertility ceremonies (see chapter 4). In central and southern California, the pit-and-groove style is often found on large outcroppings of granite and in caves. Occasionally the pits are arranged in lines, but the usual method is a ran-

106

dom scattering of the depressions on the rock surface. Of all the examples of Indian markings on rock, this type has the least claim to be classified as art. It seems to be a very early variety of aboriginal rock inscription and is found almost everywhere in the world.

North of San Francisco paintings are extremely rare and these are of the crudest finger-daubed type, but numerous pecked and incised designs have been recorded. These are very simple: concentric circles, rakes, bear tracks, and bird tracks. Often the carvings are hidden by heavy lichen growths, and in a number of instances students have had to remove the growth with chemicals or a wire brush before the design could be copied.

The Great Basin pecked technique did not penetrate far west of the Sierra passes, undoubtedly due to the unsuitability of the rock surfaces. The shallow pecking through desert varnish on basaltic rock that produced the striking designs in the Great Basin gave way to deeply pecked and incised designs on the granite and sandstone of interior California.

In the pine and madrone forests of Monterey County are a number of painted sites in sandstone caves, where smoke-blackened walls have been covered with hundreds of hand impressions in white. Many small caves in the nearby canyons have small painted stick figures in red, and diamonds, circles, and grids and ladders done with a piece of charcoal or lump of dark mineral.

The territory of the Chumash Indians, creators of the finest rock paintings in North America, begins at Morro Bay. These Indians, first described by Juan Rodriguez Cabrillo in 1542, were concentrated along the Santa Barbara Channel but their territory extended through the coastal ranges to the San Joaquin Valley, an area roughly the size of Maryland. The Spanish explorers found them superior to the other California Indians they had encountered and greatly admired their artifacts of stone, wood, shell, and basketry. They especially noted in their journals the beautiful sewn plank canoes in which the natives made long ocean voyages.

Red and white painting, mountains of northern Ventura County, California.

The Chumash paintings were done in as many as six colors though the usual range was red, black, and white, with many of the sites in red alone. The basic styles are abstract linear and abstract polychrome. With both styles, bizarre and striking anthropomorphic and zoomorphic beings occur with an endless variety of purely abstract shapes. A constantly recurring theme is the circle, with every conceivable variation of spokes, rays, cogs, and curious appendages. The abstract polychrome paintings often have circular designs with multiple outlines of contrasting colors to give a basically simple shape great richness. In almost all instances, the craftsmanship is excellent.

The coastal ranges inhabited by the Chumash are made up of ancient sedimentary rocks and most of the sites are located in shallow, wind-sculptured sandstone caves or rock shelters. I know of few pursuits more gratifying than the search for unknown or unrecorded rock-art sites. For example I remember a day spent trying to relocate a painting seen many years before by a deer hunter in the rugged San Rafael Mountains behind Santa Barbara. The trails he remembered had long since disappeared and we traveled with back packs down brush-choked ravines. With endless stops to chop brush with a machete, it was late in the day when we dropped into the main canyon and nearly dark when we found the cave, and entered through a narrow slit in the cliff face. The colors were as fresh as if applied the day before and yet they were painted at least 200 years ago. It is my belief that the paintings in the Chumash area are not very old, based on the lack of superimposition of styles, on the known rate of paint erosion at some unprotected sites, and on the association of datable artifacts with painted caves. The evidence indicates they were done in the last 1,000 years, with some dating from late prehistoric or even mission times.

The most elaborate paintings are found in the innermost mountain

Detail of a panel of more than two hundred hands painted on smoke-blackened wall, Church Creek, Monterey County, California.

The Painted Cave near Santa Barbara, California. This site has been protected with an iron grille and is the best preserved of the California paintings accessible to the public. Anderson Photo Service.

ranges and close to the western edge of the San Joaquin Valley. Farthest removed from this area are the crude red paintings of parallel lines at two sites on the Channel Islands, nearly 30 miles offshore. These islands supported a large population with a somewhat less elaborate culture than their onshore cousins. The implication is that the tradition came to the Chumash through neighboring tribes to the northeast where polychrome painting was done by the Yokuts. As there is nothing in that direction to compare to the finest Chumash paintings, it is reasonable to assume that the Chumash, like many other adaptable peoples, took over a basic idea and mightily improved on it.

Most of the Chumash paintings are unvandalized, thanks to their location in extremely rough brush-covered mountain country, where their

Polychrome panel at Carrizo Plains, California, as it appeared in 1894. The painted area was more than one hundred feet long. Site has since been destroyed by vandals. Kern County Land Company photograph.

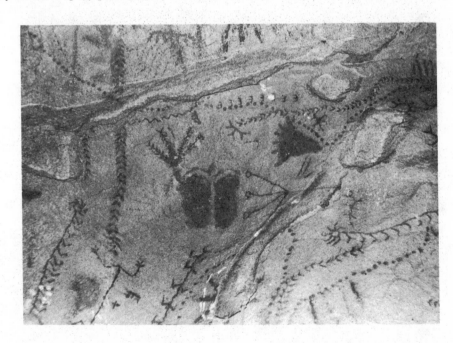

Red Chumash painting, San Rafael Range, Santa Barbara County, California.

existence was largely unknown until a survey made in 1961-63. The examples in open country or near public roads have been destroyed.

San Nicolás Island, 60 miles off the southern California coast, was inhabited by Shoshonean-speaking Indians sharing many cultural traits with the Chumash. There are incised drawings of porpoises and killer whales on the walls of a sea cave, indicating the importance of these large marine mammals in the life of the people.

Across the San Joaquin Valley lived the Yokuts, an Indian nation that was divided into about 40 tribes. It was the largest ethnic group in California before their deliberate decimation by the land-hungry settlers. Much of the valley was marshland fed by the Kern and Kings rivers, which formed large shallow lakes. Around these lakes and along the creeks in the foothills of the Sierra Nevada, the Yokuts lived in much the same manner as the Chumash. There was much trade between the two peoples and it is not surprising to find a great similarity in their paintings. The design motifs, especially the abstractions, are different but the technique is very much the same. At a few of the sites near Porterville and Exeter, the execution of the paintings is carefully done and considerable imagination is shown in the designs. There is only one example of animals drawn in a side view in Chumash territory (four mounted horsemen at a site on the extreme eastern boundary) but the occurrence of this style (as opposed to the spread-eagle or pelt convention) is frequent along the Sierra foothills in the rendering of deer, coyotes, cattle, and horses. The excellent condition of many of the Yokuts paintings and the occasional drawing of horsemen would indicate that many of them are late prehistoric and historic.

Adjoining the Yokuts territory to the southeast are the Shoshonean Tubatulabal of the Kern River and the Shoshonean Kawaiisu of the Tehachapi Mountains. Both of these peoples sporadically occupied country on the Great Basin side of the Sierra divide but their drawings rather closely follow the Yokuts design style and technique. A certain number of the pictures are polychrome in red, black, and white, but most are limited to red.

The last region with large concentrations of rock drawings is in southwestern California. With few exceptions they are paintings and are quite different from those in any other section of the state.

South of the Chumash territory were the Juaneño and Luiseño, Shoshonean tribes who shared ceremonial practices with the Chumash, including the ritual use of the narcotic jimsonweed. It has been suggested that many of the paintings were made while under narcotic influence. The Juaneño revered the condor as sacred and the great bird figured prominently in their ceremonies. In the Luiseño territory south of Riverside are numerous drawings on granite boulders and outcroppings featur-

Red, white, and black painting, Caliente Range, California.

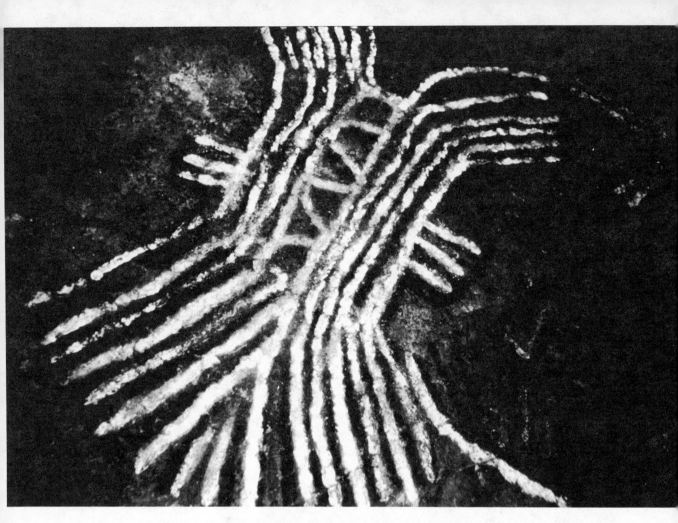

Yokuts painting in red, black, and white, Tulare County, California.

Maze pecked on granite near Hemet, California. This may not be of Indian origin as there is nothing like it in style or technique in the region.

ing red linear designs of diamonds, zigzags, parallel lines, hand prints, and cross-hatching. These were all made during puberty rites (see chapter 4).

Near Hemet, a handsome square maze design, quite unlike anything else in the region, is pecked on a granite boulder. Sixty miles to the south are somewhat similar designs in the Diegueño area, but these are all painted and are fret designs and not true mazes. There is a strong probability that this striking design has a non-Indian origin.

The areas just described were occupied by Shoshonean groups that had migrated to the west coast from the Great Basin and their rock paintings can all be described as rectilinear abstract. It seems probable that the southwestern California paintings derived from the Great Basin rectilinear abstract (pecked) and the Great Basin painted.

Near the southern border of the state are the Diegueño Indians, members of the scattered Hokan-language family that included the Chumash. These Indians were the first to come under the mission system in upper California and survived the ordeal remarkably well. Alfred Kroeber estimated their numbers in 1775 at about 3,000. Today there are over 500. Their survival must be attributed to their strong spirit of independence and resistance to the missionaries.

Elaborate fret and mazelike painting in red, Green Valley near Poway, southeastern California. These paintings are nearly eroded away and cannot be very old. San Diego Museum of Man photograph.

The only major concentration of paintings in the Diegueño territory is in Green Valley near Poway. The style is rectilinear abstract, like the basic style in the rest of southwestern California, but the design motifs are extraordinary. There are many variations on geometric fret patterns, and in some instances very large rock surfaces are entirely covered with an integrated pattern. Unfortunately the paintings, invariably in red, are on exposed granite surfaces with no protection from the elements and are rapidly eroding away. In addition, suburbia has discovered Green Valley and bulldozers are assuring the speedy and total destruction of these interesting paintings. There are a few examples in the valley of typically Great Basin style pecked designs—dotted patterns and curvilinear meanders and circles.

The Sierra Nevada of California between the San Joaquin Valley and the Great Basin sharply separates the two basic rock-drawing techniques. East of the barrier, rock pecking is overwhelmingly dominant; west of the divide, most of the drawings are painted. An equally abrupt cleavage exists between the northern and southern halves of the state. North of the San Joaquin Valley, the designs are mainly pecked and incised; south of the valley they are painted.

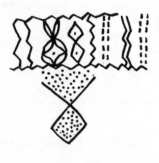

Red painting, Riverside County, California.

MAIN CALIFORNIA ROCK-DRAWING STYLES

Style	Method	Major Concentration
Abstract Linear	Painted	Southwestern California
Abstract Polychrome	Painted	Coastal ranges (Santa Barbara area) —Sierra foothills (Kern-Tulare counties)
Abstract Curvilinear	Pecked-Incised	Northern California
Pit and Groove	Pecked	Northern California

15 THE SOUTHWEST

The Southwest as defined in this study is divided into two almost equal parts by the U.S.–Mexican border. It includes the drainage areas of the Colorado and Rio Grande rivers, the southern Rockies, the Sierra Madre of Mexico, and the peninsula of Baja California. The Colorado and its tributaries have cut immense canyons through the Colorado Plateau. Particularly spectacular are the red sandstone cliffs in eastern Utah, which have attracted Indian artists for countless generations. This is a country of juniper, piñon, and sagebrush, with pines in the mountains. In Arizona, the Mogollon Rim drops off to the south and true desert conditions extend into much of Sonora and Chihuahua, where the creosote bush and cactus are characteristic plants.

A very distinctive type of rock picture is found in eastern Utah and western Colorado. Large human figures, sometimes over-life-sized, are pecked on the smooth sandstone cliffs. They are almost invariably front-faced with highly elaborate headdresses, earrings, necklaces, and belts. Often the eyes are drawn with vertical lines below them, a widespread convention known as the "weeping eye." Occasionally a figure has lines filled in with color; in rare instances the entire figure is painted.

Near Vernal, Utah, is a canyon with many beautifully carved figures of this type. The panel shown on page 117 is over 75 feet from the ground and may be the finest example of aboriginal rock-carving in the United States. A number of the ceremonial figures are depicted with shields, while others carry long-necked heads which may represent masks or trophy heads.

These designs are typical of the Fremont culture, first discovered at the Fremont River in southern Utah. Sharing many traits with the Anasazi (Basketmaker-Pueblo), including corn agriculture, this culture was wide-

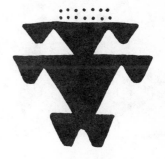

White painting, Cave Valley, Zion National Park, Utah. From photograph by Ro Wauer.

115

Ceremonial figures pecked on sandstone cliffs (chalked), Dry Fork Canyon, near Vernal, Utah. Photograph by Dale Ritter.

spread in eastern Utah and western Colorado until about 1150. What happened to these people is unknown but a good possibility is that they were overwhelmed or displaced by the Shoshoneans pushing in from the Great Basin to the west and by Navajos migrating down from the Northern Plains. The Fremont people might have moved south to live with the Anasazi of the Four Corners area, where Utah, Colorado, Arizona, and New Mexico meet.

There are many examples of both painted and pecked shield figures in the Fremont area (see chapter 7). Occasionally they occur in association with the large, highly decorated ceremonial figures but are not necessarily of the same age or culture.

In southeastern Utah near the confluence of the Green and Colorado rivers there are a number of very unusual painted sites. The typical motif is a mummylike anthropomorphic figure without arms or legs and often without features. These figures range from several feet to well over life-size. The paintings are in various shades of red-brown and the larger figures have intricate fabriclike designs incised through the paint or added in white. They are in the Fremont area but are quite unlike the typical examples. This must have been a local development that had little or no influence on the surrounding regions. A few examples of this style are known in pecked form.

In southeastern Utah, there are vast numbers of pecked designs; often a single rock surface will be covered with motifs in a completely dis-organized manner—mountain sheep, animal tracks, curvilinear meanders, etc. A well-known site of this type is in the Petrified Forest National Park in Arizona and others are in the Valley of Fire of southern Nevada. The style at these sites shows a strong Great Basin influence, not surprisingly, since during this period so many people were on the move.

Near Moab, in association with mountain sheep, there is a pecked rendering of what is locally known as the "mastodon" and widely believed to be a life portrait of that extinct beast. It is a three-toed trunked animal but the brightness of the design and its lack of patina, together with the fact that the adjoining mountain sheep and accompanying initials have some patina and so are older, brand it a hoax. The last mastodons died out about 6,000 years ago.

The western Colorado sites that have been described indicate a meeting

Life-sized figures pecked on sandstone, Dry Fork Canyon, near Vernal, Utah. Traces of red paint appear on the shield of the central figure. Photograph by Donald Martin.

of the Fremont pecked-drawing tradition with a late Plains influence. The horse never occurs in the Fremont drawings but is present at several Colorado painted sites.

In the Four Corners region, there are a great many rock drawings reflecting the very long occupation of the country by an agricultural people with ample time to develop elaborate ceremonies connected primarily with the growing of corn. The Anasazi, a peaceful, industrious people, developed the highest culture north of Middle America. Along the Glen Canyon section of the Colorado River and the San Juan, a major tributary, the earliest pictures are from the Basketmaker period (pre-A.D. 800) and are usually painted, though pecked designs have also been assigned to this period. Square and triangular-bodied anthropomorphs with small heads are common but the most abundant pecked design is the mountain sheep. The rock drawings in the Four Corners are often closely associated with spectacular ruined cliff dwellings, built into the sides of enormous sandstone cliffs. Happily the finest of these canyon ruins are rigidly protected by the government. Many of the rock drawings of this area, and indeed of the entire Colorado Plateau, strongly suggest the Great Basin and may be the work of the nonagricultural Shoshonean Utes.

During the Pueblo period, designs reached a maximum complexity. There is more pecking than painting and typical designs are the flute player, mountain sheep, and elaborate blanket or pottery designs. The *kachina* figure and *kachina* mask appear at many sites, often identical with types still used in Southwest Indian ceremonies. Many recognizable birds are depicted both realistically and stylistically—the quail, duck, roadrunner, crane, and particularly the turkey and the eagle.

Brown and white anthropomorph, Barrier Canyon, Utah. From photograph by Tom Mulhern.

In August 1680, the Pueblo Indians of New Mexico, restless under the heavy hand of their conquerors, rose in rebellion, killed four hundred Spaniards, including twenty-one missionaries, and drove the remaining Spanish from the Pueblo country. The Spanish made repeated attempts to gain back their lost province and in 1692, Santa Fe and a number of pueblos capitulated. The aggressive Navajos from the northern plains, with a long record of preying on the Pueblo Indians, now made common cause with their old enemies against the Spanish; and much hard fighting followed. By 1695, peace was restored briefly, followed by a final rebellion the following year in the Rio Grande Valley. The revolt was unsuccessful and many Indians from the pueblos of San Cristobal, Pecos, Santa Clara, Jemez, San Ildefonso, and Cochiti fled to the Navajo country in the San Juan Valley.

In this refuge area, the two groups lived together peacefully and, as a result, the Navajos underwent an intensive acculturation. They adopted many Pueblo religious practices and paraphernalia, creation myths, matrilineal descent, manufacturing techniques (especially weaving), and even, for a time, the distinctive Pueblo architecture. The Navajo rock paintings and carvings that date from this time show many ideas borrowed from the Pueblos.

Examples of Navajo rock art are found in many of the sandstone canyons of the Four Corners region, especially in Gobernador, Carrizo, Largo, and Canon de Chelly. Many of their religious paintings are remarkably like the Pueblo *kachina* figures from seventeenth- and eighteenth-century kiva paintings.

The *kachinas* are supernatural beings or gods personified by dancers in ceremonies, many of which are connected with corn growing. The Navajo *yei* is the equivalent of the Pueblo *kachina*. There are examples of *yeis*, both painted and pecked, along several of the tributaries of the San Juan River in northern New Mexico. These figures are remarkably well drawn and are undoubtedly the forerunners of the superb figures later made by the Navajo in their sand paintings.

Some of the ceremonial figures in Navajo rock drawings can be identified by their similarity to those in modern sand paintings. The *yei* shown on page 121 is the hunchback god Ganaskidi, who carries a wand and the seeds of all vegetation in his feathered hump. Other recognizable eighteenth-century *yeis* are the Twin War Gods, often represented as shields, and a *yei* with peaked cap that resembles the Fringe Mouth Gods of the Night Chant myth.

There is evidence that many of the rock paintings and engravings marked Navajo sacred places or shrines where mythological events had occurred. According to Polly Schaafsma (1966), Navajos traveled to such a decorated spot at the confluence of the Pine and San Juan rivers as recently as the 1950s to hold ceremonies.

Aside from the Pueblo-style religious paintings, the Navajos continued to make their Plains-type hunting-magic drawings, featuring hunters, mounted horsemen, and realistic game animals (often with the heart-

Pecked "mastodon" near Moab, Utah. The last mastodons died out about 6,000 years ago.

Mummylike figures in shades of red-brown, Barrier Canyon, Utah. Photograph by Tom Mulhern.

Pueblo-type figures, San Juan River, northeastern New Mexico. Museum of New Mexico photograph.

Navajo drawing on a boulder (chalked) along the Piedra River, north-western New Mexico. Museum of New Mexico photograph.

Corn plant and Navajo yei *pecked on sandstone, Largo Canyon, northwestern New Mexico.*

Navajo yei *painting from the upper San Juan River area, New Mexico, 18th century. The colors are blue-gray, red, orange-yellow, rose, blue-green, and cream. From a facsimile painting by Polly Schaafsma. Museum of New Mexico photograph.*

line). The Navajo paintings in the Canyon de Chelly date from the 18th and 19th centuries and are quite naturalistic, showing Spaniards, horses, cattle, game animals, and the like. These are in association with typical Anasazi painted and pecked square-shouldered anthropomorphs, flute players, and hand prints.

These Navajo paintings and a few Apache paintings in eastern New Mexico are the only North American examples of the naturalistic poly-chrome style and closely resemble late historic Plains paintings on buffalo hides. The Navajo rock painters used a far broader range of colors than other North American tribes. In addition to the usual red, black, and white, they had blue-gray, blue-green, dark blue, yellow, orange, rose, and many shades of brown.

Pueblo-type pecked designs are plentiful in the Santa Fe-Albuquerque region of the Rio Grande, where basaltic rock takes the place of the dominant sandstone of the Four Corners region. In the Galisteo Basin south of Santa Fe, there is a major concentration of such designs and at one huge site covering a four-mile rock outcropping, there are hundreds of designs, including many masks and *kachina* figures. These cannot date later than about 1690, when the region was abandoned. At the eastern end of the basaltic dike, there are some very fine pecked shield drawings. They resemble 15th century kiva paintings at Pottery Mound near Albuquerque and may have been influenced by a migrating band from an area where such figures were traditional. In the Pueblo-type designs and also the shield panels, a dominant motif is the four-pointed star with a circular center. The star was traditionally drawn with four points by the American Indian—often by a simple cross or X. One of the many Hopi *kachinas* is Coto, the star-*kachina*, whose head is decorated with this symbol.

Abstract pecked design near El Paso, Texas. Redrawn from A. T. Jackson.

The eastern and southern New Mexico rock-art sites continue to reflect the general styles developed in the Four Corners region. A number of highly detailed and carefully painted sites, both naturalistic and stylized, have been attributed to Athabascan Apaches who were in possession of the country during the historic period.

Thanks to A. T. Jackson's excellent *Picture Writing of the Texas Indians*, we have a great deal of information on the large concentration of rock drawings in the region of southwest Texas bounded by the Rio Grande and Pecos rivers.

In the extreme western part of the state, there are painted sites with many designs reminiscent of the Pueblo country—masks, blanket and pottery designs, and mountain sheep. A famous site is at Hueco Tanks, a rocky area near El Paso. Here the paintings are around a number of large natural rock reservoirs. First described by Bartlett in 1854, it was a favorite stopping spot for the pioneer immigrant trains and later for

Elaborate shield figures with interior clan symbols at Galisteo Basin, south of Santa Fe, New Mexico.

sightseers from El Paso. It has been badly vandalized but enjoys a measure of protection today as it is inside the Army lands at Fort Bliss.

Between the Hueco Tanks site and the Pecos River, there are a great many sites. The oldest are pecked designs similar to the typical Great Basin style with hand prints, meandering lines, and connected circles. The most recent-appearing drawings are realistic paintings, probably made by Apache Indians. An extensive site in this style is located on a large rock overhang by a spring, with many excellent paintings of mounted Indians, priests, thunderbirds, and animals, including a beautiful rendering of a deer.

Some of the most interesting paintings in the Southwest are found in the innumerable rock shelters near the junction of the Rio Grande and Pecos rivers. Over 75 per cent of the paintings are in a polychrome style. These intriguing pictures feature elongated figures usually without either faces or legs. Some of them resemble the mummylike creatures of eastern Utah. With them are stylized animals, especially antelope, cougar, insects, and plants. At some sites, historic paintings occur, undoubtedly made by the Apache. David Gebhard has described six styles from the Diablo area— the oldest, polychrome, followed by four differing red styles, and finally the historic realistic style. He suggests that the subject matter indicates not only hunting magic but also warfare magic as many of the human figures are pierced by spears and arrows.[1]

There are numerous pecked sites in central and southern Arizona featuring Pueblo design elements, with oustanding examples in the Petrified Forest National Park and south of Flagstaff along the Verde River. West of Phoenix, the drawings show strong Great Basin influence and the workmanship is much cruder—a large site near Gila Bend is in the curvilinear abstract style.

There are some immense gravel outline figures (see chapter 2) along the lower Colorado River in southeastern California. The best known are three very large spread-eagle human figures with two four-legged animals (coyotes?) and spirals in association with two of them. One writer has assumed the quadrupeds are horses and has dated them in historic times.[2] Personally I think that, with rare exceptions, the horse can be positively identified only if the artist has included the horseman. The largest human figure is 167 feet long and the creators could never have had an over-all look at their work as the only way it can be seen is from the air. The dark desert-varnish-covered stones are removed to bring out the figure detail in the light-colored sand beneath, and the removed stones are placed in ridges outlining the forms. These particular gravel drawings are in the territory of the Mojave but we do not know that these Indians were the artists. It is possibly significant that the gravel figures are located between the territories of the sand-painting people of the Southwest

Pecked design near Springville, Arizona. From photograph by Harold S. Gladwin.

Great Basin–type drawings, Newspaper Rock, Petrified Forest National Park, Arizona. Photograph by Richard O'Hanlon.

Fabric or pottery designs, Petrified Forest National Park, Arizona. Photograph by Richard O'Hanlon.

(Hopi, Navajo, Papago, Apache, etc.) and the sand-painting people of southern California (Luiseño, Diegueño, and Cahuilla).

The scope of the Southwest is so vast that it is difficult to do more than touch a few high spots. I have tried to orient the reader with geographical features rather than arbitrary political boundaries. In this next section, however, I will cover Mexico as a special unit of the Southwest.

With the exception of Baja California, we know almost nothing of the rock art of northern Mexico and until much more work is done, no firm conclusions can be drawn. It is only natural that the high cultures of Mexico with their dramatic ruins and superb artifacts have beguiled the archaeologists for over a hundred years to the almost complete exclusion of the lower culture areas to the north. A few articles have been written by French and Mexican investigators, but the map on page 17 is mostly blank for great sections of northern Mexico.

For most of our knowledge of the peninsula of Baja California, we are indebted to the investigations of Léon Diguet who in 1894 recorded many sites in central and southern Baja. In the northern mountain ranges, the few recorded sites are simple polychrome paintings done by the Diegueño Indians, whose territory extended several hundred miles south of the border. A number of pecked sites are known from the east side of the peninsula and these follow the Great Basin abstract tradition.

East of the forbidding, waterless Viscaíno Desert, there are a number of canyons cutting through the rugged mountains where sizable springs have created isolated palm oases. Diguet was the first to describe some extraordinary painted caves in these canyons. The dominant motif is the human figure, featureless and with raised arms. The figures are divided longitudinally or horizontally into red and black zones and are often life-sized or larger. Deer, mountain sheep, antelope, cougar, rabbits, and fish occur with the humans and are often very well drawn. At one site, there are many human figures pierced by arrows and figures drawn lying prone. These may represent warfare magic with all enemies happily full of arrows. In 1962, Erle Stanley Gardner, the author, prospecting the almost impassable country by helicopter, discovered a major site in this style. Since then a few more sites in the same tradition have been found by people stimulated by the publicity of Gardner's find. Clement Meighan, who made a survey of the site, has a radiocarbon date of over 500 years for a wooden artifact recovered in one of the caves. Other paintings in this section are chiefly abstract in red, black, and yellow.

The rock-pecked designs of southern Baja continue to resemble the Great Basin curvilinear abstract style, and in the mountains around La Paz there are a few simple paintings on isolated rocks. The subject matter includes hand prints, rabbits, and fish, a rare subject in rock art. All fish from Baja California are painted vertically, a convention that is found only here and across the Gulf of California in Sonora.

Red and white anthropomorphs, Sierra Santa Teressa, Sonora. These figures are about six inches high.

Several years ago, I heard of a painted site in coastal Sonora, roughly across the Gulf of California from the Baja caves with their large red-and-black figures. In the fall of 1965, I decided to investigate this site hoping to find a relationship to the Baja paintings. The Sonora paintings are in a most spectacular little gorge where the Sierra Santa Teressa rises from the coastal plain. For about a quarter of a mile, the stream, fed by the

Erle Stanley Gardner (second from left) examining large polychrome figures from a forty-four-foot panel, Sierra San Francisco, Baja California. Photograph courtesy of Erle Stanley Gardner.

summer rains, had cut a deep slit through the soft rhyolitic rock about 100 feet deep and 15 feet wide. On the almost sheer walls of the gorge and to a height of over 60 feet from the stream bed are innumerable paintings in red, white, black, and yellow. The styles were quite unlike anything in Baja California and much of the painting is in a style I have not seen anywhere else.

Many of the motifs in the bottom of the gorge, painted just above the summer flood-line, are of small anthropomorphic figures, none over a foot tall and slightly resembling the mummylike figures from eastern Utah. The bodies are long rectangles, with no arms and with three peg-like appendages in place of legs. The bodies are filled in with the most intricate and carefully executed geometric patterns, suggesting fabric designs. On the upper sections of the cliff there are many tiny human and animal drawings, some less than two inches long: horsemen, deer, dancing men with headdresses, hump-backed figures armed with bows, and hand prints. Everywhere there are beautiful geometric designs, usually enclosed in squares or rectangles. Suddenly in the center of many of the small paintings is a life-sized horseman with feathered headdress done in an entirely different style.

On the same trip we recorded eleven other sites in the region, including several on Tiburon Island and the adjacent coast. These latter are in the Seri territory and are very simple and crude compared to the Santa

Pecked drawing, Sierra de San Pablo, Sinaloa. Redrawn from A. Pompa y Pompa.

Deeply pecked designs near Saltillo, Coahuila. Photograph by Carl Compton.

Teressa sites—the paintings are of game animals and stylized humans in red and the pigment looks as though it was applied with the finger. Still another painting style, possibly also done by the Seris, is in black and white—animals and triangular human figures without legs. The fine geometric patterns may have been made by the Pima Baja, whose territory adjoins that of the Seri along the Sierra. (Woven headbands collected in Arizona in 1850 are quite similar.) Many of the paintings in this region are located at natural rock reservoirs (*tinajas*) that store the summer rains and provide the only water in this dry land.

Antonio Pompa y Pompa has recorded many painted sites in the State of Sinaloa. They are found in the Sierra from one end of the state to the other and the few published examples show them to be red and in the curvilinear abstract style. A few sites have been described from Durango. There are pecked and painted geometric designs inside squares and rectangles from Durango and simple abstract paintings in dots, circles, and diamond shapes near the Durango–Coahuila border.

The remaining examples known in northern Mexico are a few pecked sites in Coahuila with simple curvilinear abstract designs and some painted cave sites in the Sierra de Tamaulipas. The latter are rather carelessly executed drawings and are of two styles. The earliest are red and consist of short parallel lines, concentric circles, and hand prints. The second style dates from historic times (Tamaulipas was conquered by the Spanish in the late 18th century) and the crude drawings are in black of humans and horsemen. These are probably the work of hunting parties in the mountains and reflect nothing of the high culture of the Huaxtecs who lived in the fertile plains below the Sierra.[3]

All the rock-drawing styles listed in chapter 3 are found in the Southwest with the exception of the pit and groove and these may exist but have gone unrecorded. The central position of the Southwest made it the meeting ground of artistic traditions: abstract from the Great Basin to the west; naturalistic from the Columbia Plateau and the Plains to the north and east; and geometric abstract from Mexico to the south.

Pecked designs near Zape Chico, Durango. Redrawn from J. Alden Mason.

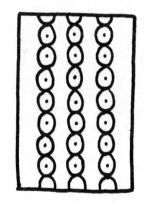

16 THE GREAT PLAINS

Incised warrior on horse, Milk River, Alberta. Redrawn from Selwyn Dewdney, 1964.

The vast area of the Great Plains, the heartland of the continent, is mainly prairie and grassland, bounded on the west by the Rocky Mountains and on the east by the forests of the Eastern Woodland. The great river of the plains is the Missouri, main tributary of the Mississippi with headwaters in the northern Rockies. The Northern Plains extend into southern Alberta, Saskatchewan, and Manitoba as far as the edge of the coniferous forests.

The typical Plains culture, dependent on buffalo hunting, dominated the entire area with the exception of south-central Texas. Before the introduction of the horse, the Northern Plains were sparsely inhabited and archaeological work in Nebraska and the Dakotas has shown an earlier culture of semisedentary people who made pottery and lived in square earth lodges. With the mobility made possible by the horse, tribes from the perimeter areas began to roam widely over the prairies following the buffalo. Prominent in this tremendous population shift were the Dakota (Sioux), Assiniboin, and Cheyenne from the northeastern Woodland; the Pawnee-Arikara and Wichita from the southeastern Woodland; and the Wind River Shoshone, Comanche, and Ute from the Great Basin. All these tribes gradually abandoned their earlier way of life and created the Plains culture. But even though these geographically diversified peoples created a common culture, their rock art often reflected the traditions of their origins.

A look at the map shows large sections of the Great Plains where no drawing sites have been recorded. This is mainly flat land with few suitable rock surfaces. There are, however, rock outcroppings, wind-eroded caves, and isolated boulders on which both paintings and carvings occur.

The rock drawings in Alberta with few exceptions lie along an old buffalo migration route taken by the immense herds moving up from Montana every year. Buffalo jumps are found along this route with rock pictures nearby. The painted sites are in the typical Algonquian style that was described in the Fraser-Columbia Plateau section. Red and black are the only colors and the drawings are crude naturalistic or stylized. The realistic subjects include humans, deer, buffalo, and bear; the stylized are shield figures, square-bodied anthropomorphs with V-neck, thunderbirds, and faces.

Glacial erratics have often been used by these Indians for their rock pictures. The rocks are sometimes painted but usually carved in the pit-and-groove style.

On the Milk River, a northern tributary of the Missouri, there is a major complex of sites. For several miles, spirited pictures are incised in the sandstone cliffs. These carvings follow the story-telling tradition of the Northern Plains so well-known from decorated buffalo robes. Successful hunts, combats between mounted and unmounted warriors, and battles are vividly portrayed. There are many examples of shield and V-necked figures, the latter often showing the heart-line. A few of the pictures are painted but most are deeply incised. This region was the territory of the Gros Ventre and the Blackfeet and these Indians probably made the rock drawings (though there is always the possibility in the plains that raiding parties from adjoining tribes made pictures outside their own country).

Throughout the Northern Plains states of Montana, Wyoming, and the Dakotas, the shield figure, both painted and incised (in many cases, simply the shield), is the most prominent motif. The subject matter, aside from the shield symbols, is naturalistic, featuring game animals, hunters, and horsemen. It is certain that the majority of these Northern Plains drawings are of the historic period. Most of the Montana sites are very crudely painted with thick red lines suggesting finger application, and many of the scratched or incised drawings are mere scrawls. In North Dakota, there are animal forms made by pebble arrangements on the ground somewhat like the gravel pictures in southeastern California. These probably have an affinity with the effigy mounds of the Eastern Woodland.

In the Wind River country of central Wyoming, there is an entirely different situation. In an area centering on Riverton, there is a large concentration of rock-pecked designs totally unlike the realistic incised drawings of the Northern Plains. This is high desert and mountain country with many sandstone cliffs and outcroppings. The typical motif is a highly stylized anthropomorph with fantastic headdress and appendages. The outlined bodies are filled with abstract designs very reminiscent of the decorated anthropomorphs of southeastern California. This is the territory of the Wind River Shoshones whose origin in southeastern California and southern Nevada (see chapter 7) is further demonstrated

Red painting along buffalo migration route, near Cayley, southwestern Alberta. Redrawn from Douglas Leechman, Margaret Hess, and Roy L. Fowler.

Pit-and-groove carvings, southern Alberta. From D. R. King and Selwyn Dewdney.

Pecked supernatural beings (chalked), northwestern Wyoming. Photograph by David Gebhard.

by their rock drawings. Abstract curvilinear drawings and the mountain-sheep motif so characteristic of the Great Basin occur along the Snake River, a natural migration route to the Wind River country.

To the east of the Bighorn River, the incised and painted Northern Plains styles are dominant, continuing through the Black Hills and the Missouri River basin of South Dakota, Sioux territory. In the eastern half of the state, there is an occasional pecked site in the Eastern Woodland style, with footprints, turkey tracks, and the like.

In southwestern Minnesota there are several interesting sites that appear

Pecked anthropomorphs (chalked), Dinwoody Lakes, Wyoming. Photograph by David Gebhard.

to have been made by the Dakota prior to their Plains culture days. At the Catlinite * quarries in Pipestone Country, there are many pecked and abraded figures on the sandstone boulders. The forms are deeply cut and include such motifs as men in bird costumes, buffalo, elk, and turtles. It is possible that the figures are totems made by the Indians before quarrying the catlinite.

Very few sites have been recorded in Nebraska, but in the northeast corner of the state are several incised rocks that seem very much out of place in the Great Plains. The drawings are of men dressed in bird costumes, hands, thunderbirds, bear tracks, turkey tracks, bisected circles, and the Winnebago medicine animal (see chapter 4). How these Eastern Woodland carvings happened to be in Nebraska is an interesting and

* Soft red stone much prized for pipe-making.

Naturalistic incised horses and riders (chalked), Hell Creek Valley, Kansas. Photograph by Thomas Witty.

depressing story. The Winnebago Indians, first described by the French in 1634 as living on Green Bay, Wisconsin, lost their ancient lands through a worthless treaty with the American government in 1825. In the following years, they were repeatedly moved from reservation to reservation as the land-hungry whites pushed farther west. In 1863, their final move brought them to a reservation in northeast Nebraska. The rock drawings therefore cannot be earlier than that date.

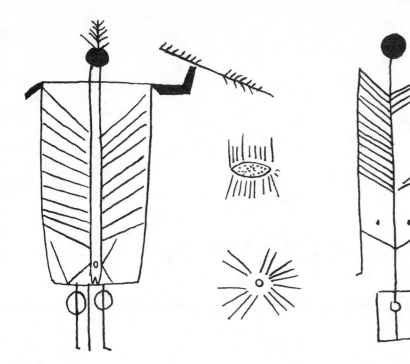

*Stylized incised figures,
Rice County, Kansas.
Redrawn from Wedel.*

The rock drawings of the central Great Plains reflect traditions from all the surrounding areas. In eastern Colorado, the Oklahoma Panhandle, and northeastern New Mexico, there is a strong Great Basin influence. The Shoshonean Utes occupied much of this territory and their origin shows in their rock-drawing style. In Kansas, central Oklahoma, and western Missouri, there is a transition zone between the naturalistic style of the Plains with its horsemen, shield figures, and game animals, and the earlier Woodland style featuring thunderbirds, footprints, and game tracks.

In Texas, the Panhandle and the central part of the state were Comanche territory, marking the farthest penetration east of the aggressive Shoshoneans in prehistoric times. There is no evidence of the Great Basin style here and the Comanche must have brought no rock-drawing tradition with them. The rock-incised pictures from the Panhandle are quite realistic, showing a strong Northern Plains influence, but farther south all but a few sites are painted in styles that seem to have originated in the Pecos-Rio Grande region. Many designs are elaborate abstractions and some are in polychrome. Historic period drawings of mission buildings, mounted men, and cattle are common and they are done in a realistic style with the figures solidly filled in with color, usually red.

Most of the rock drawings that are clearly in the typical Plains incised style occur in the Northern Plains. The situation in the Central and Southern Plains is very complex, reflecting strong influences from the Eastern Woodland and from the Southwest (particularly the Big Bend country of the Rio Grande).

*Pecked footprints and
abstract designs near
Tulare, South Dakota.*

17 THE EASTERN WOODLAND

Pecked bird with speech symbol, eastern Missouri. From photograph by Frank Magre.

This region includes most of the hardwood forests in the United States, and with its ample water and game, was a hunter's paradise supporting large hunting and food-gathering populations. The map on page 17 shows relatively few rock-drawing sites compared to the western section of the country. Parts of 31 states are included in the region, nine of which have no drawings at all. Most of the sites are concentrated along the Mississippi and some large tributaries, the Ohio, Kanawha, and Tennessee rivers.

To understand the rock-art situation in the Eastern Woodland it will be well to review briefly the history of the Woodland Indians. By 2500 B.C. Algonquian-speaking people moving into the New World had reached the Eastern Woodland, bringing with them two basic cultural traits (also found in Siberia): burial mounds and cord-marked pottery. These hunters and food gatherers occupied the river valleys, especially the upper Mississippi and Ohio drainages.

About 500 B.C. a spectacular culture was developing in the Illinois and Ohio valleys—a culture known to archaeologists as Hopewell after an enormous burial mound in Ohio. These people practiced agriculture and had an advanced technology, including large ceremonial flints, elaborately carved stone pipes, and ornaments in copper and silver. This culture had a wide influence on areas as far west as eastern Iowa and Missouri.

In the Southeast around A.D. 900 a new culture was developing from the earlier Woodland tradition. This was the Mississippi culture patterned after the Mexican civilizations in Middle America. Whether these in-

136

fluences spread through trade or Mexican settlements along the Gulf of Mexico, we do not know, but such startling innovations as huge pyramid temple mounds, highly organized towns, and systematic corn agriculture radically altered the pattern of life. The nearest high Mexican culture is that of the Huaxtecs in Tamaulipas State. Engraved shell gorgets from there are strikingly similar to some found in Missouri and Tennessee. By the time De Soto made his brutal march through the area in 1540, many large ceremonial centers had been built and the people were living in palisaded towns. The largest of these centers was Cahokia in southern Illinois, with others at Spiro, Oklahoma; Moundville, Alabama; and Etowah, Georgia. These people were of the Hokan-language stock, occupying at this time all of southeastern United States, and the principal tribes were the Cherokee, Creek, Choctaw, and Chickasaw. By 1400 a dynamic segment of the southeastern Hokan had migrated to the Northeast and had driven a wedge through the Algonquian tribes to the Saint Lawrence River. These were the Iroquois and they took with them their well-organized political system, fortified towns, and agricultural practices.

Most of the rock pictures in the Eastern Woodland are near the ceremonial centers of the Hopewell and Mississippi cultures but with few exceptions they bear little resemblance to the art forms of these cultures. The petroglyphs are almost invariably deeply incised or pecked, sometimes to a depth of over an inch. The technique and subject matter are very similar over the entire Eastern Woodland with some local variations, and the most abundant motifs are the thunderbird, hands, footprints, animal and turkey tracks.

In the upper Mississippi drainage where Minnesota, Wisconsin, and Iowa meet, there are many sites featuring these designs with deer, beaver, fish, and men as additional elements. According to an old Ojibwa who was interviewed in the 1880's, these represented totem marks. In this same region, there are many large effigy mounds in the shape of humans, animals, birds, and snakes, monuments to an obsessive cult for honoring the dead.

The only large concentration of rock drawings in the Eastern Woodland is in Missouri, near the junction of the Missouri and Mississippi rivers. Innumerable deeply pecked designs are found on the horizontal surfaces of limestone bedrock, usually in hilly and forested land. The thunderbird is the dominant design element but hand- and foot-prints, humans, arrows, and bird tracks are abundant. The thunderbird must have played a major part in the ceremonies of these Indians. Many of the drawings suggest a man in bird costume and shamans may have personated the deity during certain rituals.

The Cahokia Mound, largest earth pyramid north of Mexico (100 feet high and covering 16 acres), is located in Illinois just across the river from

Pecked footprints, Belmont County, Ohio. Redrawn from Garrick Mallery, 1893.

Pecked figures, Winona County, Minnesota. Redrawn from Dean R. Snow.

Pecked designs on limestone boulder, northeastern Missouri. Photograph by Frank Magre.

Red painting of bilobed arrow, Washington County, Missouri. From photograph by Frank Magre.

Pecked fertility symbols, Washington State Park, Missouri. From photograph by Frank Magre.

Deeply pecked figures on limestone bedrock, northeastern Missouri. Photograph by Frank Magre.

Incised drawings of fish and deer, Salt River, northeastern Missouri. Photograph by Allen Eichenberger.

Meandering patterns (chalked) incised and pecked on steatite, known as the Judaculla Rock, near Sylva, North Carolina. Photograph by Ewart Ball.

many of the Missouri sites, and motifs connected with this Mississippi ceremonial center are depicted in a few of the rock drawings such as the baton (exactly like the ceremonial flint batons excavated in many sites), and the bilobed arrow, a well-known cult symbol of the Mississippi culture. Carvings of these two symbols are also found in Tennessee and Alabama.

Other motifs in the same area that suggest Mississippi culture influence are birds with speech symbols coming from their beaks, bisected horseshoe shapes that may be fertility symbols (see page 138), and various forms of spindles that suggest the plummets or charmstones found in many parts of the Mississippi Valley and in California. A circular arrangement of one of these designs is reminiscent of similar circular arrangements of charmstones described from ceremonies of the Chumash and Yokuts in California.

There is a change of style in the Tennessee Valley, northern Georgia, and adjoining North Carolina. It is basically an elaboration on the pit-and-groove style of the western states, with added concentric circles, meandering lines, and occasional animal tracks. The most elaborate is the Judaculla Rock, North Carolina, a large carved steatite boulder. These pit-and-groove sites may be the oldest examples of rock drawing in the Eastern Woodland. Some Georgia sites show extensive erosion on designs pecked into hard granite. An interesting incised stone was found in Tennessee. It is not at all typical of the rock drawings of the region, rather resembling the Mississippi culture engravings on shell, and shows costumes, weapons, and utensils.

In the Kanawha Valley of West Virginia there were many sites described by Mallery in 1893, but they have been destroyed through dam building and road construction. A number of sites in the upper Ohio Valley near Wheeling feature meandering lines, round-headed anthropomorphs, turkey and animal tracks, and footprints. Other examples occur in Rhode Island and at the celebrated Dighton Rock in Massachusetts. This site, identical in style and technique to examples in Pennsylvania, has been discussed by armchair antiquarians for centuries (even Cotton Mather made a rather bad drawing of it in 1712), and all sorts of explanations have been offered. It has been ascribed to the Scythians, Phoenicians, and the Norsemen. Lately a new theory has appeared: the rock, moved from its original site (see chapter 9), has been placed in a small park with an adjoining display proving that the round-headed anthropomorphs are actually part of the Portuguese coat of arms, and the whole inscription is a message from Miguel Cortereal, a Portuguese explorer. The Algonquian Indians who incised the lines at least 350 years ago would have been amused.

Vast areas around Lake Michigan were occupied by Algonquian tribes

Incised stone tablet nineteen by fifteen inches found on Rocky Creek near Nashville, Tennessee. Retouched in white ink. Redrawn from Garrick Mallery, 1893.

such as the Miami and the Potawatomi. There are only a few isolated sites known in this country, which is curious as surrounding tribes made many rock pictures. In Michigan, there are two—a cliff painting in the northern part of the state done in the Northern Woodland style, and an extensive pecked and incised site in eastern Michigan. The figures are cut into sandstone bedrock and include all the main Eastern Woodland motifs with the addition of the medicine animal or water panther.

Many examples of the typical Algonquian thunderbird occur at sites in the Mississippi Valley from southern Minnesota to the junction of the Mississippi with the Ohio. The only other occurrence of this distinctive symbol in the Eastern Woodland is at Safe Harbor in Pennsylvania. The

Pecked animals, tracks, and anthropomorphs, Millsboro, Pennsylvania. Site now destroyed. Redrawn from Garrick Mallery, 1893.

Pecked designs on Dighton Rock, near Dighton, Massachusetts, from drawing made in 1830. Redrawn from Garrick Mallery, 1893.

rock design elements that can be positively linked with the Mississippi culture are the birds with speech symbols, batons, and bilobed arrows that occur at Missouri and Alabama sites. Only in eastern Missouri near the Cahokia Mound do the thunderbird and the Mississippi symbols occur together. Apparently the southeastern Indians did not share the thunderbird cult symbol with their Algonquian neighbors.

There are problems connected with dating in the Eastern Woodland. A great many of the sites are carved on horizontal surfaces of exposed bedrock, often limestone. When the drawings were freshly cut, there was undoubtedly contrast between the patinated rock and the design areas. In the humid eastern climate, however, patination and lichen growth occur rapidly, destroying all contrast and making these carvings almost impossible to photograph without chalking. This rapid patination makes relative dating difficult, as everything has the same tone. There is only one site showing evidence of European contact, suggesting that the practice of rock drawing died out slightly after the white invasions.

As a rule the Eastern Woodland rock drawings lack careful workmanship or design but there are exceptions, like the running men facing page 115 and some of the concentric circle patterns from Georgia (neither of which are typical of the Eastern Woodland).

Many of the Missouri designs were probably cult symbols that had magical as well as religious meaning, and participation in rituals at a decorated rock might have imparted the power of the symbol to the participants. There are few drawings of game animals, but in some areas animal and bird tracks might have been connected with hunting magic.

Pecked Algonquin thunderbird and other figures, Safe Harbor, Susquehanna River, Pennsylvania. Site is now destroyed. Redrawn from D. Cadzow.

Red and yellow painting, Jackson County, Alabama. Redrawn from J. W. Cambron and S. A. Waters.

EASTERN WOODLAND STYLES (PECKED AND INCISED)

Style	Locations	Main design elements
Woodland Naturalistic	Mississippi Valley north of Ohio Valley	Thunderbird, hand- and foot-prints, animal and turkey tracks
Woodland Stylized	Ohio Valley Rhode Island	Round-headed anthropomorphs, animals, footprints, tracks, snakes, meandering lines
Woodland Pit and Groove	Tennessee Valley and adjoining areas	Dots, concentric circles, tracks, meandering lines
Mississippi Stylized	Eastern Missouri Tennessee Valley	Batons, bilobed arrows, various abstract forms

There are a few scattered painted sites, mainly naturalistic, from the northern or Algonquian region, and a number of abstract painted sites from Hokan territory in the Tennessee Valley.

18 THE NORTHERN WOODLAND

Nearly all of the rock drawings of the Northern Woodland appear on the Canadian Shield, a roughly shield-shaped mass of Precambrian rocks that covers nearly half of Canada and large areas in the northern United States (see map on page 146). There are innumerable lakes and rivers on the Shield, and there is perhaps more water than land in many areas. These conditions made water travel imperative and the famous birch-bark canoe was used by all the Northern Woodland tribes. It is a heavily forested land, mostly coniferous but with deciduous trees in the southern transition zone.

The major part of the Shield region was occupied by the Algonquian-speaking tribes, and the most important of these were the Ojibwa and the Cree. The southeastern edge of the Shield was in the territory of the Hurons, part of the Iroquoian migration from the Mississippi region, and the northwestern Shield was part of the Athabascan country (the area from which the Athabascan Navajo and Apache had migrated).

The Indians of the Northern Woodland were hunters of deer, elk, caribou, moose, and occasionally buffalo. Lacking pottery, they made use of the canoe birch for containers of all kinds. This same indispensable tree furnished material for bark scrolls used in mnemonic records, and for the toboggans dragged by men on snowshoes. They traveled in small bands and their ceremonial life, dictated by the group leader or shaman, must have been of the simplest nature.

The Algonquian tribes occupied a wide territory from the Pacific Northwest to Newfoundland and their hunting and food-gathering cul-

Red painting of caribou, Rattler Creek, Saskatchewan. From photograph by Tim Jones.

145

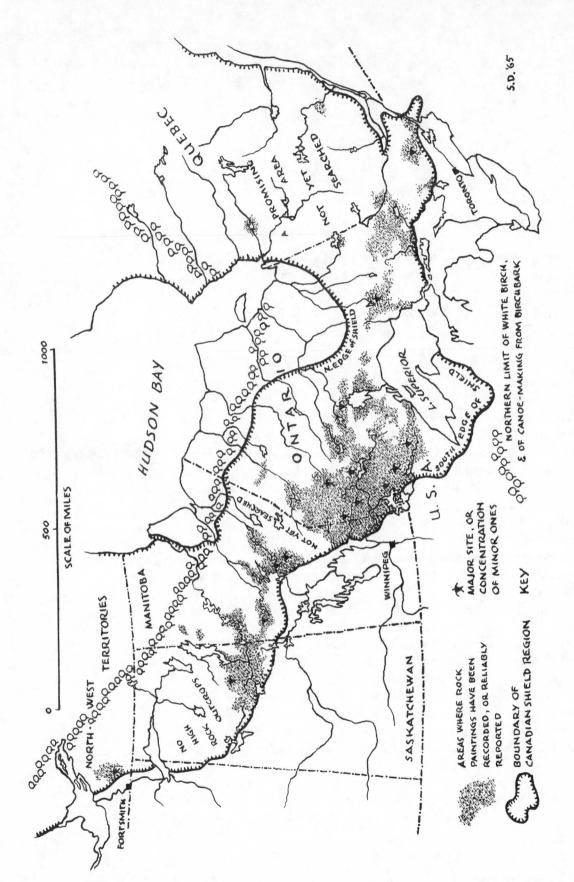

Distribution of rock paintings in the Canadian Shield area of the Northern Woodland.
Map by Selwyn Dewdney.

S.D. '65

SCALE OF MILES

0   500   1000

HUDSON BAY

QUEBEC

ONTARIO

MANITOBA

SASKATCHEWAN

NORTH WEST TERRITORIES

U. S. A.

L. SUPERIOR

PROVISIONAL AREA

NOT YET SEARCHED

NOT YET SEARCHED

N. EDGE of SHIELD

SOUTH EDGE OF SHIELD

NORTHERN LIMIT OF WHITE BIRCH, E OF CANOE-MAKING FROM BIRCHBARK

NO HIGH ROCK OUTCROPS

FORT SMITH

WINNIPEG

TORONTO

KEY

AREAS WHERE ROCK PAINTINGS HAVE BEEN RECORDED, OR RELIABLY REPORTED

BOUNDARY OF CANADIAN SHIELD REGION

MAJOR SITE, OR CONCENTRATION OF MINOR ONES

ture was remarkably the same wherever they went. Their rock drawings both in style and technique are in the same tradition from coast to coast and are like those of the Salish described in the Columbia-Fraser Plateau section. The style is predominantly naturalistic though there are many unidentified motifs. In most cases they seem to have applied the red pigment with their fingers.

Almost everything we know of these drawings has come from the excellent surveys by Selwyn Dewdney, who has been recording sites on the Shield since 1957. His field work has been by canoe and plane and considering the immense territory to be covered, he has obviously only scratched the surface. He reports that a great many paintings must have been done from canoes.

Large concentrations of paintings have been described from Ontario Province, particularly in the Lake-of-the-Woods region, and on both sides of the Ontario-Minnesota border. Aside from many unrecognizable objects, the most abundant motifs in that area are manned canoes, thunderbirds, hands, buffalo, bear, elk, moose, humans (often in ceremonial or shaman's costume), and supernatural beings. Historical subjects are rare and date from the French and English occupations. These include men with rifles, European forts, boats, and horsemen. At a few sites there are human figures smoking pipes.

Many Woodland tribes belived in an all-powerful deity, the Great Spirit or Manitou. This major supernatural figure was never personified in drawings but lesser deities figure on the rocks. The Ojibwa have a mischievous being called Maymaygwayshi, who lives in cracks and shallow caves along the water. He is very fond of fish and often robs the traps of the Indians. This spirit appears as a short, large-headed creature, sometimes with horns. The Ojibwa shaman was supposed to have the power to enter rocks and trade tobacco with the spirit for "rock medicine." [1] Other deities were the Thunderer (thunderbird); Missikinahpik, the Great Serpent; and Mishipizhiw, the Great Water Lynx. The latter is known by many names such as water panther and water monster and is the same creature as the medicine animal of the Winnebago. This sinister being was all-powerful in swift or rough water and his aid might be solicited if a dangerous water crossing was in prospect (see chapter 4). The Indians still leave small offerings such as clothing, tobacco, and bundles of colored sticks at painted rock sites. The sites are regarded as spirit rocks and the gifts are to placate the supernatural beings or to obtain their good will. Local Ojibwa have said that the offerings were made when someone was sick, different colors symbolizing different ailments. Other informants said that the offerings were for "good luck." This sort of thing is widespread in aboriginal America. In the Chumash region of southern California, the Indians often built little shrines of

Red painting of buffalo transmitting power to man, Churchill River, Saskatchewan. Redrawn from Selwyn Dewdney, 1963.

sticks and brush in which they would leave cloth, tobacco, and other articles as presents for the unseen spirits.

The drawings were doubtless made for a variety of reasons. The Salish in the Columbia-Fraser Plateau made drawings as records of dreams (see chapter 4), and this custom may have been followed in the Northern Woodland. The drawing on page 147 shows a man getting "power" from a buffalo; the power was thought to be transmitted through dreams or visions. Occasionally the pictures told a story, as in the painting of the raid across Lake Superior described in chapter 4. The large numbers of game-animal drawings suggest the hunting-magic motivation so common in the western United States. Some motifs may be clan symbols.

There are a few rock-pecked sites that have been described from Ontario and northern Minnesota. These are usually on horizontal surfaces and are crudely pecked animals, thunderbirds, and humans similar to the examples in southern Minnesota.

Investigations in the Shield country of northern Manitoba and Saskatchewan are now under way and over 50 sites have been recorded. Many of these are on the Churchill River drainage with its outlet on Hudson Bay, a region whose infinite number of lakes connected by streams or short portages make it a canoer's paradise. The paintings are in the same style as those in Ontario. There is one site with a striking drawing of a bear-headed shaman. One painting shows a man shooting a moose with a gun. The thunderbird continues as a major motif. This is mainly Cree country, a tribe with close ties with the Ojibwa, though the Churchill River region is also shared by Athabascan people. Several sites were recorded by Dewdney in 1965 between Fort Smith and Great Slave Lake in the Northwest Territories. These northernmost Shield sites seem to be in the same tradition as the Saskatchewan paintings and are in the territory of the Athabascan Slave Indians.

Scratched design by Micmac Indians, Kedgemakooge Lake, Nova Scotia. Redrawn from Garrick Mallery, 1893.

The only rock paintings from central Alaska are located on the Tanana River near Fairbanks. They depict human figures; several are inside a circle and others are in a boat that looks like a prowed dugout. This type of boat was used in southeastern Alaska.

There are a few carved sites in the Northern Woodland and the most interesting are in Nova Scotia, in the vicinity of Lake Kedgemakooge, where many rock drawings were made by the Micmac Indians. These are scratched on slabs of a smooth, slatey rock and the subjects include hands and feet, birds, animals, shields, headdresses, wigwams, etc.

A great many more paintings remain to be found in the Northern Woodland (Quebec Province, for example, has not been searched at all), but the vastness of the country, the difficulty of transportation, and the climate are formidable barriers to all but experienced and well-organized survey teams.

Female figure, possibly shaman, northern Saskatchewan. Photograph by Selwyn Dewdney.

	Far North	Northwest	Columbia-Fraser Plat.	Great Basin	California	Southwest	Great Plains	Eastern Woodland	Northern Woodland
PAINTED									
Naturalistic	X	X	X	X	X	X	X	X	X
Naturalistic Polychrome						X	X		
Stylized		X	X	X	X	X	X		X
Stylized Polychrome						X	X	X	
Abstract Linear			X	X	X	X			X
Abstract Polychrome			X	X	X	X			
PECKED									
Naturalistic			X	X		X	X	X	X
Stylized	X	X	X	X		X	X	X	X
Abstract Curvilinear			X	X	X	X		X	
Abstract Rectilinear			X	X		X	X		
Pit and Groove				X	X		X	X	
INCISED OR SCRATCHED									
Realistic *				X		X	X		X

* There are a few scattered examples of incised stylized and abstract but not enough to be classed as a main catogory.

CONCLUSIONS

In order to compress so complex a subject into a single volume it was necessary to cut the material to the bone. Many areas that would take several books to describe thoroughly have been allotted a paragraph or two.

One advantage, however, of so broad a study is that it is possible to show the extraordinary diversity of styles, techniques, and subjects created by the prehistoric North American Indians and how the different cultures each developed their characteristic rock-art forms.

Some styles were homogeneous over vast areas, such as the realistic painted tradition in the Algonquian territory stretching from Vancouver Island to Nova Scotia. Others, like the parti-colored figures in central Baja California, are confined to a few desert canyons.

Certain styles have been carried long distances by migrating tribes. The best examples of this are the Great Basin styles introduced into many areas by nomadic Shoshoneans. As contact was made with neighboring tribes having a rock-drawing tradition, there was a borrowing of ideas affecting style and subject matter but rarely technique. The Shoshoneans who pecked their designs on Great Basin basaltic rock continued their pecking technique on the sandstone of the Southwest.

There is no doubt that most of the rock drawings figured in ceremonies connected with the relation of man to the world around him, particularly the supernatural world. Specifically many of the pictures were made as visualizations of dreams during puberty rites or as hunting magic undertaken prior to a hunt.

Hunting magic was apparently not employed unless the quarry was a difficult animal to bag and a little supernatural aid was called for. There are innumerable pecked and incised drawings of the mountain sheep, a fine food animal and one of the wariest of beasts. If the game was plentiful, it rarely occurred in rock drawings. In southern Alberta, where enormous herds of buffalo migrated every year, drawings of the animal are almost nonexistent. Along the Columbia River where the Indians depended on the salmon as their main food supply, the easily procured fish was seldom pictured.

The most widespread design motif in North America, and indeed almost anywhere in the world where rock pictures are found, is the hand. It is a basic identifying sign for man, unmistakable and striking, from the Paleolithic caveprints made 30,000 years ago to the identical prints made in the Arizona canyons by the Navajo in historic times.

As the section on dating indicated, it is extremely difficult to tell the age of rock drawings though relative chronologies can be determined. The earliest rock-art sites in North America appear to be in the Great Basin, particularly southeastern California. The oldest style in the country is probably the pit and groove. This style is widely dispersed and the patterns are almost invariably pecked on isolated boulders.

The question of which Indians made which drawings can never have an entirely satisfactory answer. The constantly shifting populations in prehistoric America, with accompanying exchanges of cultural traits and art traditions, make the problem difficult indeed. However certain broad conclusions can be made. Through such clues as linguistic studies, association of drawings with archaeological remains, subject matter, and ethnographic information, we know what sort of culture produced each rock-art style and in many cases of the late prehistoric and historic periods, we know exactly what tribes made the pictures. We have convincing evidence of authorship for the Chumash and Luiseño in California, the Thompson River Salish in British Columbia, and the Hopi and Navajo in the Southwest, to name a few.

I have presented all the evidence available on the interpretation of these prehistoric drawings and in a general way we know why they were made. Only the original artist or shaman, however, would know the precise meanings of the pictures, and it is doubtful if many of us would understand him if he were here to explain. The world of the aboriginal Indian, where the supernatural was as real as the natural, is a world we cannot enter but nothing prevents us from enjoying the intriguing pictures that still exist by the thousands in caves and on cliffs.

NOTES*

CHAPTER 1

1. Kenneth Macgowan, *Early Man in the New World*, p. 196.
2. Richard S. MacNeish, "The Origins of New World Civilization," pp. 29–37.
3. M. McKusick, *Men of Ancient Iowa*, p. 81.
4. Macgowan, *op. cit.*, p. 241.

CHAPTER 2

1. Douglas Leechman *et al.*, *Some Pictographs of Southeastern British Columbia*, p. 77.

CHAPTER 3

1. Christy G. Turner, *Petrographs of the Glen Canyon Region*, p. 1.
2. David Gebhard, "Petroglyphs of Wyoming: A Preliminary Paper."
3. Frederica de Laguna, *Chugach Prehistory*.

CHAPTER 4

1. D. S. Davidson, *Aboriginal Australian and Tasmanian Rock Carvings and Paintings*, pp. 124, 125.
2. James A. Teit, *A Rock Painting of the Thompson River Indians, British Columbia*.
3. Robert F. Heizer, *Sacred Rain Rocks of Northern California*, pp. 33–38.
4. Edward L. Keithahn, "The Petroglyphs of Southeastern Alaska."
5. De Laguna, *op. cit.*, p. 105.
6. Selwyn Dewdney and Kenneth E. Kidd, *Indian Rock Paintings of the Great Lakes*, p. 14.
7. H. S. Colton, *Black Sand—Prehistory in Northern Arizona*, pp. 80, 81.

CHAPTER 6

1. G. B. M. Flamand, *Les Pierres écrites* . . .
2. C. B. Hunt, *Desert Varnish*.

* Complete publishing information can be found in Bibliography.

3. B. P. Dutton, *Sun Father's Way—The Kiva Murals of Kuaua*, pp. 19–34.
4. Ronald E. Beschel, "Dating Rock Surfaces by Lichen Growth and Its Application to Glaciology and Physiography," pp. 1044–1062.
5. Gerhard Folmann, "Lichenometrische Altersbestimmungen an Vorchristlichen Steinsetzungen der Polynesischen Osterinsel."
6. Robert F. Heizer and Martin A. Baumhoff, *Prehistoric Rock Art of Nevada and Eastern California*, pp. 231, 232.
7. Turner, *op. cit.*, pp. 1–74.

CHAPTER 7

1. W. J. Sollas, *Ancient Hunters*, pp. 238–243.
2. J. V. Young, *The Peregrinations of Kokopelli*, pp. 39–41.
3. Colton, "Is the House of Tcuhu the Minoan Labyrinth?"

CHAPTER 11

1. R. M. Underhill, *Red Man's America*, p. 294.
2. G. T. Emmons, *Petroglyphs in Southeastern Alaska*, pp. 223, 224.

CHAPTER 13

1. Zenas Leonard, *Narrative of the Adventures of Zenas Leonard*, pp. 72, 73.
2. Heizer and Baumhoff, *op. cit.*, pp. 202–208.

CHAPTER 15

1. Gebhard, *Prehistoric Paintings of the Diablo Region of Western Texas*, p. 53.
2. F. M. Setzler, "Seeking the Secret of the Giants."
3. MacNeish, "Preliminary Investigations in the Sierra de Tamaulipas, Mexico," pp. 134–136.

CHAPTER 18

1. Dewdney and Kidd, *op. cit.*, p. 14.

SUGGESTED READING*

CAIN, H. THOMAS. *Petroglyphs of Central Washington.*

CRESSMAN, L. S. *Petroglyphs of Oregon.*

DEWDNEY, SELWYN, and KIDD, KENNETH E. *Indian Rock Paintings of the Great Lakes.*

GEBHARD, DAVID. *Prehistoric Paintings of the Diablo Region of Western Texas.*

GRANT, CAMPBELL. *The Rock Paintings of the Chumash.*

HEIZER, ROBERT F., and BAUMHOFF, MARTIN A. *Prehistoric Rock Art of Nevada and Eastern California.*

JACKSON, A. T. *Picture-Writing of Texas Indians.*

MALLERY, GARRICK. *Picture Writing of the American Indians.*

SCHAAFSMA, POLLY. *Rock Art of the Navajo Reservoir District.*

STEWARD, JULIAN H. *Petroglyphs of California and Adjoining States.*

———. *Petroglyphs of the United States.*

TURNER, CHRISTY G. *Petrographs of the Glen Canyon Region.*

* Complete publishing information can be found in Bibliography.

BIBLIOGRAPHY

Pecked mythical fish,
Sproat Lake, Vancouver
Island. Redrawn from
Garrick Mallery, 1893.

ANATI, E. *Camonica Valley*. New York: Alfred A. Knopf, 1961.

ANGEL, MYRON. *La Piedra Pintada*. Los Angeles: Grafton Publishing Co., 1910.

ARTHUR, GEORGE. *Pictographs in Central Montana*. Part III: *Comments*. Montana State University, Anthropology and Sociology Papers, No. 21. Missoula, 1960.

BANDI, H. G. *et al. The Art of the Stone Age*. New York: Crown Publishers, 1961.

BEATY, J. J. "The Petroglyph Puzzle," *Pacific Discovery*, Vol. XVI, No. 3 (May–June 1963).

BECKWITH, F. "Group of Petroglyphs Near Moab, Utah," *El Palacio* (Santa Fe), XXXVI, Nos. 23–24 (1934), 177–8.

———. "Ancient Indian Petroglyphs of Utah," *ibid.*, XXXVIII, Nos. 6–9 (1935), 33–40.

———. "Glyphs That Tell the Story of an Ancient Migration," *Desert Magazine* (El Centro), III, No. 10 (1940), 4–7.

BESCHEL, RONALD E. "Dating Rock Surfaces by Lichen Growth and Its Application to Glaciology and Physiography (Lichenometry)," in G. O. Raasch, ed., *Geology of the Arctic*, Vol. II. Toronto: University of Toronto Press, 1961.

BOLTON, H. E., and MARSHALL, T. M. *The Colonization of North America 1492–1783*. New York: The Macmillan Company, 1922.

BREUIL, H. *Four Hundred Centuries of Cave Art*. Montignac, Dordogne: Centre d'Études et de Documentation Préhistoriques, 1952.

BREWER, J., and BREWER, S. "Wupatki Petroglyphs," U.S. National Park Service Southwestern Monuments Monthly Report (Santa Fe), August 1935, pp. 129–32.

BROWNLEE, RICHARD S. "The Big Moniteau Bluff Pictographs in Boone County, Missouri," *The Missouri Archaeologist*, Vol. XVIII, No. 4 (December 1956).

BRUFF, J. G. "Indian Engravings on Rocks Along Green River Valley in Sierra Nevada Range of Mountains," Annual Report of the Smithsonian Institution. Washington, D.C., 1872, pp. 409–12.

BURKITT, M. C. South Africa's Past in Stone and Paint. Cambridge: Cambridge University Press, 1928.

CADZOW, D. Petroglyphs in the Susquehanna River near Safe Harbor, Pennsylvania. Publication of the Pennsylvania Historical Commission, Vol. III (1934).

CAIN, H. THOMAS. Petroglyphs of Central Washington. Seattle: University of Washington Press, 1950.

CALDWELL, WARREN W. "An Archeological Survey of the Okanagan and Similkameen Valleys of British Columbia," Anthropology in British Columbia (Provincial Museum, Victoria) No. 4, 1953–54.

CAMBRON, J. W., and WATERS, S. A. "Petroglyphs and Pictographs in the Tennessee Valley and Surrounding Area," Journal of Alabama Archaeology, Vol. V, Issue 2 (1959).

CARSTENS, C. J., and KNUDSEN, J. P. "Petroglyphs and Pictographs of the Tennessee Valley, Part II, Spectrographic Analysis of Pigments," ibid.

CHAPMAN, C., and CHAPMAN, E. F. Indians and Archaeology of Missouri. Columbia: University of Missouri Press, 1964.

CHAPMAN, C. E. A History of California: The Spanish Period. New York: The Macmillan Company, 1921.

CHAPMAN, K. M. "Pajaritan pictography: The Cave Pictographs of the Rito de los Frijoles," in Hewett, Pajarito Plateau and Its Ancient People. Handbooks of Archaeological History. Albuquerque, 1938. Appendix 1, pp. 139–148.

COLTON, H. S. Black Sand—Prehistory in Northern Arizona, Albuquerque: University of New Mexico Press, 1960.

———. "Is the House of Tcuhu the Minoan Labyrinth?" Science (Washington, D.C.), n.s. XLV, No. 1174 (1917), 667–668.

COLTON, M. R. F., and COLTON, H. S. "Petroglyphs, the Record of a Great Adventure," American Anthropologist, XXX, No. 1 (1931), 32–37.

CONNER, STUART W. A Preliminary Survey of Prehistoric Picture Writing on Rock Surfaces in Central and South Central Montana. Billings Archaeological Society, Anthropological Paper, No. 2, 1962.

———. "The Fish Creek, Owl Canyon, and Grinnvoll Rock Shelter Pictograph Sites in Montana," Plains Anthropologist (Journal of the Plains Conference) (Billings Archaeological Society Paper, 1962).

COSGROVE, C. B. Caves of the Upper Gila and Hueco Areas in New Mexico and Texas. Papers of the Peabody Museum, Vol. XXIV, No. 2. Cambridge: Harvard University Press, 1947.

COXON, W. "Ancient Manuscripts on American Stones," Arizona Highways, September 1964.

CRAWFORD, L. F. History of North Dakota, Vol. I. Chicago and New York: American Historical Society, 1931, pp. 36–37.

CRESSMAN, L. S. Petroglyphs of Oregon. University of Oregon Publications in Anthropology. Eugene, 1937.

CUTLER, H. E. "Medicine Men and the Preservation of a Relic Gene in Maize," *Journal of Heredity*, XXXV (1944), 290–94.

DAHLGREN, B., and ROMERO, J. "La Prehistoria Baja California Redescubrimiento de Pinturas Rupestres," *Cuadernos Americanos*, LVIII (1951), 153–178.

DAHLGREN DE JORDAN, B. "Las Pinturas Rupestres de la Baja California," *Artes de Mexico*, No. 3, March, April 1954.

DANCKER, DOROTHY. "Black Hills Vacationers Puzzled by Centuries-Old Indian Carvings; Origin of Artists Remains Mystery," *The Daily Plainsman* (Huron, South Dakota), August 2, 1964.

D'ANGLURE, SALADIN. "Decouverte de petroglyphes a Qajartalik sur Ille de Qikertaaluk," (Ottawa, Department of Northern Affairs and National Resources), IX, No. 6 (1962), 34–39.

DAVIDSON, D. S. *Aboriginal Australian and Tasmanian Rock Carvings and Paintings*. Memoirs of the American Philosophical Society, Vol. V, Philadelphia, 1936.

DAVIS, E. H. "We Found the Cave of Lost Art," *Desert Magazine* (Palm Desert), XII, No. 4 (1949), 25–27.

DEETZ, J. F. "A Dateable Chumash Pictograph from Santa Barbara County," *American Antiquity* (Salt Lake City, University of Utah Press), Vol. XXIX, No. 4 (1964).

DE HARPORT, D. L. "An Archaeological Survey of Canyon de Chelly: Preliminary Report of the Field Sessions of 1948," *El Palacio*, LVIII, No. 2 (1951), 35–48.

DELABARRE, E. B. *Dighton Rock—A Study of the Written Rocks of New England*. New York: Walter Neal, 1928.

DE LAGUNA, FREDERICA. "Peintures Rupestries Eskimo," *Journal de la Société des Américanistes* (Paris), n.s. Vol. XXV (1933).

——. *The Archaeology of Cook Inlet*. Philadelphia: University of Pennsylvania Press, 1934.

——. "Chugach Prehistory," *Publications in Anthropology* (Seattle, University of Washington Press), XIII (1956), 102–109.

DEWDNEY, SELWYN. "Stone Age Art in the Canadian Shield," *Canadian Art*, XVI (1959) 164–167.

——. *Indian Art*. Saskatchewan Museum of Natural History Popular Series No. 4. Regina, 1963.

——. "Writings on Stone Along the Milk River," *The Beaver* (Winnipeg), Winter 1964.

——. *Stone Age Paintings*. Department of Mines and Natural Resources, Manitoba, 1965.

——, and KIDD, KENNETH E. *Indian Rock Paintings of the Great Lakes*. Toronto: University of Toronto Press, 1962.

DIESING, E. H., and MAGRE, F. "Petroglyphs and Pictographs in Missouri," *The Missouri Archaeologist*, Vol. VIII, No. 1 (1942).

DIGUET, L. "Note sur la pictographie de la Basse-Californie," *Anthropologie* (Paris), 1894, pp. 160–175.

——. "Rapport sur une mission scientifique dans la Basse-Californie," *Nouvelle Archives des Missions Scientifiques* (Paris), IX (1899), 1–53.

DITTERT, A. E., JR., HESTER, J. J., and EDDY, F. W. *An Archaeological Survey of the Navajo Reservoir District, Northwestern New Mexico.* A monograph of the School of American Research and the Museum of New Mexico, No. 23. Santa Fe, 1961.

DURHAM, D. "Petroglyphs at Mesa de los Padillas," *El Palacio*, Vol. LXII, No. 1 (January 1955).

DUTTON, B. P. *Sun Father's Way—The Kiva Murals of Kuaua.* Albuquerque: University of New Mexico Press, 1963.

EBERHART, H., and BABCOCK, AGNES. *An Archaeological Survey of Mutau Flat, Ventura County, California.* Contributions to California Archaeology, No. 5. Los Angeles, 1963.

ELROD, M. J. *Pictured Rocks, Indian Writings on the Rock Cliffs of Flathead Lake, Montana.* Bulletin of the University of Montana, No. 46, Biological Series No. 14. Missoula, 1908.

ELSASSER, A. B., and CONTRERAS, E. "Modern Petrography in Central California and Western Nevada," Reports of the University of California Archaeological Survey (Berkeley), No. 41 (1958), pp. 12–18.

EMMONS, G. T. "Petroglyphs in Southeastern Alaska," *American Anthropologist*, X (1908), 221–230.

ENGERRAND, J. *Nuevos Petroglifos de la Baja California.* Boletin del Museo Nacional de Arqueologia, Historia e Etnologia, No. 10, Mexico City.

———. *Nota Complementaria acera de los Petrogliphos de la Baja California, ibid.*

ERWIN, R. P. "Indian Rock Writing in Idaho," 12th Annual Report, Idaho Historical Society, Boise, 1930, pp. 35–111.

EWERS, J. C. *Plains Indian Painting.* Stanford: Stanford University Press, 1939.

FENENGA, F. *Methods of Recording and Present Status of Knowledge Concerning Petroglyphs in California.* University of California Archaeological Survey, No. 3. Berkeley, 1949.

FERGUSSON, G. J., and LIBBY, W. F. *UCLA Radiocarbon Dates II.* Los Angeles, University of California Institute of Geophysics. 1962.

———. *UCLA Radiocarbon Dates III.* Los Angeles, University of California Institute of Geophysics. 1963.

FEWKES, J. W. "A Few Tusayan Pictographs," *American Anthropologist*, o.s. V, No. 1 (1892). 9–26.

———. "Tusayan Totemic Signatures," *ibid.*, No. 1 (1897), 1–11.

———. "Tusayan Migration Traditions," Nineteenth Annual Report of the Bureau of American Ethnology, Part 2. Washington, D.C., 1900.

———. "Hopi Katcinas," Twenty-first Annual Report of the Bureau of American Ethnology. Washington, D.C., 1903, pp. 3–126.

———. *Preliminary Report on a Visit to the Navaho National Monument, Arizona.* Bureau of American Ethnology Bulletin, No. 50. Washington, D.C., 1911.

FINLEY, R. S. "Note on the Orizaba Pictograph (Olson's) Cave, Santa Cruz Island, Santa Barbara, California," National Speleological Society, Monthly Report of the Stanford Grotto (Palo Alto, California), 1951.

FLAMAND, G. B. M. *Les Pierres écrites (Hadjrat-Mektoubat): Gravures et inscriptions rupestres du Nord-africain.* Paris: Massonet Cie., Editeurs, 1921.

FOLMANN, GERHARD. "Lichenometrische Altersbestimmungen an vorchristlichen Steinsetzungen der Polynesischen Osterinsel," *Naturwissenschaften* (Berlin), 1961, pp. 627–628.

FOSSNOCK, A. "Pictographs and Murals in the Southwest," *El Palacio*, XXXIX, Nos. 16–18 (1935), 81–90.

FOSTER, G. "Petrographic Art in Glen Canyon," *Plateau* (Flagstaff), XXVII, No. 1 (1954), 6–18.

FREDERICK, M. C. "Some Indian Paintings," *Land of Sunshine*, XV, No. 4 (1901), 223–227.

FUNDABURK, L. *Sun Circles and Human Hands.* (Privately printed; Luverne, Alabama, 1957.)

GALLENKAMP, C. "Where Ancients Wrote in Stone," *Desert Magazine* (Palm Desert), XVIII, No. 5 (1955), 16–18.

GALLOWAY, E., and AGOGINO, G. A. "Pictographs at Wall Rock Cave, Albany County, Wyoming," *The Wyoming Archaeologist* (Sheridan), Vol. V, No. 3 (September 1962).

GANONG, W. F. *Upon Aboriginal Pictographs Reported From New Brunswick.* Bulletin of the Natural History Society of New Brunswick, Vol. V, No. 22, Part II. Saint John, 1904.

GARDNER, ERLE STANLEY. "The Case of the Baja Caves," *Life*, LIII (1962), 62–64.

——, *The Hidden Heart of Baja.* New York: William Morrow & Company, 1962.

GEBHARD, DAVID. "Petroglyphs of Wyoming: A Preliminary Paper," *El Palacio*, LVIII, No. 3 (1951), 67–81.

——. "Petroglyphs in the Boysen Basin, Wyoming," University of Wyoming Publication, XVIII, No. 1 (1954), 66–70.

——. "Pictographs in the Sierra Blanca Mountains," *El Palacio*, LXIV, No. 3 (1957), 215–222.

——. "Hidden Lake Pictographs," *El Palacio*, LXVIII, No. 4 (1958), 146–149.

——. "Nineteen Centuries of American Abstraction," *Art News*, LIX, No. 10 (1958), 20–23.

——. *Prehistoric Paintings of the Diablo Region of Western Texas.* Roswell Museum Publications in Art and Science, No. 3. Roswell, New Mexico, 1960.

——. "Prehistoric Rock Drawings at Painted Grotto, New Mexico," *El Palacio*, Vol. LXIX, No. 4 (1962).

——. "Rock Drawings in the Western United States," *Jahrbuch fur Prahistorische und Ethnographische Kunst* (Berlin), Vol. XX, 1963.

——. "The Shield Motif in Plains Rock Art," *American Antiquity*, 1966.

——, AGOGINO, A., and HAYNES, V. "Horned Owl Cave, Wyoming," *ibid.*, XXIX, No. 3 (1964), 360–368.

——, and CAHN, H. A. "The Petroglyphs of Dinwoody, Wyoming," *ibid.*, XV, No. 3 (1950), 219–228.

GIDDINGS, J. L. "Rock Paintings in Central Alaska," *ibid.*, Vol. VII, No. 1 (1941).

GILBERT, H. "Indian Picture Writing," *The Wyoming Archaeologist*, Vol. V, No. 3 (September 1962).

GJESSING, GUTORM. "Petroglyphs and Pictographs in British Columbia," in *Indian Tribes of Aboriginal America*. Selected Papers of the Twenty-ninth International Congress of Americanists, 1952, pp. 66–79.

———. "Petroglyphs and Pictographs in the Coast Salishan Area of Canada," in *Miscellanea Paul Rivet*. Publicationes del Instituto de Historia, Primera Serie, No. 50. Mexico City, 1958. Pp. 257–275.

GLADWIN, H. S., *Men Out of Asia*. New York: McGraw-Hill Book Company, 1947.

———. *A History of the Ancient Southwest*. Portland, Maine: Bond Wheelwright, 1957.

———, HAURY, E. W., SAYLES, E. B., and GLADWIN, N., "Excavations at Snaketown—Material Culture." Medallion papers, No. XXV. (Privately printed; Gila Pueblo: Globe, Arizona.)

GODDARD, P. E. *Life and Culture of the Hupa*. University of California Publications in American Archaeology and Ethnology, Vol. I, No. 1. Berkeley, 1903.

GOODALL, E., COOKE, C. K., and CLARK, J. D. *Prehistoric Rock Art of Central Africa*. National Publications Trust, Salisbury, Southern Rhodesia, 1959.

GRANT, CAMPBELL. "Prehistoric Paintings of the Santa Barbara Region," Santa Barbara Museum of Natural History, Museum Talk, 1960.

———. "Ancient Art in the Wilderness," *Pacific Discovery* (San Francisco), July–August 1961.

———. "Cave Paintings of the Chumash." *Arts* (New York), May–June 1962.

———. "California's Painted Caves," *Desert Magazine* (Palm Desert), May 1964.

———. *A Collection of Chumash Artifacts from the Sierra Madre Mountains of Santa Barbara County, California*. University of California Archaeological Survey, No. 63. Berkeley, 1964.

———. "California's Legacy of Indian Rock Art," *Natural History Magazine* (New York), June 1964.

———. "Rock Painting in California," *Jahrbuch fur Prahistorische und Ethnographische Kunst*, Vol. XXI (1965).

———. *The Rock Paintings of the Chumash*. Berkeley: University of California Press, 1965.

———. *Prehistoric Rock Art of the Santa Barbara Region*. An illustrated catalogue of an exhibit of rock painting facsimiles at the Art Gallery, University of California at Santa Barbara, Oct. 12–Nov. 7, 1965.

———. "Cave Paintings of Sonora," *Desert Magazine* (Palm Desert), April 1967.

GRAZIOSI, P. *Palaeolithic Art*. New York: McGraw-Hill Book Company, 1960.

GREEN, E. "Ancient Rock Inscriptions in Johnson County, Arkansas," in *Miscellaneous Papers Relating to Anthropology*. Annual Report of the Smithsonian Institution (Washington, D.C.) 1881, pp. 538–541.

GREEN, W. "Cave Painting in Ventura County." Unpublished MS in author's collection, 1935.

GREER, E. S., JR. "More 'Mystery Holes in Rock,'" *Journal of Alabama Archaeology*, Vol. IX, No. 2 (1963).

GREY, D., and SWEEM, G. D. "Pictograph Classification and Petroglyph Weathering," *The Wyoming Archaeologist*, Vol. IV, No. 2 (1961).

GRIMSHAW, RUSS, and MAY, CLYDE. "Lucerne Valley Pictographs," *The Wyoming Archaeologist*, VI, No. 4 (December 1963), 8–12.

GRUBER, A. "A Survey of Petroglyphs in Black Canyon," *The Southwest Museum Masterkey* (Los Angeles), Vol. XXXV, No. 3 (July–September 1961).

HAINES, F. "How the Indian Got the Horse," *American Heritage* (New York), 1964.

HALLISEY, N., "Sketches of Rock Paintings up the Styne Valley Near Lytton, B. C.," *British Columbia Digest*, April 1964, (Quesnel).

HARNER, M. J. "Gravel Pictographs of the Lower Colorado River Region," Reports of the University of California Archaeological Survey, No. 22. Berkeley, 1953, pp. 1–32.

HAURY, E. W. *Painted Cave: Northeastern Arizona*. Amerind Foundation Inc., No. 3, 1945.

HEDDON, M. "Surface Printing as a Method of Recording Petroglyphs," *American Antiquity*, XXIII (1958), 435–439.

HEIZER, ROBERT F. *Petroglyphs from Southwestern Kodiak Islands, Alaska*. Proceedings of the American Philosophical Society. Philadelphia, 1947, pp. 284–293.

———. *Sacred Rain Rocks of Northern California*. University of California Archaeological Survey, No. 20. Berkeley, 1953.

———., and BAUMHOFF, MARTIN A. *Prehistoric Rock Art of Nevada and Eastern California*. Berkeley: University of California Press, 1962.

HENDERSON, R. "Glyph Hunters in the Indian Country," *Desert Magazine* (El Centro), X, No. 1 (1946), 11–15.

HESTER, J. J. *Early Navajo Migrations and Acculturation in the Southwest*. Museum of New Mexico Papers in Anthropology, No. 6. Santa Fe, 1962.

HIBBEN, F. C. *A Possible Pyramidal Structure and Other Mexican Influences at Pottery Mound, New Mexico*. American Antiquity, Vol. 31, No. 4 (1966), 522–529.

HINTHORN, J. "Turner Ranch Pictographs," *The Wyoming Archaeologist*, Vol. V, No. 4 (December 1962).

HODGE, F. W. *Handbook of the American Indians North of Mexico*. Bureau of American Ethnology Bulletin, No. 30. Washington, D.C., 1907.

HUNT, C. B. "Desert Varnish," *Science*, CXX, No. 3109 (1954), 183–184.

HURST, C. T., and HENDRICKS, L. J. "Some Unusual Petroglyphs near Sapinero, Colorado," *Southwestern Lore* (Gunnison), XVIII, No. 1 (1952), 14–18.

HURT, W. L., JR. "A Method for Cataloguing Pictographs," *New Mexico Anthropologist* (Albuquerque), III, Nos. 3–4 (1939), 40–44.

HUSCHER, B. H., and HUSCHER, H. A. "Conventionalized Bear-Track Petroglyphs of the Uncompahgre Plateau," *Southwestern Lore*, VI, No. 2 (1940), 25–28.

INVERARITY, R. B. *Art of the Northwest Coast Indians*. Berkeley: University of California Press, 1950.

IOVIN, JUNE. "A Summary of Luiseño Material Culture," University of California Archaeological Survey Annual Report, 1962–1963, Los Angeles, pp. 79–134.

IRVING, WILLIAM N. "Field Work in the Western Brooks Range, Alaska: Preliminary Report," *Arctic Anthropology*, Vol. I, No. 1 (1961).

IRWIN, MARGARET C. "Petroglyphs Near Santa Barbara," Santa Barbara Museum of Natural History, Museum Talk, 1950, pp. 1–5.

JACKSON, A. T. *Picture-Writing of Texas Indians*. Bureau of Research in the Social Sciences, Study No. 27. Austin: University of Texas Press, 1938.

JASMANN, ALICE O. *Archaeology in Montana*. Montana Archaeological Society (Helena), Vol. III. No. 3. January 1962.

JENNESS, DIAMOND. *Archaeological Investigations in Bering Strait*. National Museum of Canada Bulletin, No. 50. Ottawa.

KEITHAHN, EDWARD L. "The Petroglyphs of Southeastern Alaska," *American Antiquity*, Vol. VI, No. 2 (1940), 123–132.

KELLEY, C. "Murals Painted by Ancient Tribesmen," *Desert Magazine* (Palm Desert), XIII, No. 8 (1950), 11–12.

KELLEY, J. C. "Atlatls, Bows and Arrows, Pictographs, and the Pecos River Focus," *American Antiquity*, XVI, No. 1 (1950), 71–74.

KETTL, J. W. "Project Petroglyphs," *Southwest Museum Masterkey*, Vol. XXXVI (January–March 1962).

KIDDER, A. V., and GUERNSEY, S. J. *Archaeological Explorations in Northwestern Arizona*. Bureau of American Ethnology Bulletin, No. 65. Washington, D.C., 1919.

KING, D. R., and DEWDNEY, SELWYN. "Prehistoric Rock Art in Alberta." To be published by Glenbow Foundation of Archaeology.

KIRKLAND, F. *A Description of Texas Pictographs*. Bulletin of Texas Archaeological and Paleontological Society (Abilene), X (1938), 11–39.

KLEIBER, H., and LEWIS, O. "Dinwoody Lakes Pictograph Site," *The Wyoming Archaeologist*, Vol. V, No. 4 (December 1962).

KROEBER, A. L. *Handbook of the Indians of California*. Bureau of American Ethnology Bulletin, No. 78. Washington D.C., 1925.

KUHN, H. *Wenn Steine Reden*. Wiesbaden: Brockhaus, 1966.

LA MONK, CHARLES S. "Pictograph Cave, Burro Flats," Archaeological Survey Association of Southern California *Newsletter* (Los Angeles), I, No. 2 (1953), 8–9.

———. "Painted Rock," *ibid*., Vol. II, No. 4 (1954), 3–5.

LA PAZ, L. "Meteoritical Pictographs," Contributions of the Meteoritical Society, IV, No. 2, 122–128. Los Angeles, 1948.

LATHRAP, D. *A Distinctive Pictograph from the Carrizo Plains, San Luis Obispo County*. University of California Archaeological Survey, No. 9, 1950.

LATTA, F. F. *Handbook of the Yokuts Indians*. Oildale, California: Bear State Books, 1949.

LAUDERMILK, J. D. "On the Origin of Desert Varnish," *American Journal of Science* (New Haven), Fifth Series, XXI, No. 121 (1931), 51–66.

LAWSON, A. C. "Ancient Rock Inscriptions on the Lake of the Woods," *American Naturalist*, XIX (1885), 654–657.

LAWTON, SHERMAN P. "Petroglyphs and Pictographs in Oklahoma: An Introduction," *Plains Anthropologist*, Vol. VII, No. 17 (1962).

LEECHMAN, DOUGLAS, HESS, MARGARET, and FOWLER, ROY L. *Pictographs in Southwestern Alberta*. Bulletin No. 136, Annual Report of the National Museum. Ottawa, 1953–54.

——, et al. *Some Pictographs of Southeastern British Columbia*. Transactions of the Royal Society of Canada, Third Series, XLVIII (1954), 77–85.

LEONARD, ZENAS. *Narrative of the Adventures of Zenas Leonard*. Norman: University of Oklahoma Press, 1959.

LEWIS, T. H. "Incised Boulders in the Upper Mississippi Valley," *American Naturalist*, September 1889.

LEWIS, T. M. N., and KNEBERG, M., eds. *Ten Years of the Tennessee Archaeologist: Selected Subjects*. Knoxville: University of Tennessee, 1954.

LHOTE, H. *The Search for the Tassili Frescoes*. New York: E. P. Dutton & Co., 1959.

LIBBY, WILLARD F. *Radiocarbon Dating*. Chicago: The University of Chicago Press, 1955.

MAC GOWAN, KENNETH. *Early Man in the New World*. New York: The Macmillan Company, 1950.

MAC NEISH, RICHARD S. "Preliminary Investigations in the Sierra de Tamaulipas, Mexico," American Philosophical Society, Vol. 48, Part 6, 1958.

——. "The Origins of New World Civilization," *Scientific American*, Vol. CCXI, No. 5 (1964).

MC ADAMS, W. *Records of Ancient Races in the Mississippi Valley*. St. Louis: Barns, 1887.

MC KUSICK, M. *Men of Ancient Iowa*. Ames: Iowa State University Press, 1964.

MAGRE, FRANK. "The Petrographs of Missouri." Unpublished MS in the possession of the author.

MALLERY, GARRICK. *Pictographs of the North American Indians*. Fourth Annual Report of the Bureau of American Ethnology. Washington, D.C., 1886.

——. *Picture Writing of the American Indians*. Tenth Annual Report of the Bureau of American Ethnology. Washington, D.C., 1893.

MALOUF, CARLING. *Pictographs and Petroglyphs*. Archaeological Society of Montana, Vol. III, No. 1 (1961).

MASON, J. ALDEN. *Some Unusual Petroglyphs and Pictographs of Durango and Coahuila, Mexico*. Homenaje a Pablo Martinez del Rio, Instituto Nacional de Antropologia e Historia. Mexico, 1961.

MAYNARD, C. C. "Hieroglyphics Near Benjamin, Utah," *Improvement Era* (Salt Lake City), 1911, pp. 582–591.

MEIGHAN, CLEMENT W. "Prehistoric Rock Paintings in Baja California," *American Antiquity*, XXXI, No. 3 (January 1966), 372–392.

MILLER, W. C. "Two Possible Astronomical Pictographs Found in Northern Arizona," *Plateau*, XXVII, No. 4 (1955), 6–13.

MITCHELL, J. R. "Petroglyphs and Pictographs in the Tennessee Valley and Surrounding Area: Part II," *Journal of Alabama Archaeology*, Vol. IX, No. 2 (1963).

MOMYER, G. *Indian Picture Writing in Southern California.* (Privately printed; San Bernardino, 1937).

MONTGOMERY, C. M. "The Corn Shrines of the Tanos," *Desert Magazine* (Palm Desert), Vol. XXVII, No. 12 (December 1964).

MORRISON, A. L. "The Painted Rocks of the Carisa (Carrizo Plains)," *National Motorist*, January 30, 1926.

MORSS, N. *The Ancient Culture of the Fremont River in Utah.* Papers of the Peabody Museum, Vol. XII, No. 3. Cambridge: Harvard University Press, 1931.

MOUNTFORD, C. P. "Art, Myth, and Symbolism," in *Records of the American-Australian Scientific Expedition to Arnhem Land.* Vol. I. Melbourne, 1956.

MULLOY, W. *A Preliminary Historical Outline for the Northwest Plains.* University of Wyoming Publications, Vol. XXII, No. 1. Laramie, 1958.

NEWCOMBE, C. F. "Petroglyphs in British Columbia," *Victoria Daily Times*, September 7, 1907.

NIBLACK, A. P. "The Coast Indians of Southern Alaska and Northern British Columbia," Annual Report for 1887–88, U.S. National Museum. Washington, D.C., 1890, pp. 225–386.

OBERMAIER, H., and WEINERT, P. *Las Pinturas Rupestres del Narranco de Valltorta.* Madrid: Castellon, 1919.

ORELLANA, R. *Petroglifos y Pinturas Rupestres de Sonora.* Organo oficial del Centro de Investigaciones antropologicas de Mexico, Vol. I. Mexico City, 1953.

ORR, PHIL C. "Who Painted Painted Cave?" Archaeological Survey Association of Southern California *Newsletter*, II, No. 2 (1954), 7–8.

OSBURN, D. N. "Petroglyph and Pictograph Sites in the Finlay Mountains," *Field and Laboratory* (Southern Methodist University), IX, No. 1 (1941), 30–35.

OVER, W. H. *Indian Picture Writing in South Dakota.* University of South Dakota Archaeological Circular, No. 4, 1941.

PARKER, M. "A Study of the Rocky Creek Pictoglyph," *Tennessee Archaeologist* (Knoxville), Vol. V, No. 2 (1948).

PAYEN, L. A. "Petroglyphs of Sacramento and Adjoining Counties," University of California Archaeological Survey. Berkeley, 1959.

PEITHMAN, IRVING M. "Pictographs and Petroglyphs in Southern Illinois," *Journal of Illinois State Archaeological Society* (Springfield), Vol. II, No. 4 (1952).

———. "A Petroglyph Site at Fountain Bluff, Jackson County, Illinois," *Central States Archaeological Journal* (Carbondale), II, No. 1 (1955), pp. 11–13.

PEPPER, CHORAL. "Bewitched by Baja," *Desert Magazine* (Palm Desert), Vol. XXVII, No. 8 (August 1964).

———. "Petroglyphs, the Unsolved Mystery," *ibid.*, Vol. XXVI, No. 11 (November 1964).

PERRYMAN, M. "Georgia Petroglyphs," *Archaeology* (New York), 1964, pp. 54–56.

PETERSEN, EUGENE T. "Michigan's Mysterious Rock Painting," *Ford Times*, July 1960.

POMPA Y POMPA, ANTONIO. "La Escritura Petroglifica Rupestre y su Expresion en el Noroeste Mexicano," *Anales* (Mexico, Instituto Nacional de Antropologia e Historia), Epoca 6a, 1956, pp. 213–225.

PRENTICE, R. A. "Pictograph Story of Konate," *El Palacio*, LVIII, No. 3 (1951), 90–96.

Present Status of Knowledge Concerning Petroglyphs in Nova Scotia. Nova Scotia Museum. Halifax, 1956.

RAFN, C. C. *Antiquites Americanae.* Plate 13. Copenhagen, 1845.

REAGAN, A. B. "The Pictographs of Ashley and Dry Fork Valleys in Northeastern Utah," *Transactions* of the Kansas Academy of Science (Topeka), XXXIV (1931), 168–216.

——. "Some Notes on the Picture Writing North of Mexico," Bulletin of the Wagner Free Institute of Science of Philadelphia, VII, No. 4 (1932), 38–54.

——. *Some Notes on an Ancient Culture of the Provo-Salt Lake Region.* Reprinted from *Northwest Science*, Vol. IX, No. 2 (1935).

RENAUD, E. B. *Archaeological Survey of Eastern Colorado, First Report.* University of Denver, Department of Anthropology, 1931.

——. *Archaeological Survey of Eastern Wyoming, Summer 1931.* University of Denver, Department of Anthropology, and University of Wyoming. Denver, 1932.

——. *Archaeological Survey of Eastern Colorado, Second Report.* University of Denver, Department of Anthropology, 1932.

——. *Archaeological Survey of Eastern Colorado, Third Report.* University of Denver, Department of Anthropology, 1933.

——. *Archaeological Survey of the High Western Plains, Eighth Report.* University of Denver, Department of Anthropology, 1936.

——. *Archaeological Survey of North Central New Mexico, Eleventh Report.* University of Denver, Department of Anthropology, 1938.

——. *Archaeology of the High Western Plains, Seventeen Years of Archaeological Research.* University of Denver, Department of Anthropology, 1947.

RICHARDS, A., and RICHARDS, D. "Petroglyphs of the Russell Site," in *Science of Man, I*, No. 1 (1960), 18–21.

RICHARDS, D. J. *The Sanilac Petroglyphs.* Cranbrook Institute of Science, Bulletin 36. Bloomfield Hills, Michigan, 1958.

RITTER, D. "Petroglyphs, a Few Outstanding Sites," Oregon Archaeological Society *Screenings* (Portland), Vol. XIV, No. 8 (1965).

RITZENTHALER, R. E. "Wisconsin Petroglyphs and Pictographs," *Wisconsin Archaeologist*, XXXI, No. 4 (1950), 83–129.

ROSS, E. T. "A Preliminary Survey of the Petroglyphs of Southern California." Unpublished MS, 1938.

ROZAIRE, C. E. "Pictographs at Burro Flats," Ventura Historical Society Quarterly, February 1959.

——, and KRITZMAN, C. "A Petroglyph Cave on San Nicolas Island," *Southwest Museum Masterkey*, Vol. XXXIV, No. 4 (1960).

RUDY, J. R. *Archaeological Survey of Western Utah.* University of Utah Anthropological Paper No. 12. Salt Lake City, 1953.

RUL, FRANCISCO GONZALEZ. *Petroglifos en un Lugar Denominado "El Sol."* Homenaje a Pablo Martinez del Rio, Instituto Nacional de Antropologia e Historia. Mexico, 1961.

SCHAAFSMA, POLLY. "Rock Art of the Navajo Reservoir," *El Palacio*, Vol. LXIX, No. 4 (1962).

———. *Rock Art in the Navajo Reservoir District.* Museum of New Mexico Papers in Anthropology, No. 7. Santa Fe: Museum of New Mexico Press, 1963.

———. *Southwest Indian Pictographs and Petroglyphs.* Santa Fe: Museum of New Mexico Press, 1965.

———. *Early Navajo Rock Paintings and Carvings.* Museum of Navaho Ceremonial Art, Sante Fe, 1966.

SCHOOLCRAFT, H. R. *Historical and Statistical Information Respecting the Indians of the United States.* Vol. II: plate 41; Vol. III: plate 41. Philadelphia: J. B. Lippincott Company, 1852–54.

SECRIST, K. G. *Pictographs in Central Montana.* Part I: *Fergus County.* Montana State University Anthropology and Sociology Papers, No. 20. Missoula, 1960.

SETZLER, F. M. "Seeking the Secret of the Giants," *National Geographic Magazine*, Vol. CII, No. 3 (1952).

SHUMATE, MAYNARD. *Pictographs in Central Montana.* Part II: *Panels Near Great Falls, Montana.* Montana State University Anthropology and Sociology Papers, No. 21. Missoula, 1960.

SHUTLER, R., and SHUTLER, M. E. *Archaeological Survey in Southern Nevada.* Nevada State Museum Anthropological Papers, No. 7. Reno, 1962.

SIMS, A. C. "An Artist Analyses New Mexico's Petroglyphs," *El Palacio*, LV, No. 10 (1948), 302–309.

———. *San Cristobal Petroglyphs.* Santa Fe: Southwest Editions, 1950.

SKINNER, A. *A Staten Island Petroglyph.* Heye Foundation Indian Notes, Vol. X. New York, 1925.

SMITH, G. A., et al. *Indian Picture Writing of San Bernardino and Riverside Counties.* San Bernardino County Museum Association Publication, Vol. 7, No. 3, 1961.

SMITH, H. I. *An Album of Prehistoric Canadian Art.* Victoria Memorial Museum, Bulletin 37. Ottawa, 1923.

———. "A List of Petroglyphs in British Columbia," *American Anthropologist*, XXIX, No. 4 (1927), 605–610.

———. "A Pictograph on the Lower Skeena River, British Columbia," *ibid.*, pp. 611–614.

SMITH, M. W. "Petroglyph Complexes in the History of the Columbia-Fraser Region," *Southwestern Journal of Anthropology* (Santa Fe), II, No. 3 (1946), 306–322.

SMITH, V. "Sheep Hunting Artists of Black Canyon Walls," *Desert Magazine*, VII, No. 5 (1944), 5–7.

SMITH, W. *Kiva Mural Decorations at Awatovi and Kawaika-a, with a Survey of Other Wall Paintings in the Pueblo Southwest.* Papers of the Peabody Museum, Vol. 37, No. 5. Cambridge: Harvard University Press, 1952.

SNOW, DEAN R. "Petroglyphs of Southern Minnesota," *The Minnesota Archaeologist*, XXIV, No. 4 (October 1962), 102–128.

SOLECKI, RALPH S. "A Petrograph in Northern Alaska," *American Antiquity*, XVIII, No. 1 (1952), 63–64.

SOLLAS, W. J. *Ancient Hunters*. New York: The Macmillan Company, 1924.

STEWARD, JULIAN H. *Petroglyphs of California and Adjoining States*. University of California Publications in American Archaeology and Ethnology, Vol. 24, No. 2. Berkeley, 1929.

————. "Petroglyphs of the United States," Annual Report of the Smithsonian Institution. Washington, D.C., 1936.

————. *Archaeological Reconnaissance of Southern Utah*. Smithsonian Institution Bulletin, No. 128. Washington, D.C., 1941.

STRONG, E. *Stone Age on the Columbia River*. Portland, Oregon: Binfords and Mort, 1959.

STRONG, W. D., and SCHENCK, W. E. "Petroglyphs near The Dalles of the Columbia River," *American Anthropology*, XXVII, (1925), 77–90.

————, ————, and STEWARD, J. H. *Archaeology of The Dalles-Deschutes Region*. University of California Publications in American Archaeology and Ethnology, Vol. 29, No. 1. Berkeley and Los Angeles, 1930.

SWANTON, J. D. *The Indian Tribes of North America*. Bureau of American Ethnology Bulletin, No. 145. Washington, D.C., 1953.

SWAUGER, JAMES L. "An X-Ray Figure on the Timmons Farm Petroglyphs Site, 46-Oh-64," *The West Virginia Archaeologist* (Moundsville), No. 14, February 1962.

————. "Petroglyphs at the Hamilton Farm Site, Monongalia County, West Virginia," *ibid.*, No. 15, February 1963.

————. "The Table Rock Petroglyphs Site, 46-Oh-38," *ibid.*, No. 16, December 1963.

————. *The East Liverpool Petroglyph Data: A Tribute*. Reprint from *Pennsylvania Archaeologist* (Philadelphia, Bulletin of the Society for Pennsylvania Archaeology), Vol. XXXIII, No. 3 (1963).

————. "The Francis Farm Petroglyphs Site, 36-Fa-35," *ibid.*, Vol. XXXIV, No. 2 (1964).

————. "The New Geneva Petroglyphs Site, 36-Fa-37," *ibid.*

SWEETMAN, P. W. "A Preliminary Report on the Peterborough Petroglyphs," *Ontario History*, Vol. XLVII, No. 3 (1955).

SWIFT, R. H. "Prehistoric Paintings in Santa Barbara," Southern California Archaeological Society Publication, No. 3, 1931, pp. 35–38.

TAFT, G. E. "An Arizona Pictograph," *American Antiquarian* (Philadelphia), XXXV (1913), 140–145.

TANNER, C. L., and CONNOLLY, F. "Petroglyphs of the Southwest," Kiva (Tucson), III, No. 4 (1938), 13–16.

TATUM, R. M. "Distribution and Bibliography of the Petroglyphs of the United States," *American Antiquity*, XII, No. 2 (1946), 122–125.

————. "The Importance of Petroglyphs in Tennessee," *Tennessee Archaeologist*, III, No. 2 (1946), 40–41.

TAYLOR, H. C. *An Archaeological Reconnaissance in Northern Coahuila.* Bulletin of the Texas Archaeological and Paleontological Society, Vol. 19. Lubbock, 1848. Pp. 74–87.

TEIT, JAMES A. *A Rock Painting of the Thompson River Indians, British Columbia.* American Museum of Natural History Bulletin, 1896. Pp. 227–230.

———. "The Salishan Tribes of the Western Plateaus," in Franz Boas, ed., Forty-fifth Annual Report of the Bureau of American Ethnology, 1930, pp. 23–396.

TREGANZA, A. E. "An Archaeological Reconnaissance of Northeastern Baja California and Southeastern California," *American Antiquity,* VIII, No. 2 (1942), 160–161.

TRUE, D. L. "Pictographs of the San Luis Rey Basin," *ibid.,* XX, No. 1 (1954), 68–72.

TRUMBO, T. M. "Ancient Artist Lived on Rattlesnake Peak," *Desert Magazine* (Palm Desert), XII, No. 8 (1949), 13–16.

TURNER, CHRISTY G. *Petrographs of the Glen Canyon Region.* Museum of Northern Arizona, Bulletin 38, Glen Canyon Series, No. 4. Flagstaff, 1963.

UNDERHILL, R. M. *Red Man's America.* Chicago: University of Chicago Press, 1953.

VAN VALKENBURGH, R. "We Found the Glyphs in the Guijus," *Desert Magazine* (El Centro), IX, No. 3 (1946), 17–20.

VOEGLIN, E. W. *Tubatulabal Ethnography.* University of California Anthropological Records, Vol. 2, No. 1. Berkeley, 1938.

VON WERLHOF, J. C. "Granite Galleries," *Pacific Discovery,* Vol. XI. No. 4 (July–August 1958).

———. *Rock Art of the Owens Valley, California.* University of California Archaeological Survey, No. 65. Berkeley, 1965.

WATERS, F. *Book of the Hopi.* New York: Viking Press, 1963.

WEDEL, WALDO R. *An Introduction to Kansas Archaeology.* Bureau of American Ethnology Bulletin, No. 174. Washington, D. C., 1959.

WETHERILL, M. A. "Pictographs at Betatakin Ruin," U.S. National Park Service Southwestern Monuments Monthly Report. Santa Fe, May 1935, pp. 263–264.

WILBURN, H. C. *Judaculla Rock.* Southern Indian Studies, Vol. IV, October 1952.

WILLOUGHBY, C. C. *Antiquities of the New England Indians.* Papers of the Peabody Museum. Cambridge: Harvard University Press, 1935.

WINTEMBERG, W. J. *Petroglyphs of Roche Percee and Vicinity, Saskatchewan.* Transactions of the Royal Society of Canada, Third Series, XXXIII (1939), 175–184.

WITTY, THOMAS A., JR. *Archaeological Investigations of the Hell Creek Valley in the Wilson Reservoir, Russell and Lincoln Counties, Kansas.* Kansas State Historical Society Anthropological Series 1, 1962.

WOODS, E. B. *La Piedra Pintada de la Carrisa.* (Privately printed, 1900.)

WORMINGTON, H. M. *A Reappraisal of the Fremont Culture.* Denver Museum of Natural History Proceedings, No. 1, 1955.

———, and LISTER, R. H. *Archaeological Investigations on the Uncompahgre*

Plateau in West Central Colorado. Denver Museum of Natural History Proceedings, No. 2, 1956.

YATES, L. G. "Indian Pictoglyphs in California," *Overland Monthly*, 2d Series, 1896, pp. 657–661.

YOUNG, J. V. "The Peregrinations of Kokopelli," *Westways* (Los Angeles), Vol. LVII, No. 9 (1965).

INDEX

abstract style:
  abstract linear painted, 23
  defined, 20
  distribution of, 19–20
  painted abstract polychrome, 23
  pecked, 19–20, 25, 27
  pit and groove, 20, 27
Afognak Island, Alaska, 82
Agawa Rock, 36
agriculture, 8, 11, 18, 136, 137
Alabama, 57, 137, 140, 143
Alaska, 6, 7, 8, 15, 20, 23, 25, 32, 81, 82,
  83, 84, 85, 149
Alberta, Canada, 15, 27, 32, 36, 61, 62,
  130, 131, 152
Aleut, 81, 82
Algonquian, 6, 10, 11, 106, 131, 136, 137,
  140, 144, 145, 151
  rock art, 141, 143, 146, 147
Altamira Cave, 3
Alton, Illinois, sites, 4, 34–35
Anasazi, 9, 18, 21, 50, 115, 116, 118, 123
Anati, Emmanuel, 70, 72
animals, extinction of, 8
Antelope Mesa, Arizona, 57
Apache, 9, 10, 21, 62, 123, 124, 126, 145
Arizona, 4, 8, 9, 10, 13, 18, 20, 21, 31,
  36, 37, 38, 39, 48, 49, 55, 57, 58, 60, 61,
  62, 65, 66, 78, 115, 116, 117, 119, 123,
  124, 125, 129, 152
art, rock art as, 40–42

artifacts, association with:
  rock art dating, 48
Athabascan, 5, 9, 10, 42, 123, 145, 149
Awatovi kiva, Arizona, 57, 61, 62
Aztec, 9, 57, 101

Baja California, 42, 46, 57, 115, 126, 127,
  128, 151
Bannock Indians, 60
Bartlett, J. R., 123
Basketmaker culture, 9, 60, 62, 104, 118
Baumhoff, Martin A., 4, 32, 47, 59, 104
Bautista de Anza, Juan, 52
bear tracks as design motif, 54, 55–56, 98,
  133
Bella Coola, 83, 84, 86, 91
Beschel, Ronald E., 46–47
Big Eddy, Washington, 98
Bighorn River, 132
bird tracks in design, 56
Blackfeet, 52, 131
Black Hills, 132
Breuil, Henri, 3
British Columbia (see also Columbia-
  Fraser Plateau), 14, 15, 29, 32, 37, 53,
  59, 83, 84, 85, 86, 87, 92, 93, 94, 152
Brooks Range Alaska, 81
brushes for pictographs, 14
burial mounds, see effigy mounds
Buttress Canyon hand prints, 55

Cabrillo, Juan Rodríguez, 107
Cahokia Mound, 137, 140, 143
Calgary, Canada, 61
California, 3, 4, 5, 7, 10, 12, 13, 14, 15, 17,
    19, 20, 21, 23, 24, 25, 26, 27, 30, 31, 32,
    33, 34, 37, 39, 41, 44, 45, 46, 48, 49, 52,
    53, 55, 56, 57, 59, 60, 68, 74, 75, 78, 83,
    100, 101, 102, 103, 104, 106–114, 124,
    126, 131, 140, 150, 152
    rock art, 15, 19–21, 23, 30–34, 41, 44, 46,
    52–53, 55–56, 59, 60, 78, 104, 106, 107,
    111, 114, 119, 124, 150
Camonica Valley, Italy, 72
Canada (see also specific area), 5, 8, 9,
    10, 15, 20, 36, 37, 81, 145, 149
Canadian Shield, 145, 146, 147–149, 150
Canyon de Chelly, Arizona, 20, 49, 78,
    119, 123
Cape Alitak, Alaska, 81
Carrizo Canyon, 21, 119
Carrizo Plains, 74
carbon-14 dating method, 45–46
carving, Northern Woodland, 149
Casa Grande ruin, Arizona, 65
Cascade Range, 92, 100, 106
Castle Gardens, Wyoming, 56
"Cave of 200 Hands," Utah, 55
ceremonial function of rock art, 28–35,
    151–152
Chaco Canyon National Monument, 78
chalking, in rock art reproduction, 69–70
Channel Islands, California, 109
Cherokee, 58, 137
Chicksaw, 137
Chihuahua, Mexico, 10, 115a
Chickasaw, 137
chronology, see dating rock art
Chumash, 13, 33–34, 41, 45, 56, 107–111,
    113, 140, 147, 152
Churchill River, Canada, 149
clan symbol(s), 38, 49
    grizzly, 56
    thunderbird, 59
cleaning rock art for recording, 72–73
Coahuila, Mexico, 74, 128, 129
Coast Salish, see Salish
Coeur d'Alene, Lake, 98
Colorado, 4, 9, 44, 115, 116, 117, 118, 135
Colorado River, 10, 13, 19, 38, 44, 48, 77,
    115, 116–117, 117–118, 124
Colton, Harold S., 66
Columbia-Fraser Plateau, 15, 19, 29–30,
    86, 92–99, 129, 131, 147, 149, 150

Columbia River, 10, 67, 76, 86, 91, 92,
    93–94, 98, 99, 152
Comanche, 62, 130, 135
Comanche Gap, New Mexico, 62
Cook Inlet, 82
copying in rock art, 38–39, 49
cord-marked pottery, 136
Coronado, Francisco Vásquez de, 10, 50
Cortereal, Miguel, 140
Cortés, Hernando, 50
Coso Range, California, 49, 59, 60
creation myth, 84
Cree, 145, 149
Creek Indians, 58, 137
cult symbols in rock art, 143
Cupeño, 30
curvilinear drawings, abstract pecked, 19,
    25, 27

Dakota Indians, 35, 130, 133
Dalles, The, 76, 78, 91, 93, 94, 98
d'Anglure, Saladin, 82
dating rock art, 43–53
    artifact association in, 48
    California, 108
    Columbia-Fraser Plateau, 93
    by deposits covering, 47
    Eastern Woodland, 143
    erosion rate in, 47–48
    Eskimo, 82
    ethnographic identification in, 49
    Great Basin, 152
    lichen overgrowth in, 46–47
    Mexico, 126
    Northwest, 83, 91
    patination in, 43–45
    radiocarbon tests in, 45–46
    Southwest, 118, 123, 124, 126
    style superimposition in, 45
    subject matter in, 49–53
Death Valley, California, 49, 60, 104
deer track designs, 56
deposits covering designs, 47
Deschutes River, Oregon, 99
desert varnish, 12–13, 43–45
design motifs (see also specific area or
    motif), 54–67, 107, 111, 113, 114
    bear tracks, 54, 55–56
    Canadian Shield, 147, 149
    Columbia-Fraser Plateau, 92, 93, 94, 98
    conventions in, 66–67
    in dating 49–53
    Eastern Woodland, 137, 140, 143, 144

design motifs (*cont.*)
  Eskimo, 81, 82
  four-pointed star, 98, 123
  Great Basin, 101, 104, 105
  Great Plains, 131–132, 135
  hand, 54–55
  humped-back flute player, 54, 60–61
  Mexico, 126, 128–129
  Minoan maze, 65–66
  mountain sheep, 59–60
  Northwest, 84, 86, 91
  occurrence, 151–152
  origin of, 65
  plumed serpent, 56–58
  rayed semicircle design, 93, 94, 98
  shield figure, 54, 61–62, 63, 64
  Southwest, 115–119, 123, 124, 126, 128–
    129
  thunderbird, 58–59
De Soto, Hernando, 137
Dewdney, Selwyn, 5, 15, 36, 68, 147, 149
Diablo Area, Texas, 124
Diegueño, 113, 114, 126, 127
Dighton Rock, Massachusetts, 4, 78, 140
Diguet, Lèon 126,
doodling in rock art, 38–39
Durango, Mexico, 10, 129

Easter Island, 47
Eastern Woodland, 10, 23, 27, 31, 36, 51,
    58, 62, 67, 130, 131, 132, 135, 136–
    144, 157
Effigy mounds, 131, 136, 137
El Morro National Monument, New
    Mexico, 76
erosion of rock art, 47–48, 74
Escalante, Father Silvestre de, 4
Eskimo, 7, 8, 10, 15, 17, 20, 25, 32, 46,
    47, 81, 82, 84, 106
Esteban, 61
ethnography in dating, 49
Etolin Island, 84
Etowah, Georgia, 57, 137
Exeter, California, 111

Far North, 81–82, 150
fertility:
  Kokopelli as symbol, 61
  rites, 106; rock art and, 30–31
fishing, *see* hunting and fishing
Folmann, Gerhard, 47
Fort Smith, Canada, 149
Four Corners area, 9, 13, 21, 60, 118, 119,
    123

four-pointed star design, *see* design motifs
France, rock art of, 3, 41, 54
Fraser Canyon, 92
Fremont culture, 25, 41, 61, 62, 115–116

Galisteo Basin, New Mexico, 33, 57, 62,
    66, 70, 123
Gardner, Erle Stanley, 126
Gebhard, David, 19, 124
Georgia, 57, 58, 137, 140, 143
Gila Bend, Arizona, 78
Ginkgo Petrified Forest Museum, 78
Giotto, 42
Gladwin, Harold, 7
Glen Canyon area, 19, 48, 77, 118
Gobernador, 119
gods:
  Aztec, 57
  Chumash, 34, 147, 149
  Eskimo, 32
  Hopi, 57, 65
  Maya, 57
  Navajo, 119
  Ojibwa, 32, 34, 147
  in rock art, 57–59, 147, 149
  Salish, 29, 59
  Winnebago, 58
  Woodland, 31, 32, 58
  Zuñi, 57
Great Basin, 10, 18, 23, 25, 27, 32, 39, 43,
    45, 49, 53, 55, 59, 60, 62, 98, 99, 100–
    105, 106, 107, 111, 113, 116, 117, 118,
    129, 135, 150, 151, 152
  rock art, 15, 18–20, 43, 45, 55, 59, 101–
    105, 124, 126, 150, 151
Great Plains, 10, 15, 19, 25, 35, 36, 50, 52,
    61, 62, 67, 94
  rock art, 35, 36, 52, 130–135, 150
Great Lakes country, 34
Great Salt Lake, 7, 100
Great Slave Lake, Canada, 149
Green River, Utah, 116–117
Green Valley, California, 114
grizzly motif, 56
Gros Ventre Indians, 131
Gulf of Georgia, Washington, 86, 91

Haida Indians, 83
hand design motif, 54–55, 152
  California, 55
  Eastern Woodland, 137, 144
  France, 54
  Great Basin, 55
  Great Plains, 133

hand design motif (*cont.*)
   Mexico, 126, 129
   Southwest, 55, 129
Hano, New Mexico, 61
Haury, Emil, 48
heart-line design convention, 67, 119, 123, 131
Heizer, Robert F., 4, 32, 47, 59, 104
Hemet, California, 113
Hermosillo, Mexico, 21, 23
Hokan, 137, 144
Hohokam, 9, 60, 61
Hollywood stone, 66
Hopewell culture, 136, 137
Hopi, 8, 21, 31, 33, 36, 38, 41, 45, 49, 56, 57, 59, 60, 61, 65, 66, 100, 101, 123, 126. 152
horned serpent, *see* plumed serpent, design motifs
horse in rock art, 50, 52
Hoyle, Fred, 37
Huaxtec, 129, 137
Hueco Tanks, Texas, 123–124
Humboldt Lake, 100
humped-back flute player motif, 54, 60–61
hunting and fishing, 8, 82
   rock art and magic for, 32, 56, 151–152; California, 32; Eskimo, 32; heart-line and, 67
Hupa, 31
Huron, 145

Idaho, 30, 49, 56, 61, 68, 97, 98, 99
Illinois, 4, 34, 137
incised or scratched styles:
   area classification, 150
   defined, 12
   Eastern Woodland, 137
   Eskimo, 15
   Great Basin, 15, 104, 105
   Great Plains, 131, 132, 133, 135
   naturalistic, 19, 27
   rock types for, 79
Inland Salish, *see* Salish
Inscription Rock, New Mexico, 76
interpretation of rock art, 28–39, 152
   ceremonial use, 28–35
   as clan symbol, 38
   doodling and copying, 38–39
   as mnemonic, 35–37
Iowa, 6, 58, 136, 137
Iroquois, 11, 137
Jackson, A. T., 123

Jimsonweed, 34, 111
John Day River, Oregon, 99
Joshua Tree National Monument, 104
Juaneño rock art, 111
Judaculla Rock, North Carolina, 140

kachina masks and figures, 21, 33, 47, 61, 118, 119, 123
Kanawha River, West Virginia, 136, 140
Kansas, 134, 135
Karok Indians, 31
Kawaika ruins, Arizona, 61
Kedgemakooge, Lake, 149
Keithahn, Edward L., 32
Kern River, California, 44, 111
Kings River, California, 111
Kino, Father Eusebio, 4, 78
kiva paintings, 42, 45, 57, 61, 62
Klamath, 31, 101
Kodiak Island, 15, 20, 25, 32, 81, 82
Kokopelli, 60–61
Kroeber, Alfred, 113
Kuaua kiva, New Mexico, 45, 57
Kwakiutl, 37, 53, 83, 86

Labrador, 81
Laguna, Frederica de, 82
Lake of the Woods, Ontario, 32, 147
La Paz, Mexico, 126
Largo Canyon, 21, 119
Leechman, Douglas, 15
Leonard, Zenas, 100
Lewis and Clark expedition, 52, 94
Lhote, Henri, 68, 72
Libby, Willard, 45
lichen overgrowth in dating, 46–47
linear drawing style, 23
Long Narrows, Washington, 98
Los Angeles, California, 23
Lovelock Cave, Nevada, 49–50
Luiseño Indians, 30, 49, 111, 113, 126, 152

MacNeish, Richard S., 8
Maine, 77
Mallery, Colonel Garrick, 4, 5, 48, 140
Manitoba, Canada, 15, 130, 149
Manitou, 147
Maori, 8
Marquette, Father Jacques, 4, 34, 35
Martin, Donald, 44
masks:

masks (*cont.*)
  ceremonial, 32–33
  Eskimo, 32, 82
  kachina, 33, 118, 119, 123
  Northwest, 83
Massachusetts, 4, 78, 140, 142
Mather, Cotton, 140
Maya, 57
maze, Minoan, *see* Minoan maze
Meighan, Clement, 4, 46, 126
Menomini, 38
Mesa Verde, 10
Mexico, 4, 5, 7, 8, 9, 10, 17, 21–23, 25, 50,
    58, 59, 60, 61, 66, 67, 79, 106, 115, 126,
    127, 128, 129, 136, 137
  rock art, 56–57, 126–129
Miami Indians, 141
Michigan, 140
Michigan, Lake, 140, 141
Micmac, 55, 149
Middle America, 11, 137
Milk River sites, 36, 131
Mimbres pottery, 60
Minoan maze, 65–66
Minnesota, 67, 132, 137, 138, 141, 147, 149
Mississippi culture, 57, 67, 136–137, 140,
    143, 144
Mississippi Valley, 4, 5, 11, 34, 35, 136,
    137, 140, 141, 143, 144
Missouri, 135, 136, 137, 138, 139, 140, 143
Missouri River, 130, 131, 132, 137
Mnemonic role of rock art, 35–37
Modoc Indians, 101
Mojave Desert, 44, 59, 124
molds, rock art, 69
Monk, Charles la, 68
Montana, 23, 61, 67, 98, 131
Monterey County, California, 4, 54, 55,
    106, 107
Monument Valley, Utah, 60
Morro Bay, 107
Moundville, Alabama, 57, 137
mountain sheep motif, 59–60, 151–152
  California, 59–60
  Columbia-Fraser Plateau, 98
  Great Basin, 59, 104, 105
  Southwest, 117, 118, 126
mutilation, hand, 54
mysticism, Indian, 28
mythology:
  bear in, 55
  creation myth, 84
  humped-back flute player in, 60–61

serpent in, 56–58
thunderbird in, 58–59

Nanaimo, Vancouver Island, 91
narcotic, use of, 34, 111
Nass River sites, 37, 84
Natchez Indians, 58
naturalistic style:
  defined, 20
  distribution of, 19, 20
  incised, 19, 27
  painted, 20
  pecked, 19, 23
Navajo, 9, 10, 21, 23, 28, 29, 33, 41, 42, 45,
    48, 49, 116, 118, 119, 123, 126, 145, 152
  rock art, 19, 123, 152
Nayarit, Mexico, 66
Nebraska, 35, 130, 133, 134
Nevada, 9, 21, 23, 26, 32, 47, 49, 50, 53, 59,
    60, 61, 64, 100, 103, 104, 105, 117
New Brunswick, Canada, 15
New Mexico, 9, 10, 21, 31, 33, 42, 45, 47,
    48, 50, 57, 58, 61, 62, 66, 67, 70, 76, 77,
    116, 118, 119
Newfoundland, Canada, 8, 15, 145
Nez Percé, 30
Niza, Fray Marco de, 61
Nojoqui Valley, 48
Nootka, 53, 83, 91
North Carolina, 139, 140
North Dakota, 13, 31, 35, 130, 131, 132
Northern Plains, 27, 32, 61, 116, 130, 131,
    132, 135
Northern Woodland, 19, 36, 141, 145–150
Northwest, 10, 19, 23, 32, 36–37, 41, 53,
    54, 58, 59, 82–91, 94, 98
  rock art, 32, 36–37, 41, 53, 83–91, 150
Nova Scotia, Canada, 7, 15, 27, 55, 56, 106,
    149, 151

Ohio, 4, 34, 35, 136, 137, 144
Ohio Valley, 136, 140, 144
Ojibwa, 20, 32, 34, 35–36, 38, 41, 67, 137,
    145, 147, 149
Okanogan, 92–93
Oklahoma, 57, 58, 135, 137
Oñate, Juan de, 50
Ontario, Canada, 5, 15, 21, 32, 147, 149
Oraibi, Arizona, 65
Oregon, 15, 59, 78, 90, 99, 100, 101, 104
Osage, 58

Painted Cave, California, 48, 55, 78

INDEX

176

painted rock art:
  California, 107–109, 111, 114, 150
  Canadian Shield, 147, 149, 150
  Great Basin, 105, 150
  Great Plains, 131, 132, 150
  Mexico, 126, 128, 129
  rock type for, 79
  Southwest, 116–119, 123, 124, 126, 128, 129, 150
  styles of, 19–21, 23, 150
"Painted Rocks," Arizona, 4
Paiute, 8, 13, 49, 59, 100, 104, 123
Paleolithic rock art, 3, 29, 40–43, 54, 56
palettes, 14
Papago Indians, 126
patina, 12–13
patination in dating, 43–45
Pawnee, 63, 130
pecked rock art:
  California, 19–20, 107, 114, 150
  Columbia-Fraser Plateau, 19, 20, 94, 98, 150
  dating, 43, 152
  Eastern Woodland, 137, 150
  Great Basin, 19–20, 104, 105, 150
  Great Plains, 19, 131–133, 150
  Mexico, 126, 129
  Northern Woodland, 19, 149, 150
  rock type for, 79
  Southwest, 19–20, 116–118, 123, 124, 126, 129, 150
  styles: abstract pit and groove, 20, 27; naturalistic, 19, 23
Pecos River, 123, 124, 135
Pend d'Oreille, Lake, 56, 98
Pennsylvania, 77, 140, 141, 142, 143
Petley Point, 37
Petrified Forest National Park, Arizona, 117, 124
petroglyph (see also pecked rock art), 12–13, 18–20, 32, 36, 38, 46, 61, 91
Petroglyph Canyon, California, 59, 78
photography in recording, 69–70, 72
pictograph 12, 13–14
Piedra Pintadas, Arizona, 78
Pima Indians, 65, 66, 144
pigments, 13–14
Pipestone County, Minnesota, 133
pit-and-groove styles, 20, 27
  age of, 152
  California, 106–107
  Eastern Woodland, 140
  Great Basin, 105
  Great Plains, 131
Plains Indians, 11, 19, 50, 62, 130

plumed serpent motif, 56–58
  Eastern Woodland, 57-58
  Hopi, 57
  Mexico, 56–57
  Southwest, 56–58
polychrome styles, 19–21, 23
Pompa y Pompa, Antonio, 129
Porterville, California, 111
Potawatomi Indians, 141
potlatch ceremonies, 36–37
Pottery Mound, New Mexico, 61
Powell, Lake, 19, 48, 77
preservation of rock art, 74, 76–78
Prince William Sound, 82, 84
puberty rites, 29–30, 113, 151
Pueblo Bonito, 9
Pueblo Indians, 8, 9–10, 33, 37, 42, 48, 49, 62, 115, 118, 119
Puget Sound, Washington, 86, 91

Quebec, Canada, 15, 32, 82, 149
Quetzalcoatl, 56–57
Quinault Indians, 30

radiocarbon dating, 45–46
rainmaking, 31, 106
rayed semicircle design, see design motifs
recording techniques, 68–73
records, rock art as, 35–37, 149, 151
rectilinear abstract drawings, 20, 27
Renegade Canyon, California, 59, 78
Rhode Island, 140, 144
Rio Grande, 10, 14, 53, 60, 115, 123, 124, 135
Riverside, California, 111, 113
rock types for art, 12–13, 79
Rocky Mountains, 5, 7, 9, 61, 92, 98, 115

Safe Harbor, Pennsylvania, 141, 143
Sahaptin Indians, 99
Salish, 29–30, 53, 83, 86, 91, 92, 93, 147, 149, 152
Salmon River, Idaho, 98
sand paintings, 28, 45
San Francisco Mountains, Baja California, 57
San Ildefonso, 57, 118
San Joaquin Valley, California, 14, 106, 107, 109, 111, 114
San Juan River, 118
San Nicolás Island, California, 111
San Rafael Mountains, California, 108
Santa Barbara-Kern-Tulare regions, California, 21, 23, 33, 41, 46, 48, 74, 78, 107

Santa Lucia Mountains, California, 55

Saskatchewan, Canada, 15, 130, 147, 148, 149

Sautuola, Marcelino de, 3

Schaafsma, Polly, 119

Schoolcraft, Henry, 36

Schuster, Carl, 66

scratched styles, *see* incised or scratched styles

Seri, 127, 128

Seward Peninsula, Alaska, 81

shaman, 28–29, 31, 32, 40, 54–56, 59

Shasta Indians, 31

shield figure motif, 61–62, 63, 64
  Columbia-Fraser Plateau, 98
  Great Plains, 61–62, 131, 135
  Southwest, 61–62, 116, 123

Shipaulovi, Arizona, 65

Shoshonean, 8, 59–60, 98–99, 100–101, 104, 111, 113, 116, 130, 131–132, 135, 151

Siberia, 6, 101, 143

Sierra de Tamaulipas, Mexico, 129

Sierra Madre, Mexico, 7, 10, 115

Sierra Nevada, 23, 49, 60, 104, 106, 107, 111, 114, 129

Sierra Santa Teressa, Mexico, 21, 61, 127–128

Sinaloa, Mexico, 128, 129

Sioux, *see* Dakota Indians

sites of rock art (*see also* specific area and/or topic), 5, 14–17
  California, 106–114
  Columbia-Fraser Plateau, 92–99
  Eastern Woodland, 136–144
  Far North, 81–82
  Great Basin, 100–105
  Great Plains, 130–135
  maps, 16–17, 80
  Mexico, 126–129
  Northern Woodland, 145–149
  Northwest, 83–91
  petroglyphs, 12, 16–17
  preservation of, 74, 76–78
  Southwest, 115–129
  style distribution, 19–27, 150

Sitka, Alaska, 84

Skeena River sites, 37, 84

Smith, H. I., 32

Snake River sites, 98, 132

Sonora, Mexico, 10, 20, 21, 61, 62, 65, 71, 115, 126, 127–128

South America, 4, 5, 8, 60

South Dakota, 26, 31, 61, 130, 131, 135

Southwest, 4, 5, 7, 9–11, 12, 13, 18, 20, 21, 23, 25, 27, 33, 36, 38, 41, 43, 44, 50,

55, 58, 60, 61, 67, 78, 79, 115–129, 135, 150, 151, 152
  rock art, 15, 18, 19–20, 36, 37, 50, 52–53, 55, 56, 57, 58, 60–62, 78, 115–129, 150, 152

Spain, rock art of, 3, 18, 41–42, 54

speech motif convention, 66, 67

Spedis owl design, 98

Spiro, Oklahoma, 57, 137

Sproat Lake sites, 91

states, *see* specific area: and/or site

styles of rock art, 4, 18–27, 151
  area in classification, 150
  California, 106–107, 111, 113, 114, 150
  dating, 45, 152
  Columbia-Fraser Plateau, 93, 99, 150
  Eastern Woodland, 137, 140, 143, 144, 150
  Great Basin, 104, 105, 150
  Great Plains, 131–133, 135, 150
  Mexico, 126, 128–129
  Southwest, 117, 123, 124, 126, 128–129, 150

stylized style:
  defined, 20
  distribution, 19–20
  painted, 20–21
  pecked, 19

subject matter, *see* design motifs

Superior, Lake, 7, 36, 37

supernatural beings, 34–35

Susquehanna River sites, 77

Tamaulipas, Mexico, 129, 137

Tanana Rivers, Alaska, 149

Tassili drawing complex, 3, 68, 72

techniques of rock art (*see also* styles of rock art), 12–27
  California, 107, 111, 114
  Columbia-Fraser Plateau, 94
  distribution, 14–17
  Eastern Woodland, 137, 143
  Eskimo, 81, 82
  Great Basin, 101, 104, 105
  Northwest, 83, 84, 86, 91
  petroglyphs, 12–13
  pictographs, 13–14
  rock types and, 79
  Southwest, 116

Tehachapi Mountains, California, 111

Tennessee, 58, 137, 140, 141

Tennessee Valley, 140, 144

Tewa, 57

Texas, 6, 9, 13, 17, 19, 21, 23, 43, 52, 53, 54, 58, 61, 122, 123, 124, 130, 135
Thompson River Indians, 29–30, 152
thunderbird motif, 31, 38, 58–59
  Canadian Shield, 149
  Eastern Woodland, 31, 137, 144
  Great Plains, 131, 133, 135
  Southwest, 124
Tiburon Island, Mexico, 128–129
Tlingit, 32, 36–37, 54, 83, 84
toloache, 34
Tolowa Indians, 31
Toltec, 56–57
totem pole, 84
tracing, in recording, 68–69
Tsimshian Indians, 83, 84
Tubatulabal Indians, 111
Tule Lake, 101, 104
Turner, Christy G., 18, 48, 77
turtle fertility figure, 31
Twana Reservation, Washington, 31
twinned brothers design, 93
twin war gods motif, 119

Utah, 9, 17, 24, 25, 33, 40, 41, 44, 55, 56, 60, 61, 62, 67, 79, 100, 104, 115, 116, 117, 118, 119, 124, 128
Ute, 49, 60, 118, 123, 124, 135

Valley of Fire, Nevada, 117
Vancouver Island, 86, 88, 91, 151, 156
vandalism of rock art sites, 74–76
Vantage site, Washington, 94
Verde River, Arizona, 124

Vernal, Utah, 115
Viscaíno Desert, Mexico, 126

Wakehan Bay, Quebec, 82
Washington, 31, 78, 86, 91, 92, 93, 94, 95, 96, 98
weapons, in rock art, 49–50
weeping eye convention, 66, 67
Wenatchee, Washington, 94
West Virginia, 67, 70, 77, 140
Western Plains (*see also* Great Plains), 6, 7
White Mesa region, Arizona, 37
Wichita Indians, 130
Willow Springs, Arizona, 38
Wind River, Wyoming, 130, 131, 132
Winnebago Indians, 35, 133, 134, 147
Winquatt Museum, 78
Wisconsin, 38, 46, 134, 137
wondjina paintings, 28–29
Woodland Indians culture (*see also* Eastern Woodland, Northern Woodland), 8, 10, 11, 134, 136, 137
Wormington, H. M., 62
Wrangell Island, 84, 86, 91
Writing-on-Stone, Alberta, 62
Wyoming, 11, 19, 56, 61, 67, 131, 132, 133

Yakima sites, Washington, 94
Yavapai, 49
yei figures, 33, 119
Yokuts, 10, 33, 109, 111, 140
Yucatan, 57

Zion National Park, 78
Zuñi, 10, 57, 61, 76

STUDY GUIDE *for*

MEMMLER'S

Structure and Function of the Human Body

9TH EDITION

Barbara Janson Cohen

Kerry L. Hull

Professor
Department of Biology
Bishop's University
Sherbrooke, Quebec
Canada

Wolters Kluwer | Lippincott
Health | Williams & Wilkins

Senior Acquisitions Editor: David Troy
Developmental Editor: Dana Knighten
Managing Editor: Renee Thomas
Marketing Manager: Allison Noplock
Managing Editor, Production: Eve Malakoff-Klein
Designer: Doug Smock
Artist: Dragonfly Media Group
Compositor: Maryland Composition, Inc.
Printer: Victor Graphics

9th Edition

351 West Camden Street   530 Walnut Street
Baltimore, MD 21201   Philadelphia, PA 19106

Printed in the United States

9 8 7 6 5 4 3 2

Library of Congress Cataloging-in-Publication Data

Cohen, Barbara J.
 Study guide for Memmler's structure and function of the human body / Barbara Janson Cohen, Kerry L. Hull. — 9th ed.
  p. cm.
 To be used with the textbook: Memmler's structure and function of the human body, 9th ed.
 ISBN 978-0-7817-6596-1
 1. Human physiology—Examinations, questions, etc. 2. Human anatomy—Examinations, questions, etc. 3. Body, Human—Examinations, questions, etc. I. Hull, Kerry L. II. Cohen, Barbara J. Memmler's structure and function of the human body. 9th ed. III. Title. IV. Title: Memmler's structure and function of the human body.
 QP36.M54 2009 Suppl.
 612.0076—dc22

2008034089

DISCLAIMER

Care has been taken to confirm the accuracy of the information present and to describe generally accepted practices. However, the authors, editors, and publisher are not responsible for errors or omissions or for any consequences from application of the information in this book and make no warranty, expressed or implied, with respect to the currency, completeness, or accuracy of the contents of the publication. Application of this information in a particular situation remains the professional responsibility of the practitioner; the clinical treatments described and recommended may not be considered absolute and universal recommendations.

The authors, editors, and publisher have exerted every effort to ensure that drug selection and dosage set forth in this text are in accordance with the current recommendations and practice at the time of publication. However, in view of ongoing research, changes in government regulations, and the constant flow of information relating to drug therapy and drug reactions, the reader is urged to check the package insert for each drug for any change in indications and dosage and for added warnings and precautions. This is particularly important when the recommended agent is a new or infrequently employed drug.

Some drugs and medical devices presented in this publication have Food and Drug Administration (FDA) clearance for limited use in restricted research settings. It is the responsibility of the health care provider to ascertain the FDA status of each drug or device planned for use in their clinical practice.

To purchase additional copies of this book, call our customer service department at **(800) 638-3030** or fax orders to **(301) 223-2320**. International customers should call **(301) 223-2300**.

Visit Lippincott Williams & Wilkins on the Internet: http://www.lww.com. Lippincott Williams & Wilkins customer service representatives are available from 8:30 am to 6:00 pm, EST.

Preface

The *Study Guide for Memmler's Structure and Function of the Human Body*, 9th edition, assists the beginning student to learn basic information required in the health occupations. Although it will be more effective when used in conjunction with the 9th edition of *Memmler's Structure and Function of the Human Body*, the *Study Guide* may also be used to supplement other textbooks on basic anatomy and physiology.

The questions in this edition reflect revisions and updating of the text. Students can work through the exercises in "Addressing the Learning Outcomes" using their textbook, as necessary. Different types of exercises, including labeling and coloring exercises, matching, true-false, and short answer, will help students master the material. The "Testing Your Knowledge" section should be tackled after students finish the chapter, since it integrates information from different learning outcomes. The "Practical Applications" questions of this section use clinical situations to test understanding of a subject.

The exercises are planned to help in student learning, not merely to test knowledge. A certain amount of repetition has been purposely incorporated as a means of reinforcement. Matching questions require the student to write out complete answers, giving practice in spelling as well as recognition of terms. Other question formats include multiple choice, completion, true–false, and short essays. The true–false questions must be corrected if they are false. The essay answers provided are examples of suitable responses, but other presentations of the material are acceptable.

All answers to the *Study Guide* questions are in the *Instructor's Manual* that accompanies the text.

Introduction

Learning about the Human Body

You already have some ideas about the human body that will influence how you learn the information in this textbook. Many of your theories are correct, and this Study Guide, created to accompany the 9th edition of *Memmler's Structure and Function of the Human Body*, will simply add detail and complexity to these ideas. Other theories, however, may be too simplistic. It can be difficult to replace these ingrained beliefs with more accurate information. For instance, many students think that the lungs actively inflate and deflate as we breathe, but it is the diaphragm and the rib-cage muscles that accomplish all of the work. Learning physiology or any other subject therefore involves:

1. **Construction**: Adding to and enhancing your previous store of ideas.
2. **Reconstruction**: Replacing misconceptions (prior views and ideas) with scientifically sound principles.
3. **Self-monitoring**. Construction and reconstruction require that you also monitor your personal understanding of a particular topic and consciously formulate links between what you are learning and what you have previously learned. Rote learning is not an effective way to learn anatomy and physiology (or almost anything else, for that matter). **Metacognition** is monitoring your own understanding. Metacognition is very effective if it takes the form of self-questioning during the lectures. Try to ask yourself questions during lectures, such as "What is the prof trying to show here?" "What do these numbers really mean?" or "How does this stuff relate to the stuff we covered yesterday?" Self-questioning will help you create links between concepts. In other words, try to be an active learner during the lectures. Familiarity with the material is not enough. You w have to internalize it and apply it to succeed. You can greatly enhance your ability to be an active learner by reading the appropriate sections of the textbook before the lecture.

Each field in biology has its own language. This language is not designed to make your life difficult; the terms often represent complex concepts. Rote memorization of definitions will not help you learn. Indeed, because biological terms often have different meanings in everyday conversation, you probably hold some definitions that are misleading and must be revised. For example, you may say that someone has a "good metabolism" if they can eat enormous meals and stay slender. However, the term "metabolism" actually refers to all of the chemical reactions that occur in the body, including those that build muscle and fat. We learn a new language not by reading about it but by using it. The *Study Guide* you hold in your hands employs a number of learning techniques in every chapter to help you become comfortable with the language of anatomy and physiology.

Addressing the Learning Outcomes

This section will help you master the material both verbally and visually. The *Study Guide* uses different question formats to address each learning outcome. Coloring and labeling exercises, for instance, are especially useful for mastering anatomy. Follow the instructions to label and color (when appropriate) each exercise. You will use the same color to write the name of the structure and to color it. Colored pencils work best, but you may have to outline in black names written in light colors. Coloring exercises are fun, and have been shown to enhance learning. You can also use the completed exercise as a study aid. Other learning outcomes are addressed using other question formats, such as matching or short answer. Use the textbook as needed to complete these exercises.

"Making the Connections": Learning through Concept Maps

This learning activity uses concept mapping to master definitions and concepts. You can think of concept mapping as creating a web of information. Individual terms have a tendency to get lost, but a web of terms is more easily maintained in memory. You can make a concept map by following these steps:

1. Select the concepts to map (6–10 is a good number). Try to use a mixture of nouns, verbs, and processes.
2. If one exists, place the most general, important, or over-riding concept at the top or in the center and arrange the other terms around it. Organize the terms so that closely related terms are close together.
3. Draw arrows between concepts that are related. Write a sentence to connect the two concepts that begins with the term at the beginning of the arrow and ends with the term at the end of the arrow.

For instance, consider a simple concept map composed of three terms: student learning, professors, and textbooks. Write the three terms at the three corners of a triangle, separated from each other by 3–4 inches. Next is the difficult part: devising connecting phrases that explain the relationship between any two terms. What is the essence of the relationship between student learning and professors? An arrow could be drawn from professors to student learning, with the connecting phrase "*can explain difficult concepts to facilitate.*" The relationship would be "*Professors can explain difficult concepts to facilitate student learning.*" Draw arrows between all other term pairs (*student learning* and *textbooks*, *textbooks* and *professors*) and try to come up with connecting phrases. Make sure that the phrase is read in the direction of the arrow.

There are two concept mapping exercises for most chapters. The first exercise consists of filling in boxes and, in the later maps, connecting phrases. The guided concept maps for Chapters 1 through 7 ask you to think of the appropriate term for each box. The guided concept maps for Chapters 8 through 21 are more traditional concept maps. Pairs of terms are linked together by a connecting phrase. The phrase is read in the direction of the arrow. For instance, an arrow leading from "*genes*" to "*chromosomes*" could result in the phrase "*Genes are found on pieces of DNA called chromosomes.*" The second optional exercise provides a suggested list of terms to use to construct your own map. This second exercise is a powerful learning tool, because you will identify your own links between concepts. The act of creating a concept map is an effective way to understand terms and concepts.

Testing Your Knowledge

These questions should be completed after you have read the textbook and completed the other learning activities in the study guide. Try to answer as many questions as possible without referring to your notes or the text. As in the end-of-chapter questions, there are three different levels of questions. Type I questions (Building Understanding) test simple recall: how well have you learned the material? Type II questions (Understanding Concepts) examine your ability to integrate and apply the information in simple practical situations. Type III questions (Conceptual Thinking) are the most challenging. They ask you to apply your knowledge to new situations and concepts. There is often more than one right answer to Conceptual Thinking questions. The answers to all questions are available from your instructor.

Learning from the World Around You

The best way to learn anatomy and physiology is to immerse yourself in the subject. Tell your friends and family what you are learning. Discover more about recent health advances from television, newspapers, magazines, and the Internet. Our knowledge about the human body is constantly changing. The work you will do using the *Study Guide* can serve as a basis for lifelong learning about the human body.

Contents

Preface iii

Introduction v

Unit 1 **The Body as a Whole 1**

Chapter 1. Organization of the Human Body 2

Chapter 2. Chemistry, Matter, and Life 19

Chapter 3. Cells and Their Functions 34

Chapter 4. Tissues, Glands, and Membranes 51

Chapter 5. The Integumentary System 64

Unit II **Movement and Support 73**

Chapter 6. The Skeleton: Bones and Joints 74

Chapter 7. The Muscular System 98

Unit III **Coordination and Control 117**

Chapter 8. The Nervous System: The Spinal Cord and Spinal Nerves 118

Chapter 9. The Nervous System: The Brain and Cranial Nerves 136

Chapter 10. The Sensory System 152

Chapter 11. The Endocrine System: Glands and Hormones 169

Unit IV **Circulation and Body Defense 183**

Chapter 12. The Blood 184

Chapter 13. The Heart 199

Chapter 14. Blood Vessels and Blood Circulation 212

Chapter 15. The Lymphatic System and Body Defenses 232

Unit V **Energy: Supply and Use 253**

Chapter 16. The Respiratory System 254

Chapter 17. The Digestive System 267

Chapter 18 Metabolism, Nutrition, and Body Temperature 288

Chapter 19. The Urinary System and Body Fluids 299

Unit VI **Perpetuation of Life 323**

Chapter 20. The Male and Female Reproductive Systems 324

Chapter 21. Development and Heredity 341

UNIT
I

The Body as a Whole

➤ **Chapter 1**

Organization of
the Human Body

➤ **Chapter 2**

Chemistry, Matter,
and Life

➤ **Chapter 3**

Cells and Their
Functions

➤ **Chapter 4**

Tissues, Glands,
and Membranes

➤ **Chapter 5**

The
Integumentary
System

Organization of the Human Body

Overview

Anatomy is the study of body structure, whereas **physiology** is the study of how the body functions.

Living things are organized from simple to complex levels. The simplest living form is the **cell**, the basic unit of life. Specialized cells are grouped into **tissues**, which in turn are combined to form **organs**; these organs form systems, which work together to maintain the body.

The systems are the:

- integumentary system, the body's covering, which includes the skin and its associated structures;
- skeletal system, the framework of the body;
- muscular system, which moves the bones;
- nervous system, the central control system that includes the organs of special sense;
- endocrine system, which produces regulatory hormones;
- circulatory system, consisting of the heart, blood vessels, and lymphatic vessels, which transport vital substances;
- respiratory system, which adds oxygen to the blood and removes carbon dioxide;
- digestive system, which converts raw food materials into products usable by cells;
- urinary system, which removes wastes and excess water; and the
- reproductive system, by which new individuals of the species are produced.

All the cellular reactions that sustain life together make up **metabolism**, which can be divided into **catabolism** and **anabolism**. In catabolism, complex substances are broken down into simpler molecules. When the nutrients from food are broken down by catabolism, energy is released. This energy is stored in the compound **ATP** (adenosine triphosphate) for use by the cells. In anabolism, simple compounds are built into substances needed for cellular activities.

All the systems work together to maintain a state of balance, or **homeostasis**. The main mechanism for maintaining homeostasis is **negative feedback**, by which the state of the body is the signal to keep conditions within set limits.

The human body is composed of large amounts of fluid, the amount and composition of which must be constantly regulated. The **extracellular fluid** consists of the fluid that surrounds the cells as well as the fluid circulated in blood and lymph. The fluid within cells is the **intracellular fluid**.

Study of the body requires knowledge of directional terms to locate parts and relate various parts to each other. Several planes of division represent different directions in which cuts can be made through the body. Separation of the body into areas and regions, together with the use of the special terminology for directions and locations, makes it possible to describe an area within the human body with great accuracy.

The large internal spaces of the body are cavities in which various organs are located. The **dorsal cavity** is subdivided into the **cranial cavity** and the **spinal cavity (canal)**. The **ventral cavity** is subdivided into the **thoracic** and **abdominopelvic cavities**. Imaginary lines are used to divide the abdomen into regions for study and diagnosis.

The metric system is used for all scientific measurements. This system is easy to use because it is based on multiples of 10.

Addressing the Learning Outcomes

1. Define the terms *anatomy* and *physiology*.

EXERCISE 1-1.

INSTRUCTIONS

Write a definition of each term in the spaces below.

1. Anatomy _____
2. Physiology _____

2. Describe the organization of the body from chemicals to the whole organism.

EXERCISE 1-2: Levels of Organization (Text Fig. 1-1)

INSTRUCTIONS

1. Write the name or names of each labeled part on the numbered lines in different colors.
2. Color the different structures on the diagram with the corresponding color. For instance, if you wrote "cell" in blue, color the cell blue.

1. _____
2. _____
3. _____
4. _____
5. _____
6. _____

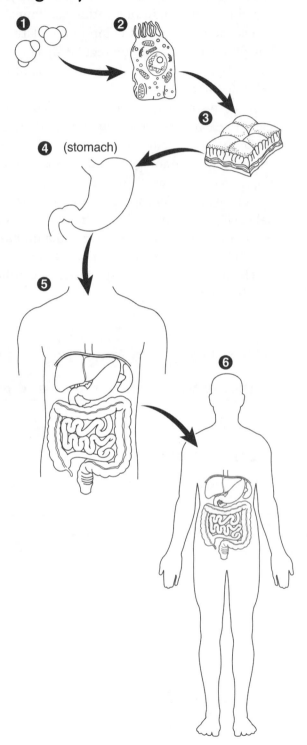

3. List 11 body systems and give the general function of each.

EXERCISE 1-3.

INSTRUCTIONS

Write the appropriate term in each blank.

nervous sytem   integumentary system   circulatory system
respiratory system   skeletal system   urinary system
endocrine system   lymphatic system   digestive system

1. The system that processes sensory information   _____
2. The system that delivers nutrients to body tissues   _____
3. The system that breaks down and absorbs food   _____
4. The system that includes the fingernails   _____
5. The system that includes the bladder   _____
6. The system that includes the joints   _____
7. The system that delivers oxygen to the blood   _____
8. The system that includes the tonsils   _____

4. Define *metabolism* and name the two phases of metabolism.

5. Briefly explain the role of ATP in the body.

EXERCISE 1-4.

INSTRUCTIONS

Fill in the blanks in the paragraph below using the following terms: ATP, metabolism, catabolism, and anabolism.

The term _____ (1) refers to all life-sustaining reactions that occur within the body. The reactions involved in _____ (2) assemble simple components into more complex ones. The reactions of _____ (3) break down substances into simpler components, generating energy in the form of (4) _____. This energy can be used to fuel cellular activities.

6. Differentiate between extracellular and intracellular fluids.

EXERCISE 1-5.

INSTRUCTIONS

Fill in the blank after each statement. Does it apply to extracellular fluid (EC) or intracellular fluid (IC)?
1. includes lymph and blood _____
2. refers to fluid inside cells _____
3. includes fluid between cells _____

7. Define and give examples of homeostasis.

8. Compare negative feedback and positive feedback.

EXERCISE 1-6.

INSTRUCTIONS

Fill in the blanks in the paragraph below using the following terms: negative feedback, positive feedback, homeostasis.

The maintenance of a constant internal body state, known as _____ (1), is critical for health. Different body parameters, such as body temperature and blood glucose concentration, are kept constant using _____ (2). Conversely, _____ (3) does not keep a body parameter constant. Instead, it reinforces the stimulus. This form of feedback facilitates dramatic events, such as childbirth.

9. List and define the main directional terms for the body.

EXERCISE 1-7: Directional Terms (Text Fig. 1-7)

INSTRUCTIONS

1. Write the name of each directional term on the numbered lines in different colors.
2. Color the arrow corresponding to each directional term with the corresponding color.

1. _____
2. _____
3. _____
4. _____
5. _____
6. _____
7. _____
8. _____

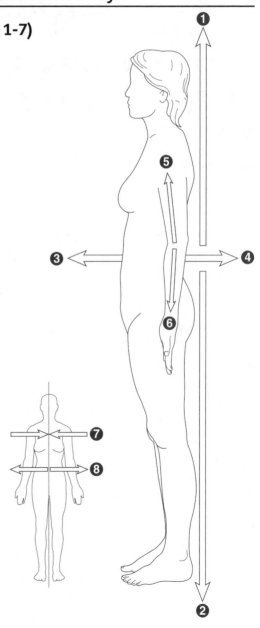

EXERCISE 1-8.

INSTRUCTIONS

Write the appropriate term in the blank.

posterior   anterior   medial   distal
caudal   lateral   horizontal

1. A term that indicates a location toward the front   _____
2. A term that means farther from the origin of a part   _____
3. A directional term that means away from the midline
   (toward the side)   _____
4. A term that means nearer to the sacral (lowermost) region
   of the spinal cord   _____
5. A term that describes the position of the shoulder blades in
   relation to the collar bones   _____

10. List and define the three planes of division of the body.

EXERCISE 1-9: Planes of Division (Text Fig. 1-8)

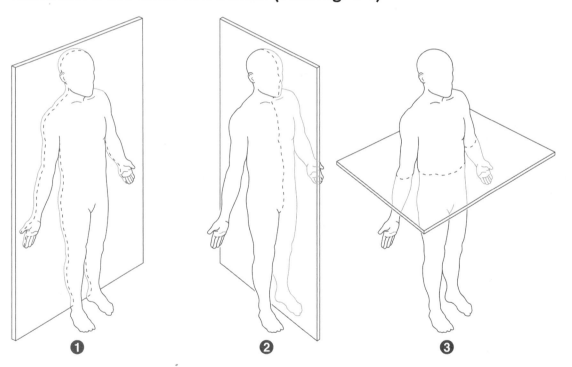

❶   ❷   ❸

INSTRUCTIONS

1. Write the names of the three planes of division on the correct numbered lines in different
   colors.
2. Color each plane in the illustration with the corresponding color.

1. _____
2. _____
3. _____

11. Name the subdivisions of the dorsal and ventral cavities.

EXERCISE 1-10: Lateral View of Body Cavities (Text Fig. 1-11)

INSTRUCTIONS

1. Write the names of the different body cavities and other structures in the appropriate spaces in different colors. Try to choose related colors for the dorsal cavity subdivisions and ventral cavity subdivisions.
2. Color parts 2, 3, and 6 to 9 with the corresponding color.

1. _____

2. _____

3. _____

4. _____

5. _____

6. _____

7. _____

8. _____

9. _____

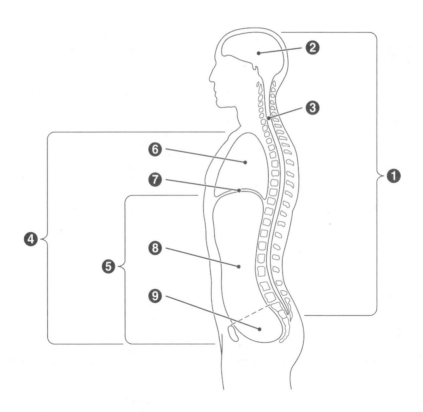

12. Name and locate the subdivisions of the abdomen.

EXERCISE 1-11: Regions of the Abdomen (Text Fig. 1-13)

INSTRUCTIONS

1. Write the names of the nine regions of the abdomen on the appropriate numbered lines in different colors.
2. Color each region with the corresponding color.

1. _____
2. _____
3. _____
4. _____
5. _____
6. _____
7. _____
8. _____
9. _____

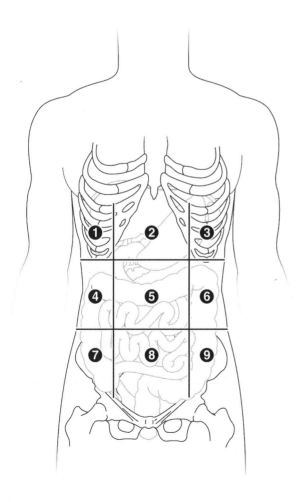

EXERCISE 1-12: Quadrants of the Abdomen (Text Fig. 1-14)

INSTRUCTIONS

1. Write the names of the four quadrants of the abdomen on the appropriate numbered lines in different colors.
2. Color each quadrant with the corresponding color.

1. _____

2. _____

3. _____

4. _____

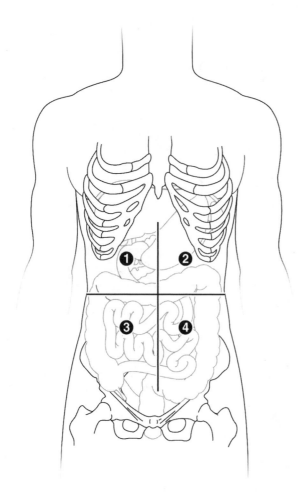

13. Name the basic units of length, weight, and volume in the metric system.

14. Define the metric prefixes *kilo-*, *centi-*, *milli-*, and *micro-*.

EXERCISE 1-13.

INSTRUCTIONS

Write the appropriate term in the space provided.

kilo-	milli-	centi-	micro-
gram	liter	meter	

1. A prefix meaning *one hundredth*   _____
2. The basic unit of length   _____
3. A prefix meaning *one millionth*   _____
4. The basic unit of weight   _____
5. A prefix meaning *one thousand*   _____

15. Show how word parts are used to build words related to the body's organization.

EXERCISE 1-14.

INSTRUCTIONS

Complete the following table by writing the correct word part or meaning in the space provided. Write a word that contains each word part in the Example column.

Word Part	Meaning	Example
1. -tomy	_____	_____
2. -stasis	_____	_____
3. _____	nature, physical	_____
4. homeo-	_____	_____
5. _____	apart, away from	_____
6. _____	down	_____
7. _____	upward	_____

Making the Connections

The following concept map deals with the body's cavities and their divisions. Complete the concept map by filling in the blanks with the appropriate word or phrase for the cavity, division, subdivision, or region.

Internally the body is divided into two main cavities.

They are the ❶ [ ] and the ❷ [ ]

The two subdivisions of this cavity are the

❸ [ ] and the [spinal cavity]

The two subdivisions of this cavity are the

[thoracic cavity] and the ❹ [ ]

They are separated by a muscle called the

❺ [ ]

This cavity can be divided into the

[abdominal cavity]

and the

❻ [ ]

For the purpose of examination the abdominal cavity can be divided into nine regions. From superior to inferior they are:

Right Lateral   Central   Left Lateral

❼ [ ]   [Epigastric region]   [Hypochondriac region]

[Lumbar region]   ❾ [ ]   ⓫ [ ]

❽ [ ]   ❿ [ ]   [Iliac region]

Testing Your Knowledge

Building Understanding

I. Multiple Choice

Select the best answer and write the letter of your choice in the blank.

1. The coronal plane is also called the:　　　　　　　　　　　1. _____
   a. frontal plane
   b. transverse plane
   c. cross-sectional plane
   d. sagittal plane

2. The diaphragm separates:　　　　　　　　　　　　　　　2. _____
   a. the cranial and spinal cavities
   b. the dorsal and ventral cavities
   c. the thoracic and abdominal cavities
   d. the abdominal and pelvic cavities

3. The breakdown of complex molecules into more simple ones is called:　3. _____
   a. anabolism
   b. synthesis
   c. negative feedback
   d. catabolism

4. Lymph is an example of which type of fluid?　　　　　　　4. _____
   a. extracellular
   b. intracellular
   c. superior
   d. extraneous

5. The heart and the blood vessels compose the:　　　　　　5. _____
   a. cardiovascular system
   b. nervous system
   c. integumentary system
   d. digestive system

6. The navel is found in the:　　　　　　　　　　　　　6. _____
   a. lumbar region
   b. umbilical region
   c. iliac region
   d. hypogastric region

7. The study of normal body function is called:　　　　　　7. _____
   a. physiology
   b. homeology
   c. anatomy
   d. chemistry

8. A penny-shaped slice of a banana is probably which type of section?　8. _____
   a. longitudinal section
   b. sagittal section
   c. cross section
   d. coronal section

II. Completion Exercise

➤ **Group A: General Terminology**

Write the word or phrase that correctly completes each sentence.

1. In the anatomic position, the body is upright and palms are facing   _____
2. Fluid inside cells is called   _____
3. Catabolism releases energy in the form of   _____
4. Negative feedback is a mechanism for maintaining an internal state of balance known as   _____
5. The sum of all catabolic and anabolic reactions in the body is called   _____
6. The process of childbirth is an example of a type of feedback called   _____

➤ **Group B: Body Cavities, Directional Terms, and Planes of Division**

1. The term that means nearer to the head is   _____
2. The space enclosing the brain and spinal cord forms a continuous cavity called the   _____
3. The abdomen may be divided into four regions, each of which is called a(n)   _____
4. The cavity that houses the bladder is the   _____
5. The plane that divides the body into anterior and posterior parts is the   _____
6. The ventral body cavity that contains the stomach, most of the intestine, the liver, and the spleen is the   _____
7. The abdomen may be subdivided into nine regions, including three along the midline. The region closest to the sternum (breastbone) is the   _____
8. The space between the lungs is called the   _____
9. The diaphragm separates the abdominopelvic cavity from the   _____

➤ **Group C: The Metric System**

Write the word that correctly completes each sentence.

1. The number of milligrams in a gram is   _____
2. The number of centimeters in an inch is   _____
3. The number of millimeters in a centimeter is   _____
4. Using the metric system, your height would probably be calculated in   _____
5. A liter is a slightly greater volume than a(n)   _____

Understanding Concepts

I. True/False

For each question, write *T* for true or *F* for false in the blank to the left of each number. If a statement is false, correct it by replacing the underlined term and write the correct statement in the blank below the question.

_____ 1. Proteins are broken down into their component parts by the process of anabolism.

_____

_____ 2. Your mouth is inferior to your nose.

_____

_____ 3. The brain is caudal to the spine.

_____

_____ 4. Your umbilicus is lateral to the left lumbar region.

_____

_____ 5. The right iliac region is found in the right lower quadrant.

_____

II. Practical Applications

Study each discussion. Then write the appropriate word or phrase in the space provided.

➤ **Group A: Directional Terms**

1. The gallbladder is located just above the colon. The directional term that describes the position of the gallbladder with regard to the colon is _____.
2. The kidneys are closer to the sides of the body than is the stomach. The directional term that describes the kidneys with regard to the stomach is _____.
3. The entrance to the stomach is nearest the point of origin or beginning of the stomach, so this part is said to be _____.
4. The knee is located closer to the hip than is the ankle. The term that describes the position of the ankle with regard to the knee is _____.
5. The ears are closer to the back of the head than is the nose. The term that describes the position of the ears with regard to the nose is _____.
6. The stomach is below the esophagus; it may be described as _____.
7. The head of the pancreas is nearer the midsagittal plane than is its tail portion, so the head part is more _____.

➤ **Group B: Body Cavities and the Metric System**

Study the following cases and answer the questions based on the nine divisions of the abdomen and your knowledge of the metric system.

1. Mr. A bruised his ribs in a dirt buggy accident. He experienced tenderness in the upper left side of his abdomen. In which of the nine abdominal regions are the injured ribs located? _____

2. Ms. D had a history of gallstones. The operation to remove these stones involved the upper right part of the abdominal cavity. Which abdominal division is this? _____

3. Following her operation, Ms. D was able to bring her stones home in a jar. She was told that her stones weighed 0.025 kg in total. How many milligrams do her stones weigh? _____

4. Ms. C is 8 weeks pregnant. Her uterus is still confined to the most inferior division of the abdomen. This region is called the _____.

5. Ms. C is experiencing heartburn as a result of her pregnancy. The discomfort is found just below the breastbone, in the _____.

6. Following the birth of her child, Ms. C opted for a tubal ligation. The doctor threaded a fiberoptic device through a small incision in her navel as part of the surgery. Ms. C will now have a very small incision in which portion of the abdomen? _____

7. Ms. C's incision was 2 mm in length. What is the length of her incision in centimeters? _____

➤ **Group C: Body Systems**

The triage nurse in the emergency room was showing a group of students how she assessed patients with disorders in different body systems. Study each situation, and answer the following questions based on your knowledge of the 11 body systems.

1. One person was complaining of dizziness and blurred vision. Vision is controlled by the _____.

2. One person had been injured in a snowboarding accident, spraining his wrist joint. The wrist joint is part of the _____.

3. A woman had attempted a particularly onerous yoga pose and felt a sharp pain in her left thigh. Now she was limping. The nurse suspected a tear to structures belonging to the _____.

4. An extremely tall individual entered the clinic, complaining of a headache. The nurse suspected that he had excess production of a particular hormone. The specialized glands that synthesize hormones make up the _____.

5. A middle-aged woman was brought in with loss of ability to move the right side of her body. The nurse felt that a blood clot in a blood vessel of the brain was producing the symptoms. Blood vessels are part of the _____.

6. A man complaining of pain in the abdomen and vomiting blood was brought in by his family. A problem was suspected in the system responsible for taking in food and converting it to usable products. This system is the _____.

7. Each client was assessed for changes in the color of the outer covering of the body. The outer covering is called the skin, which is part of the _____.

8. A young woman was experiencing pain in her pelvic region. The doctor suspected a problem with her ovaries. The ovaries are part of the _____.

9. An older man was experiencing difficulty with urination. The production of urine is the function of the _____.

III. Short Essays

1. Compare and contrast the terms **anabolism** and **catabolism**. List one similarity and one difference.

   _____

   _____

   _____

   _____

   _____

2. Which type of feedback, negative or positive, is used to maintain homeostasis? Defend your answer, referring to the definition of homeostasis.

   _____

   _____

   _____

   _____

   _____

3. Explain why specialized terms are needed to indicate different positions and directions within the body. Provide a concrete example.

   _____

   _____

   _____

   _____

   _____

Conceptual Thinking

1. Consider the role of negative feedback in the ability of a thermostat to keep your house at the same temperature. What would happen on a hot day if your thermostat worked according to the principles of positive feedback?

   _____

   _____

   _____

   _____

2. Consider the role of positive feedback in childbirth. Is childbirth a good example of homeostasis? Would the baby be delivered if stretching of the uterine muscles inhibited oxytocin secretion?

_____

_____

_____

_____

_____

3. A disease at the chemical level can have an effect on the whole body. That is, a change in a chemical affects a cell, which alters the functioning of a tissue, which disrupts an organ, which disrupts a system, which results in body dysfunction. Illustrate this concept by rewriting the following description in your own words using the different levels of organization: chemical, cell, tissue, organ, system, and body. (Hint: blood is a tissue.) Which of the **bold** terms applies to each level of organization? Which level of organization is not explicitly stated?

   Mr. S. experiences pain throughout his **body**. The movement of **blood** through his vessels is impaired. His **blood cells** are misshapen. A chemical found in red blood cells called **hemoglobin** is abnormal.

_____

_____

_____

_____

_____

Expanding Your Horizons

As a student of anatomy and physiology, you have joined a community of scholars stretching back into prehistory. The history of biological thought is a fascinating one, full of murder and intrigue. We think that scientific knowledge is entirely objective. However, as the following books will show, theories of anatomy and physiology, depend upon societal factors such as economic class, religion, and gender issues.

Resources

1. Serafini A. _The Epic History of Biology_. Cambridge, MA: Perseus; 1993.
2. Magner LN. _A History of the Life Sciences_. New York: Dekker; 1993.
3. Asimov I. _A Short History of Biology_. Westport, CT: Greenwood; 1980.

CHAPTER 2

Chemistry, Matter, and Life

Overview

Chemistry is the physical science that deals with the composition of matter. To appreciate the importance of chemistry in the field of health, it is necessary to know about elements, atoms, molecules, compounds, and mixtures. An **element** is a substance consisting of just one type of atom. Although exceedingly small particles, atoms possess a definite structure. The **nucleus** contains **protons** and **neutrons**, and the element's **atomic number** indicates the number of protons in its nucleus. The **electrons** surround the nucleus, where they are arranged in specific orbits called **energy levels**.

The union of two or more atoms produces a **molecule**; the atoms in the molecule may be alike (as in the oxygen molecule) or different (sodium chloride, for example). In the latter case, the substance is called a **compound**. A combination of compounds, each of which retains its separate properties, is a **mixture**. Mixtures include solutions, such as salt water, and suspensions. In the body, chemical compounds are constantly being formed, altered, broken down, and recombined into other substances.

Water is a vital substance composed of hydrogen and oxygen. It makes up more than half of the body and is needed as a solvent and a transport medium. Hydrogen, oxygen, carbon, and nitrogen are the elements that constitute about 96% of living matter, whereas calcium, sodium, potassium, phosphorus, sulfur, chlorine, and magnesium account for most of the remaining 4%.

When atoms combine with each other to form compounds they are held together by chemical bonds. Bonds that form as the result of the attraction between oppositely charged ions are called **ionic bonds**. Bonds that form when two atoms share electrons between them are called **covalent bonds**.

Inorganic compounds include acids, bases, or salts. **Acids** are compounds that can donate hydrogen ions (H^+) when in solution. **Bases** usually contain the hydroxide ion (OH^-) and can accept hydrogen ions. The **pH scale** is used to indicate the strength of an acid or base. **Salts** are formed when an acid reacts with a base.

Isotopes (forms of elements) that give off radiation are said to be **radioactive**. Because they can penetrate tissues and can be followed in the body, they are useful in diagnosis. Radioactive substances also have the ability to destroy tissues and can be used in the treatment of many types of cancer.

Proteins, carbohydrates, and lipids are the organic compounds characteristic of living organisms. **Enzymes**, an important group of proteins, function as catalysts in metabolism.

Addressing the Learning Outcomes

1. Define an element.

2. Describe the structure of an atom.

EXERCISE 2-1.

INSTRUCTIONS

Write the appropriate term in each blank.

nucleus	proton	element	electrons
neutrons	atom	ions	

1. A positively charged particle inside the atomic nucleus   _____
2. The smallest complete unit of matter   _____
3. An uncharged particle inside the atomic nucleus   _____
4. A substance composed of one type of atom   _____
5. The part of the atom containing protons and neutrons   _____
6. A negatively charged particle outside the atomic nucleus   _____

EXERCISE 2-2: Parts of the Atom, Molecule of Water (Text Figs. 2-1 and 2-2)

INSTRUCTIONS

1. Write the names of the types of atoms in this figure (2 hydrogen and 1 oxygen) on the numbered lines in two different light colors.
2. LIGHTLY color the hydrogen and oxygen atoms in the figure with the corresponding color.
3. Write the names of the parts of the atom (electron, proton, neutron) on the numbered lines in different, darker colors.
4. Color the electrons, protons, and neutrons on the figure in the appropriate colors. You should find 10 electrons, 10 protons, and 8 neutrons in total.

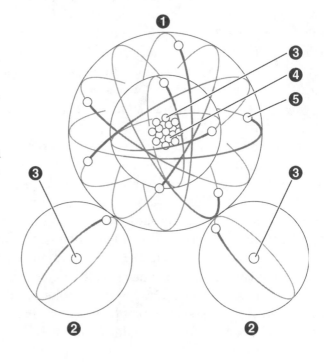

1. _____
2. _____
3. _____
4. _____
5. _____

3. Differentiate between molecules and compounds.

EXERCISE 2-3.

INSTRUCTIONS

Indicate which of the following statements apply to molecules (M), compounds (C), or both (B) by writing the appropriate letter in the blank.

1. contain two or more atoms   _____

2. contain two or more identical atoms   _____

3. contain two or more different atoms   _____

4. Explain why water is so important to the body.

EXERCISE 2-4.

Which of the following properties are NOT true of water? There is one correct answer.

A. all substances can dissolve in water
B. water participates in chemical reactions
C. water is a stable liquid at ordinary temperatures
D. water carries substances to and from cells

5. Define mixture; list the three types of mixtures and give two examples of each.

EXERCISE 2-5.

INSTRUCTIONS

Write the appropriate term in each blank.

solution   suspension   solute   colloid
solvent   aqueous   mixture

1. A substance that is dissolved in another substance   _____

2. A mixture in which substances will settle out unless the mixture is shaken   _____

3. Term used to describe a solution mostly formed of water   _____

4. The substance in which another substance is dissolved   _____

5. Cytoplasm and blood plasma are examples of this type of mixture   _____

6. Any combination of two or more substances in which each constituent maintains its identity   _____

6. Differentiate between ionic and covalent bonds.

7. Define an electrolyte.

EXERCISE 2-6.

INSTRUCTIONS

Write the appropriate term in each blank.

cations   ionic   covalent   electrolytes   anions

1. Negatively charged ions   _____

2. A bond formed by the sharing of electrons between two atoms   _____

3. Compounds that form ions when in solution   _____

4. Positively charged ions   _____

5. A bond formed by the transfer of electron(s) from one atom to another   _____

8. Define the terms *acid, base,* and *salt.*

9. Explain how the numbers on the pH scale relate to acidity and basicity (alkalinity).

10. Define *buffer* and explain why buffers are important in the body.

EXERCISE 2-7.

INSTRUCTIONS

Fill in the blanks in the paragraph below using the following terms: pH scale, salt, acid, base, buffer, hydroxide, alkali, hydrogen, high, low.

Any substance that can donate a hydrogen ion to another substance is called a(n) _____(1). Any substance that can accept a hydrogen ion is called a(n) _____ (2) or a(n) _____ (3). Many of these contain a(n) _____ ion (4). A reaction between a hydrogen-accepting substance and a hydrogen-donating substance produces a _____ (5). The _____ (6) measures the concentration of hydrogen ions in a solution. A solution with a large concentration of hydrogen ions will have a _____ (7) pH; a solution with a large concentration of hydroxyl ions will have a ____ (8) pH. A substance that helps to maintain a stable hydrogen ion concentration in a solution is called a(n) _____ (9); these substances are critical for health.

11. Define *radioactivity* and cite several examples of how radioactive substances are used in medicine.

EXERCISE 2-8.

Which of the following statements about radioactivity are TRUE? There are four correct statements.

A. All isotopes are radioactive.
B. Isotopes have the same atomic weight.
C. Isotopes have the same number of protons.
D. Isotopes have the same number of electrons.
E. Isotopes have the same number of neutrons.
F. Radioactive isotopes disintegrate easily.
G. Radioactive isotopes can be used for diagnosis and treatment.

12. List three characteristics of organic compounds.

EXERCISE 2-9.

The three characteristics of organic compounds are:

1. _____

2. _____

3. _____

13. Name the three main types of organic compounds and the building blocks of each.

EXERCISE 2-10.

INSTRUCTIONS

Write the appropriate term in each blank.

protein   amino acid   phospholipid   carbohydrate
monosaccharide   steroid   disaccharide

1. Two simple sugars linked together   _____

2. A building block of proteins   _____

3. A lipid containing a ring of carbon atoms   _____

4. A lipid that contains phosphorus in addition to carbon, hydrogen,
   and oxygen   _____

5. A category of organic compounds that includes simple sugars
   and starches   _____

EXERCISE 2-11: Carbohydrates (Text Fig. 2-7)

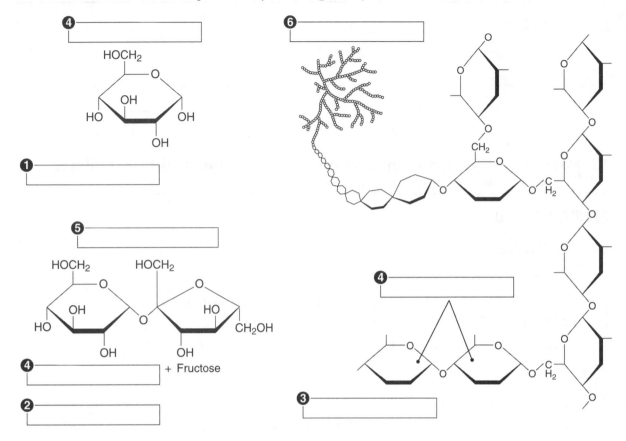

INSTRUCTIONS

1. Write the terms *monosaccharide*, *disaccharide*, and *polysaccharide* in the appropriate numbered boxes 1-3.
2. Write the terms *glucose*, *sucrose*, and *glycogen* in the appropriate numbered boxes 4-6 in different colors.
3. Color the glucose, sucrose, and glycogen molecules with the corresponding colors. To simplify your diagram, only use the glucose color to shade the glucose molecule in the monosaccharide.

EXERCISE 2-12: Lipids (Text Fig. 2-8)

INSTRUCTIONS

1. Write the terms *glycerol* and *fatty acids* on the numbered lines in two different colors.
2. Find the boxes surrounding these two components on the diagram and color them lightly in the corresponding colors.
3. Write the terms *triglyceride* and *cholesterol* in the boxes under the appropriate diagrams.

1. _____

2. _____

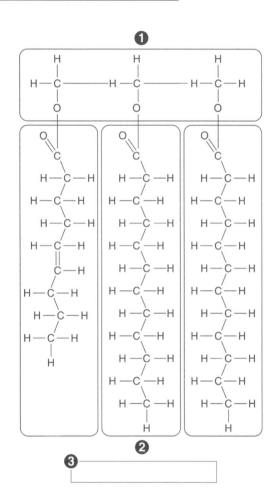

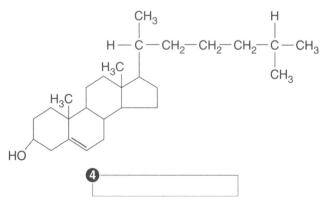

EXERCISE 2-13: Proteins (Text Fig. 2-9)

INSTRUCTIONS

1. Write the terms *amino group* and *acid group* on the numbered lines in different colors.
2. Find the shapes surrounding these two components on the diagram, and color them lightly in the corresponding colors.
3. Place the following terms in the appropriate numbered boxes: amino acid, coiled, pleated, folded.

1. _____

2. _____

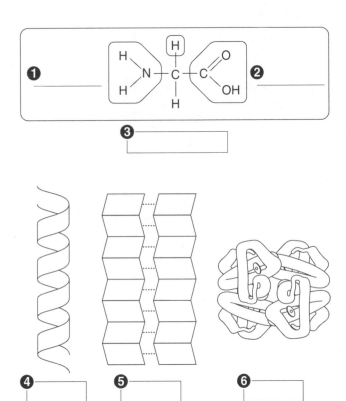

14. Define *enzyme*; describe how enzymes work.

EXERCISE 2-14: Enzyme Action (Text Fig. 2-10)

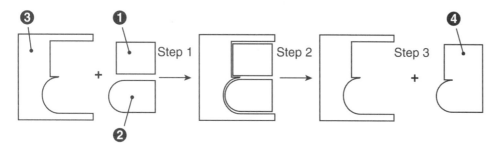

INSTRUCTIONS:

1. Write the terms *substrate 1, substrate 2,* and *enzyme* on the appropriate numbered lines in different colors (red and blue are recommended).
2. Color the structures on the diagram with the corresponding color.
3. What color will result from the combination of your two substrate colors? Write "product" in this color on the appropriate line, and then color the product.

1. _____
2. _____
3. _____
4. _____

15. Show how word parts are used to build words related to chemistry, matter, and life.

EXERCISE 2-15.

INSTRUCTIONS

Complete the following table by writing the correct word part or meaning in the space provided. Write a word that contains each word part in the Example column.

Word Part	Meaning	Example
1. _____	to fear	_____
2. _____	to like	_____
3. glyc/o	_____	_____
4. _____	different	_____
5. hydr/o	_____	_____
6. hom/o-	_____	_____
7. _____	many	_____
8. aqu/e	_____	_____
9. sacchar/o	_____	_____
10. _____	together	_____

Making the Connections

The following concept map deals with the components of matter. Complete the concept map by filling in the blanks with the appropriate word or phrase.

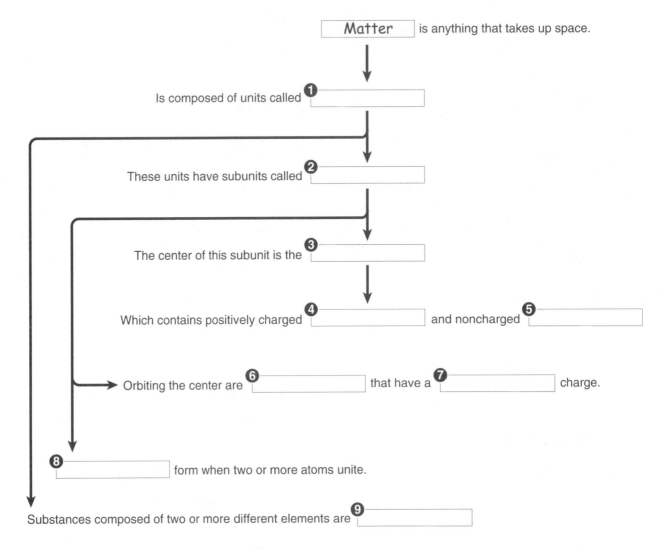

Matter is anything that takes up space.

Is composed of units called ❶

These units have subunits called ❷

The center of this subunit is the ❸

Which contains positively charged ❹ and noncharged ❺

Orbiting the center are ❻ that have a ❼ charge.

❽ form when two or more atoms unite.

Substances composed of two or more different elements are ❾

Optional Exercise: Construct your own concept map using the following terms: amino acid, protein, monosaccharide, enzyme, polysaccharide, glycogen, glucose, lipid, and triglyceride.

Testing Your Knowledge

Building Understanding

I. Multiple Choice

Select the best answer and write the letter of your choice in the blank.

1. The element that is the basis for organic chemistry is:
   a. nitrogen
   b. carbon
   c. oxygen
   d. hydrogen

   1. _____

2. The smallest particle of an element that has all the properties of that element is a(n):
   a. proton
   b. neutron
   c. electron
   d. atom

   2. _____

3. If an electron is added to an atom it becomes a type of charged particle known as a(n):
   a. proton
   b. anion
   c. cation
   d. electrolyte

   3. _____

4. Electrons are arranged around the nucleus in specific orbits called:
   a. energy levels
   b. ellipses
   c. pathways
   d. isotopes

   4. _____

5. A pH of seven is said to be:
   a. basic
   b. neutral
   c. acidic
   d. radioactive

   5. _____

6. The building blocks for sugars are:
   a. amino acids
   b. free fatty acids
   c. glycerol molecules
   d. monosaccharides

   6. _____

7. Covalent bonds are:
   a. formed between two ions
   b. polar or nonpolar
   c. never used in organic molecules
   d. usually very unstable

   7. _____

8. Salt completely dissolved in water is an example of a(n):   8. _____
   a. colloid
   b. suspension
   c. aqueous solution
   d. isotope
9. A fat can also be called a(n):   9. _____
   a. polysaccharide
   b. lipid
   c. inorganic molecule
   d. isotope

II. Completion Exercise

Write the word or phrase that correctly completes each sentence.

1. The most abundant element by mass in the human body is _____.
2. An isotope that disintegrates, giving off rays of atomic particles, is said to be _____.
3. The number of electrons lost or gained by an atom in a chemical reaction is called its _____.
4. Water can dissolve many different things. For this reason it is called the _____.
5. Sugar water is a mixture in which one substance is dissolved in another and remains evenly distributed. This type of mixture is a(n)_____.
6. A mixture that is not a solution but does not separate because the particles in the mixture are so small is a(n) _____.
7. Metabolic reactions require organic catalysts called _____.
8. Many essential body activities depend on certain compounds that form ions when in solution. Such compounds are called _____.
9. The name given to a chemical system that prevents changes in hydrogen ion concentration is _____.
10. The study of the composition and properties of matter is called _____.

Understanding Concepts

I. True-False

For each question, write *T* for true or *F* for false in the blank to the left of each number. If a statement is false, correct it by replacing the underlined term and write the correct statement in the blank below the question.

_____ 1. Sodium chloride (NaCl) is an example of an underlined element.

_____

_____ 2. If a neutral atom has 12 protons, it will have 11 electrons.

_____

_____ 3. An atom with an atomic number of 15 will have 15 protons.

_____

_____ 4. Butter dissolves poorly in water. Butter is thus an example of a <u>hydrophobic</u> substance.

_____

_____ 5. When table salt is dissolved in water, the sodium ion donates one electron to the chloride ion. The chloride ion thus has 17 protons and <u>17</u> electrons.

_____

_____ 6. You put some soil in water and shake well. After 10 minutes, you note that some of the dirt has settled to the bottom of the jar. With respect to the dirt at the bottom of the jar, your mixture is a <u>colloid</u>.

_____

_____ 7. A pH of 10.0 is <u>basic</u>.

_____

_____ 8. Carbon dioxide is composed of two oxygen atoms and one carbon atom bonded by the sharing of electrons. The shared electrons are usually closer to the oxygens than to the carbon. Carbon dioxide is formed by <u>ionic bonds</u>.

_____

_____ 9. Maltose, a <u>disaccharide</u>, is composed of two glucose molecules.

_____

_____ 10. Hemoglobin, a protein, is composed of long chains of <u>phospholipids</u>.

_____

II. Practical Applications

Study each discussion. Then write the appropriate word or phrase in the space provided. The following medical tests are based on principles of chemistry and physics.

1. Young Ms. M was experiencing intense thirst and was urinating more than usual. Her doctor suspected that she might have diabetes mellitus. This diagnosis was confirmed by findings of glucose in her urine and high glucose levels in her blood. Glucose and other sugars belong to a group of organic compounds classified as _____.

2. Young Mr. L was brought to the clinic because he had suffered two convulsions during the night. The doctor suspected that he might have epilepsy. He obtained a graphic record of his brain wave activity to aid in this diagnosis. This brain wave record is called a(n) _____.

3. Ms. F. just ran a 50-kilometer ultramarathon in the Sahara desert. She was brought into the clinic with symptoms of decreased function of many systems. Her history revealed poor fluid intake for several weeks. Her symptoms were due to a shortage of the most abundant compound in the body, which is _____.

4. Mr. Q has been experiencing diarrhea, intestinal gas, and bloating whenever he drinks milk. He was diagnosed with a deficiency in an enzyme called lactase, which digests the sugar in milk. Enzymes, like all proteins, are composed of building blocks called _____.

5. Mr. V came to the clinic complaining of severe headaches. The doctor ordered a PET scan that measures the use of a monosaccharide by the brain. This monosaccharide, which can be assembled into a glycogen molecule in body tissues, is called _____.

6. Daredevil Mr. L was riding his skateboard on a high wall when he fell. He had pain and swelling in his right wrist. His examination included a procedure in which rays penetrate body tissues to produce an image on a photographic plate. The rays used for this purpose are called _____.

7. Ms. F. was given an intravenous solution containing sodium, potassium, and chloride ions. These elements come from salts that separate into ions in solution and are referred to as _____.

III. *Short Essays*

1. Describe the structure of a protein. Make sure you include the following terms in your answer: pleated sheet, helix, protein, amino acid.

    _____

    _____

    _____

    _____

    _____

2. What is the difference between a solvent and a solute? Name the solvent and the solute in salt water.

    _____

    _____

    _____

3. What is the difference between inorganic and organic chemistry?

    _____

    _____

    _____

4. Why is the shape of an enzyme important in its function?

    _____

    _____

    _____

5. Compare and contrast solutions and suspensions. Name one similarity and one difference.

_____

_____

_____

Conceptual Thinking

1. Using the periodic table of the elements in Appendix 3, answer the following questions:
   a. How many protons does silicon (Si) have? _____
   b. How many electrons does copper (Cu) have? _____
   c. Phosphorus (P) exists as many isotopes. One isotope is called P^{32}, based on its atomic weight. The atomic weight can be calculated by adding up the number of protons and the number of neutrons. How many neutrons does P^{32} have? _____
   d. How many electrons does the magnesium ion Mg^{2+} have? (The 2+ indicates that the magnesium atom has lost two electrons). _____

2. There is much more variety in proteins than in carbohydrates. Explain why.

_____

_____

_____

Expanding Your Horizons

Drink Your Orange Juice: The Benefits of Vitamin C

You may have read the term "antioxidant" in newpaper articles or on the Internet. But what is an antioxidant, and why do we want them? An understanding of atomic structure is required to answer this question. Radiation or chemical reactions can cause molecules to pick up or lose an electron, resulting in an unpaired electron. Molecules with unpaired electrons are called **free radicals**. For instance, an oxygen molecule can gain an electron, resulting in superoxide (O_2-), and a hydroxyl ion (OH^-) can lose an electron, resulting in a neutral OH free radical. Unpaired electrons are very unstable; thus, free radicals steal electrons from other substances, converting them into free radicals. This chain reaction disrupts normal cell metabolism and can result in cancer. Antioxidants, including vitamin C, give up electrons without converting into free radicals, thereby stopping the chain reaction. The two references listed below will tell you more about free radicals and how antioxidants may fight the aging process and protect against Parkinson disease.

Resources

1. Brown K. A radical proposal. _Scientific American Presents_ 2000; 11:38–43.
2. Youdim MB, Riederer P. Understanding Parkinson's disease. _Sci Am_ 1997; 276:52–59.

CHAPTER 3

Cells and Their Functions

Overview

The **cell** is the basic unit of life; all life activities result from the activities of cells. The study of cells began with the invention of the light microscope and has continued with the development of electron microscopes. Cell functions are carried out by specialized structures within the cell called **organelles**. These include the nucleus, ribosomes, mitochondria, Golgi apparatus, endoplasmic reticulum (ER), lysosomes, peroxisomes, and centrioles. Two specialized organelles, cilia and flagella, function in cell locomotion and the movement of materials across the cell surface.

An important cell function is the manufacture of proteins, including enzymes (organic catalysts). Protein manufacture is carried out by the ribosomes in the cytoplasm according to information coded in the deoxyribonucleic acid (DNA) of the nucleus. Specialized molecules of RNA called messenger RNA play a key role in the process by carrying copies of the information in DNA to the ribosomes. DNA also is involved in the process of cell division or mitosis. Before cell division can occur, the DNA must replicate so each daughter cell produced by mitosis will have exactly the same kind and amount of DNA as the parent cell.

The **plasma (cell) membrane** is important in regulating what enters and leaves the cell. Some substances can pass through the membrane by **diffusion**, which is simply the movement of molecules from an area where they are in higher concentration to an area where they are in lower concentration. The diffusion of water through the plasma membrane is termed **osmosis**. Because water can diffuse very easily across the membrane, cells must be kept in solutions that have the same concentrations as the cell fluid. If the cell is placed in a solution of higher concentration, a **hypertonic solution**, it will shrink; in a solution of lower concentration, a **hypotonic solution**, it will swell and may burst. The plasma membrane can also selectively move substances into or out of the cell by **active transport**, a process that requires energy (ATP) and transporters. Large particles and droplets of fluid are taken in by the processes of **phagocytosis** and **pinocytosis**.

Addressing the Learning Outcomes

1. List three types of microscopes used to study cells.

EXERCISE 3-1.

INSTRUCTIONS

Write the appropriate term in each blank.

compound light microscope   transmission electron microscope
scanning electron microscope   micrometer   centimeter

1. 1/1,000 of a millimeter   _____
2. Microscope that provides a three-dimensional view of an object   _____
3. The most common microscope, which magnifies an object up
   to 1,000 times   _____
4. A microscope that magnifies an object up to one million times   _____

2. Describe the function and composition of the plasma membrane.

EXERCISE 3-2: Structure of the Plasma Membrane (Text Fig. 3-3)

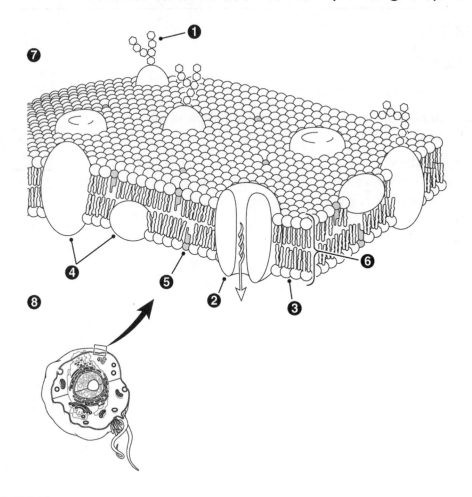

INSTRUCTIONS

1. Write the name of each labeled membrane component on the numbered lines in different colors. Choose a light color for component number 3.
2. Color the different structures on the diagram with the corresponding color (except for structures 6 to 8). Color ALL of components 1 and 3 to 5, not just those indicated by the leader lines. For instance, component 1 is found in three locations.

1. _____

2. _____

3. _____

4. _____

5. _____

6. _____

7. _____

8. _____

EXERCISE 3-3: Membrane Proteins (Text Table 3-2)

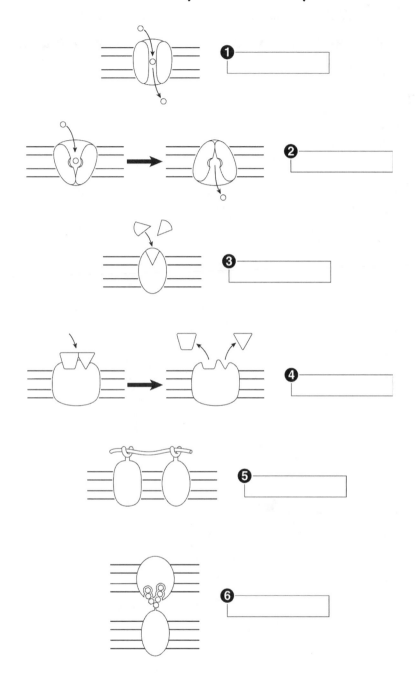

INSTRUCTIONS

1. Write the appropriate membrane protein function in boxes 1 to 6 in different colors.
2. Color the protein in each diagram with the corresponding color.

3. Describe the cytoplasm of the cell, including the name and function of the main organelles.

EXERCISE 3-4: Typical Animal Cell Showing the Main Organelles (Text Fig. 3-2)

INSTRUCTIONS

1. Write the name of each labeled part on the numbered lines in different colors. Make sure you use light colors for structures 1 and 7.
2. Color the different structures on the diagram with the corresponding color.

*Note: Parts 12 and 15 have the same appearance in this diagram; write the name of one of the possible parts in blank 12 and the other in blank 15.

1. _____
2. _____
3. _____
4. _____
5. _____
6. _____
7. _____
8. _____
9. _____
10. _____
11. _____
12. _____
13. _____
14. _____
15. _____
16. _____

EXERCISE 3-5.

INSTRUCTIONS

Write the appropriate term in each blank.

lysosome   nucleolus   cilia   ribosome
Golgi apparatus   vesicle   mitochondrion   nucleus

1. A structure that assembles ribosomes   _____
2. A structure that assembles amino acids into proteins   _____
3. A set of membranes involved in packaging proteins for export   _____
4. A small saclike structure used to transport substances within
   the cell   _____
5. A membraneous organelle that generates ATP   _____
6. A small saclike structure that degrades waste products   _____
7. The site of DNA storage   _____

4. Describe the composition, location, and function of the DNA in the cell.

EXERCISE 3-6: Basic Structure of a DNA Molecule (Text Fig. 3-6)

INSTRUCTIONS

1. Write the name of each part of the DNA
   molecule on the numbered lines in contrasting colors.
2. Color the different parts on the diagram with
   the corresponding color. Try to color each
   part everywhere it occurs in the DNA molecule.

1. _____
2. _____
3. _____
4. _____
5. _____
6. _____

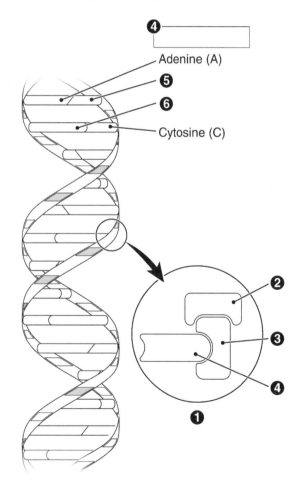

Adenine (A)

Cytosine (C)

5. Compare the function of three types of RNA in the cells.

6. Explain briefly how cells make proteins.

EXERCISE 3-7.

INSTRUCTIONS

Write the appropriate term in each blank from the list below.

DNA   nucleotide   transcription   translation
transfer RNA (tRNA)   messenger RNA (mRNA)   ribosomal RNA (rRNA)

1. The process by which RNA is synthesized from the DNA   _____
2. A building block of DNA and RNA   _____
3. An important component of ribosomes   _____
4. The structure that carries amino acids to the ribosome   _____
5. The nucleic acid that carries information from the nucleus to
   the ribosomes   _____
6. The process by which amino acids are assembled into a protein   _____

7. Name and briefly describe the stages in mitosis.

EXERCISE 3-8: Stages of Mitosis (Text Fig. 3-9)

INSTRUCTIONS

Identify interphase and the indicated stages of mitosis. Find the DNA in each stage and color it.

1. _____

2. _____

3. _____

4. _____

5. _____

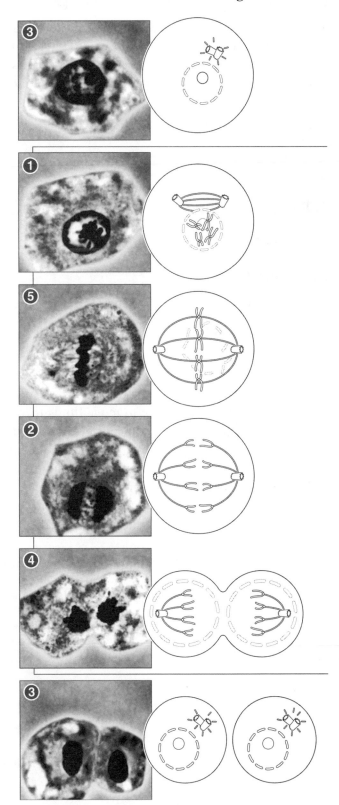

EXERCISE 3-9.

INSTRUCTIONS

Write the appropriate term in each blank from the list below.

mitosis   anaphase   telophase   meiosis
metaphase   prophase   interphase

1. The process by which one cell divides into two identical
   daughter cells   _____
2. The nuclear membrane reforms during this phase   _____
3. Centrioles begin to form and chromosomes condense during
   this phase   _____
4. The phase of mitosis when chromosomes are aligned in the
   middle of the cell   _____
5. DNA synthesis occurs during this phase   _____
6. The chromosomes are being pulled apart in this phase   _____

8. Define eight methods by which substances enter and leave cells.

EXERCISE 3-10.

INSTRUCTIONS

Write the appropriate term in each blank using the terms listed below.

exocytosis   endocytosis   active transport   facilitated diffusion
osmosis   diffusion   filtration   pinocytosis

1. The process that utilizes a transporter to move materials across the
   plasma membrane against the concentration gradient using ATP   _____
2. The use of hydrostatic force to move fluids through a membrane   _____
3. The process that utilizes a transporter to move materials across the
   plasma membrane in the direction of the concentration gradient   _____
4. A special form of diffusion that applies only to water   _____
5. The spread of molecules throughout an area   _____
6. The process by which a cell takes in large particles   _____
7. The process by which materials are expelled from the cell
   using vesicles   _____
8. Small fluid droplets are brought into the cell using this method   _____

9. Explain what will happen if cells are placed in solutions with concentrations the same as or different from those of the cell fluids.

EXERCISE 3-11: Osmosis (Text Fig. 3-18)

INSTRUCTIONS

Label each of the following solutions using the term that indicates the solute concentration in the solution relative to the solute concentration in the cell.

1. _____
2. _____
3. _____

10. Show how word parts are used to build words related to cells and their functions.

EXERCISE 3-12.

INSTRUCTIONS

Complete the following table by writing the correct word part or meaning in the space provided. Write a word that contains each word part in the Example column.

Word Part	Meaning	Example
1. phag/o	_____	_____
2. _____	to drink	_____
3. -some	_____	_____
4. lys/o	_____	_____
5. _____	cell	_____
6. _____	above, over, excessive	_____
7. hem/o	_____	_____
8. _____	same, equal	_____
9. hypo-	_____	_____
10. _____	in, within	_____

Making the Connections

The following concept map deals with the movement of materials through the plasma membrane. Complete the concept map by filling in the blanks with the appropriate word or phrase that describes the indicated process.

1. Processes that move small quantities of material through the plasma membrane include...

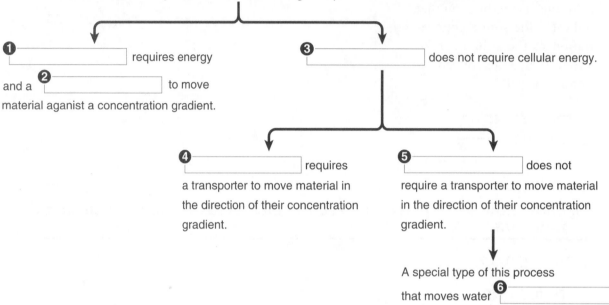

❶ _____ requires energy

and a ❷ _____ to move

material aganist a concentration gradient.

❸ _____ does not require cellular energy.

❹ _____ requires
a transporter to move material in
the direction of their concentration
gradient.

❺ _____ does not
require a transporter to move material
in the direction of their concentration
gradient.

A special type of this process
that moves water ❻ _____

2. Processes that move large quantities of material through the plasma membrane include...

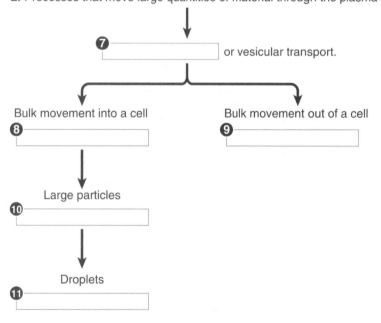

❼ _____ or vesicular transport.

Bulk movement into a cell
❽ _____

Bulk movement out of a cell
❾ _____

Large particles
❿ _____

Droplets
⓫ _____

Optional Exercise: Make your own concept map, based on the components of the cell. Choose your own terms to incorporate into your map, or use the following list: nucleus, mitochondria, cell membrane, protein, RNA, DNA, ATP, vesicle, ribosome, and endoplasmic reticulum.

Testing Your Knowledge

Building Understanding

I. Multiple Choice

Select the best answer and write the letter of your choice in the blank.

1. Which of the following organelles consists of a series of membranes studded with ribosomes?   1. _____
    a. mitochondrion
    b. rough endoplasmic reticulum
    c. smooth endoplasmic reticulum
    d. Golgi apparatus
2. A natural part of growth and remodeling involves the process of programmed cell death known as   2. _____
    a. mitosis
    b. mutation
    c. apoptosis
    d. phagocytosis
3. Which of the following are required for active transport?   3. _____
    a. vesicles and cilia
    b. transporters and ATP
    c. osmotic pressure and centrioles
    d. osmosis and lysosomes
4. The stage of mitosis during which the DNA condenses into visible chromosomes is called: 4. _____
    a. metaphase
    b. anaphase
    c. prophase
    d. telophase
5. Large proteins can be secreted from the cell using the process of: 5. _____
    a. pinocytosis
    b. osmosis
    c. endocytosis
    d. exocytosis
6. Which of the following substances is NOT a constituent of the plasma membrane?   6. _____
    a. DNA
    b. proteins
    c. carbohydrates
    d. phospholipids
7. Which of the following tools has the greatest magnification?   7. _____
    a. scanning electron microscope
    b. transmission electron microscope
    c. light microscope
    d. magnifying glass

8. A membrane protein that permits the passage of specific substances is
    called a(n):   8. _____
    a. channel
    b. receptor
    c. linker
    d. enzyme

II. Completion Exercise

Write the word or phrase that correctly completes each sentence.

1. The type of light microscope in use today is the _____.
2. The plasma membrane contains two kinds of lipids: cholesterol and _____.
3. In some cells the plasma membrane is folded outward into multiple small projections called _____.
4. The four nitrogen bases found in DNA are A, C, G, and _____.
5. The four nitrogen bases found in RNA are A, C, G, and _____.
6. The assembly of amino acids into proteins is called _____.
7. When a red blood cell draws in water and bursts it is said to undergo _____.
8. The chromosomes replicate during the period between mitoses, which is called _____.
9. A cell has four chromosomes before entering the process of mitosis. After mitosis, the number of chromosomes in each daughter cell will be _____.
10. Transporters are used for the processes of active transport and _____.
11. Droplets of water and dissolved substances are brought ino the cell by the process of _____.
12. The number of daughter cells formed when a cell undergoes mitosis is _____.
13. Bacteria are brought into the cell by the process of _____.

Understanding Concepts

I. True/False

For each question, write *T* for true or *F* for false in the blank to the left of each number. If a statement is false, correct it by replacing the underlined term and write the correct statement in the blank below the question.

_____ 1. The nucleotide sequence "ACCUG" would be found in DNA.

_____

_____ 2. A living cell (with a tonicity equivalent to 0.9% NaCl) is placed in a solution containing 2% NaCl. This solution is hypertonic.

_____

_____ 3. Glucose is moving into a cell, down its concentration gradient, using a carrier protein. Glucose is travelling by active transport.

_____

_____ 4. A toxin has entered a cell. The cell is no longer capable of generating ATP. The most likely explanation for this effect is that the toxin has destroyed the <u>mitochondria</u>.

_____

_____ 5. The best microscope to view a ribosome would be a <u>scanning electron microscope</u>.

_____

_____ 6. It is impossible to count individual chromosomes during <u>interphase</u>.

_____

II. Practical Applications

Study each discussion. Then write the appropriate word or phrase in the space provided. The following are observations you might make while working for the summer in a hospital laboratory.

1. A sample of breast tissue that was thought to be cancerous arrived at the pathology lab. Breast cells that produce milk synthesize large amounts of protein. The small RNA-containing bodies that synthesize proteins are called _____.
2. The tissue was in a liquid called normal saline so that the cells would neither shrink nor swell. Normal saline contains 0.9% salt and is thus considered to be _____.
3. The pathologist (Dr. C) sliced the tissue very thinly and placed it on a microscope slide, but he was unable to see anything. Unfortunately, he had forgotten to add a dye to the tissue. These special dyes are called _____.
4. Dr. C went back to his bench in order to get the necessary dye. He noticed that there were many impurities floating in the dye, and he decided to screen them out. He separated the solid particles from the liquid by forcing the liquid through a membrane, a process called _____.
5. Dr. C was clumsy and accidentally spilled the dye into a sink full of dishes. The water in the sink rapidly turned pink. The dye molecules had moved through the water by the process of _____.
6. Dr. C made up some new dye and treated the tissue. Finally, the tissue was ready for examination. Which type of microscope uses light to view stained tissues? _____.
7. The pathologist looked at the tissue and noticed that the nuclei of many cells were in the process of dividing. This division process is called _____.
8. Some cells were in the stage of cell division called prophase. The DNA was condensed into structures called _____.

III. Short Essays

1. Compare and contrast active transport and facilitated diffusion. List at least one similarity and at least one difference.

   _____

   _____

   _____

2. You are in the hospital for a minor operation, and the technician is hooking you up to an IV. He knows you are a nursing student and jokingly asks if you would like a hypertonic, hypotonic, or isotonic solution to be placed in your IV. Which solution would you pick? Explain your answer.

   _____

   _____

   _____

3. Compare the transmission electron microscope with the scanning electron microscope. List one similarity and one difference.

   _____

   _____

   _____

Conceptual Thinking

1. Compare the structure of a cell to a factory or a city. Try to find cell structures that accomplish all of the different functions of the city or factory.

   _____

   _____

   _____

   _____

   _____

2. Your great-aunt M is 96 years old and loves to hear about what you are learning in class. She recently attended an Elderhostel camp, where people were talking about this new-fangled notion called DNA.

  a. She asks you to explain why DNA is so important. Explain the role of DNA in protein synthesis, using clear, uncomplicated language. You must define any term that your great-aunt might not know. You can use an analogy if you like.

_____

_____

_____

_____

_____

  b. Next, your great-aunt wonders how the proteins get out of the cell. Explain the pathway a protein takes from the ribosome to the blood. You can use an illustration if you like.

_____

_____

_____

_____

_____

3. You are a xenobiologist studying an alien cell isolated on Mars. Surprisingly, you notice that the cell contains some of the same substances as our cells. You quantify the concentration of these substances and determine that the cell contains 10% glucose and 0.3% calcium. The cell is placed in a solution containing 20% glucose and 0.1% calcium. The plasma membrane of this cell is is very different from ours. It is permeable to glucose but not to calcium. That is, only glucose can cross the plasma membrane without using transporters. Use this information to answer the following questions:

  a. Will glucose move into the cell or out of the cell? Which transport mechanism will be involved?

_____

_____

  b. Carrier proteins are present in the membrane that can transport calcium. If calcium moves down its concentration gradient, will calcium move into the cell or out of the cell? Which transport mechanism will be involved?

_____

_____

c. You place the cell in a new solution to study the process of osmosis. You know that sodium does not move across the alien cell membrane. You also know that the concentration of the intracellular fluid is equivalent to 1% sodium. The new solution contains 2% sodium.
   (i) Is the 2% sodium solution hypertonic, isotonic, or hypotonic? _____
   (ii) Will water flow into the cell or out of the cell? _____
   (iii) What will be the effect of the water movement on the cell? _____

Expanding Your Horizons

Trees can be dated by counting the rings. Is it possible to tell the age of a cell? The answer is a qualified "yes." It is usually possible to estimate the number of divisions a cell has undergone. The DNA region at the end of chromosomes (the telomere) shortens every time a cell undergoes mitosis. Older cells thus have shorter telomeres. When telomeres become very short, the cell stops dividing or dies. Abnormally short telomeres result in premature aging of skin and other tissues. Some cells have a special enzyme (telomerase) that restores the telomeres, making the cells essentially immortal. Perhaps this enzyme can be inserted into human heart and skin cells—a true fountain of youth. You can read about telomeres and their importance in cell aging and cancer in the following article:

Resources

1. Strauss E. Counting the lives of a cell. *Sci Am* 2000; 11:50–55.

CHAPTER 4

Tissues, Glands, and Membranes

Overview

The cell is the basic unit of life. Individual cells are grouped according to function into **tissues**. The four main groups of tissues include **epithelial tissue**, which forms glands, covers surfaces, and lines cavities; **connective tissue**, which gives support and form to the body; **muscle tissue**, which produces movement; and **nervous tissue**, which conducts nerve impulses.

Glands produce substances used by other cells and tissues. **Exocrine glands** produce secretions that are released through ducts to nearby parts of the body. **Endocrine glands** produce hormones that are carried by the blood to all parts of the body.

The simplest combination of tissues is a **membrane**. Membranes serve several purposes, a few of which are mentioned here: they may serve as dividing partitions, line hollow organs and cavities, and anchor various organs. Membranes that have epithelial cells on the surface are referred to as **epithelial membranes**. Two types of epithelial membranes are **serous membranes**, which line body cavities and cover the internal organs, and **mucous membranes**, which line passageways leading to the outside.

Connective tissue membranes cover or enclose organs, providing protection and support. These membranes include the fascia around muscles, the meninges around the brain and spinal cord, and the tissues around the heart, bones, and cartilage.

The study of tissues—**histology**—requires much memorization. In particular, you may be challenged to learn the different types of epithelial and connective tissue as well as the classification scheme of epithelial and connective membranes. Learning the structure of these different tissues and membranes will help you understand the amazing properties of the body—how we can jump from great heights, swim without becoming waterlogged, and fold our ears over without breaking them.

Addressing the Learning Outcomes

1. Name the four main groups of tissues and give the location and general characteristics of each.

EXERCISE 4-1: Three Types of Epithelium (Text Fig. 4-1)

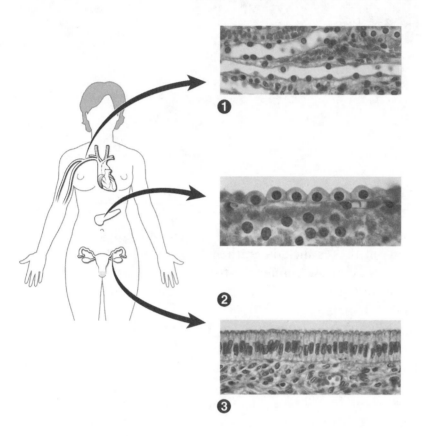

INSTRUCTIONS

Label each of the following types of epithelium.

1. _____
2. _____
3. _____

EXERCISE 4-2: Muscle Tissue (Text Fig. 4-7)

INSTRUCTIONS

Write the names of the three types of muscle tissue in the appropriate blanks in different colors. Color some of the muscle cells with the corresponding color. Look for the nuclei, and color them a different color.

1. _____
2. _____
3. _____

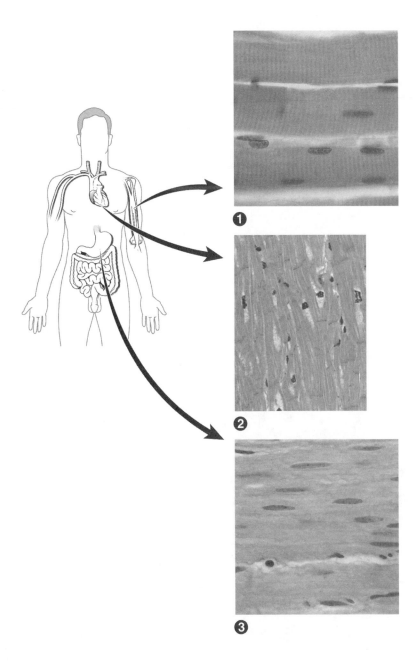

EXERCISE 4-3: Nervous Tissue (Text Fig. 4-8)

INSTRUCTIONS

1. Write the names of each tissue (indicating the plane of the section where appropriate) in boxes 7 to 9.
2. Label each of the following neural structures and tissues using different colors. Where possible, color each structure or tissue with the corresponding color.

1. _____
2. _____
3. _____
4. _____
5. _____
6. _____

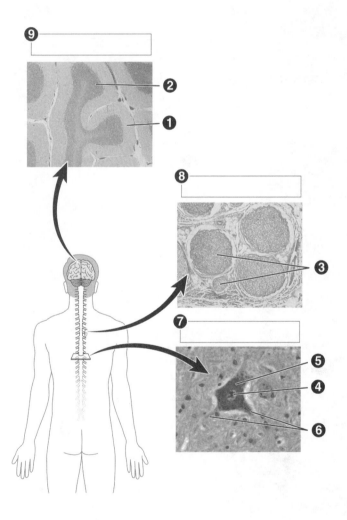

EXERCISE 4-4.

INSTRUCTIONS

Write the appropriate term in each blank.

tissue   squamous   stratified   transitional
columnar   simple   cuboidal

1. A group of cells similar in structure and function   _____
2. Term that describes flat, irregular epithelial cells   _____
3. A term that means *in layers*   _____
4. Term that describes long and narrow epithelial cells   _____
5. Term that describes square epithelial cells   _____
6. Cells arranged in a single layer   _____

EXERCISE 4-5.

INSTRUCTIONS

Write the appropriate term in each blank.

bone   myocardium   voluntary muscle   epithelial tissue
neuron   smooth muscle   neuroglia   connective tissue

1. The tissue that makes up the thigh muscle   _____
2. Tissue that forms when cartilage gradually becomes impregnated
   with calcium salts   _____
3. The thick, muscular layer of the heart wall   _____
4. A type of tissue found in membranes and glands   _____
5. Another name for visceral muscle   _____
6. A cell that carries nerve impulses is called a(n)   _____
7. A tissue in which cells are separated by large amounts of acellular
   material called matrix   _____

2. Describe the difference between exocrine and endocrine glands and give examples of each.

EXERCISE 4-6.

INSTRUCTIONS

Do each of the following characteristics apply to exocrine glands (EX), endocrine glands (EN), or both (B)? Write the appropriate abbreviation in each blank.

1. A gland that secretes into the blood   _____
2. A gland that secretes through ducts   _____
3. A gland that secretes onto the body surface   _____
4. The pituitary gland, for example   _____
5. A group of cells that produces substances for use by other parts
   of the body   _____
6. Salivary glands, for example   _____

3. Give examples of circulating, generalized, and structural connective tissues.

EXERCISE 4-7: Connective Tissue (Text Figs. 4-5 and 4-6)

INSTRUCTIONS

Write the names of the six examples of connective tissue in the appropriate blanks. Use red for the circulating connective tissue (1), three different shades of green for the generalized tissues (2 to 4), and two shades of blue for the structural tissues (5 to 6). Color some of the **cells** of each tissue type with the corresponding color.

1. _____

2. _____

3. _____

4. _____

5. _____

6. _____

EXERCISE 4-8.

INSTRUCTIONS

Write the appropriate term in each blank.

ligament   tendon   collagen   chondrocyte
capsule   fibrocartilage   hyaline cartilage elastic cartilage

1. A cord of connective tissue that connects a muscle to a bone   _____
2. A tough membranous connective tissue that encloses an organ   _____
3. The cartilage found between the bones of the spine   _____
4. A fiber found in most connective tissues   _____
5. A cell that synthesizes cartilage   _____
6. A strong, gristly cartilage that makes up the trachea   _____

4. Describe three types of epithelial membranes.

EXERCISE 4-9.

INSTRUCTIONS

Write the appropriate term in each blank.

mesothelium   serous membrane   cutaneous membrane   parietal layer
visceral layer mucous membrane   peritoneum   serous pericardium

1. An epithelial membrane that lines a body cavity or covers an
   internal organ   _____
2. The epithelial membrane also known as the skin   _____
3. A membrane that lines a space open to the outside of the body   _____
4. The portion of a serous membrane attached to an organ   _____
5. The portion of a serous membrane attached to the body wall   _____
6. The epithelial portion of serous membranes   _____
7. The serous membrane covering the heart   _____

5. List several types of connective tissue membranes.

Exercise 4-10.

INSTRUCTIONS

Write the appropriate term in each blank.

periosteum   fibrous pericardium   perichondrium   epithelial membrane
synovial membrane   superficial fascia   deep fascia   connective tissue membrane

1. The sheet of tissue that underlies the skin   _____
2. The connective tissue membrane that lines joint cavities   _____
3. A tough membrane composed entirely of connective tissue that
   serves to anchor and support an organ or to cover a muscle   _____
4. A layer of fibrous connective tissue around a bone   _____
5. The membrane that covers cartilage   _____

6. A general term describing a membrane composed of epithelial
and connective tissue   _____

7. A general term describing a membrane composed exclusively
of connective tissue   _____

6. Show how word parts are used to build words related to tissues, glands, and membranes.

EXERCISE 4-11.

INSTRUCTIONS

Complete the following table by writing the correct word part or meaning in the space provided.
Write a word that contains each word part in the Example column.

Word Part	Meaning	Example
1. _____	cartilage	_____
2. _____	on, upon	_____
3. oste/o-	_____	_____
4. _____	heart	_____
5. osse/o	_____	_____
6. -blast	_____	_____
7. peri-	_____	_____
8. _____	muscle	_____
9. _____	false	_____
10. hist/o	_____	_____
11. neur/o-	_____	_____
12. _____	side, rib	_____

Making the Connections

The following concept map deals with the classification of tissues. Complete the concept map by filling in the appropriate word or phrase that classifies or describes the tissue.

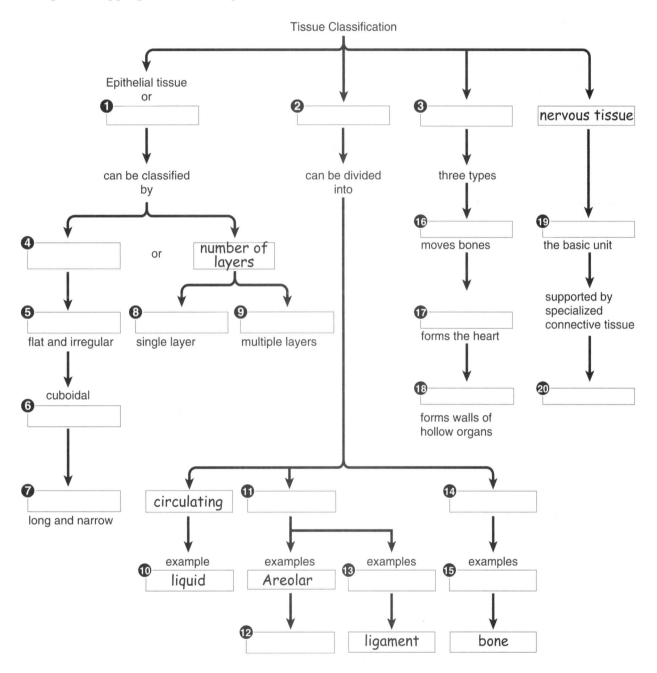

Optional Exercise: Assemble your own concept map summarizing the classification of membranes. Use the following terms: membrane, epithelial tissue membrane, connective tissue membrane, serous, mucous, cutaneous, peritoneum, pleurae, serous pericardium, parietal layer, visceral layer, meninges, fascia, deep, superficial, fibrous pericardium, periosteum, and perichondrium. You could also provide some examples of the different membranes, as shown in the concept map provided.

Testing Your Knowledge

Building Understanding

I. Multiple Choice

Select the best answer and write the letter of your choice in the blank.

1. Which of the following is a type of connective tissue?   1. _____
   a. transitional
   b. squamous
   c. cuboidal
   d. areolar

2. The phrase *stratified cuboidal epithelium* describes: 2. _____
   a. flat, irregular epithelial cells in a single layer
   b. square epithelial cells in many layers
   c. long, narrow epithelial cells in a single layer
   d. flat, irregular epithelial cells in many layers

3. The only type of muscle that is under voluntary control is: 3. _____
   a. smooth
   b. skeletal
   c. cardiac
   d. visceral

4. The proper scientific name for a nerve cell is: 4. _____
   a. neuroglia
   b. nevus
   c. neuron
   d. axon

5. Mucus is secreted from: 5. _____
   a. endocrine glands
   b. goblet cells
   c. areolar tissue
   d. tendons

6. Cartilage is produced by: 6. _____
   a. chondrocytes
   b. fibroblasts
   c. osteoblasts
   d. osteocytes

7. An example of structural connective tissue is: 7. _____
   a. an organ capsule
   b. adipose
   c. tendon
   d. bone

8. The tough connective tissue membrane that covers most parts of all
   bones is the: 8. _____
   a. perichondrium
   b. periosteum
   c. fascia
   d. ligament

II. *Completion Exercise*

Write the word or phrase that correctly completes each sentence.

1. The secretion that traps dust and other inhaled foreign particles is _____
2. Cells that form bone are called _____
3. The cartilage found at the end of long bones is called _____
4. The axons of some neurons have an insulating coating called _____
5. The study of tissues is called _____
6. The epithelial membrane that lines the walls of the abdominal cavity is called the _____
7. A mucous membrane can also be called the _____
8. A lubricant that reduces friction between the ends of bones is produced by a(n) _____
9. The microscopic, hairlike projections found in the cells lining most of the respiratory tract are called _____

Understanding Concepts

I. *True/False*

For each question, write *T* for true or *F* for false in the blank to the left of each number. If a statement is false, correct it by replacing the underlined term and write the correct statement in the blank below the question.

_____ 1. The mouth is lined by a type of epithelial membrane called a serous membrane.

_____

_____ 2. The heart is an example of skeletal muscle.

_____

_____ 3. The strip of tissue connecting the kneecap to the thigh muscle is an example of a tendon.

_____

_____ 4. Inflammation of the large abdominal serous membrane is pleuritis.

_____

_____ 5. The pituitary gland releases prolactin into the bloodstream. The pituitary gland is thus an exocrine gland.

_____

_____ 6. The visceral layer of the peritoneum is in contact with the stomach.

_____

_____ 7. You have identified a new gland in the neck. This gland is connected to the mouth by a duct. Your new gland is an example of an <u>exocrine</u> gland.

_____

II. Practical Applications

You are working as a sports therapist for a wrestling team. At a particularly brutal competition, you are asked to evaluate a number of injuries.

1. Mr. K suffered a crushing injury to the lower leg yesterday in a sumo wrestling match when his opponent fell on him. Initially, he had little pain. Now, he complains of numbness and pain in the foot and leg. This type of injury is made worse by the tight, fibrous covering of the muscles, known as the _____.

2. Mr. K is also complaining of pain in the knee. You suspect an injury to the membrane that lines the joint cavity, a membrane called the _____.

3. You note that Mr. K has a significant amount of fat. Fat is contained in a type of connective tissue called _____.

4. Ms. J suffered a bloody nose in her wrestling match. Blood is a liquid form of the tissue classified as _____.

5. Ms. J also suffered a painful bump on her ankle in the same match. The swelling involved the superficial tissues and the fibrous covering of the bone, or the _____.

6. Mr. S was involved in a closely fought match when his opponent bent his ear back. Thankfully, the cartilage in his ear was able to spring back into shape. This kind of cartilage is called _____.

7. Later, Mr. S suffered a penetrating wound to his abdomen when his opponent accidentally threw him into the seating area. You fear that the wound may have penetrated the membrane that lines his abdomen, called the _____.

8. The wrestling coach comes over to talk to you during a break in the match. He has a question about his favorite shampoo. The advertisement stated that it contained collagen. He asks you which cells in the body synthesize collagen. These cells are _____.

III. Short Essays

1. Compare and contrast epithelial tissue membranes, and give an example of each. List at least one similarity and one difference in your answer.

_____

_____

_____

_____

2. Differentiate between epithelial tissue, connective tissue, and muscle in terms of the amount and composition of the extracellular matrix.

_____

_____

_____

_____

Conceptual Thinking

1. Why is bone considered to be connective tissue? Define connective tissue in your answer.

   _____

   _____

   _____

2. Which tissue, epithelial or connective, would be best suited to the following functions?
   a. cushioning the kidneys against a blow
   b. creating a virtually waterproof barrier between the body and the environment
   c. preventing toxins from entering the blood from the gastrointestinal tract

   _____

   _____

   _____

Expanding Your Horizons

Text Box 4-1 talks about some of the possibilities and ethical dilemmas surrounding stem cell use. Although stem cells have enormous potential, the technical and political difficulties involved sometimes seem insurmountable. Indeed, it has proved difficult to find true stem cells that can differentiate into any cell type. Many alleged stem cell lines can only produce certain types of cells. Much research remains to be done regarding techniques to identify stem cells and the factors that cause differentiation into different cell types (say, a liver cell or a skin cell). You can learn more about the politics, difficulties, and potential of stem cell research in the following article.

Resources

1. Lanza R, Rosenthal N. The Stem Cell Challenge. *Sci Am* 2004; 290:92–100.

CHAPTER 5
The Integumentary System

Overview

Because of its various properties, the skin can be classified as a membrane, an organ, or a system. The outermost layer of the skin is the **epidermis**. Beneath the epidermis is the **dermis** (the true skin), where glands and other accessory structures are mainly located. The **subcutaneous tissue** underlies the skin. It contains fat that serves as insulation. The accessory structures of the skin are the **sudoriferous** (sweat) **glands**, the oil-secreting **sebaceous glands**, **hair**, and **nails**.

The skin protects deeper tissues against drying and against invasion by harmful organisms. It regulates body temperature through evaporation of sweat and loss of heat at the surface. It collects information from the environment by means of sensory receptors.

The protein **keratin** in the epidermis thickens and protects the skin and makes up hair and nails. **Melanin** is the main pigment that gives the skin its color. It functions to filter out harmful ultraviolet radiation from the sun. Skin color is also influenced by the hemoglobin concentration and quantity of blood circulating in the surface blood vessels.

This chapter does not contain any particularly difficult material. However, you must be familiar with the different tissue types discussed in Chapter 4 in order to understand the structure and function of the integument.

Addressing the Learning Outcomes

1. Name and describe the layers of the skin.

EXERCISE 5-1.

INSTRUCTIONS

Write the appropriate term in each blank.

melanocyte   integument   keratin   dermis   epidermis
stratum corneum   dermal papillae   stratum basale   subcutaneous tissue

1. A pigment-producing cell that becomes more active in the
   presence of ultraviolet light   _____
2. The protein in the epidermis that thickens and protects the skin   _____
3. The true skin, or corium   _____
4. The uppermost layer of skin, consisting of flat, keratin-filled cells   _____
5. Another name for the skin as a whole   _____
6. Portions of the dermis that extend into the epidermis   _____
7. The deepest layer of the epidermis, which contains living,
   dividing cells   _____

2. Describe the subcutaneous tissue.

EXERCISE 5-2.

INSTRUCTIONS

Match the structures in the list below with their functions.

adipose tissue   elastic fibers   blood vessels   nerves

1. Connect the subcutaneous tissue with the dermis   _____
2. Insulates the body and acts as an energy reserve   _____
3. Carry sensory information from the skin to the brain   _____
4. Supply skin with nutrients and oxygen   _____

3. Give the location and function of the accessory structures of the skin.

EXERCISE 5-3.

INSTRUCTIONS

Write the appropriate term in each blank.

apocrine   eccrine   ceruminous   ciliary   sudoriferous
sebaceous   sebum   wax   vernix caseosa

1. A general term for any gland that produces sweat   _____
2. Sweat glands found throughout the skin that help cool the body _____
3. Glands that are found only in the ear canal   _____
4. Excess activity of these glands contributes to acne vulgaris   _____
5. The product of ceruminous glands   _____
6. Sweat glands in the armpits and groin that become active at puberty _____
7. Glands that are only found on the eyelids   _____

EXERCISE 5-4: The Skin (Text Fig. 5-1)

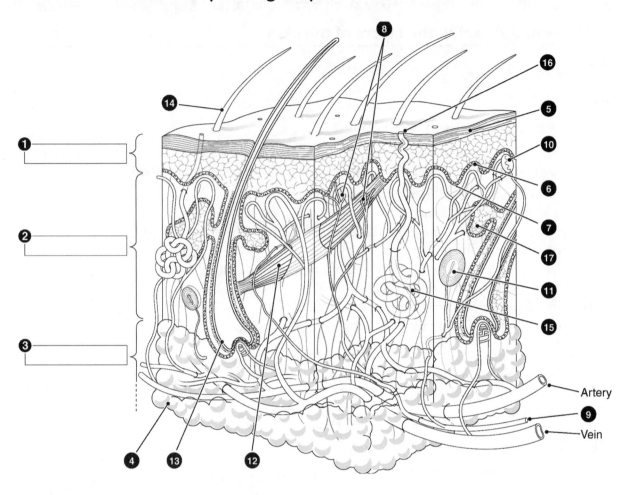

INSTRUCTIONS

1. Write the names of the three skin layers in the numbered boxes 1 to 3.
2. Write the name of each labeled part on the numbered lines in different colors. Use a light color for structures 4 and 12. Use the same color for structures 15 and 16, for structures 13 and 14, and for structures 8 and 9.
3. Color the different structures on the diagram with the corresponding color. Try to color every structure in the figure with the appropriate color. For instance, structure number 8 is found in three locations.

4. _____   11. _____

5. _____   12. _____

6. _____   13. _____

7. _____   14. _____

8. _____   15. _____

9. _____   16. _____

10. _____   17. _____

4. List the main functions of the skin.

EXERCISE 5-5.

INSTRUCTIONS

Fill in the numbered blanks of the table below.

Function	Structures Involved
(1)	Stratum corneum, shedding skin cells
Protection against dehydration	(2)
Regulation of body temperature	(3)
(4)	Nerve endings, specialized receptors

5. Discuss the factors that contribute to skin color.

EXERCISE 5-6.

INSTRUCTIONS

Write the appropriate term in each blank below.

carotene   hemoglobin   albinism   melanin

1. A disorder characterized by a lack of pigment in the hair,
   skin and eyes.   _____
2. A yellowish pigment stored in fatty tissue and skin.   _____
3. The pigment that gives blood its color.   _____

6. Show how word parts are used to build words related to the skin.

EXERCISE 5-7.

INSTRUCTIONS

Complete the following table by writing the correct word part or meaning in the space provided. Write a word that contains each word part in the Example column.

Word Part	Meaning	Example
1. sub-	_____	_____
2. _____	dark, black	_____
3. _____	white	_____
4. hair	_____	_____
5. dermat/o-	_____	_____
6. _____	horny	_____
7. ap/o-	_____	_____

Making the Connections

The following concept map deals with the structural features of the skin. Complete the concept map by filling in the appropriate word or phrase that describes the indicated skin structure.

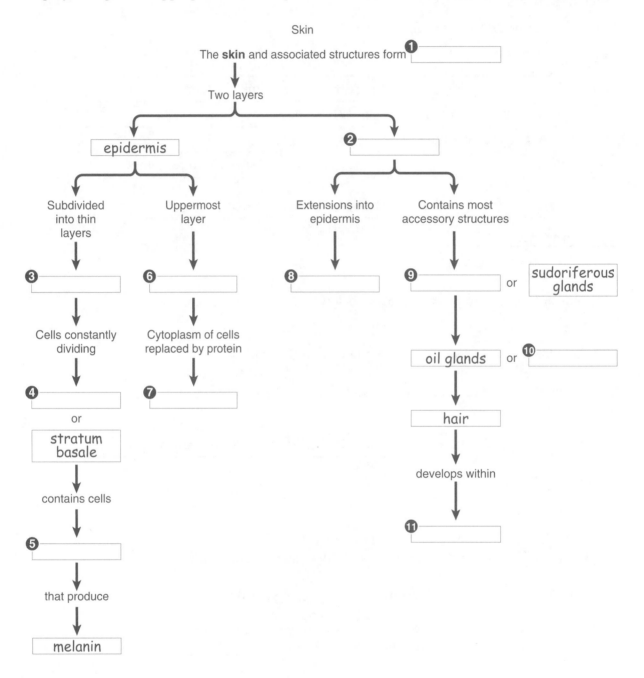

Testing Your Knowledge

Building Understanding

I. Multiple Choice

Select the best answer and write the letter of your choice in the blank.

1. New epidermal cells are produced by the
   a. dermis
   b. stratum corneum
   c. stratum basale
   d. subcutaneous layer

   1. _____

2. Which of the following glands is NOT a modified sweat gland?
   a. mammary gland
   b. sebaceous gland
   c. ceruminous gland
   d. ciliary gland

   2. _____

3. Blood vessels are made smaller in order to decrease blood flow. This decrease in size is called
   a. dilation
   b. constriction
   c. closure
   d. merger

   3. _____

4. Which of the following is NOT an accessory structure of the skin?
   a. hair
   b. nails
   c. blood vessels
   d. sweat glands

   4. _____

5. A gland that produces ear wax is a
   a. ciliary gland
   b. ceruminous gland
   c. sudoriferous gland
   d. eccrine gland

   5. _____

6. Many babies are born with a cheesy covering known as
   a. keratin
   b. melanin
   c. cerumen
   d. vernix caseosa

   6. _____

II. Completion Exercise

Write the word or phrase that correctly completes each sentence.

1. The outer layer of the epidermis, which contains flat, keratin-filled cells, is called _____.

2. Fingerprints are created by extensions of the dermis into the epidermis. These extensions are _____.

3. The main pigment of the skin is _____.

4. The light-colored, proximal end of a nail that overlies the thicker growing region is _____.

5. The muscle attached to a hair follicle that produces a "goose bump" when it contracts is the _____.

6. The subcutaneous layer is also called the hypodermis or the _____.

7. The ceruminous glands and the ciliary glands are modified forms of _____.

8. Hair and nails are composed mainly of a protein named _____.

Understanding Concepts

I. True/False

For each question, write *T* for true or *F* for false in the blank to the left of each number. If a statement is false, correct it by replacing the <u>underlined</u> term and write the correct statement in the blank below the question.

_____ 1. The nail cuticle, which seals the space between the nail plate and the skin above the nail root, is an extension of the <u>stratum basale</u>.

_____

_____ 2. In cold weather, the blood vessels in the skin <u>constrict</u> in order to conserve heat.

_____

_____ 3. Changes in temperature are detected by <u>Meissner corpuscles</u>.

_____

_____ 4. Sebum is produced by <u>sudoriferous glands</u>.

_____

_____ 5. The <u>stratum corneum</u> is the deepest layer of the epidermis.

_____

II. Practical Applications

Mr. B has experienced a fall in a downhill mountain biking competition. You are a first-aid volunteer at the competition and are the first person to the scene of the accident. Study each discussion. Then write the appropriate word or phrase in the space provided.

1. Mr. B has light scratches on his cheek. The scratches are not bleeding, indicating that they have only penetrated the uppermost layer of the epidermis, known as the _____.
2. A branch tore a long jagged wound in his right arm. This wound has penetrated into the tissue underneath the dermis, known as the superficial fascia or _____.
3. The skin of Mr. B's nose is very brown. The brown color reflects the presence of a pigment called _____.
4. Mr. B has difficulties hearing your questions. You examine his ears, and discover that they are full of ear wax. Ear wax is synthesized by modified sweat glands called _____.
5. You note that Mr. B has a rather strong body odor. Body odor reflects the secretions of glands called _____.
6. Mr. B, like many young men, suffers from acne vulgaris. This skin disease, which is characterized by pimples and blackheads, involves infection of the oil-producing glands of the skin called the _____.

III. Short Essays

1. Compare and contrast eccrine and apocrine sweat (sudoriferous) glands.

   _____

   _____

   _____

2. Describe the role that the skin plays in the regulation of body temperature.

   _____

   _____

   _____

   _____

Conceptual Thinking

1. Describe the location and structure of the different tissue types (epithelial, muscle, nervous, connective) present in the integumentary system.

   _____

   _____

   _____

Expanding Your Horizons

Why did different skin tones evolve? It is often thought that darker pigmentation (more melanin) has evolved to protect humans from skin cancer. However, since skin cancer occurs later in life (usually postreproduction), it cannot exert much evolutionary pressure. The advantages and disadvantages of darker skin tone are discussed in a *Scientific American* article.

Resources

1. Jablonski NG, Chaplin G. Skin deep. *Sci Am* 2002; 287:74–81.

Movement and Support

➤ **Chapter 6**

The Skeleton:
Bones and Joints

➤ **Chapter 7**

The Muscular
System

CHAPTER 6

The Skeleton: Bones and Joints

Overview

The skeletal system protects and supports the body parts and serves as attachment points for the muscles, which furnish the power for movement. The bones also store calcium salts and are the site of blood cell production. The skeletal system includes some 206 bones; the number varies slightly according to age and the individual.

Although bone tissue contains a matrix of nonliving material, bones also contain living cells and have their own systems of blood vessels, lymphatic vessels, and nerves. Bone tissue may be either **spongy** or **compact**. Compact bone is found in the **diaphysis** (shaft) of long bones and in the outer layer of other bones. Spongy bone makes up the **epiphyses** (ends) of long bones and the center of other bones. **Red marrow**, present at the ends of long bones and the center of other bones, manufactures blood cells; **yellow marrow**, which is largely fat, is found in the central (medullary) cavities of the long bones.

Bone tissue is produced by cells called **osteoblasts**, which gradually convert cartilage to bone during development. The mature cells that maintain bone are called **osteocytes**, and the cells that break down (resorb) bone for remodeling and repair are the **osteoclasts**.

A **joint** is the region of union of two or more bones. Joints are classified into three main types on the basis of the material between the connecting bones. In **fibrous joints** the bones are held together by fibrous connective tissue, and in **cartilaginous joints** the bones are joined by cartilage. In **synovial joints**, the material between the bones is synovial fluid, which is secreted by the synovial membrane lining the joint cavity. The bones in synovial joints are connected by ligaments. Synovial joints show the greatest degree of movement, and the six types of synovial joints allow for a variety of movements in different directions.

Addressing the Learning Outcomes

1. List the functions of bones.

EXERCISE 6-1.

INSTRUCTIONS

List 5 functions of bones in the spaces provided.

1. _____

2. _____

3. _____

4. _____

5. _____

2. Describe the structure of a long bone.

EXERCISE 6-2: Structure of a Long Bone (Text Fig. 6-2)

INSTRUCTIONS

1. Write the names of the three parts of a long bone in the numbered boxes 1 to 3.
2. Write the name of each labeled part on the numbered lines in different colors. Use a dark color for structure 5.
3. Color the different structures on the diagram with the corresponding color.

4. _____

5. _____

6. _____

7. _____

8. _____

9. _____

10. _____

11. _____

12. _____

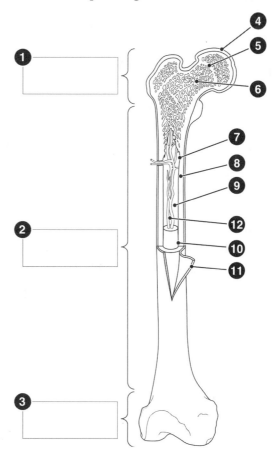

3. Differentiate between compact bone and spongy bone with respect to structure and location.

EXERCISE 6-3.

INSTRUCTIONS

Do the following statements apply to compact bone (C) or spongy bone (S)?

1. Makes up the interior of the epiphyses of long bones _____
2. Makes up the center of short bones_____
3. Makes up the shaft of a long bone _____
4. A meshwork of small, bony plates _____
5. Very hard bone with few spaces _____

4. Differentiate between red and yellow marrow with respect to function and location.

EXERCISE 6-4.

INSTRUCTIONS

Do the following statements apply to red marrow (R) or yellow marrow (Y)?

1. Found in the spaces of spongy bone _____
2. Composed largely of fat ____
3. Site of blood cell synthesis ____
4. Found in the shaft of a long bone ____

EXERCISE 6-5.

INSTRUCTIONS

Write the appropriate term in each blank.

diaphysis	epiphysis	medullary cavity	haversian canal
periosteum	endosteum	spongy bone	osteon

1. The shaft of a long bone   _____
2. The tough connective tissue membrane that covers bones   _____
3. The end of a long bone   _____
4. The type of bone tissue found at the end of long bones   _____
5. The thin membrane that lines the central cavity of long bones   _____
6. The hollow portion of a long bone containing yellow marrow   _____

5. Name the three different types of cells in bone and describe the functions of each.

EXERCISE 6-6.

INSTRUCTIONS

Write the name of the appropriate bone cell in each blank.

osteoblast   osteocyte   osteoclast

1. A cell that resorbs bone matrix   _____
2. A mature bone cell that is completely surrounded by hard bone tissue _____
3. A cell that builds bone tissue   _____

6. Explain how a long bone grows.

EXERCISE 6-7.

INSTRUCTIONS

Label each of the following statements as true (T) or false (F).

1. Long bones grow in length after birth by producing new bone tissue in the middle of the diaphysis. ____
2. Once bone growth is complete, the epiphyseal plate turns into the epiphyseal line. ____
3. Long bones elongate by converting cartilage in the bone ends into bone tissue. ____
4. Osteoclasts and osteoblasts stop working once bone growth is complete. ____
5. As a bone lengthens, the medullary cavity becomes larger. ____

7. Name and describe various markings found on bones.

EXERCISE 6-8.

INSTRUCTIONS

Write the appropriate term in each blank.

crest   condyle   head   process
foramen   fossa   sinus   meatus

1. A short channel or passageway   _____
2. An air space found in some skull bones   _____
3. A rounded knoblike end separated by a slender region from the rest of the bone   _____
4. A rounded projection   _____
5. A distinct border or ridge   _____
6. A depression on a bone surface   _____
7. A hole that permits the passage of a vessel or nerve   _____

8. List the bones in the axial skeleton.

EXERCISE 6-9: The Skull (Text Fig. 6-5A)

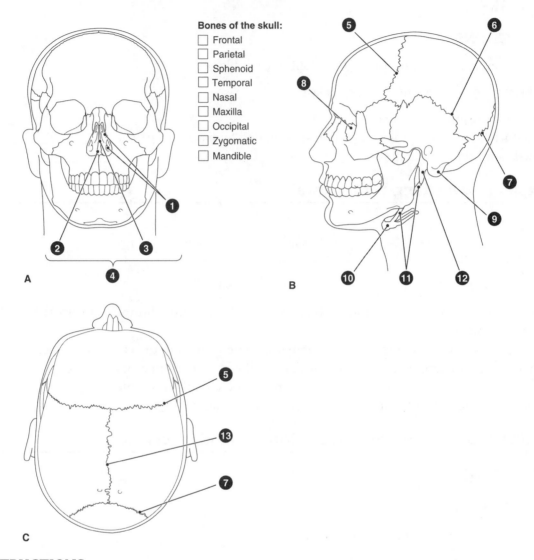

Bones of the skull:
- ☐ Frontal
- ☐ Parietal
- ☐ Sphenoid
- ☐ Temporal
- ☐ Nasal
- ☐ Maxilla
- ☐ Occipital
- ☐ Zygomatic
- ☐ Mandible

INSTRUCTIONS

1. Color the boxes next to the names of the skull bones in different, light colors.
2. Color the skull bones in parts A, B, and C of the diagram with the corresponding color.
3. Label each of the following numbered bones and bone features. If you wish, you can use different dark colors to write the names and color or outline the corresponding part for all structures except structures 4, 9, and 12.

1. _____   8. _____

2. _____   9. _____

3. _____   10. _____

4. _____   11. _____

5. _____   12. _____

6. _____   13. _____

7. _____

EXERCISE 6-10: The Skull: Inferior, Superior, and Sagittal Views (Text Figs. 6-6, 6-7, and 6-8)

Bones of the skull:

☐ Frontal ☐ Occipital
☐ Parietal ☐ Zygomatic
☐ Temporal ☐ Mandible
☐ Sphenoid ☐ Maxilla

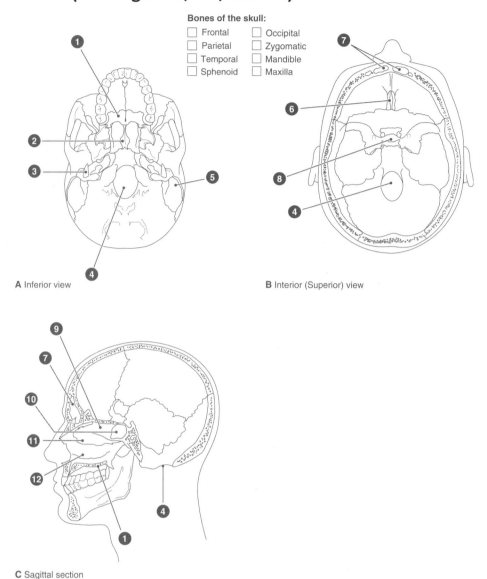

A Inferior view

B Interior (Superior) view

C Sagittal section

INSTRUCTIONS

1. Use the same colors you used in Exercise 6-9 to color the boxes next to the skull bone names.
2. Color the skull bones in parts A, B, and C of the diagram with the corresponding color.
3. Label each of the following numbered bones and bone features. If you wish, you can use different colors to write the name and color the corresponding part for all structures except structures 3, 5, and 8.

1. _____
2. _____
3. _____
4. _____
5. _____
6. _____

7. _____
8. _____
9. _____
10. _____
11. _____
12. _____

EXERCISE 6-11: Bones of the Thorax Anterior View (Text Fig. 6-14)

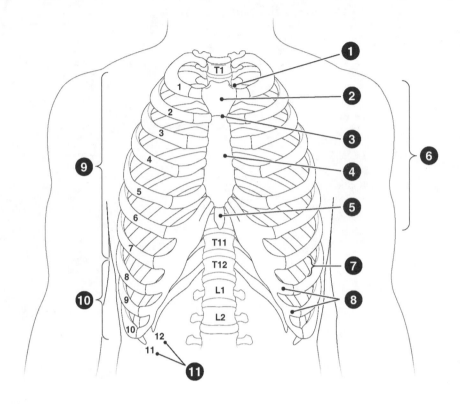

INSTRUCTIONS

1. Write the name of each labeled part on the numbered lines in different colors. Structures 1, 3, 6, 7 will not be colored, so write their names in black.
2. Color the different structures on the diagram with the corresponding color.

1. _____
2. _____
3. _____
4. _____
5. _____
6. _____
7. _____
8. _____
9. _____
10. _____
11. _____

EXERCISE 6-12: Vertebral Column Lateral View (Text Fig. 6-10)

INSTRUCTIONS

1. Color each of the following bones the indicated color.
   a. cervical vertebrae—blue
   b. thoracic vertebrae—red
   c. lumbar vertebrae—green
   d. sacrum—yellow
   e. coccyx—violet
2. Label each of the indicated bones and bone parts.

1. _____
2. _____
3. _____
4. _____
5. _____
6. _____
7. _____

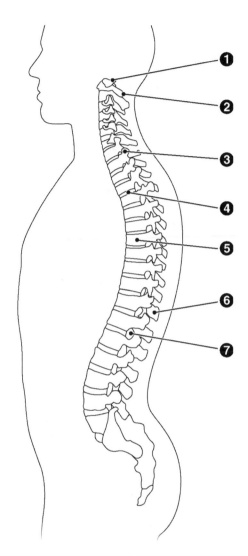

EXERCISE 6-13: Vertebral Column Anterior View (Text Fig. 6-11)

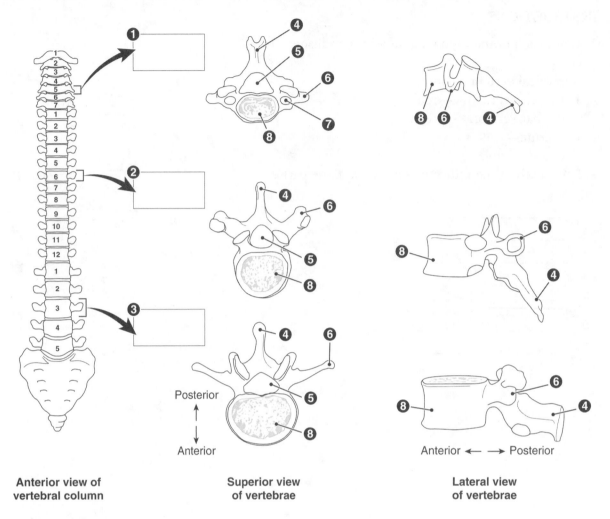

Anterior view of
vertebral column

Superior view
of vertebrae

Lateral view
of vertebrae

INSTRUCTIONS

1. Write the names of the three vertebral divisions in the numbered boxes 1 to 3.
2. Write the name of each labeled part on the numbered lines in different colors.
3. Color the different structures on the diagram with the corresponding color.

4. _____

5. _____

6. _____

7. _____

8. _____

EXERCISE 6-14.

INSTRUCTIONS

Write the appropriate term in each blank.

parietal	temporal	frontal	hyoid	nasal
maxilla	mandible	sphenoid bone	zygomatic bone	occipital

1. The only movable bone of the skull   _____
2. A bone of the upper jaw   _____
3. The U-shaped bone lying just below the mandible   _____
4. The bone that articulates with the parietal and temporal bones
   and forms the posterior inferior part of the cranium   _____
5. The bone that forms the forehead   _____
6. One of two slender bones that form the bridge of the nose   _____
7. One of two large bones that articulate with the frontal bone and
   form the superior lateral portions of the cranium   _____
8. The anatomical name for the cheekbone   _____

9. Explain the purpose of the infant fontanels.

EXERCISE 6-15.

INSTRUCTIONS

Write the appropriate term in each blank.

floating ribs	true ribs	fontanel	costal
xiphoid process	manubrium	clavicular notch	foramina

1. The T-shaped, superior portion of the sternum   _____
2. The portion of the sternum that is made of cartilage in children   _____
3. An adjective that refers to the ribs   _____
4. A soft spot in the infant skull that later closes   _____
5. The last two pairs of ribs, which are very short and do not
   extend to the front of the body   _____
6. The point of articulation between the sternum and the collarbone   _____
7. Ribs that attach to the sternum by individual cartilagenous
   extensions   _____

10. Describe the normal curves of the spine and explain their purpose.

EXERCISE 6-16.

INSTRUCTIONS

Write the appropriate term in each blank.

cervical region   thoracic region   lumbar region   coccyx
thoracic curve   lumbar curve   cervical curve

1. A primary curve of the spine   _____
2. The second part of the vertebral column, made up of 12 vertebrae   _____
3. The spinal curve that appears when the infant holds her head up   _____
4. The spinal curve that appears when the infant begins to walk   _____
5. The most caudal part of the vertebral column   _____
6. The region of the spine that contains the largest, strongest vertebrae _____
7. The region of the vertebral column made up of the first seven
   vertebrae   _____

11. List the bones in the appendicular skeleton.

EXERCISE 6-17: The Skeleton (Text Fig. 6-1)

INSTRUCTIONS

1. Write the name of each labeled part on the numbered lines in different colors. Use the same color for structures 24 and 25 and for structures 19 and 20.
2. Color the different structures on the diagram with the corresponding color. Try to color every structure in the figure with the appropriate color. For instance, structure number 3 is found in two locations.

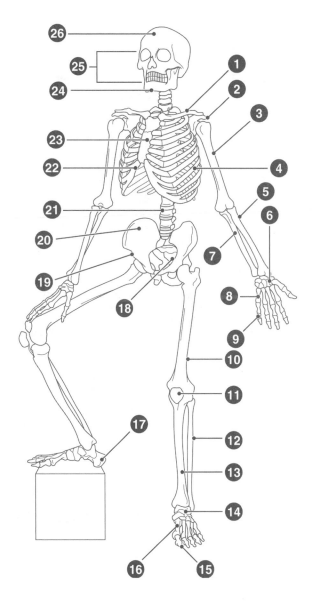

1. _____
2. _____
3. _____
4. _____
5. _____
6. _____
7. _____
8. _____
9. _____
10. _____
11. _____
12. _____
13. _____
14. _____
15. _____
16. _____
17. _____
18. _____
19. _____
20. _____
21. _____
22. _____
23. _____
24. _____
25. _____
26. _____

EXERCISE 6-18: Bones of the Shoulder Girdle (Text Fig. 6-15)

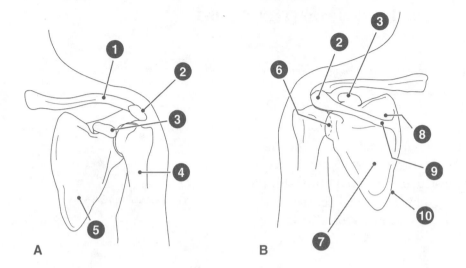

A   B

INSTRUCTIONS

1. Write the name of each labeled part on the numbered lines in different colors. Structures 1, 3, 6, 7 will not be colored, so write their names in black.
2. Color the different structures on the diagram with the corresponding color.

1. _____   6. _____
2. _____   7. _____
3. _____   8. _____
4. _____   9. _____
5. _____   10. _____

EXERCISE 6-19: Left Elbow Lateral View (Text Fig. 6-19)

INSTRUCTIONS

Label each of the indicated parts. The identity of parts 7 and 8 can be found in Fig. 6-17.

1. _____
2. _____
3. _____
4. _____
5. _____
6. _____
7. _____
8. _____

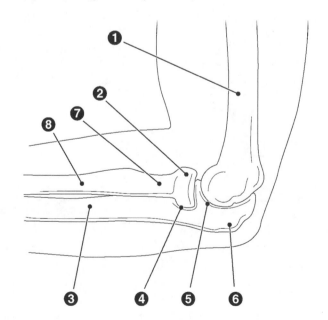

EXERCISE 6-20: Pelvic Bones (Text Fig. 6-21)

☐ Ilium   ☐ Pubis   ☐ Ischium

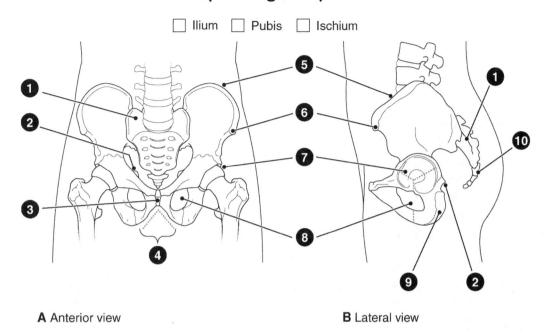

A Anterior view   **B** Lateral view

INSTRUCTIONS

1. Color the boxes next to the names of the pelvic bones in different, light colors.
2. Color the pelvic bones in parts A and B of the diagram with the corresponding color.
3. Label each of the following numbered bones and bone features. If you wish, you can use different dark colors to write the names and color or outline the corresponding part for structures 1, 3, 8, and 10.

1. _____
2. _____
3. _____
4. _____
5. _____

6. _____
7. _____
8. _____
9. _____
10. _____

EXERCISE 6-21.

INSTRUCTIONS

Write the appropriate term in each blank.

olecranon   carpal bones   clavicle   ulna   radius
metacarpal bones   phalanges   scapula   humerus

1. The anatomical name for the collarbone   _____
2. The five bones in the palm of the hand   _____
3. The medial forearm bone (in the anatomical position)   _____
4. The upper part of the ulna, which forms the point of the elbow   _____
5. The 14 small bones that form the framework of the fingers on
   each hand   _____
6. The bone located on the thumb side of the forearm   _____
7. The bone containing the supraspinous and infraspinous fossae   _____

EXERCISE 6-22.

INSTRUCTIONS

Write the appropriate term in each blank.

greater trochanter   patella   tibia   calcaneus   pubis
fibula   ilium   ischium   acetabulum

1. The deep socket in the hip bone that holds the head of the femur   _____
2. The most inferior bone in the pelvis   _____
3. The lateral bone of the leg   _____
4. A bone that is wider and more flared in females   _____
5. The scientific name for the kneecap   _____
6. The largest of the tarsal bones; the heel bone   _____
7. The large, rounded projection at the upper and lateral portion
   of the femur   _____

12. Compare the structure of the female pelvis and the male pelvis.

EXERCISE 6-23.

INSTRUCTIONS

Write "male" or "female" in the spaces below to make each statement true.

1. The pelvic outlet is narrower in the _____ than in the _____.
2. The angle of the pubic arch is broader in the _____ than in the _____.
3. The sacrum and coccyx are shorter and less curved in the _____ than in the _____.
4. The ilia are narrower in the _____ than in the _____.

13. Describe how the skeleton changes with age.

EXERCISE 6-24.

INSTRUCTIONS

Write the appropriate term in each blank, from the following list: protein, intervertebral discs, collagen, calcium, intercostal cartilages.

In older adults, bones are weaker because of a loss in _____ (1) salts and a general decline in the manufacture of _____ (2). Height may be reduced because the _____ (3) become thinner. The chest may become smaller because the _____ (4) become calcified and less flexible. The reduction in levels of the protein _____ (5) in tendons and ligaments makes movement more difficult.

14. Describe the three types of joints.

EXERCISE 6-25.

INSTRUCTIONS

Write the most appropriate term in each blank. Each term will be used once.

cartilaginous joint   articulation   diarthrosis   synarthrosis
fibrous joint   synovial joint   amphiarthrosis

1. The region of union of two or more bones; a joint   _____
2. A slightly moveable joint, defined by its function   _____
3. A freely moveable joint, defined by its function   _____
4. An immovable joint, defined by its function   _____
5. A joint held together by fibrous connective tissue   _____
6. A joint held together by cartilage   _____
7. A joint in which there is a fluid-filled space between the bones   _____

15. Describe the structure of a synovial joint and give six examples of synovial joints.

EXERCISE 6-26: The Knee Joint (Text Fig. 6-27)

INSTRUCTIONS

1. Write the name of each labeled part on the numbered lines in different colors. Use a dark color for part 7, which can be outlined.
2. Color the different structures on the diagram with the corresponding color. Try to color every structure in the figure with the appropriate color. For instance, structure number 2 is found in two locations.

1. _____
2. _____
3. _____
4. _____
5. _____
6. _____
7. _____
8. _____
9. _____
10. _____
11. _____
12. _____
13. _____

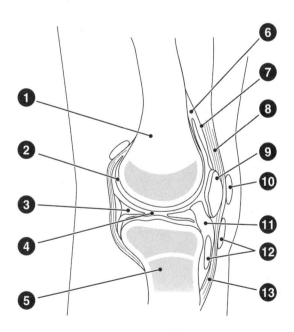

EXERCISE 6-27: Types of Synovial Joints (Text Table 6-3)

INSTRUCTIONS

Label each of the different types of synovial joints.

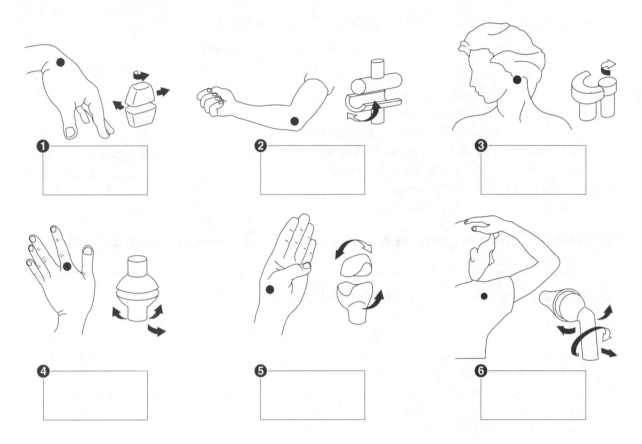

16. Demonstrate six types of movement that occur at synovial joints.

EXERCISE 6-28: Movements at Synovial Joints (Text Fig. 6-28)

INSTRUCTIONS

Label each of the illustrated motions with the correct term for that movement.

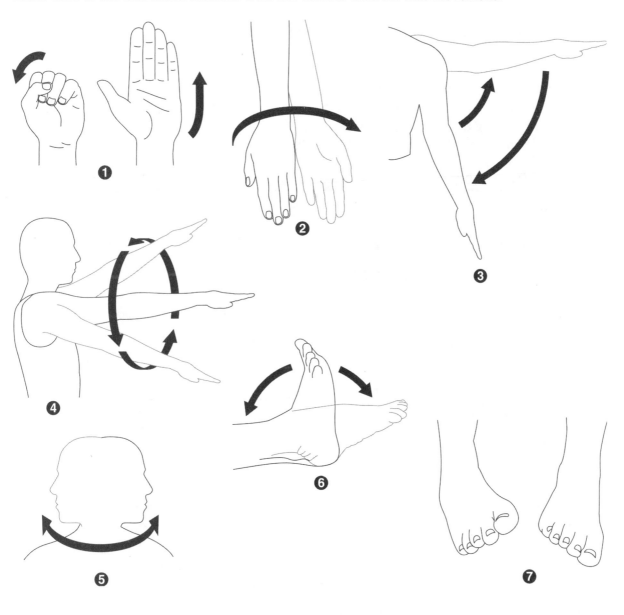

1. _____

2. _____

3. _____

4. _____

5. _____

6. _____

7. _____

EXERCISE 6-29.

INSTRUCTIONS

Write the appropriate term in each blank.

flexion   rotation   abduction   extension   adduction
supination   circumduction   dorsiflexion   plantar flexion

1. A movement that increases the angle between two bones   _____
2. Movement away from the midline of the body   _____
3. Motion around a central axis   _____
4. A bending motion that decreases the angle between two parts   _____
5. Movement toward the midline of the body   _____
6. The act of turning the palm up or forward   _____
7. The act of pointing the toes downward   _____

17. Show how word parts are used to build words related to the skeleton.

EXERCISE 6-30.

INSTRUCTIONS

Complete the following table by writing the correct word part or meaning in the space provided. Write a word that contains each word part in the Example column.

Word Part	Meaning	Example
1. _____	near, beyond	_____
2. -clast	_____	_____
3. _____	rib	_____
4. amphi-	_____	_____
5. arthr/o	_____	_____
6. _____	away from	_____
7. _____	around	_____
8. _____	toward, added to	_____
9. dia-	_____	_____
10. pariet/o	_____	_____

Making the Connections

The following concept map deals with bone structure. Complete the concept map by filling in the appropriate term or phrase that describes the indicated structure or process.

Bone Structure and Organization

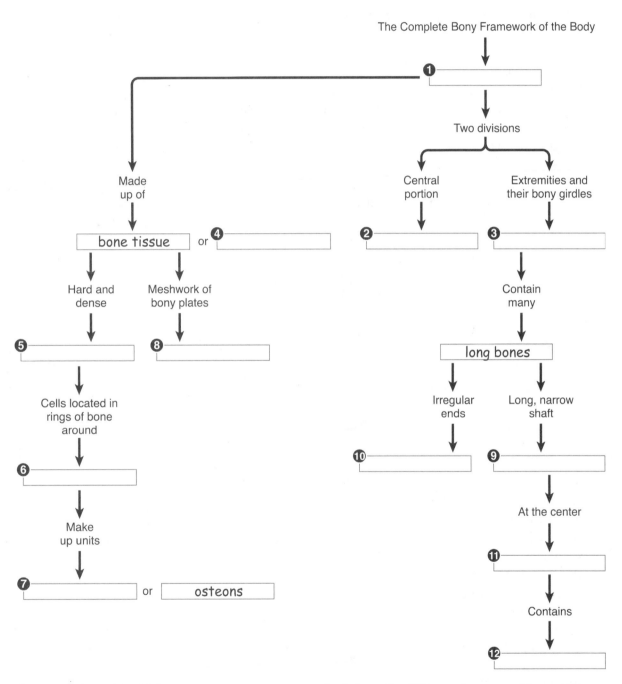

Optional Exercise: Make your own concept map, based on the different bone markings. Choose your own terms to incorporate into your map or use the following list: bone markings, projections, depressions, head, process, condyle, crest, spine, foramen, sinus, fossa, meatus, sella turcica, mastoid sinus, foramen magnum, acromion, intervertebral foramina, supraspinous fossa, and scapula spine. Try to find an example of each bone marking.

Testing Your Knowledge

Building Understanding

I. Multiple Choice

Select the best answer and write the letter of your choice in the blank.

1. The bone cells that synthesize new bone matrix are called   1. _____
   a. osteoblasts
   b. osteocytes
   c. osteoclasts
   d. osteons

2. A suture is an example of an immovable joint also called a(n)   2. _____
   a. synovial joint
   b. diarthrosis
   c. synarthrosis
   d. amphiarthrosis

3. Which of the following is a projection?   3. _____
   a. process
   b. fossa
   c. foramen
   d. sinus

4. The back of the hard palate is formed by the   4. _____
   a. vomer bone
   b. palatine bones
   c. hyoid bone
   d. mandible

5. The os coxae is a fused bone consisting of the ilium, ischium, and   5. _____
   a. femur
   b. acetabulum
   c. sacrum
   d. pubis

6. The patella is the largest of a type of bone that develops within a
   tendon or a joint capsule. It is described as   6. _____
   a. sesamoid
   b. axial
   c. tarsal
   d. symphysis

7. The shoulder girdle consists of the the clavicle and the   7. _____
   a. sternum
   b. tibia
   c. scapula
   d. os coxae

8. Ribs that individually attach to the sternum are called the   8. _____
   a. false ribs
   b. floating ribs
   c. xiphoid ribs
   d. true ribs

9. The foramen magnum is   9. _____
   a. a large hole in a hip bone near the symphysis pubis
   b. the curved rim along the top of the hip bone
   c. a hole between vertebrae that allows for passage of a spinal nerve
   d. a large opening at the base of the skull through which the spinal
       cord passes
10. Which of the following is an example of a cartilaginous joint?   10. _____
   a. condyloid
   b. pivot
   c. saddle
   d. pubic symphysis

II. Completion Exercise

Write the word or phrase that correctly completes each sentence.

1. The first cervical vertebra is called the _____.
2. The bat-shaped bone that extends behind the eyes and also forms part of the base of the skull
   is called the _____.
3. The bone located between the eyes that extends into the nasal cavity, eye sockets, and cranial floor is called the _____.
4. The hard bone matrix is composed mainly of salts of the element _____.
5. The part of the skull that encloses the brain is the _____.
6. A joint between bones of the skull is a(n) _____.
7. Pivot, hinge, and gliding joints are examples of freely movable joints, also called
   _____.
8. Swimming the overhead crawl requires a broad circular movement at the shoulder that is a
   combination of simpler movements. This combined motion is called _____.
9. When you bend your foot upward to walk on your heels, the position of the foot is technically called _____.
10. In the embryo, most of the developing bones are made of _____.
11. The type of bone tissue that makes up the shaft of a long bone is called _____.
12. The skull, vertebrae, ribs, and sternum make up the division of the skeleton called the
    _____.

Understanding Concepts

I. True/False

For each question, write *T* for true or *F* for false in the blank to the left of each number. If a statement is false, correct it by replacing the underlined term and write the correct statement in the
blank below the question.

_____   1. The shaft of a long bone contains underlined yellow marrow.

_____

_____   2. The ethmoid bone is in the axial skeleton.

_____

_____ 3. Moving a bone toward the midline is <u>abduction</u>.

_____

_____ 4. The second cervical vertebra is called the <u>axis</u>.

_____

_____ 5. Increasing the angle at a joint is <u>extension</u>.

_____

_____ 6. There are <u>six</u> pairs of false ribs.

_____

_____ 7. A mature bone cell is an <u>osteocyte</u>.

_____

_____ 8. <u>Immovable</u> joints are called synovial joints.

_____

_____ 9. The ends of a long bone are composed mainly of <u>spongy</u> bone.

_____

_____ 10. The medial malleolus is found at the distal end of the <u>fibula</u>.

_____

II. Practical Applications

Ms. M, aged 67, suffered a serious fall at a recent bowling tournament. As a physician assistant trainee, you are responsible for her preliminary evaluation.

1. Her right forearm is bent at a peculiar angle. You suspect a fracture to the radius or to the _____.

2. The arm x-ray also reveals a number of fractures in the wrist bones, which are also called the _____.

3. Ms. M also reports pain in the hip region. The hip joint consists of the femur and a deep socket called the _____.

4. An x-ray reveals a crack in the "sitting bones" that support the weight of the trunk when sitting. This bone is called the _____.

5. The physician prescribes a new medication designed to increase the activity of cells that synthesize new bone tissue. These cells are called _____.

III. *Short Essays*

1. What is the function of the fontanels?

_____
_____
_____

2. Describe the four curves of the adult spine and explain the purpose of these curves.

_____
_____
_____

3. What is the difference between true ribs, false ribs, and floating ribs?

_____
_____
_____

Conceptual Thinking

1. The following questions relate to the knee joint.
    A. Classify the knee joint in terms of the **degree** of movement permitted.

_____

    B. Classify the knee joint based on the **types** of movement permitted.

_____

    C. Classify the knee joint in terms of the material between the adjoining bones.

_____

    D. List the bones that articulate within the capsule of the knee joint.

_____

    E. List the types of movement that can occur at the knee joint.

_____

Expanding Your Horizons

The human skeleton has evolved from that of four-legged animals. Unfortunately, the adaptation is far from perfect; thus, our upright posture causes problems like backache and knee injuries. If you could design the human skeleton from scratch, what would you change? A *Scientific American* article suggests some improvements.

Resources

1. Olshansky JS, Carnes BA, Butler RN. If humans were built to last. Sci Am 2001; 284:50–55.

CHAPTER 7

The Muscular System

Overview

There are three basic types of muscle tissue: skeletal, smooth, and cardiac. This chapter focuses on **skeletal muscle**, which is usually attached to bones. Skeletal muscle is also called **voluntary muscle**, because it is normally under conscious control. The muscular system is composed of more than 650 individual muscles.

Skeletal muscles are activated by electrical impulses from the nervous system. A nerve fiber makes contact with a muscle cell at the **neuromuscular junction**. The neurotransmitter **acetylcholine** transmits the signal from the neuron to the muscle cell by producing an electrical change called the **action potential** in the muscle cell membrane. The action potential causes the release of **calcium** from the endoplasmic reticulum into the muscle cell cytoplasm. Calcium enables two types of intracellular filaments inside the muscle cell, made of **actin** and **myosin**, to contact each other. The myosin filaments pull the actin filaments closer together, resulting in muscle contraction. **ATP** is the direct source of energy for the contraction. To manufacture ATP, the cell must have adequate supplies of **glucose** and **oxygen** delivered by the blood. A reserve supply of glucose is stored in muscle cells in the form of **glycogen**. Additional oxygen is stored by a muscle cell pigment called **myoglobin**.

When muscles do not receive enough oxygen, as during strenuous activity, they can produce a small amount of ATP and continue to function for a short period. As a result, however, the cells produce **lactic acid**, which may contribute to muscle fatigue. A person must then rest and continue to inhale oxygen, which is used to convert the lactic acid into other substances. The amount of oxygen needed for this purpose is referred to as the **oxygen debt**.

Muscles usually work in groups to execute a body movement. The muscle that produces a given movement is called the **prime mover**; the muscle that produces the opposite action is the **antagonist**.

Muscles act with the bones of the skeleton as lever systems, in which the joint is the pivot point or fulcrum. Exercise and proper body mechanics help maintain muscle health and effectiveness. Continued activity delays the undesirable effects of aging.

This chapter contains some challenging concepts, particularly in respect to muscle contractions, and many muscles to memorize. Try to learn the muscle names and actions by using your own body. You should be familiar with the different movements and the anatomy of joints from Chapter 6 before you tackle this chapter.

Addressing the Learning Outcomes

1. Compare the three types of muscle tissue.

EXERCISE 7-1.

INSTRUCTIONS

Write the appropriate term in each blank.

cardiac muscle   skeletal muscle   smooth muscle   fascicle   ligament
endomysium   perimysium   epimysium   tendon

1. A cordlike structure that attaches a muscle to bone
2. A bundle of muscle fibers   _____
3. A connective tissue layer surrounding muscle fiber bundles   _____
4. Muscle under voluntary control   _____
5. The only muscle type that does not have visible striations   _____
6. An involuntary muscle containing intercalated disks   _____
7. The innermost layer of the deep fascia that surrounds the
   entire muscle   _____

EXERCISE 7-2: Structure of a Skeletal Muscle (Text Fig. 7-1)

INSTRUCTIONS

Label each of the indicated parts.

1. _____
2. _____
3. _____
4. _____
5. _____
6. _____
7. _____
8. _____
9. _____

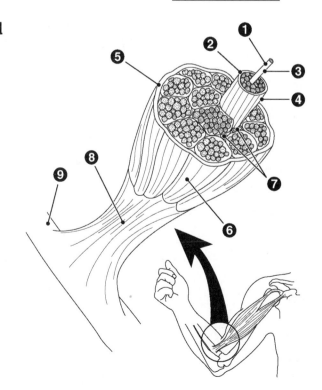

2. Describe three functions of skeletal muscle.

EXERCISE 7-3.

INSTRUCTIONS

List three functions of skeletal muscle in the spaces below.

1. _____
2. _____
3. _____

3. Briefly describe how skeletal muscles contract.

EXERCISE 7-4: Neuromuscular Junction (Text Fig. 7-3)

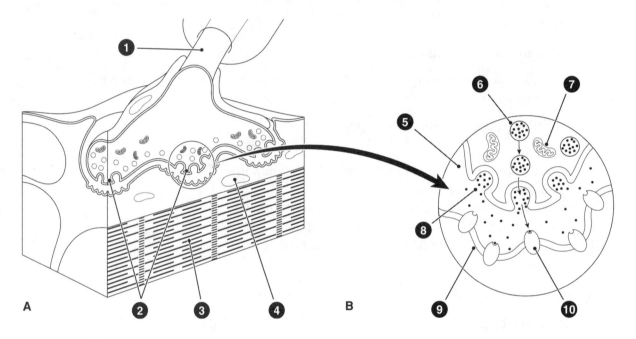

INSTRUCTIONS

Label each of the indicated parts.

1. _____
2. _____
3. _____
4. _____
5. _____
6. _____
7. _____
8. _____
9. _____
10. _____

EXERCISE 7-5.

INSTRUCTIONS

Write the appropriate term in each blank.

synaptic cleft   motor end plate   motor unit   actin
myosin   troponin   sarcomere

1. The protein that makes up muscle's lighter, thin filaments   _____
2. The protein that interacts with actin to form crossbridges   _____
3. The membrane of the muscle cell that binds ACh   _____
4. The space between the neuron and the muscle cell   _____
5. A single neuron and all of the muscle fibers it stimulates   _____
6. A protein that binds calcium during muscle contraction   _____

4. List the substances needed in muscle contraction and describe the function of each.

EXERCISE 7-6.

INSTRUCTIONS

In the blanks, write the name of the substance that is accomplishing each action. Each term may be used more than once.

ATP   calcium   acetylcholine

1. Substance released into the synpatic cleft   _____
2. The immediate source of energy for muscle contraction   _____
3. Binds to troponin when muscle contracts   _____
4. Used to detach the myosin head   _____
5. Pumped back into the smooth ER when muscle relaxes   _____
6. Causes an action potential when it binds the motor end plate   _____

5. Define the term *oxygen debt*.

EXERCISE 7-7.

INSTRUCTIONS

Circle all correct answers. (There are two.)
Oxygen debt:

A. Occurs when muscles are operating aerobically.
B. Occurs when muscles are operating anaerobically.
C. Results from the accumulation of glycogen in working muscles.
D. Is the amount of oxygen required to convert accumulated lactic acid into other substances.

6. Describe three compounds stored in muscle that are needed to generate energy in highly active muscle cells.

EXERCISE 7-8.

INSTRUCTIONS

Write the appropriate term in each blank.

glycogen   creatine phosphate   myoglobin

1. A compound similar to ATP that can be used to generate ATP   _____
2. A polysaccharide that can be used to generate glucose   _____
3. A compound that stores additional oxygen   _____

7. Cite the effects of exercise on muscles.

EXERCISE 7-9.

INSTRUCTIONS

In the blank following each statement, write (T) if it is true and (F) if it is false.

1. Resistance exercise causes muscle hypertrophy.   _____
2. Blood vessels constrict in actively contracting muscles.   _____
3. Weight lifting is the most efficent way to improve endurance.   _____
4. Regular exercise increase the number of capillaries in muscles.   _____
5. Regular exercise decreases the number of mitochondria in muscles.   _____

8. Compare isotonic and isometric contractions (see Exercise 7-10).

9. Explain how muscles work in pairs to produce movement.

EXERCISE 7-10.

INSTRUCTIONS

Write the appropriate term in each blank.

origin   prime mover   antagonist   synergist
isotonic   isometric   insertion

1. A muscle acting as a helper to accomplish a particular movement   _____
2. The muscle attachment joined to a moving part of the body   _____
3. The muscle attachment joined to a more fixed part of the body   _____
4. The muscle that produces a given movement   _____
5. A muscle that relaxes during a given movement   _____
6. A contraction in which the muscle shortens but muscle tension remains the same   _____
7. A contraction in which muscle tension increases but muscle length is unchanged   _____

EXERCISE 7-11: Muscle Attachment to Bones (Text Fig. 7-7)

INSTRUCTIONS

Label each of the indicated parts.

1. _____
2. _____
3. _____
4. _____
5. _____
6. _____
7. _____
8. _____

10. Compare the workings of muscles and bones to lever systems.

EXERCISE 7-12.

INSTRUCTIONS

For each of the following muscle actions, state which class of lever (1st, 2nd, or 3rd) is the most applicable.

1. Nodding the head _____
2. Performing a biceps curl _____
3. Standing on tiptoes _____

11. Explain how muscles are named.

EXERCISE 7-13.

INSTRUCTIONS

For each muscle name, write the characteristic(s) used for the name. Choose between the following 6 options: location, size, shape, direction of fibers, number of heads, action. The number of blanks indicates how many characteristics apply to each muscle. Note that femoris means thigh, brachii means arm, carpii means wrist, teres means long and round.

1. trapezius _____
2. quadriceps femoris _____ _____
3. rectus abdominus _____ _____
4. flexor carpii _____ _____
5. teres minor _____ _____

12. Name some of the major muscles in each muscle group and describe the main function of each.

EXERCISE 7-14: Superficial Muscles: Anterior View (Text Fig. 7-9)

INSTRUCTIONS

1. Write the name of each labeled muscle on the numbered lines in different colors.
2. Color the different muscles on the diagram with the corresponding color.

1. _____
2. _____
3. _____
4. _____
5. _____
6. _____
7. _____
8. _____
9. _____
10. _____
11. _____
12. _____
13. _____
14. _____
15. _____
16. _____
17. _____
18. _____
19. _____
20. _____
21. _____
22. _____
23. _____
24. _____
25. _____

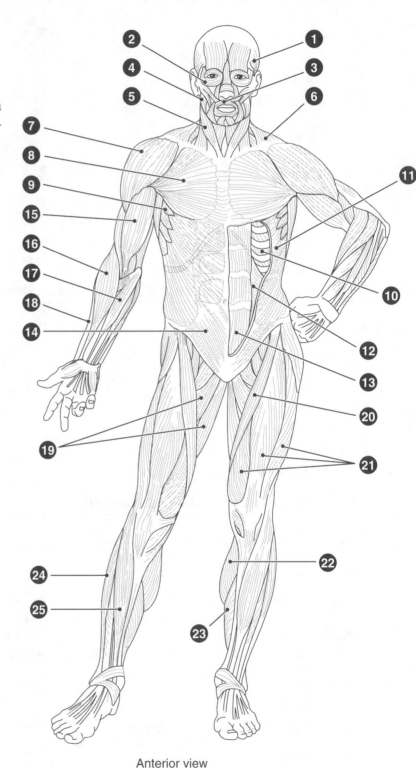

Anterior view

EXERCISE 7-15: Superficial Muscles: Posterior View (Text Fig. 7-10)

INSTRUCTIONS

1. Write the name of each labeled muscle or tendon on the numbered lines in different colors. If possible, use the same color you used for the muscle in Exercise 7-14.
2. Color the different muscles and tendons on the diagram with the corresponding color.

1. _____
2. _____
3. _____
4. _____
5. _____
6. _____
7. _____
8. _____
9. _____
10. _____
11. _____
12. _____
13. _____
14. _____
15. _____
16. _____
17. _____
18. _____
19. _____
20. _____

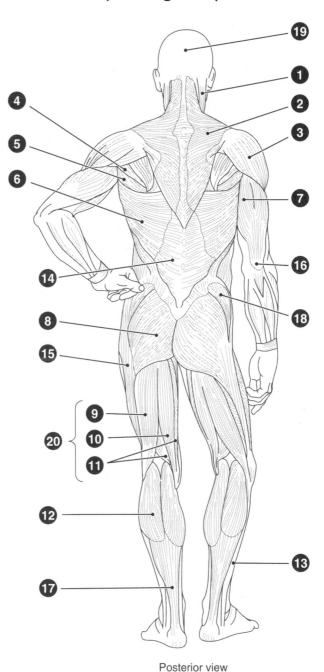

Posterior view

EXERCISE 7-16: Muscles of the Head (Text Fig. 7-11)

INSTRUCTIONS

1. Write the name of each labeled muscle or tendon on the numbered lines in different colors. If possible, use the same color you used for the muscle in Exercises 7-14 and 7-15.
2. Color the different muscles and tendons on the diagram with the corresponding color.

1. _____
2. _____
3. _____
4. _____
5. _____
6. _____
7. _____
8. _____
9. _____
10. _____
11. _____
12. _____
13. _____
14. _____
15. _____
16. _____

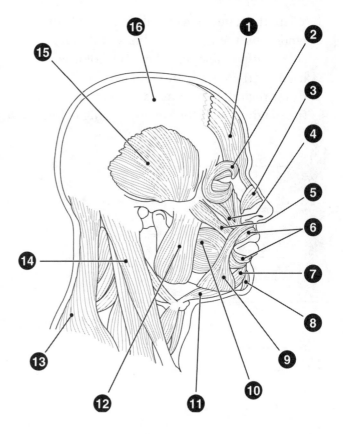

EXERCISE 7-17: Muscles of the Thigh: Anterior View (Text Fig. 7-16A)

INSTRUCTIONS

1. Write the name of each labeled muscle, tendon, or bone on the numbered lines in different colors. If possible, use the same color you used for the muscle in Exercise 7-14.
2. Color the different structures on the diagram with the corresponding color.

1. _____
2. _____
3. _____
4. _____
5. _____
6. _____
7. _____
8. _____
9. _____
10. _____
11. _____

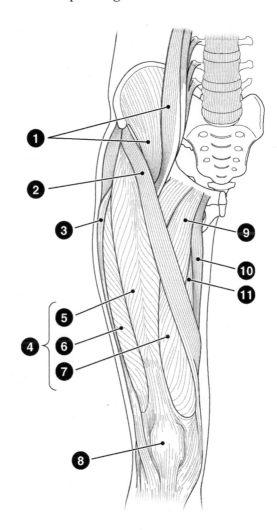

EXERCISE 7-18.

INSTRUCTIONS

Write the appropriate term in each blank.

sternocleidomastoid   buccinator   masseter   trapezius   orbicularis oris
deltoid   rotator cuff   latissimus dorsi   orbicularis oculi   brachialis

1. The muscle capping the shoulder and upper arm   _____
2. A deep muscle group that supports the shoulder joint   _____
3. A muscle that closes the eye   _____
4. The muscle that makes up the fleshy part of the cheek   _____
5. A muscle that closes the jaw   _____
6. A muscle on the side of the neck that flexes the head   _____
7. The main flexor of the forearm   _____
8. A triangular muscle on the back of the neck and the upper back
   that extends the head   _____

EXERCISE 7-19.

INSTRUCTIONS

Write the appropriate term in each blank.

triceps brachii   serratus anterior   brachioradialis   biceps brachii   trapezius
intercostals   levator ani   erector spinae   latissimus dorsi

1. A large muscle of the middle and lower back that inserts in the
   humerus and extends the arm at the shoulder behind the back   _____
2. The muscle in the pelvic floor that aids in defecation   _____
3. A muscle on the front of the arm that flexes the elbow and
   supinates the hand   _____
4. The large muscle on the back of the arm that extends the elbow   _____
5. A chest muscle inferior to the axilla that moves the scapula forward   _____
6. A deep muscle that extends the vertebral column   _____
7. Muscles between the ribs that can enlarge the thoracic cavity   _____

EXERCISE 7-20.

INSTRUCTIONS

Write the appropriate term in each blank.

rectus abdominis   transversus abdominis   gluteus maximus   gluteus medius rectus femoris
iliopsoas   adductor longus   gracilis   biceps femoris

1. Part of the quadriceps femoris muscle   _____
2. The muscle that forms much of the fleshy part of the buttock   _____
3. A deep muscle of the buttock that abducts the thigh   _____
4. A vertical muscle covering the anterior surface of the abdomen   _____
5. A muscle that aids in pressing the thighs together   _____
6. A muscle extending from the pubic bone to the tibia that adducts
   the thigh at the hip   _____
7. A powerful flexor of the thigh that arises from the ilium   _____

EXERCISE 7-21.

INSTRUCTIONS

Write the appropriate term in each blank.

sartorius	gastrocnemius	soleus	peroneus longus
tibialis anterior	quadriceps femoris	semimembranosus	flexor digitorum group

1. The thin muscle that travels down and across the medial surface
   of the thigh   _____
2. The chief muscle of the calf of the leg   _____
3. The muscle that inverts and dorsiflexes the foot   _____
4. Muscles that flex the toes   _____
5. The muscle that everts the foot   _____
6. A deep muscle that plantar flexes the foot at the ankle   _____

13. Describe how muscles change with age.

EXERCISE 7-22.

INSTRUCTIONS

List two changes that occur in aging muscles.

1. _____

2. _____

14. Show how word parts are used to build words related to the muscular system.

EXERCISE 7-23.

INSTRUCTIONS

Complete the following table by writing the correct word part or meaning in the space provided. Write a word that contains each word part in the Example column.

Word Part	Meaning	Example
1. _____	muscle	_____
2. brachi/o	_____	_____
3. _____	nutrition, nurture	_____
4. erg/o	_____	_____
5. metr/o	_____	_____
6. _____	four	_____
7. _____	tone, tension	_____
8. _____	flesh	_____
9. vas/o	_____	_____
10. iso-	_____	_____

Making the Connections

The following concept map deals with substances and structures required for muscle contraction. Each pair of terms is linked together by a connecting phrase into a sentence. The sentence should be read in the direction of the arrow. Complete the concept map by filling in the appropriate term or phrase. There is one right answer for each term. However, there are many correct answers for the connecting phrases.

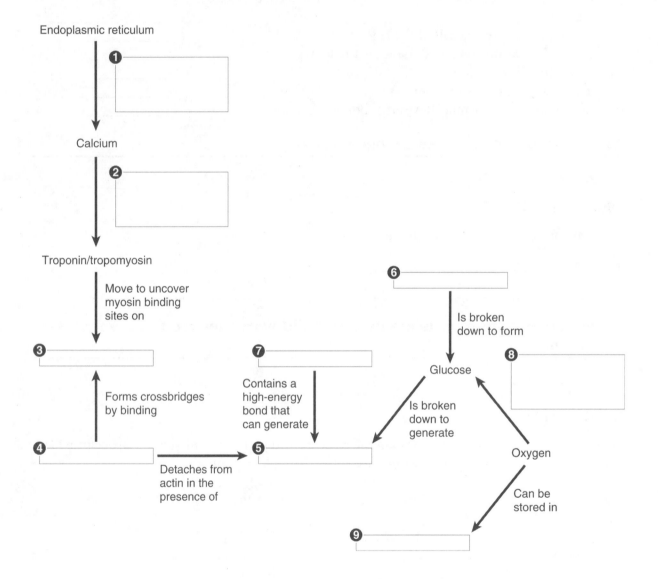

Optional Exercise: Make your own concept map, based on the events of muscle contraction. Choose your own terms to incorporate into your map or use the following list: neuron, acetylcholine, neuromuscular junction, snaptic cleft, motor end plate, myosin, actin, endoplasmic reticulum, calcium, sarcomere, troponin/tropomyosin, and ATP.

Testing Your Knowledge

Building Understanding

I. Multiple Choice

Select the best answer and write the letter of your choice in the blank.

1. Which of the following statements is NOT true of skeletal muscle?   1. _____
   a. The cells are long and threadlike.
   b. It is involuntary.
   c. It is described as striated.
   d. The cells are multinucleated.

2. When muscles and bones act together in the body as a lever system,
   the pivot point or fulcrum of the system is the   2. _____
   a. joint
   b. tendon
   c. ligament
   d. myoglobin

3. The quadriceps muscles act to   3. _____
   a. flex the thigh
   b. extend the leg
   c. adduct the leg
   d. abduct the thigh

4. Which of the following is NOT a muscle of the hamstring group?   4. _____
   a. biceps femoris
   b. rectus femoris
   c. semimembranosus
   d. semitendinosus

5. The connective tissue layer around individual muscle fibers is called the   5. _____
   a. epimysium
   b. perimysium
   c. superficial fascia
   d. endomysium

6. During muscle contraction, ATP binds to   6. _____
   a. tropomyosin
   b. myosin
   c. actin
   d. troponin

II. Completion Exercise

Write the word or phrase that correctly completes each sentence.

1. Normally, muscles are in a partially contracted state, even when not in use. This state of mild constant tension is called _____.
2. The hemoglobin-like compound that stores oxygen in muscle is _____.
3. The muscle attachment that is usually relatively fixed is called its _____.
4. A contraction that generates tension but does not shorten the muscle is called _____.
5. The band of connective tissue that attaches the gastrocnemius muscle to the heel is the _____.
6. The muscles of the pelvic floor together form the _____.
7. A muscle that must relax during a given movement is called the _____.
8. The ion that binds tropinin/tropomyosin is _____.
9. The muscular partition between the thoracic and abdominal cavities is the _____.
10. A superficial muscle of the neck and upper back acts at the shoulder. This muscle is the _____.
11. The large muscle of the upper chest that flexes the arm across the body is the _____.
12. The muscle responsible for dorsiflexion and inversion of the foot is the _____.

Understanding Concepts

I. True/False

For each question, write *T* for true or *F* for false in the blank to the left of each number. If a statement is false, correct it by replacing the <u>underlined</u> term and write the correct statement in the blank below the question.

_____ 1. The triceps brachii <u>flexes</u> the arm at the elbow.

_____

_____ 2. Muscles enter into oxygen debt when they are functioning <u>anaerobically</u>.

_____

_____ 3. In an <u>isometric</u> contraction, muscle tension increases but the muscle does not shorten.

_____

_____ 4. The neurotransmitter used at the neuromuscular junction is <u>norepinephrine</u>.

_____

_____ 5. A contracting subunit of skeletal muscle is called a(n) <u>crossbridge</u>.

_____

_____ 6. The storage form of glucose is called <u>creatine phosphate</u>.

_____

_____ 7. The element that binds to the troponin and tropomyosin complex is <u>calcium</u>.

_____

II. Practical Applications

Study each discussion. Then write the appropriate word or phrase in the space provided.

➤ Group A

Ms. J is sitting at her desk studying for her anatomy final exam.

1. She has excellent posture, with her back straight. The deep back muscle responsible for her erect posture is the _____.
2. Despite her excellent posture, Ms. J has developed a muscle spasm that has fixed her head in a flexed, rotated position. This condition is called wryneck, or _____.
3. Ms. J has a cheerful disposition, and she likes to whistle while she works. The cheek muscle involved in whistling is the _____.
4. Ms. J is furiously writing notes, and her hand is flexed around the pen. The muscle groups that flex the hand are called the _____.
5. After several hours of intense studying, Ms. J takes a break. Stretching, she straightens her leg at the knee joint. The muscle that accomplishes this action is the _____.

➤ Group B

Mr. L, age 72, is a retired concert pianist.

1. He reports numbness and weakness in his right hand. He can no longer flex and extend his fingers rapidly enough to play Rachmaninoff. The muscles that extend his fingers are the

    _____.
2. Mr. L also experiences pain when he sits. He has lost muscle mass in the muscle forming the fleshy part of the buttock, known as the _____.
3. The healthcare worker recommends that he undertakes a regular exercise program, incorporating stretching, aerobic exercise, and resistance training. This type of varied program is called interval training, or _____.
4. Mr. L asks if the resistance training will give him bigger muscles. He is told that his muscle cells may increase in size, a change called _____.

III. Short Essays

1. Mr. Q has embarked on an exercise program based solely on jogging. Name three distinct changes that will occur in his muscles.

   _____

   _____

   _____

2. Ms. L has suffered an embarrassing (but relatively painless) fall. Mr. L is staring at her with his mouth open. Ms. L asks him to activate two muscles to close his jaw. Name these two muscles.

   _____

   _____

   _____

Conceptual Thinking

1. Ms. S is competing in an endurance event at the Olympics. She is consuming a special herbal product that reputedly degrades lactic acid in the absence of oxygen. Explain the potential benefit of this product, discussing the production and effects of lactic acid.

   _____

   _____

   _____

2. While attending the ballet, you notice a dancer raising her heel to stand on her tiptoes.
   A. What is the name of this action (i.e., adduction)? _____
   B. What is the prime mover for this action? _____
   C. Name a synergistic muscle involved in this action. _____
   D. Name an antagonist muscle involved. _____
   E. Which class of lever is represented by this action? _____
   F. Name the fulcrum and resistance, and describe the relative positions of the fulcrum, resistance, and effort.

   _____

   _____

   _____

Expanding Your Horizons

Are world-class athletes born or made? It is no coincidence that athletic performance tends to run in families. Genetic influences on muscular function are discussed in an article in *Scientific American*. This information could be used to screen for elite athletes—perhaps children of the future will know which sports they can excel in based on their genetic profile. This possibility is discussed in a special *Scientific American* issue entitled "Building the Elite Athlete."

Resources

1. Andersen JL, Schjerling P, Saltin B. Muscle, genes and athletic performance. *Sci Am* 2000; 283:48–55.
2. Olshansky JS, Carnes BA, Butler RN. If humans were built to last. *Sci Am* 2001; 284:50–55.
3. Taubes G. Toward Molecular Talent Scouting. Scientific American Presents: Building the Elite Athlete 2000; 11:26–31.

UNIT III

Coordination and Control

➤ **Chapter 8**

The Nervous System: The Spinal Cord and Spinal Nerves

➤ **Chapter 9**

The Nervous System: The Brain and Cranial Nerves

➤ **Chapter 10**

The Sensory System

➤ **Chapter 11**

The Endocrine System: Glands and Hormones

CHAPTER 8

The Nervous System: The Spinal Cord and Spinal Nerves

Overview

The nervous system is the body's coordinating system—receiving, sorting, and controlling responses to both internal and external changes (stimuli). The nervous system as a whole is divided structurally into the **central nervous system** (**CNS**), made up of the brain and the spinal cord, and the **peripheral nervous system** (**PNS**), made up of the cranial and spinal nerves. The PNS connects all parts of the body with the CNS. The brain and cranial nerves are the subject of Chapter 10. Functionally, the nervous system is divided into the somatic (voluntary) system and the autonomic (involuntary) system.

The nervous system functions by means of the **nerve impulse**, an electrical current or **action potential** that spreads along the membrane of the **neuron** (nerve cell). Each neuron is composed of a cell body and fibers, which are threadlike extensions from the cell body. A **dendrite** is a fiber that carries impulses toward the cell body, and an **axon** is a fiber that carries impulses away from the cell body. Some axons are covered with a sheath of fatty material called **myelin**, which insulates the fiber and speeds conduction along the fiber. In the PNS, neuron fibers are collected in bundles to form **nerves**. Bundles of fibers in the CNS are called **tracts**. Nerve cells make contact at a junction called a **synapse**. Here, a nerve impulse travels across a very narrow cleft between the cells by means of a chemical referred to as a **neurotransmitter**. Neurotransmitters are released from axons of presynaptic cells to be picked up by receptors in the membranes of responding cells, the postsynaptic cells.

A neuron may be classified as either a sensory (afferent) type, which carries impulses toward the central nervous system, or a motor (efferent) type, which carries impulses away from the central nervous system. **Interneurons** are connecting neurons within the central nervous system.

The basic functional pathway of the nervous system is the **reflex arc**, in which an impulse travels from a receptor, along a sensory neuron to a synapse or synapses in the central nervous system, and then along a motor neuron to an effector organ that carries out a response. The spinal cord carries impulses to and from the brain. It is also a center for simple reflex activities in which responses are coordinated within the cord.

The **autonomic nervous system** controls unconscious activities. This system regulates the actions of glands, smooth muscle, and the heart muscle. The autonomic nervous system has two divisions, the **sympathetic nervous system** and the **parasympathetic nervous system**, which generally have opposite effects on a given organ.

Addressing the Learning Outcomes

1. Describe the organization of the nervous system according to structure and function.

EXERCISE 8-1: Anatomic Divisions of the Nervous System (Text Fig. 8-1)

INSTRUCTIONS

Label the parts and divisions of the nervous system shown below.

1. _____
2. _____
3. _____
4. _____
5. _____
6. _____

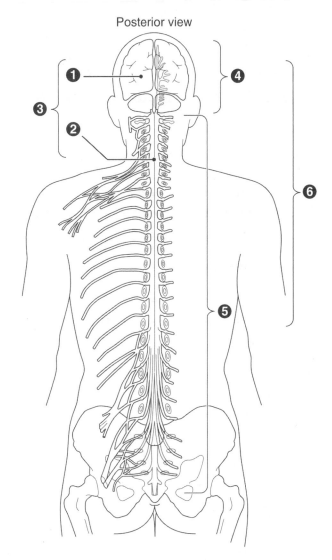

Posterior view

EXERCISE 8-2.

INSTRUCTIONS

Write the appropriate term in each blank.

central nervous system   peripheral nervous system   somatic nervous system
sympathetic nervous system   parasympathetic nervous system   autonomic nervous system

1. The functional division of the nervous system that is also called the visceral nervous system   _____
2. The functional division of the nervous system that controls skeletal muscles   _____
3. The system that promotes the fight-or-flight response   _____
4. The system that stimulates the activity of the digestive tract   _____
5. The structural division of the nervous system that includes the brain   _____
6. The structural division of the nervous system that includes the cranial nerves   _____

2. Describe the structure of a neuron.

EXERCISE 8-3: The Motor Neuron (Text Fig. 8-2)

INSTRUCTIONS

1. Write the name of each labeled part on the numbered lines in different colors. Structures 4 to 6 will not be colored, so write their names in black.
2. Color the different structures on the diagram with the corresponding color.
3. Add large arrows showing the direction the nerve impulse will travel, from the dendrites to the muscle.

1. _____
2. _____
3. _____
4. _____
5. _____
6. _____
7. _____
8. _____

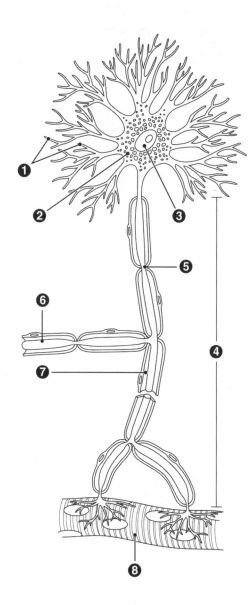

EXERCISE 8-4.

INSTRUCTIONS

Write the appropriate term in each blank.

dendrite	neurilemma	axon
white matter	gray matter	node

1. A nerve cell fiber that carries impulses away from the cell body   _____
2. The part of a neuron that receives a stimulus   _____
3. The sheath around some neuron fibers that aids in regeneration   _____
4. A gap in the neuron sheath   _____
5. The portion of the spinal cord made up of myelinated axons   _____

3. Describe how neuron fibers are built into a nerve.

EXERCISE 8-5.

INSTRUCTIONS

Write the appropriate term in each blank.

afferent neurons	efferent neurons	neuron	tract
endoneurium	perineurium	epineurium	nerve

1. The scientific name for a nerve cell   _____
2. A bundle of neuron fibers located outside the central nervous system   _____
3. A bundle of neuron fibers located within the central nervous system   _____
4. Neurons that conduct impulses towards the brain   _____
5. Neurons that conduct impulses away from the brain   _____
6. The coating of individual nerve fibers   _____
7. The coating of an entire nerve   _____

4. Explain the purpose of neuroglia.

EXERCISE 8-6.

INSTRUCTIONS

List five functions of neuroglia in the spaces below.

1. _____
2. _____
3. _____
4. _____
5. _____

5. Diagram and describe the steps in an action potential.

EXERCISE 8-7.

INSTRUCTIONS

In the space below, draw an action potential tracing as illustrated in Fig. 8-7. On your diagram, indicate which event is occurring (depolarization, repolarization, or resting) and which ion is moving (sodium [Na] or potassium [K], if any.

EXERCISE 8-8.

INSTRUCTIONS

Write the appropriate term in each blank.

depolarization   action potential   repolarization Na^+ K^+
resting

1. The step in which the membrane potential returns to rest   _____
2. The ion that crosses the neuron membrane to cause depolarization   _____
3. The result of positive ions entering the neuron   _____
4. A sudden change in membrane potential that is transmitted
   along axons   _____
5. The ion that leaves the neuron to cause repolarization   _____

6. Briefly describe the transmission of a nerve impulse.

EXERCISE 8-9.

INSTRUCTIONS

Place the following events in the order in which they occur.

A. The action potential opens sodium channels in adjacent portions of the membrane.
B. Sodium entry into the cell causes another action potential in the adjacent portion of the membrane.
C. A stimulus initiates an action potential.
D. Open sodium channels let sodium enter the cell.

1. _____
2. _____
3. _____
4. _____

7. Explain the role of myelin in nerve conduction.

EXERCISE 8-10: Formation of a Myelin Sheath (Text Fig. 8-4)

INSTRUCTIONS

1. Write the name of each labeled part on the numbered lines in different colors. Structures 4 and 7-9 will not be colored, so write their names in black.
2. Color the different structures on the diagram with the corresponding color. Make sure you color the structure in all parts of the diagram. For instance, structure 3 is visible in 3 locations.

1. _____
2. _____
3. _____
4. _____
5. _____
6. _____
7. _____
8. _____
9. _____

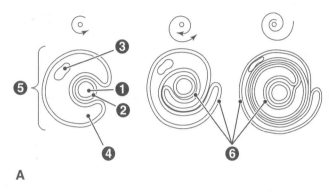

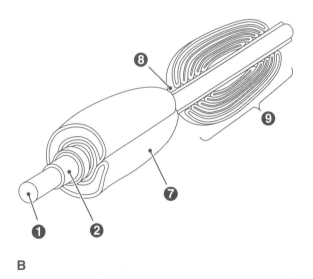

EXERCISE 8-11.

INSTRUCTIONS

Label each of the following statements as true (T) or false (F).

1. Action potentials occur in axon regions surrounded by myelin.   _____
2. Action potential transmission is faster in myelinated neurons.   _____
3. Action potentials occur at nodes.   _____

8. Briefly describe transmission at a synapse.

EXERCISE 8-12: A Synapse
(Text Fig. 8-9)

INSTRUCTIONS

Label the parts of the synapse shown below.

1. _____
2. _____
3. _____
4. _____
5. _____
6. _____
7. _____
8. _____
9. _____
10. _____

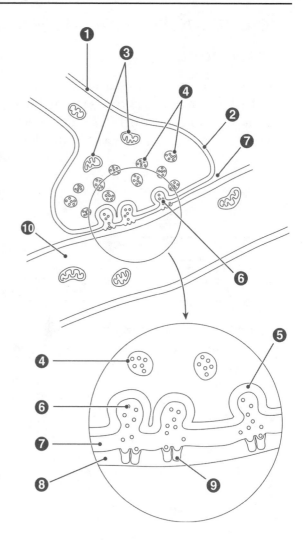

EXERCISE 8-13.

INSTRUCTIONS

Place the following synaptic events in order.

A. Neurotransmitter molecules bind receptors in the postsynaptic membrane.
B. Neurotransmitter molecules are released into the synaptic cleft.
C. The nerve impulse arrives at the end of the presynaptic neuron.
D. Vesicles containing neurotransmitter fuse with the cell membrane.
E. The activity of the postsynaptic cell is altered.

1. ____   4. ____
2. ____   5. ____
3. ____

9. Define *neurotransmitter* and give several examples of neurotransmitters.

EXERCISE 8-14.

INSTRUCTIONS

List three examples of neurotransmitters in the spaces below.

1. _____
2. _____
3. _____

10. Describe the distribution of gray and white matter in the spinal cord.

EXERCISE 8-15: Spinal Cord (Text Fig. 8-12)

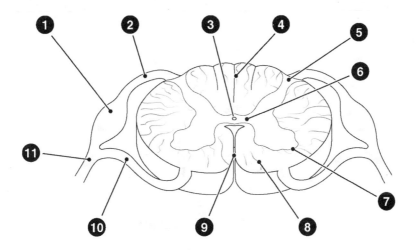

INSTRUCTIONS

1. Write the name of each labeled part on the numbered lines. Use the following color scheme:
   - 1 and 2: red
   - 3, 4, 9: different dark colors
   - 5: pink
   - 6: any light color
   - 7: light bluer
   - 10: medium blue
   - 11: purple
2. Color or outline the different structures on the diagram with the corresponding color.

1. _____
2. _____
3. _____
4. _____
5. _____
6. _____

7. _____
8. _____
9. _____
10. _____
11. _____

11. List the components of a reflex arc.

EXERCISE 8-16: Reflex Arc (Text Fig. 8-13)

INSTRUCTIONS

1. Write the names of the five components of a reflex arc on the numbered lines 1 to 5 in different colors, and color the components with the corresponding color. Follow the color scheme provided below.
2. Write the names of the parts of the spinal cord on numbered lines 6 to 12 in different colors, and color the structures with the appropriate color. Follow the color scheme provided below.

   Color Scheme
   - 1, 2, 6, 7, 8: red
   - 3: green
   - 4, 10: medium blue
   - 5: purple
   - 9: do not color (write name in black)
   - 11: pink
   - 12: light blue

1. _____
2. _____
3. _____
4. _____
5. _____
6. _____
7. _____
8. _____
9. _____
10. _____
11. _____
12. _____

12. Define a simple reflex and give several examples of reflexes.

EXERCISE 8-17.

INSTRUCTIONS

Fill in the blanks in the discussion below using the following terms: patellar reflex, simple reflex, somatic reflexes, and autonomic reflexes.

A _____ (1) describes any rapid automatic response involving very few neurons. Reflexes involving skeletal muscles are called _____ (2); reflexes involving smooth muscle or glands are _____ (3). An example of the former type is the _____ (4), a stretch reflex that involves striking a tendon at the top of the leg.

13. Describe and name the spinal nerves and three of their main plexuses.

EXERCISE 8-18: Spinal Cord (Text Fig. 8-11)

INSTRUCTIONS

1. Label the parts of the central nervous system (structures 1 to 5).
   • Spinal nerves are named based on the site they emerge from the spinal column. Write the names of the nerve groups on the appropriate line (lines 6 to 10).
   • Some of the anterior branches of the spinal nerves interlace to form plexuses. Identify the plexuses (structures 11 to 13).
   • Label the specific nerves (structures 14 to 20).
2. Color or outline the different structures on the diagram with the corresponding color.

1. _____   8. _____   15. _____

2. _____   9. _____   16. _____

3. _____   10. _____   17. _____

4. _____   11. _____   18. _____

5. _____   12. _____   19. _____

6. _____   13. _____   20. _____

7. _____   14. _____

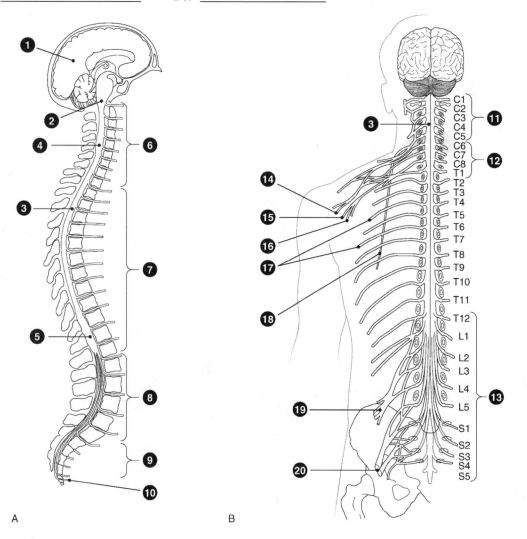

A   B

14. Compare the location and functions of the sympathetic and parasympathetic nervous systems.

EXERCISE 8-19.

INSTRUCTIONS

Do each of the following statements apply to the sympathetic nervous system (S) or the parasympathetic nervous system (P)?

1. Also described as the adrenergic system
2. Also described as the cholinergic system
3. Motor neurons originate in the thoracolumbar region of the spinal cord
4. Motor neurons originate in the craniosacral region of the spinal cord
5. Activation causes the pupils to dilate
6. Activation causes blood vessels in digestive organs to dilate
7. Terminal ganglia located in or near the effector
8. Ganglia located near the spinal cord or in collateral ganglia
9. Activation decreases kidney activity
10. Activation stimulates the sweat glands

15. Explain the role of cellular receptors in the action of neurotransmitters.

EXERCISE 8-20.

INSTRUCTIONS

Write the appropriate term in each blank.

muscarinic receptor   nicotinic receptor   adrenergic receptor

1. binds norepinephrine
2. binds acetylcholine and induces muscle contraction
3. acetylcholine receptor found on effector organs of the parasympathetic system

16. Show how word parts are used to build words related to the nervous system.

EXERCISE 8-21.

INSTRUCTIONS

Complete the following table by writing the correct word part or meaning in the space provided. Write a word that contains each word part in the Example column.

Word Part	Meaning	Example
1. _____	sheath	_____
2. re-	_____	_____
3. soma-	_____	_____
4. _____	nerve, nervous tissue	_____
5. _____	remove	_____
6. aut/o	_____	_____
7. post-	_____	_____

Making the Connections

The following concept map deals with the organization of the nervous system. Each pair of terms is linked together by a connecting phrase into a sentence. The sentence should be read in the direction of the arrow. Complete the concept map by filling in the appropriate term or phrase. There is one right answer for each term. However, there are many correct answers for the connecting phrases (2, 8, 9, and 12).

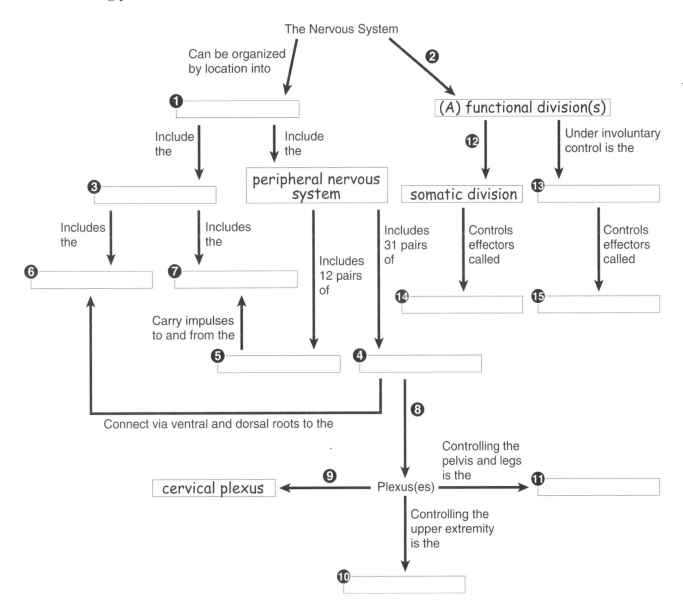

Optional Exercise: Make your own concept map, based on the structures of the spinal cord and the components of a reflex loop. Choose your own terms to incorporate into your map, or use the following list: dorsal root ganglion, gray matter, white matter, ventral root ganglion, afferent fibers, efferent fibers, sensory fibers, motor fibers, receptor, muscle, gland, and effector.

Testing Your Knowledge

Building Understanding

I. Multiple Choice

Select the best answer and write the letter of your choice in the blank.

1. The skin region supplied by a single spinal nerve is called a(n)
   a. dermatome
   b. ganglion
   c. plexus
   d. synapse

   1. _____

2. The voluntary nervous system controls
   a. visceral muscle
   b. skeletal muscle
   c. glands
   d. cardiac muscle

   2. _____

3. Which of the following are effectors of the nervous system?
   a. sensory neurons and ganglia
   b. muscles and glands
   c. synapses and dendrites
   d. receptors and neurotransmitters

   3. _____

4. Cell bodies of sensory neurons are collected in ganglia in the
   a. dorsal root of the spinal nerve
   b. sympathetic chain
   c. ventral horn of the spinal cord
   d. effector organ

   4. _____

5. Which of the following substances is a neurotransmitter?
   a. myelin
   b. actin
   c. epinephrine
   d. sebum

   5. _____

6. White matter contains
   a. neuronal cell bodies
   b. myelinated axons
   c. unmyelinated axons
   d. cerebrospinal fluid

   6. _____

7. Neurons that relay impulses within the spinal cord are called
   a. afferent neurons
   b. motor neurons
   c. interneurons
   d. mixed nerves

   7. _____

II. Completion Exercise

Write the word or phrase that correctly completes each sentence.

1. Fibers that carry impulses towards the neuron cell body are called _____.
2. The portion of the spinal cord made up of cell bodies and unmyelinated axons is called the
   _____.
3. The fatty material that covers some axons is called _____.
4. Dilation of the bronchial tubes is increased by the part of the autonomic nervous system
   called the _____.
5. The junction between two neurons is called a(n) _____.
6. The network of spinal nerves that supplies the pelvis and legs is the _____.
7. The brain and spinal cord together are referred to as the _____.
8. The neurotransmitter used at cholinergic synapses is _____.
9. The small channel in the center of the spinal cord that contains cerebrospinal fluid is the
   _____.
10. A nerve cell is also called a(n) _____.
11. The bridge of gray matter connecting the right and left horns of the spinal cord is the
    _____.

Understanding Concepts

I. True/False

For each question, write *T* for true or *F* for false in the blank to the left of each number. If a statement is false, correct it by replacing the underlined term and write the correct statement in the blank below the question.

_____ 1. Motor impulses leave the underline{dorsal} horn of the spinal cord.

_____

_____ 2. An underline{axon} conducts impulses toward the cell body.

_____

_____ 3. A underline{tract} is a bundle of neuron fibers within the central nervous system.

_____

_____ 4. The underline{parasympathetic} system has terminal ganglia.

_____

_____ 5. The underline{brachial plexus} controls the shoulder and arm.

_____

_____ 6. The parasympathetic system is <u>adrenergic</u>.

_____

_____ 7. The spinal nerves are part of the <u>central</u> nervous system.

_____

_____ 8. Neurotransmitters bind to specific proteins on the postsynaptic cell called <u>transporters</u>.

_____

_____ 9. At a synapse, a neurotransmitter is released from the <u>postsynaptic</u> cell.

_____

_____ 10. A reflex arc that passes through the spinal cord but not the brain is called a <u>spinal</u> reflex.

_____

II. Practical Applications

Study the discussion. Then write the appropriate word or phrase in the space provided.

1. Mr. W, a patient with diabetes mellitus for 10 years, complained of pain and numbness of his feet. In observing Mr. W walk, the physician noted there was weakness in the muscles responsible for dorsiflexion of the foot. These symptoms are caused by a degenerative disorder of nerves to the extremities. The nerves that supply the foot are found in a plexus called the _____

2. The physician pricked Mr. W's foot with a needle. Mr. W did not feel the needle prick, suggesting that there was a problem with the nerves that carry impulses to the brain. These nerves are called _____

3. The physician tapped below Mr. W's knee to elicit a knee-jerk response. The tendon she struck was the _____

4. The effector in this reflex arc is the _____

III. Short Essays

1. List the events that occur in an action potential.

_____

_____

_____

2. What are neuroglia, and what are some functions of neuroglia?

_____

_____

_____

Conceptual Thinking

1. Ms. J is teaching English in Japan. She dines on a local delicacy called pufferfish, and shortly thereafter her lips become numb. She later discovers that pufferfish contain a toxin that blocks sodium channels. Explain why her lips are numb.

_____

_____

_____

2. Dopamine is a neurotransmitter involved in feelings of pleasure. Cocaine blocks the reuptake of dopamine. Use this information to discuss how cocaine affects mood.

_____

_____

_____

Expanding Your Horizons

Paralysis resulting from spinal cord injuries is generally thought to be irreversible, because neurons in the central nervous system do not easily regenerate. However, there is new hope for patients with spinal cord injuries. New therapies are discussed in a recent *Scientific American* article.

Resources

1. McDonald JW. Repairing the damaged spinal cord. *Sci Am* 1999; 281:64–73.

CHAPTER 9

The Nervous System: The Brain and Cranial Nerves

Overview

The brain consists of the two cerebral hemispheres, diencephalon, brainstem, and cerebellum. Each cerebral hemisphere is covered by a layer of gray matter, the **cerebral cortex**, which is further divided into four lobes (the frontal, parietal, temporal, and occipital lobes). Specific functions have been localized to the different lobes. For instance, the interpretation of visual images is performed by an area of the occipital lobe. The diencephalon consists of the **thalamus**, an important relay station for sensory impulses, and the **hypothalamus**, which plays an important role in homeostasis. The brainstem links the spinal cord to the brain and regulates many involuntary functions necessary for life, whereas the cerebellum is involved in coordination and balance. The **limbic system** is not found in a specific brain division. It consists of several structures located between the cerebrum and diencephalon that are involved in emotion, learning, and memory.

The brain and spinal cord are covered by three layers of fibrous membranes called the **meninges.** The **cerebrospinal fluid** (CSF) also protects the brain and spinal cord by providing support and cushioning. The CSF is produced by the choroid plexuses (capillary networks) in four ventricles (spaces) within the brain.

Connected with the brain are 12 pairs of **cranial nerves,** most of which supply structures in the head. Most of these, like all the spinal nerves, are mixed nerves containing both sensory and motor fibers. A few of the cranial nerves contain only sensory fibers, whereas others are motor in function.

Addressing the Learning Outcomes

1. Give the location and functions of the four main divisions of the brain.

EXERCISE 9-1: Brain, Sagittal Section (Text Fig. 9-1)

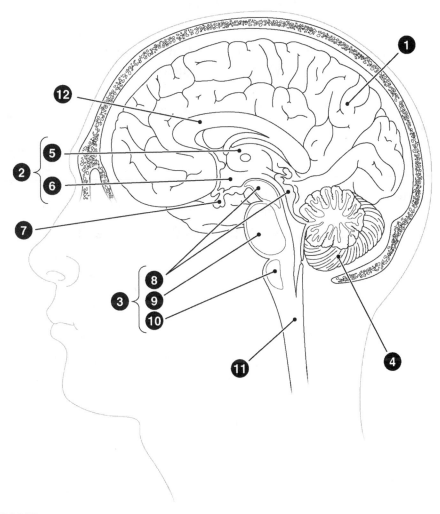

INSTRUCTIONS

1. Write the names of the four labeled brain divisions in lines 1 to 4, using four different colors. Use red for no. 2 and blue for no. 3. DO NOT COLOR THE DIAGRAM YET.
2. Write the name of each labeled structure on the appropriate numbered line in different colors. Use different shades of red for structures 5 and 6 and different shades of blue for structures 8 to 10.
3. Color each structure on the diagram with the corresponding color.

1. _____   7. _____
2. _____   8. _____
3. _____   9. _____
4. _____   10. _____
5. _____   11. _____
6. _____   12. _____

EXERCISE 9-2.

INSTRUCTIONS

Write the appropriate term in each blank.

lobe   hemisphere   cerebrum   cerebellum
brainstem   meninges   diencephalon

1. Each half of the cerebrum   _____
2. The "little" brain that coordinates voluntary muscle movements   _____
3. An individual subdivision of the cerebrum that regulates
   specific functions   _____
4. The portion of the brain that contains the thalamus and
   hypothalamus   _____
5. Connects the spinal cord with the brain   _____
6. The largest part of the brain   _____

2. Name and describe the three meninges.

EXERCISE 9-3: Meninges and Related Parts (Text Fig. 9-3)

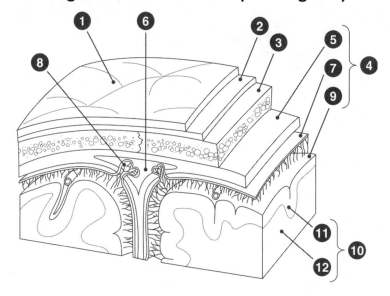

INSTRUCTIONS

1. Write the name of each labeled part on the numbered lines in different colors. Use the same
   color for structures 7 and 8. Write the name of structures 9, 10, and 12 in black.
2. Color the structures on the diagram with the corresponding color. Do not color structures
   4, 10, and 12.

1. _____   7. _____

2. _____   8. _____

3. _____   9. _____

4. _____   10. _____

5. _____   11. _____

6. _____   12. _____

3. Cite the function of cerebrospinal fluid and describe where and how this fluid is formed.

_____

EXERCISE 9-4: Flow of Cerebrospinal Fluid (Text Fig. 9-4)

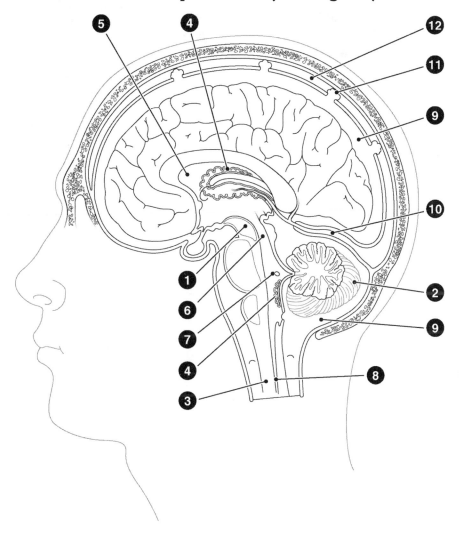

INSTRUCTIONS

1. Write the name of each labeled part on the numbered lines in different colors. Use light colors for structures 5 to 12.
2. Color the structures on the diagram with the corresponding color. The boundaries between structures 5 to 12 (inclusive) are not always well defined. For instance, structure 6 is continuous with structure 7. You can overlap your colors to signify this fact.
3. Draw arrows to indicate the direction of CSF flow.

1. _____ 7. _____

2. _____ 8. _____

3. _____ 9. _____

4. _____ 10. _____

5. _____ 11. _____

6. _____ 12. _____

EXERCISE 9-5: Ventricles of the Brain (Text Fig. 9-5)

INSTRUCTIONS

1. Write the name of each labeled part on the numbered lines in different colors.
2. Color the structures on the diagram with the corresponding color. The boundaries between structures are not always well defined. For instance, structure 2 is continuous with structure 4. You can overlap your colors to signify this fact.

1. _____
2. _____
3. _____
4. _____
5. _____
6. _____
7. _____
8. _____
9. _____

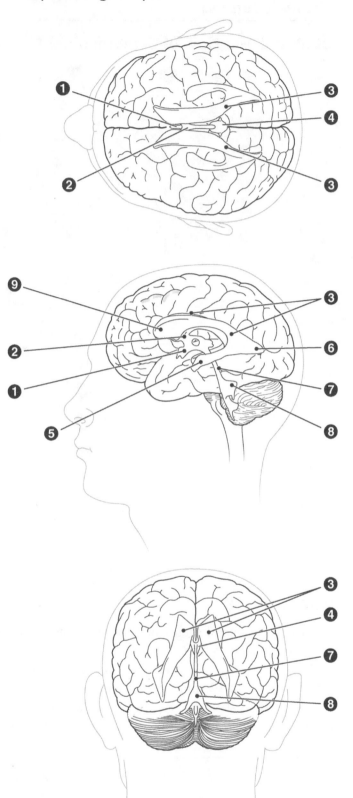

EXERCISE 9-6.

INSTRUCTIONS

Write the appropriate term in each blank.

dura mater   pia mater   arachnoid   choroid plexus   cerebral aqueduct
subarachnoid space   arachnoid villi   ventricle   dural sinus

1. The weblike middle meningeal layer   _____
2. Venous channel between the two outermost meninges   _____
3. The innermost layer of the meninges, the delicate
   membrane in which there are many blood vessels   _____
4. The area in which cerebrospinal fluid collects before
   its return to the blood   _____
5. The vascular network in a ventricle that forms
   cerebrospinal fluid   _____
6. The projections in the dural sinuses through which
   CSF is returned to the blood   _____
7. The outermost layer of the meninges, which is the
   thickest and toughest   _____

4. Name and locate the lobes of the cerebral hemispheres (also see Exercise 9-8).

EXERCISE 9-7.

INSTRUCTIONS

Write the appropriate term in each blank.

gyrus   central sulcus   lateral sulcus   basal ganglia
dopamine   corpus callosum   internal capsule   cortex

1. A shallow groove that separates the temporal lobe from the
   frontal and parietal lobes   _____
2. Masses of gray matter deep within the cerebrum that help
   regulate body movement and the muscles of facial expression   _____
3. A band of white matter that carries impulses between the
   cerebrum and the brainstem   _____
4. An elevated portion of the cerebral cortex   _____
5. The thin layer of gray matter on the surface of the cerebrum   _____
6. A band of myelinated fibers that bridges the two cerebral
   hemispheres   _____
7. The neurotransmitter used by the basal nuclei neurons   _____

5. Cite one function of the cerebral cortex in each lobe of the cerebrum.

EXERCISE 9-8: Functional Areas of the Cerebral Cortex (Text Fig. 9-8)

☐ Frontal lobe   ☐ Parietal lobe   ☐ Temporal lobe   ☐ Occipital lobe

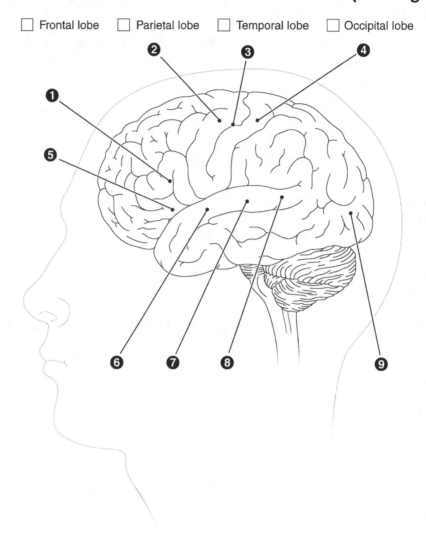

INSTRUCTIONS

1. Color the boxes next to the cerebral lobe names as follows: frontal lobe, pink; parietal lobe, light purple; temporal lobe, light blue; occipital lobe, light green.
2. Lightly color the four cerebral lobes on the diagram with corresponding colors.
3. Write the names of structures 1 to 9 on the appropriate lines in different colors. For all structures except 3, use a darker color than the one used for the corresponding cerebral lobe. For instance, a structure found in the frontal lobe could be colored red. Use the same color for structures 6 to 8. Use a dark color for structure 3.
4. Color or outline the structures on the diagram with the corresponding color.

1. _____   6. _____
2. _____   7. _____
3. _____   8. _____
4. _____   9. _____
5. _____

EXERCISE 9-9.

INSTRUCTIONS

Write the appropriate term in each blank.

temporal lobe　　　parietal lobe　　　occipital lobe　　　frontal lobe

1. The portion of the cerebral cortex where visual impulses
from the retina are interpreted　　　　　　　　　　　　　　　　　_____
2. The portion of the cerebral cortex where auditory impulses
are interpreted　　　　　　　　　　　　　　　　　　　　　　　_____
3. Location of a sensory area for interpretation of pain, touch,
and temperature　　　　　　　　　　　　　　　　　　　　　　_____
4. The lobe controlling voluntary muscles　　　　　　　　　　　_____

6. Name two divisions of the diencephalon and cite the functions of each (see Exercise 9-10).

7. Locate the three subdivisions of the brainstem and give the functions of each.

EXERCISE 9-10.

INSTRUCTIONS

Write the appropriate term in each blank.

thalamus　　　　　　　medulla oblongata　　　　　　pons　　　　　　　midbrain
vasomotor center　　　cardiac center　　　　　　　　limbic system　　　hypothalamus

1. The portion of the brainstem composed of myelinated nerve fibers
that connects to the cerebellum　　　　　　　　　　　　　　　　_____
2. The superior portion of the brainstem　　　　　　　　　　　　_____
3. The part of the brain between the pons and the spinal cord　　_____
4. The region of the diencephalon that acts as a relay center
for sensory stimuli　　　　　　　　　　　　　　　　　　　　　_____
5. The region consisting of portions of the cerebrum and
diencephalon that is involved in emotional states and behavior　_____
6. Nuclei that regulate the contraction of smooth muscle in blood
vessel walls　　　　　　　　　　　　　　　　　　　　　　　_____
7. The portion of the brain controlling the autonomic nervous system　_____

8. Describe the cerebellum and cite its functions.

EXERCISE 9-11.

INSTRUCTIONS

List three functions of the cerebellum in the spaces below.

1. _____

2. _____

3. _____

9. Name some techniques used to study the brain.

EXERCISE 9-12.

INSTRUCTIONS

Write the appropriate term in each blank.

MRI   CT   PET   EEG

1. Technique that produces a picture of brain activity levels in the different parts of the brain   _____

2. Technique that measures electric currents in the brain   _____

3. X-ray technique that provides photos of bone, cavities, and lesions   _____

4. Technique used to visualize soft tissue, such as scar tissue, hemorrhages, and tumors that does not use x-rays   _____

10. Cite the names and functions of the 12 cranial nerves.

EXERCISE 9-13: Cranial Nerves (Text Fig. 9-18)

INSTRUCTIONS

1. Write the number and name of each labeled cranial nerve on the numbered lines in different colors. Use the same color for structures 1 and 2.
2. Color the nerves on the diagram with the corresponding color.

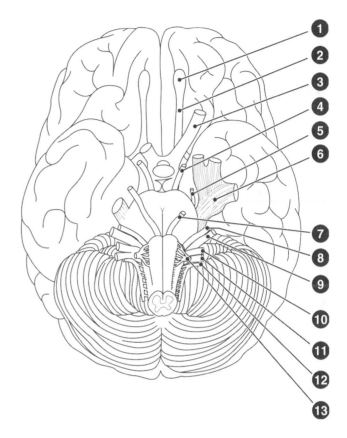

1. _____
2. _____
3. _____
4. _____
5. _____
6. _____
7. _____
8. _____
9. _____
10. _____
11. _____
12. _____
13. _____

EXERCISE 9-14.

INSTRUCTIONS

Write the appropriate term in each blank.

glossopharyngeal nerve   optic nerve   vagus nerve   trochlear nerve   abducens nerve
vestibulocochlear nerve   facial nerve   trigeminal nerve   accessory nerve

1. A motor nerve controlling the trapezius, sternocleidomastoid, and larynx muscles _____
2. The nerve that controls contraction of a single eye muscle _____
3. The nerve that carries visual impulses from the eye to the brain _____
4. The most important sensory nerve of the face and head _____
5. The nerve that supplies most of the organs in the thoracic and abdominal cavities _____
6. The nerve that supplies the muscles of facial expression _____
7. The nerve that carries sensory impulses for hearing and equilibrium _____

11. Show how word parts are used to build words related to the nervous system.

EXERCISE 9-15.

INSTRUCTIONS

Complete the following table by writing the correct word part or meaning in the space provided. Write a word that contains each word part in the Example column.

Word Part	Meaning	Example
1. _____	cut	_____
2. chori/o	_____	_____
3. _____	tongue	_____
4. encephal/o	_____	_____
5. cerebr/o	_____	_____
6. _____	opposed, against	_____
7. _____	lateral, side	_____
8. gyr/o	_____	_____

Making the Connections

The following concept map deals with the structure of the brain. Each pair of terms is linked together by a connecting phrase into a sentence. The sentence should be read in the direction of the arrow. Complete the concept map by filling in the appropriate term or phrase. There is one right answer for each term. However, there are many correct answers for the connecting phrases (4, 8, 11, 14, 17). There are many other connections that could be made on this map. For instance, how could you connect structures 2 and 16? Can you add more terms to the map?

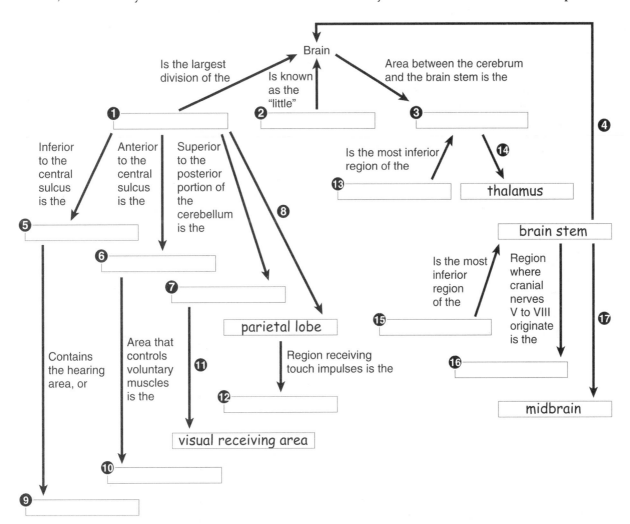

Optional Exercise: Make your own concept map, based on structures involved in the synthesis and movement of cerebrospinal fluid. Choose your own terms to incorporate into your map, or use the following list: ventricle, choroid plexus, lateral ventricles, third ventricle, fourth ventricle, foramina, horns, cerebral aqueduct, spinal cord, cerebrospinal fluid, dural sinuses, subarachnoid space, and arachnoid villi.

Testing Your Knowledge

Building Understanding

I. Multiple Choice

Select the best answer and write the letter of your choice in the blank.

1. The shallow groove lying between the frontal and parietal lobe is the
   a. lateral sulcus
   b. central sulcus
   c. longitudinal fissure
   d. basal nuclei

   1. _____

2. The dura mater is
   a. the innermost layer of the meninges
   b. the outermost layer of the meninges
   c. the network of vessels that produces cerebrospinal fluid
   d. the part of the brain that connects with the spinal cord

   2. _____

3. Impulses for the sense of taste travel to the
   a. parietal lobe
   b. temporal lobe
   c. hippocampus
   d. occipital lobe

   3. _____

4. The cerebrospinal fluid is formed in the
   a. cerebral aqueduct
   b. central sulcus
   c. choroid plexus
   d. internal capsule

   4. _____

5. The abducens nerve supplies the
   a. eye
   b. ear and pharynx
   c. face and salivary gland
   d. tongue and pharynx

   5. _____

6. The reticular formation is
   a. a region of the limbic system that controls wakefulness and sleep
   b. a deep groove that divides the cerebral hemispheres
   c. the part of the temporal lobe concerned with the sense of smell
   d. the fifth lobe of the cerebrum

   6. _____

II. Completion Exercise

Write the word or phrase that correctly completes each sentence.

1. The four chambers within the brain where cerebrospinal fluid is produced are the
_____.

2. Sounds are interpreted in the area of the temporal lobe called the _____.

3. The region of the diencephalon that helps maintain homeostasis (e.g., water balance, appetite, and body temperature) and controls the autonomic nervous system is the
_____.

4. The storage of information to be recalled at a later time is called _____.

5. Records of the electrical activity of the brain can be made with an instrument called a(n)
_____.

6. Extensions of the lateral ventricles into the cerebral lobes are called _____.

7. Except for the first two pairs, all the cranial nerves arise from the _____.

8. The three layers of membranes that surround the brain and spinal cord are called the
_____.

9. The clear liquid that helps to support and protect the brain and spinal cord is
_____.

10. The number of pairs of cranial nerves is _____.

11. The area of the brainstem concerned with eye-tracking reflexes involved in reading is the
_____.

12. The middle portion of the cerebellum is called the _____.

Understanding Concepts

I. True/False

For each question, write *T* for true or *F* for false in the blank to the left of each number. If a statement is false, correct it by replacing the underlined term and write the correct statement in the blank below the question.

_____ 1. The <u>pia mater</u> is the middle layer of the meninges.

_____

_____ 2. The interventricular foramina form channels between the lateral ventricles and the <u>fourth ventricle</u>.

_____

_____ 3. The primary motor cortex is found in the <u>parietal lobe</u>.

_____

_____ 4. The <u>internal capsule</u> consists of myelinated fibers linking the cerebral hemispheres with the brainstem.

_____

_____ 5. The <u>parietal lobe</u> lies posterior to the central sulcus and superior to the occipital lobe.

_____

_____ 6. The raised areas on the surface of the cerebrum are called <u>gyri</u>.

_____

_____ 7. Auditory (sound) impulses are carried by the <u>third</u> cranial nerve.

_____

_____ 8. The <u>hypoglossal</u> nerve transmits sensory information from the tongue.

_____

II. Practical Applications

Study each discussion. Then write the appropriate word or phrase in the space provided.

1. Mr. B, age 87, drove his car into a ditch. When the paramedics arrived, he was unable to speak, a disorder called _____.
2. Mr. B also experienced paralysis on his right side, indicating a problem within the largest division of the brain, the _____.
3. The right side of Mr. B's face droops, and he cannot control his facial expressions. The facial muscles are controlled by the cranial nerve numbered _____.
4. Imaging studies showed damage to the left side of the brain. The anatomical name for the left side of the brain is the left _____.
5. Mr. B's speech disorder indicates that the bleed affected his motor speech area, also called _____.

III. Short Essays

1. Describe the structures that protect the brain and spinal cord.

_____

_____

_____

2. List some functions of the structures in the diencephalon.

_____

_____

_____

3. List the name, number, and sensory information conveyed for each of the purely sensory cranial nerves.

_____

_____

_____

Conceptual Thinking

1. Describe the journey of cerebrospinal fluid (CSF), beginning with its synthesis and ending with its entry into the circulatory system.

_____

_____

_____

Expanding Your Horizons

Do you use herbal supplements like gingko biloba to boost your learning power? As discussed in this _Scientific American_ article, gingko biloba does boost memory—to the same extent as a candy bar! Mental exercise may be the best way to improve your academic performance.

Resources

1. Gold PE, Cahill L, Wenk GL. The lowdown on Gingko biloba. _Sci Am_ 2003;288:86–91.
2. Holloway M. The mutable brain. _Sci Am_ 2003;289:78–85.

CHAPTER 10

The Sensory System

Overview

The sensory system enables us to detect changes taking place both internally and externally. These changes are detected by specialized structures called receptors. Any change that acts on a receptor to produce a response in the nervous system is termed a stimulus. The special senses, so called because the receptors are limited to a few specialized sense organs in the head, include the senses of vision, hearing, equilibrium, taste, and smell. The receptors of the eye are the rods and cones located in the retina. The receptors for both hearing (the organ of Corti) and equilibrium (the vestibule and semicircular canals) are located within the inner ear. Receptors for the chemical senses of taste and smell are located on the tongue and in the upper part of the nose, respectively. The general senses are scattered throughout the body; they respond to touch, pressure, temperature, pain, and position. Receptors for the sense of position, known as proprioceptors, are found in muscles, tendons, and joints. The nerve impulses generated in a receptor cell by a stimulus must be carried to the central nervous system by way of a sensory (afferent) neuron. Here, the information is processed and a suitable response is made.

This chapter is quite challenging, because it contains both difficult concepts and large amounts of detail. You can use concept maps to assemble all of the details into easy-to-remember frameworks.

Addressing the Learning Outcomes

1. Describe the function of the sensory system.

EXERCISE 10-1.

INSTRUCTIONS

Fill in the blanks in the following paragraph using these terms:

central nervous system, homeostasis, sensory neuron, sensory receptor

The sensory system protects people by detecting changes in the internal and external environment that threaten to disrupt _____ (1), which is the maintenance of a constant internal environment. The change is detected by a _____ (2), which sends an impulse through a _____ (3) to the _____ (4).

2. Differentiate between the special and general senses and give examples of each.

EXERCISE 10-2.

INSTRUCTIONS

Classify each of the following senses as general senses (G) or special senses (S).

1. sense of position _____
2. smell _____
3. vision _____
4. touch _____
5. temperature _____
6. equilibrium _____

3. Describe the structure of the eye.

EXERCISE 10-3: The Eye (Text Fig. 10-3)

INSTRUCTIONS

1. Write the name of each labeled part on the numbered lines in different colors. Use the same color for structures 3 and 4 and structures 6 to 9 (inclusive). Write the name of structures 1 and 2 in black, because they will not be colored.
2. Color the different structures on the diagram with the corresponding color. Some structures are present in more than one location on the diagram. Try to color all of a particular structure in the appropriate color. For instance, only one of the suspensory ligaments is labeled, but color both suspensory ligaments.

1. _____
2. _____
3. _____
4. _____
5. _____
6. _____
7. _____
8. _____
9. _____
10. _____
11. _____
12. _____
13. _____
14. _____
15. _____
16. _____

4. List and describe the structures that protect the eye.

EXERCISE 10-4: The Lacrimal Apparatus (Text Fig. 10-2)

INSTRUCTIONS

Label the indicated parts.

1. _____
2. _____
3. _____
4. _____
5. _____
6. _____
7. _____

5. Define *refraction* and list the refractive parts of the eye.

EXERCISE 10-5.

INSTRUCTIONS

List 4 eye structures that bend (refract) light in the spaces below.

1. _____
2. _____
3. _____
4. _____

6. Differentiate between the rods and the cones of the eye.

EXERCISE 10-6.

INSTRUCTIONS

Write the appropriate term in each blank below.

cone   cornea   rhodopsin   sclera
optic disk   retina   rod   fovea centralis

1. A vision receptor that is sensitive to color   _____
2. The part of the eye that light rays pass through first as they
   enter the eye   _____
3. Another name for the blind spot, the region where the optic
   nerve connects with the eye   _____
4. The innermost coat of the eyeball, the nervous tissue layer that
   includes the receptors for the sense of vision   _____
5. A vision receptor that functions well in dim light   _____
6. A pigment needed for vision   _____
7. The depressed area in the retina that is the point of clearest vision   _____

7. Compare the functions of the extrinsic and intrinsic muscles of the eye.

EXERCISE 10-7: Extrinsic Muscles of the Eye (Text Fig. 10-6)

INSTRUCTIONS

1. Write the name of each labeled muscle on the
   numbered lines in different colors.
2. Color the different muscles on the diagram with
   the corresponding color.

1. _____
2. _____
3. _____
4. _____
5. _____

EXERCISE 10-8.

INSTRUCTIONS

Write the appropriate term in each blank.

aqueous humor   vitreous body   lens   ciliary muscle
choroid   conjunctiva   pupil   iris

1. The structure that alters the shape of the lens for accommodation   _____
2. The watery fluid that fills much of the eyeball in front of the crystalline lens   _____
3. The vascular, pigmented middle tunic of the eyeball   _____
4. Structure with two sets of muscle fibers that regulate the amount of light entering the eye   _____
5. The jellylike material located behind the crystalline lens that maintains the spherical shape of the eyeball   _____
6. The central opening of the iris   _____
7. The membrane that lines the eyelids   _____

8. Describe the nerve supply to the eye.

EXERCISE 10-9: Nerves of the Eye (Text Fig. 10-10)

INSTRUCTIONS

Label the indicated nerves.

1. _____
2. _____
3. _____
4. _____
5. _____
6. _____

(also see Exercise 10-15)

9. Describe the three divisions of the ear.

EXERCISE 10-10: The Ear (Text Fig. 10-11)

INSTRUCTIONS

1. Write the names of the three ear divisions on the appropriate lines (1 to 3).
2. Write the names of the labeled parts on the numbered lines in different colors.
3. Color each part with the corresponding color.

1. _____
2. _____
3. _____
4. _____
5. _____
6. _____
7. _____
8. _____
9. _____
10. _____
11. _____
12. _____
13. _____
14. _____

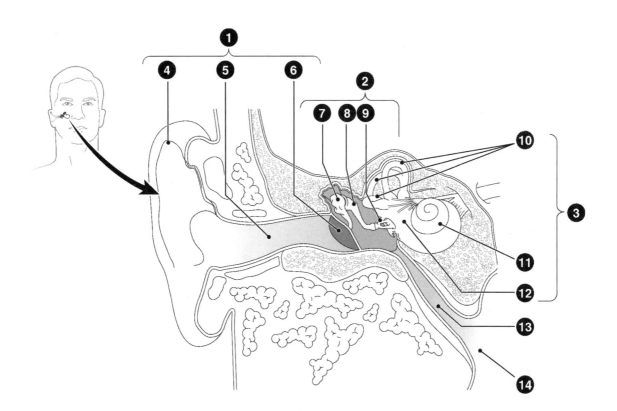

EXERCISE 10-11: The Inner Ear (Text Fig. 10-13)

INSTRUCTIONS

Label the indicated parts.

1. _____
2. _____
3. _____
4. _____
5. _____
6. _____
7. _____
8. _____

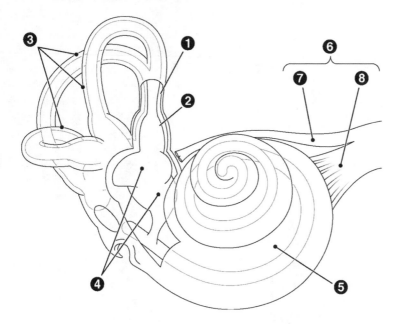

10. Describe the receptor for hearing and explain how it functions.

EXERCISE 10-12: Cochlea and Organ of Corti (Text Fig. 10-14)

INSTRUCTIONS

1. Write the name of each labeled part on the numbered lines. Use colors for structures 3 to 7, 11, and 12. Use black for the other structures.
2. Color structures 3 to 7, 11, and 12 with the corresponding color.

1. _____
2. _____
3. _____
4. _____
5. _____
6. _____
7. _____
8. _____
9. _____
10. _____
11. _____
12. _____
13. _____

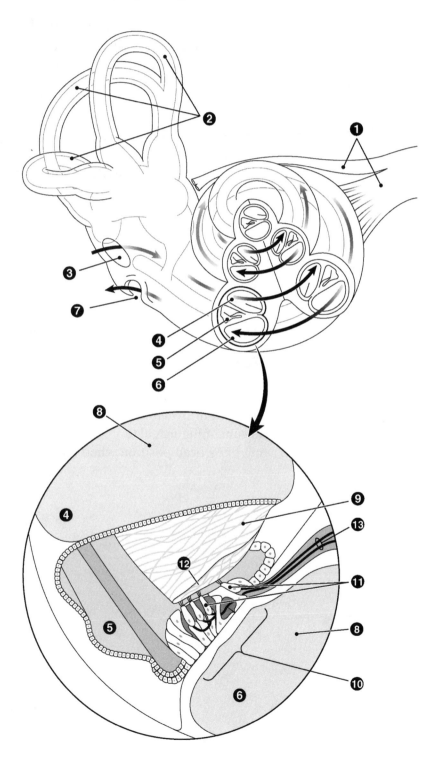

EXERCISE 10-13.

INSTRUCTIONS

Write the appropriate term in each blank.

oval window   organ of Corti   malleus   eustachian tube   bony labyrinth
perilymph   incus   pinna   cochlear duct endolymph

1. The fluid contained within the membranous labyrinth of the
   inner ear   _____
2. The bone that interacts with the tympanic membrane   _____
3. Another name for the projecting part, or auricle, of the ear   _____
4. The channel connecting the middle ear cavity with the pharynx   _____
5. The fluid of the inner ear contained within the bony labyrinth and
   surrounding the membranous labyrinth   _____
6. Ciliated receptor cells that detect sound waves   _____
7. The skeleton of the inner ear   _____

11. Compare static and dynamic equilibrium and describe the location and function of these receptors.

EXERCISE 10-14.

INSTRUCTIONS

Write the appropriate term in each blank.

vestibule   dynamic equilibrium   semicircular canals   cristae
cochlear duct   static equilibrium   otoliths

1. The sense of knowing the position of the head in relation to gravity   _____
2. Small crystals that activate maculae   _____
3. The sense organ involved in dynamic equilibrium   _____
4. The receptor cells involved in dynamic equilibrium   _____
5. Two small chambers containing maculae   _____
6. The sense of knowing one's head position when the body is spinning   _____

12. Explain the function of proprioceptors.

EXERCISE 10-15.

INSTRUCTIONS

Write the appropriate term in each blank.

kinesthesia   proprioception   tactile corpuscle   cochlear nerve
vestibular nerve   oculomotor nerve   ophthalmic nerve   equilibrium
optic nerve   free nerve endings

1. The branch of the vestibulocochlear nerve that carries hearing impulses   _____
2. The nerve that carries visual impulses from the retina to the brain   _____
3. The branch of the fifth cranial nerve that carries impulses of pain, touch, and temperature from the eye to the brain   _____
4. The largest of the three cranial nerves that carry motor fibers to the eyeball muscles   _____
5. The sense of knowing the position of one's body and the relative positions of different muscles   _____
6. The sense of body movement   _____
7. Receptors that detect changes in temperature   _____

13. List several methods for treatment of pain.

EXERCISE 10-16.

INSTRUCTIONS

Write the appropriate term in each blank.

NSAID   narcotic   anesthetic   endorphin   analgesic

1. Term describing any drug that relieves pain   _____
2. A substance produced by the brain that relieves pain   _____
3. Drug that acts on the CNS to alter pain perception, such as morphine _____
4. Drug that acts locally to reduce inflammation   _____

14. Describe sensory adaptation and explain its value.

EXERCISE 10-17.

INSTRUCTIONS

Define "sensory adaptation" in the space below.

_____

_____

15. Show how word parts are used to build words related to the sensory system.

EXERCISE 10-18.

INSTRUCTIONS

Complete the following table by writing the correct word part or meaning in the space provided. Write a word that contains each word part in the Example column.

Word Part	Meaning	Example
1. presby-	_____	_____
2. _____	stone	_____
3. kine	_____	_____
4. narc/o	_____	_____
5. _____	drum	_____
6. _____	yellow	_____
7. propri/o-	_____	_____
8. _____	pain	_____
9. -esthesia	_____	_____
10. _____	hearing	_____

Making the Connections

The concept map on the next page deals with the structure and function of the eye. Each pair of terms is linked together by a connecting phrase into a sentence. The sentence should be read in the direction of the arrow. Complete the concept map by filling in the appropriate term or phrase. There is one right answer for each term. However, there are many correct answers for the connecting phrases (2, 9).

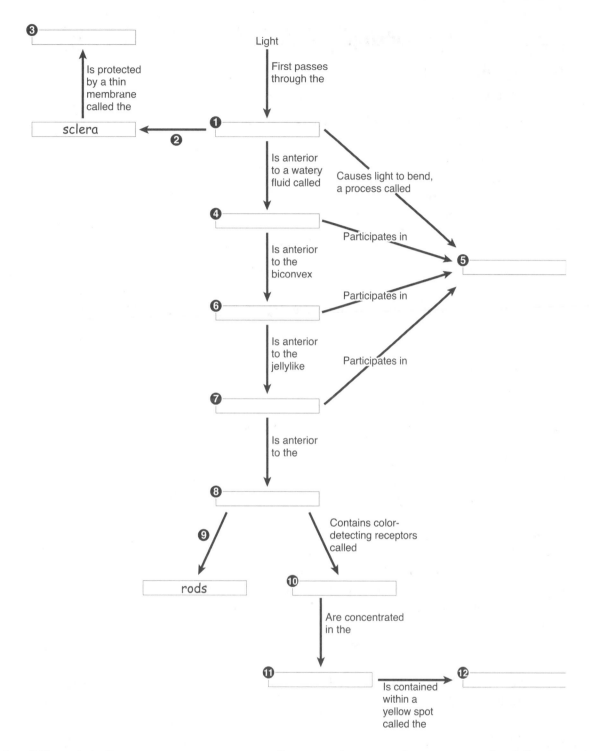

Light

First passes
through the

❸ [_____]

Is protected
by a thin
membrane
called the

sclera ◀— ❷ — ❶ [_____]

Is anterior
to a watery
fluid called

Causes light to bend,
a process called

❹ [_____]

Is anterior
to the
biconvex

Participates in

❻ [_____]

Is anterior
to the
jellylike

Participates in

❼ [_____]

Is anterior
to the

Participates in

❺ [_____]

❽ [_____]

❾

Contains color-
detecting receptors
called

rods

❿ [_____]

Are concentrated
in the

⓫ [_____] —Is contained
within a
yellow spot
called the→ ⓬ [_____]

Optional Exercise: Construct a concept map of terms relating to the ear using the following terms and any others you would like to include: tympanic membrane, stapes, malleus, incus, pinna, bony labyrinth, organ of Corti, oval window, round window, cochlear duct, tectorial membrane, and cochlear nerve. You may also want to construct concept maps relating to the other special senses (equilibrium, taste, smell) and the general senses (touch, pressure, temperature, proprioception).

Testing Your Knowledge

Building Understanding

I. Multiple Choice

1. A physician who specializes in disorders of the eye is a(n)   1. _____
    a. ophthalmologist
    b. internist
    c. allergist
    d. orthopedic surgeon

2. A term related to the sense of taste is   2. _____
    a. tactile
    b. gustatory
    c. proprioceptive
    d. thermal

3. Alterations in the lens' shape to allow for near or far vision is called   3. _____
    a. accommodation
    b. convergence
    c. divergence
    d. dark adaptation

4. The term *lacrimation* refers to the secretion of   4. _____
    a. mucus
    b. wax
    c. tears
    d. aqueous humor

5. Painkillers that are released from certain regions of the brain are   5. _____
    a. narcotics
    b. endorphins
    c. anaesthetics
    d. nonsteroidal anti-inflammatory drugs

6. A person who lacks cones in the retina will suffer from   6. _____
    a. complete blindness
    b. color blindness
    d. night blindness
    d. deafness

7. The organ of Corti is the receptor for   7. _____
    a. taste
    b. smell
    c. hearing
    d. equilibrium

II. Completion Exercise

1. The transparent portion of the sclera is the   _____

2. The glands that secrete ear wax are called   _____

3. The nerve endings that aid in judging position and changes in location of body parts are the   _____

4. The sense of position is partially governed by equilibrium receptors in the internal ear, including two small chambers in the vestibule and the three   _____

5. The tactile corpuscles are the receptors for the sense of   _____

6. Any drug that relieves pain is called a(n)   _____

7. When you enter a darkened room, it takes a while for the rods to begin to function. This interval is known as the period of   _____

8. The receptor tunic (layer) of the eye is the   _____

9. The bending of light rays as they pass through the media of the eye is   _____

Understanding Concepts

I. True/False

For each question, write *T* for true or *F* for false in the blank to the left of each number. If a statement is false, correct it by replacing the underlined term and write the correct statement in the blank below the question.

_____ 1. <u>Extrinsic</u> eye muscles control the diameter of the pupil.

_____

_____ 2. There are <u>seven</u> extrinsic muscles connected to each eye.

_____

_____ 3. The iris is an <u>intrinsic</u> muscle of the eye.

_____

_____ 4. The sense of temperature is a <u>general</u> sense.

_____

_____ 5. The <u>rods</u> of the eye function in bright light and detect color.

_____

_____ 6. When the eyes are exposed to a bright light, the pupils <u>constrict</u>.

_____

_____ 7. Sound waves leave the ear through the <u>round window</u>.

_____

_____ 8. The ciliary muscle <u>contracts</u> to allow thickening of the lens.

_____

_____ 9. The sense of smell is also called <u>olfaction</u>.

_____

II. Practical Applications

Study each discussion. Then write the appropriate word or phrase in the space provided.

➤ Group A

Baby L was brought in by his mother because he awakened crying and holding the right side of his head. He had been suffering from a cold, but now he seemed to be in pain. Complete the following descriptions relating to his evaluation and treatment.

1. Examination revealed a bulging red eardrum. The eardrum is also called the _____.
2. The cause of Baby L's painful bulging eardrum was an infection of the middle ear. The middle ear contains three small bones: the malleus, incus, and _____.
3. Antibiotic treatment of Baby L's middle ear infection was begun, because this early treatment usually prevents complications. The middle ear is prone to infections, because it is connected to the pharynx by the _____.
4. Baby L was returned to the emergency room the next day because he was falling down repeatedly. The physician suspected a problem with his sense of balance, or _____.
5. Baby L's mother asked how an ear infection could affect balance. The physician explained that two structures were located within the inner ear that are involved with balance, named the semicircular canals and the _____.
6. In particular, the physician feared that the middle ear infection had spread to the fluid within the membranous labyrinth. This fluid is called _____.

➤ Group B

Sixty-year-old Mr. S had ridden his scooter over some broken glass. A fragment of glass bounced up and flew into one eye. Complete the following descriptions relating to his evaluation and treatment.

1. Examination by the eye specialist showed that there was a cut in the transparent window of the eye, the _____.
2. On further examination of Mr. S, the colored part of the eye was seen to protrude from the wound. This part of the eye is the _____.
3. Mr. S's treatment included antiseptics, anesthetics, and suturing of the wound. Medication was instilled in the saclike structure at the anterior of the eyeball. This sac is lined with a thin epithelial membrane, the _____.

➤ Group C

You are conducting hearing tests at a senior citizens' home. During the course of the afternoon, you encounter the following patients. Complete the following descriptions relating to the evaluation and treatment of hearing loss.

1. Mrs. B complained of some hearing loss and a sense of fullness in her outer ear. Examination revealed that her ear canal was plugged with hardened ear wax, which is scientifically called _____.

2. Mr. J, age 72, complained of gradually worsening hearing loss, although he had no symptoms of pain or other ear problems. Examination revealed that his hearing loss was due to nerve damage. The cranial nerve that carries hearing impulses to the brain is called the _____.

3. In particular, the endings of this nerve were damaged. These nerve endings are located in the spiral-shaped part of the inner ear, a part of the ear that is known as the _____.

III. Short Essays

1.   Describe several different structural forms of sensory receptors and give examples of each.

       _____

       _____

       _____

2.   List three methods to relieve pain that do not involve administration of drugs.

       _____

       _____

       _____

Conceptual Thinking

1. You have probably been sitting in a chair for quite a while, yet you have not been constantly aware of your legs contacting the chair. Why not?

       _____

       _____

       _____

2. Write your name at the bottom of this sheet of paper. Explain the contributions of different sensory receptors that were required to successfully complete that simple task. For instance, proprioceptors are required to indicate the fingers' location at every moment.

       _____

       _____

       _____

Expanding Your Horizons

Imagine if you could taste a triangle, or hear blue. This is reality for individuals with a disorder called synesthesia. Read about some exceptional artists that suffer from this disorder, and how synesthesia has helped us understand how the brain processes sensory information in the article below.

Here is an exercise you can do to find your own blind spot. Draw a cross (on the left) and a circle (on the right) on a piece of paper that are separated by a handwidth. Focus on the cross and notice (but do not focus on) the circle. Move the paper closer and further away until the circle disappears. Weird activities to investigate your blind spot can be found at the website http://serendip.brynmawr.edu/bb/blindspot1.html.

Resources

1. Ramachandran VS, Hubbard EM. Hearing colors, tasting shapes. *Sci Am* 2003; 288:52–59.

CHAPTER 11

The Endocrine System: Glands and Hormones

Overview

The endocrine system and the nervous system are the main coordinating and controlling systems of the body. Chapter 8 discusses how the nervous system uses chemical and electrical stimuli to control very rapid, short-term responses. This chapter discusses the endocrine system, which uses specific chemicals called hormones to induce short- or long-term changes in the growth, development, and function of specific cells. Although some hormones act locally, most travel in the blood to distant sites and exert their effects on any cell (the target cell) that contains a specific receptor for the hormone. Although hormones are produced by many tissues, certain glands, called endocrine glands, specialize in hormone production. These endocrine glands include the pituitary (hypophysis), thyroid, parathyroids, adrenals, pancreas, gonads, thymus, and pineal. Together, these glands comprise the endocrine system. The activity of endocrine glands is regulated by negative feedback, other hormones, nervous stimulation, and/or biological rhythms. One of the most important endocrine glands is the pituitary gland, which comprises the anterior and posterior pituitary. The posterior pituitary gland is made of nervous tissue—it contains the axons and terminals of neurons that have their cell bodies in a part of the brain called the hypothalamus. Hormones are synthesized in the hypothalamus and released from the posterior pituitary. The anterior pituitary secretes a number of hormones that act on other endocrine glands. The cells of the anterior pituitary are controlled in part by releasing hormones made in the hypothalamus. These releasing hormones pass through the blood vessels of a portal circulation to reach the anterior pituitary. Hormones are also made outside the traditional endocrine glands. Other structures that secrete hormones include the stomach, small intestine, kidney, heart, skin, and placenta.

This chapter contains a lot of details for you to learn. Try to summarize the material using concept maps and summary tables. You should also understand positive and negative feedback (Chapter 1) before you tackle the concepts in this chapter.

Addressing the Learning Outcomes

1. Compare the effects of the nervous system and the endocrine system in controlling the body.

EXERCISE 11-1.

INSTRUCTIONS

Identify the following characteristics as belonging to the nervous system (N) or the endocrine system (E).

1. controls rapid responses ___
2. used to regulate growth ___
3. uses chemical stimuli only ___
4. uses both chemical and electrical stimuli ____

2. Describe the functions of hormones.

EXERCISE 11-2.

INSTRUCTIONS

Define the following terms:

1. receptor _____
2. target tissue _____
3. hormone _____

3. Discuss the chemical composition of hormones.

EXERCISE 11-3.

INSTRUCTIONS

Do each of the following statements apply to amino acid compounds (A) or lipids (L)?

1. protein hormones _____
2. can be formed by modifying cholesterol ____
3. hormones of the sex glands and the adrenal cortex ____
4. hormones not produced by the sex glands or adrenal cortex _____
5. prostaglandins ____

4. Explain how hormones are regulated.

EXERCISE 11-4.

INSTRUCTIONS

Define negative and positive feedback.

_____

_____

5. Identify the glands of the endocrine system on a diagram.

EXERCISE 11-5: The Endocrine Glands (Text Fig. 11-2)

INSTRUCTIONS

1. Write the name of each labeled part on the numbered lines in different colors.
2. Color the different structures on the diagram with the corresponding color. Some structures are present in more than one location on the diagram. Try to color all of a particular structure in the appropriate color. For instance, color both adrenal glands, although only one is indicated by a leader line.

1. _____

2. _____

3. _____

4. _____

5. _____

6. _____

7. _____

8. _____

9. _____

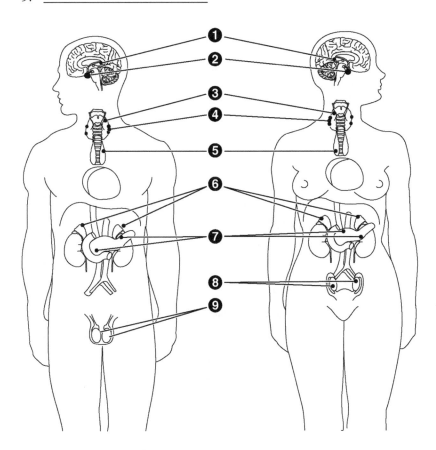

EXERCISE 11-6.

INSTRUCTIONS

Write the term in the appropriate blank.

parathyroid   thymus   pineal   hypothalamus
thyroid   adrenal   pancreas

1. One of the tiny glands located behind the thyroid gland   _____
2. The largest of the endocrine glands, located in the neck   _____
3. The gland in the brain that is regulated by light   _____
4. An organ that contains islets   _____
5. The endocrine gland composed of a cortex and medulla, each
   with specific functions   _____

6. List the hormones produced by each endocrine gland and describe the effects of each on the body.

EXERCISE 11-7.

INSTRUCTIONS

Fill in the missing information in the chart below. This table does not cover all of the hormones and their actions discussed in the text. Do not fill in the column at the far right yet. These columns will be discussed under Outcome 9.

Hormone	Gland	Effects	Medical Uses
ADH (antidiuretic hormone)			N/A
	Adrenal cortex	Nutrient metabolism during stress	
		Uterine contraction, milk ejection	
	Anterior pituitary	Promotes growth of all body tissues	
Parathyroid hormone			N/A
	Pancreas	Necessary for glucose uptake into cells	
Thyroid hormones: thyroxine (T4) and triiodothyronine (T3)			
	Adrenal cortex	Helps regulate water and electrolyte balance	N/A
		Stimulates glucose release from the liver	N/A
Melatonin			N/A

EXERCISE 11-8.

INSTRUCTIONS

Write the appropriate term in each blank.

epinephrine   antidiuretic hormone   ACTH   aldosterone
follicle-stimulating hormone   estrogen   calcitonin   prolactin

1. The anterior pituitary hormone that stimulates milk synthesis   _____
2. The main hormone of the adrenal medulla that, among other
   actions, raises blood pressure and increases the heart rate   _____
3. The anterior pituitary hormone that stimulates the adrenal cortex   _____
4. A hormone produced by the ovaries   _____
5. The hormone from the adrenal cortex that regulates sodium and
   potassium reabsorption in the kidney tubules   _____
6. A gonadotropic hormone   _____
7. A hormone synthesized in the hypothalamus   _____

EXERCISE 11-9.

INSTRUCTIONS

Write the appropriate term in each blank

insulin   glucagon   parathyroid hormone   testosterone
thymosin   cortisol

1. A hormone that raises the blood calcium level   _____
2. A hormone that lowers the blood glucose level   _____
3. A pancreatic hormone that raises the blood glucose level   _____
4. An adrenal hormone that raises the blood glucose level   _____
5. A hormone that promotes T cell development   _____

7. Describe how the hypothalamus controls the anterior and posterior pituitary.

EXERCISE 11-10: The Pituitary Gland (Text Fig. 11-3)

INSTRUCTIONS

1. Label the parts of the hypothalamo-pituitary system.
2. Color blood vessels red and nerves yellow.

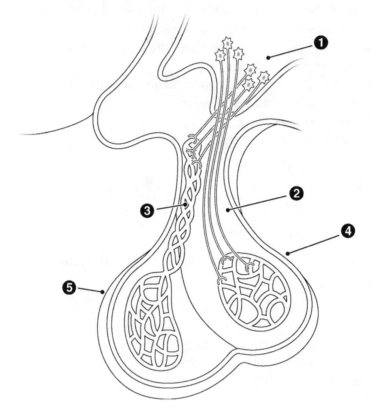

1. _____
2. _____
3. _____
4. _____
5. _____

EXERCISE 11-11.

Do the following characteristics apply to the anterior pituitary (AP) or the posterior pituitary (PP)?

1. Secretes hormones synthesized in the hypothalamus ____
2. Consists of neural tissue ____
3. Releases hormones under the regulation of hypothalamic releasing hormones ____

8. List tissues other than the endocrine glands that produce hormones.

EXERCISE 11-12.

INSTRUCTIONS

Fill in the missing information in the chart below.

Hormone	Site of Synthesis	Effects
Atrial natriuretic peptide		
	Kidney	Stimulates erythrocyte production

9. List some medical uses of hormones.

EXERCISE 11-13.

INSTRUCTIONS

Fill in the column "Medical Uses" in the table prepared for Exercise 11-7 for the following hormones: insulin, cortisol (a glucocorticoid), epinephrine, thyroid hormones, and oxytocin.

10. Explain how the endocrine system responds to stress.

EXERCISE 11-14.

INSTRUCTIONS

Explain why cortisol and epinephrine are released during stressful situations.

1. _____

_____

_____

2. _____

_____

_____

11. Show how word parts are used to build words related to the endocrine system.

EXERCISE 11-15.

INSTRUCTIONS

Complete the following table by writing the correct word part or meaning in the space provided. Write a word that contains each word part in the Example column.

Word Part	Meaning	Example
1. trop/o	_____	_____
2. _____	cortex	_____
3. –poiesis	_____	_____
4. natri	_____	_____
5. _____	male	_____
6. _____	milk	_____
7. ren/o	_____	_____
8. glyc/o	_____	_____
9. oxy	_____	_____
10. nephr/o	_____	_____

Making the Connections

The following concept map deals with the relationship between the hypothalamus, pituitary gland, and some target organs. Each pair of terms is linked together by a connecting phrase into a sentence. The sentence should be read in the direction of the arrow. Complete the concept map by filling in the appropriate term or phrase. There is one right answer for each term. However, there are many correct answers for the connecting phrases (1, 4, 5, 9, 12).

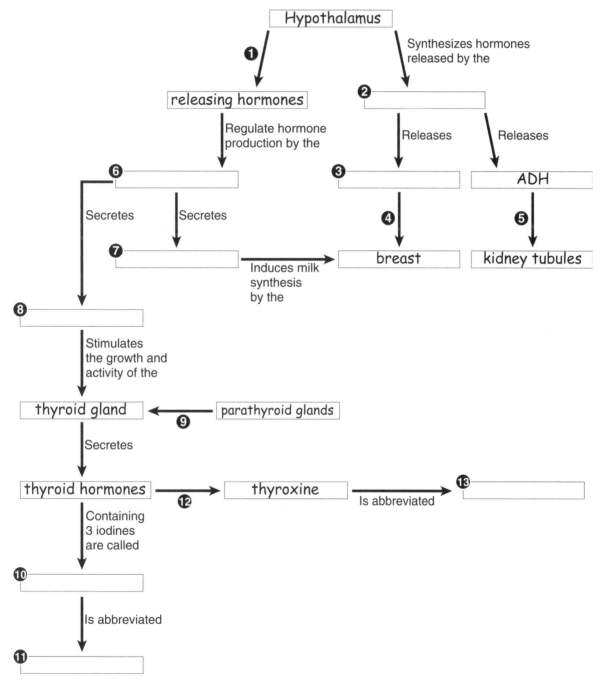

Optional Exercise: Construct your own concept map using the following terms: pancreas, insulin, glucagon, adrenal gland, medulla, cortex, epinephrine, cortisol, aldosterone, raises blood sugar, lowers blood sugar, and diabetes mellitus. You can also add other appropriate terms (for instance, target sites or hormone actions).

Testing Your Knowledge

Building Understanding

I. Multiple Choice

1. An androgen is a(n)
   a. female sex hormone
   b. glucocorticoid
   c. male sex hormone
   d. atrial hormone

   1. _____

2. Which of the following hormones is NOT produced by the thyroid gland?
   a. calcitonin
   b. thyroxine
   c. triiodothyronine
   d. thymosin

   2. _____

3. The hormone that causes milk ejection from the breasts is
   a. oxytocin
   b. prolactin
   c. progesterone
   d. estrogen

   3. _____

4. Which of the following hormones is derived from cholesterol?
   a. progesterone
   b. thyroid hormone
   c. growth hormone
   d. luteinizing hormone

   4. _____

5. The pituitary hormone that regulates the activity of the thyroid gland is
   a. TSH
   b. GH
   c. ACTH
   d. MSH

   5. _____

6. Erythropoietin is synthesized in the
   a. kidneys
   b. skin
   c. heart
   d. placenta

   6. _____

II. Completion Exercise

1. An abnormal increase in production of the hormone epinephrine may result from a tumor of the _____.

2. Releasing hormones are sent from the hypothalamus to the anterior pituitary by way of a special circulatory pathway called a(n) _____.

3. When the blood glucose level decreases to less than average, the islet cells of the pancreas release less insulin. The result is an increase in blood glucose. This is an example of the regulatory mechanism called _____.

4. The hypothalamus stimulates the anterior pituitary to produce ACTH, which in turn stimulates hormone production by the _____.

5. The element needed for the production of thyroxine is _____.

6. Local hormones that have a variety of effects, including the promotion of inflammation and the production of uterine contractions, are the _____.

7. A hormone secreted from the posterior pituitary that is involved in water balance is _____.

8. The primary target tissue for prolactin is the _____.

Understanding Concepts

I. True/False

For each question, write *T* for true or *F* for false in the blank to the left of each number. If a statement is false, correct it by replacing the underlined term and write the correct statement in the blank below the question.

_____ 1. ACTH acts on the adrenal medulla.

_____

_____ 2. Cortisol and the pancreatic hormone insulin both raise blood sugar.

_____

_____ 3. The ovaries and testes produce steroid hormones.

_____

_____ 4. Cortisol is produced by the adrenal cortex.

_____

_____ 5. Islet cells are found in the adrenal gland.

_____

_____ 6. ADH and oxytocin are secreted by the anterior lobe of the pituitary.

_____

_____ 7. Atrial natriuretic peptide (ANP) is produced by the kidneys.

_____

II. Practical Applications

Write the appropriate word or phrase in the space provided.

1. Mr. L, age 42, reported to the hospital emergency room with complaints of shortness of breath and heart palpitations. His metabolic rate was extremely high, and a gland located in the anterior neck was abnormally large. Laboratory tests confirmed the diagnosis of overactivity of the _____.

2. After surgery for his endocrine problem, Mr. L had tetany, or contractions of the muscles of the hands and face. This was caused by the incidental surgical removal of the glands that control the release of calcium into the blood. The glands that maintain adequate blood calcium levels are the _____.

3. Ms. M has just been stung by a bee. She is extremely allergic to bees. Her sister gives her a life-saving injection of an adrenal hormone. This hormone is called _____.

4. Ms. Q was supposed to have her baby 10 days ago. Her relatives are anxiously awaiting the birth of her child, so she asks her obstetrician if he can do something to hasten the birth of her child. The obstetrician agrees to induce labor using a hormone called _____.

5. Mr. S is preparing for his final law exams and is feeling very stressed. His partner is studying for a physiology exam and mentions that he probably has elevated levels of an anterior pituitary hormone that acts on the adrenal cortex. This hormone is called _____.

6. Ms. J, age 35, is preparing for a weight-lifting competition. She wants to build muscle tissue very rapidly, so a friend recommends that she tries injections of a male steroid known to stimulate tissue building. This steroid is mainly produced by the _____.

III. Short Essays

1. Explain why hormones, although they circulate throughout the body, exercise their effects only on specific target cells.

   _____

   _____

   _____

2. List two differences between the endocrine system and the nervous system.

   _____

   _____

   _____

3. Name three organs other than endocrine glands that produce hormones, and name a hormone produced in each organ.

   _____

   _____

   _____

4. Compare the anterior and the posterior lobes of the pituitary.

_____

_____

_____

Conceptual Thinking

1. Young Ms. K suffers from asthma. She uses an inhaler containing epinephrine to treat her attacks. However, lately she has been suffering from a very rapid heart beat. Her physician advises her to use her inhaler less frequently. Why?

_____

_____

_____

Expanding Your Horizons

In the past, the only source of protein hormones for therapeutic use was cadavers. Hormone supplies were very limited and only used in severe cases of hormone deficiency. Hormones can now be synthesized in unlimited quantities in a test tube. Some hormones, including growth hormone and anabolic steroids, are now abused by some athletes. They are also used by the elderly to treat some age-related deficits, such as reduced bone mass and impaired muscle strength, even though their safety has not been proven. Hormone use and abuse can be investigated using websites (http://www.hormone.org/ and http://www.nlm.nih.gov/medlineplus/). Hormone abuse in athletes is discussed in a _Scientific American_ article.

Resources

1. Zorpette G. The athlete's body: the chemical games. _Scientific American_ Presents: Building the Elite Athlete 2000;11:16–23.

UNIT IV

Circulation and Body Defense

➤ **Chapter 12**
The Blood

➤ **Chapter 13**
The Heart

➤ **Chapter 14**
Blood Vessels and
Blood Circulation

➤ **Chapter 15**
The Lymphatic
System and Body
Defenses

The Blood

Overview

The blood maintains the constancy of the internal environment through its functions of transportation, regulation, and protection. Blood is composed of two portions: the liquid portion, or plasma, and the formed elements, consisting of the cells and cellular products. The plasma is 91% water and 9% proteins, carbohydrates, lipids, electrolytes, and waste products. The formed elements are composed of the erythrocytes, which carry oxygen to the tissues; the leukocytes, which defend the body against invaders; and the platelets, which are involved in the process of blood coagulation (clotting). The forerunners of the blood cells are called hematopoietic stem cells. These are formed in the red bone marrow, where they then develop into the various types of blood cells.

Blood coagulation is a protective mechanism that prevents blood loss when a blood vessel is ruptured by an injury. The steps in the prevention of blood loss (hemostasis) include constriction of the blood vessels, formation of a platelet plug, and formation of a clot, a complex series of reactions involving many different factors.

If the quantity of blood in the body is severely reduced because of hemorrhage or disease, the cells suffer from lack of oxygen and nutrients. In such instances, a transfusion may be given after typing and matching the blood of the donor with that of the recipient. Donor red cells with different surface antigens (proteins) than the recipient's red cells will react with antibodies in the recipient's blood, causing harmful agglutination reactions and destruction of the donated cells. Blood is most commonly tested for the ABO system involving antigens A and B. Blood can be packaged and stored in blood banks for use when transfusions are needed. Whenever possible, blood components such as cells, plasma, plasma fractions, or platelets are used. This practice is more efficient and can reduce the chances of incompatibility and transmission of disease.

The Rh factor, another red blood cell protein, also is important in transfusions. If blood containing the Rh factor (Rh positive) is given to a person whose blood lacks that factor (Rh negative), the recipient will produce antibodies to the foreign Rh factor. If an Rh-negative mother is thus sensitized by an Rh-positive fetus, her antibodies may damage fetal red cells in a later pregnancy, resulting in hemolytic disease of the newborn (erythroblastosis fetalis).

Scientists have devised numerous studies to measure the composition of blood. These include the hematocrit, hemoglobin measurements, cell counts, blood chemistry tests, and coagulation studies. These techniques can diagnose blood diseases, some infectious diseases, and some metabolic diseases. Modern laboratories are equipped with automated counters, which rapidly and accurately count blood cells, and with automated analyzers, which measure enzymes, electrolytes, and other constituents of blood serum.

Addressing the Learning Outcomes

1. List the functions of the blood.

EXERCISE 12-1.

INSTRUCTIONS

List three functions of blood, and provide an example for each.

1. _____
2. _____
3. _____

2. List the main ingredients in plasma.

EXERCISE 12-2.

INSTRUCTIONS

Which of the following substances are found in plasma? Circle all that apply.

A. erythrocytes
B. water
C. proteins
D. platelets
E. nutrients
F. electrolytes

3. Describe the formation of blood cells.

EXERCISE 12-3.

INSTRUCTIONS

Name the type of stem cell that can develop into all types of blood cells.

_____

4. Name and describe the three types of formed elements in the blood and give the function of each.

EXERCISE 12-4: Composition of Whole Blood (Text Fig. 12-1)

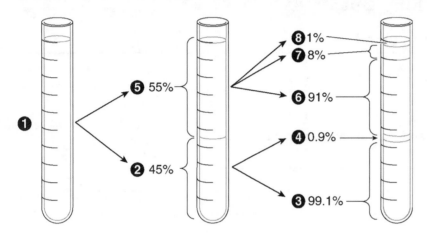

INSTRUCTIONS

1. Write the names of the different blood components on the appropriate numbered lines in different colors. Use the color red for parts 1, 2, and 3.
2. Color the blood components on the diagram with the corresponding color.

1. _____
2. _____
3. _____
4. _____
5. _____
6. _____
7. _____
8. _____

5. Characterize the five types of leukocytes.

EXERCISE 12-5: Leukocytes (Text Fig. 12-4)

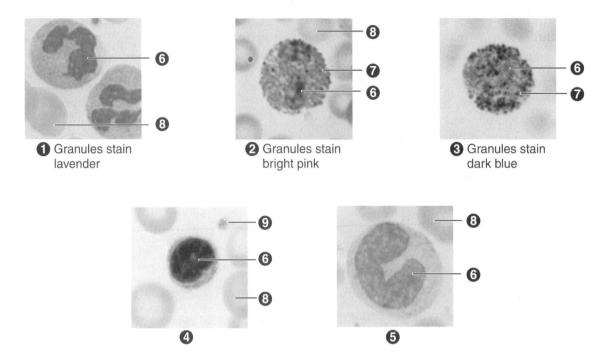

❶ Granules stain
lavender

❷ Granules stain
bright pink

❸ Granules stain
dark blue

INSTRUCTIONS

1. Write the names of the five types of leukocytes on lines 1 to 5.
2. Write the names of the labeled cell parts and other blood cells on lines 6 to 9.

1. _____

2. _____

3. _____

4. _____

5. _____

6. _____

7. _____

8. _____

9. _____

EXERCISE 12-6.

INSTRUCTIONS

Write the appropriate term in each blank.

erythrocyte   platelet   leukocyte   serum
albumin   antibodies   complement   plasma

1. A red blood cell   _____
2. Another name for thrombocyte   _____
3. The most abundant protein(s) in blood   _____
4. The liquid portion of blood   _____
5. A white blood cell   _____
6. Enzymes that assist antibodies to battle pathogens   _____
7. The watery fluid that remains after a blood clot is removed   _____

EXERCISE 12-7.

INSTRUCTIONS

Write the appropriate term in each blank.

neutrophil   macrophage   monocyte   pus
eosinophil   basophil   plasma cell

1. The most abundant type of white blood cell in whole blood   _____
2. A mature monocyte   _____
3. A lymphocyte that produces antibodies   _____
4. A leukocyte that stains with acidic dyes   _____
5. The largest blood leukocyte   _____
6. A substance that often accumulates when leukocytes are actively
   destroying bacteria   _____

6. Define *hemostasis* and cite three steps in hemostasis.

EXERCISE 12-8.

What is the difference between hemostasis and homeostasis?

_____

_____

_____

EXERCISE 12-9.

INSTRUCTIONS

Write the appropriate term in each blank.

vasoconstriction   coagulation   hemorrhage   platelet plug

1. A collection of cell fragments that temporarily repairs a vessel injury   _____
2. The process of blood clot formation   _____
3. Contraction of smooth muscles in the blood vessel wall   _____
4. Another term for profuse bleeding   _____

7. Briefly describe the steps in blood clotting.

EXERCISE 12-10: Formation of a Blood Clot (Text Fig. 12-8)

INSTRUCTIONS

Write the correct term in each of the numbered boxes.

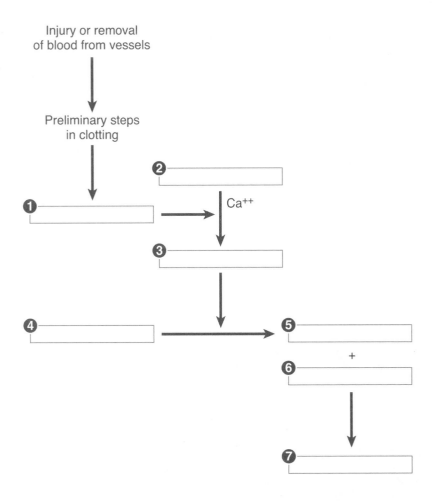

Injury or removal
of blood from vessels

Preliminary steps
in clotting

2 _____

Ca^{++}

1 _____

3 _____

4 _____

5 _____

+

6 _____

7 _____

8. Define *blood type* and explain the relation between blood type and transfusions.

EXERCISE 12-11: Blood Typing (Text Fig. 12-9)

INSTRUCTIONS

Based on the agglutination reactions, write the name of each blood type on the numbered lines.

1. _____

2. _____

3. _____

4. _____

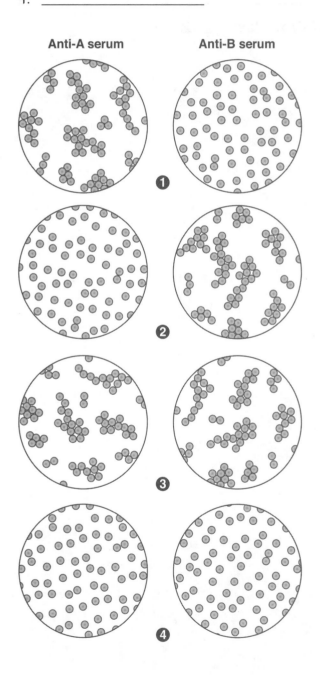

Anti-A serum   Anti-B serum

9. List the possible reasons for transfusions of whole blood and blood components.

EXERCISE 12-12.

INSTRUCTIONS

Write the appropriate term in each blank.

hematocrit   Rh factor   autologous   AB antigen   agglutination
hemapheresis   plasmapheresis   transfusion   antigen

1. The blood antigen involved in hemolytic disease of the newborn, which results from a blood incompatibility between a mother and fetus   _____
2. The procedure for removing plasma and returning formed elements to the donor   _____
3. The procedure for removing specific components and returning the remainder of the blood to the donor   _____
4. Term describing blood donated by an individual for his or her own use   _____
5. The volume percentage of red cells in whole blood   _____
6. The administration of blood or blood components from one person to another person   _____
7. A general term describing a protein on blood cells that causes incompatibility reactions   _____
8. The process by which cells become clumped when mixed with a specific antiserum   _____

10. Specify the tests used to study blood.

EXERCISE 12-13.

INSTRUCTIONS

Which blood test would you use to diagnose each disease? Choose from the list below. Each test can be used only once.

red cell count   coagulation study   bone marrow biopsy
platelet count   blood smear

1. hemophilia   _____
2. polycythemia vera or anemia   _____
3. thrombocytopenia   _____
4. leukemia   _____
5. malaria   _____

11. Show how word parts are used to build words related to the blood.

EXERCISE 12-14.

INSTRUCTIONS

Complete the following table by writing the correct word part or meaning in the space provided. Write a word that contains each word part in the Example column.

Word Part	Meaning	Example
1. erythr/o	_____	_____
2. _____	blood clot	_____
3. pro-	_____	_____
4. morph/o	_____	_____
5. _____	white, colorless	_____
6. _____	producing, originating	_____
7. hemat/o	_____	_____
8. _____	nucleus	_____
9. macr/o	_____	_____
10. _____	dissolving	_____

Making the Connections

The following concept map deals with the classification of blood cells. Each pair of terms is linked together by a connecting phrase into a sentence. The sentence should be read in the direction of the arrow. Complete the concept map by filling in the appropriate term or phrase. There is one right answer for each term. However, there are many correct answers for the connecting phrases (5, 6, 8, 10, 12, 14, and 16).

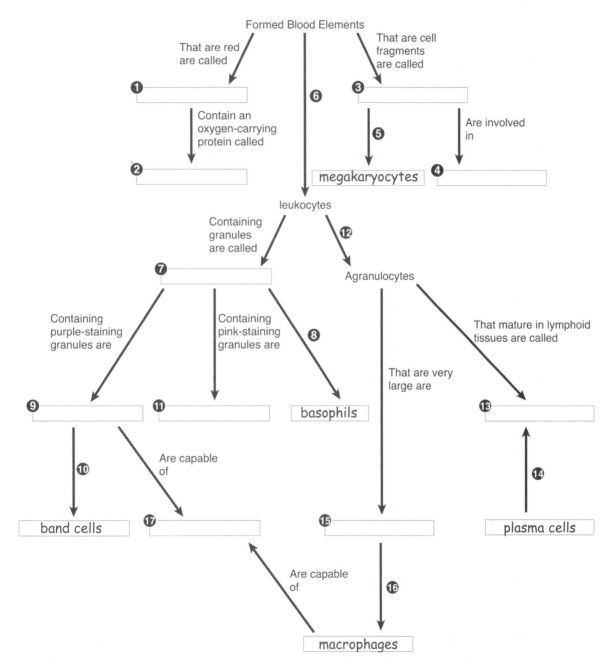

Optional Exercise: Construct your own concept map using the following terms and any others you would like to include: procoagulants, anticoagulants, platelet plug, hemostasis, vasoconstriction, blood clot, fibrinogen, fibrin, prothrombinase, thrombin, serum.

Testing Your Knowledge

Building Understanding

I. Multiple Choice

1. Plasma can be given to anyone without danger of incompatibility because it lacks
   a. serum
   b. red cells
   c. protein
   d. clotting factors

   1. _____

2. Polymorphs, PMNs, and segs are alternate names for
   a. monocytes
   b. neutrophils
   c. basophils
   d. lymphocytes

   2. _____

3. Which of the following is NOT a type of white blood cell?
   a. thrombocyte
   b. lymphocyte
   c. eosinophil
   d. monocyte

   3. _____

4. Blood clotting occurs in a complex series of steps. The substance that finally forms the clot is
   a. albumin
   b. anticoagulant
   c. thromboplastin
   d. fibrin

   4. _____

5. Which of the following might result in an Rh incompatibility problem?
   a. an Rh-positive mother and an Rh-negative fetus
   b. an Rh-negative mother and an Rh-positive fetus
   c. an Rh-negative mother and a type AB fetus
   d. an Rh-positive mother and an Rh-negative father

   5. _____

6. Intrinsic factor is
   a. the first factor activated in blood clotting
   b. a substance needed for absorption of folic acid
   c. a type of hereditary bleeding disease
   d. a substance needed for absorption of vitamin B_{12}

   6. _____

7. Electrophoresis is the process by which
   a. the volume proportion of red cells is determined
   b. normal and abnormal types of hemoglobin can be separated
   c. red blood cells are counted
   d. white blood cells are counted

   7. _____

8. An immature neutrophil is called a(n):
   a. band cell
   b. monocyte
   c. eosinophil
   d. lymphocyte

   8. _____

9. Which of the following cells is NOT a granulocyte?   9. _____
   a. monocyte
   b. eosinophil
   c. neutrophil
   d. polymorph

II. Completion Exercise

1. Blood that contains antibodies against the A antigen is termed type   _____
2. The conversion of prothrombin into thrombin requires the element   _____
3. The gas that is necessary for life and that is transported to all parts of the body by the blood is   _____
4. Some monocytes enter the tissues, mature, and become active phagocytes. These cells are called   _____
5. One waste product of body metabolism is carried to the lungs to be exhaled. This gas is   _____
6. The hormone that stimulates red blood cell production is   _____
7. Blood cells are formed in the   _____
8. The most important function of certain lymphocytes is to engulf disease-producing organisms by the process of   _____
9. The chemical element that characterizes hemoglobin is   _____

Understanding Concepts

I. True/False

For each question, write *T* for true or *F* for false in the blank to the left of each number. If a statement is false, correct it by replacing the underlined term and write the correct statement in the blank below the question.

_____ 1. Eosinophils and basophils are granular leukocytes.

_____

_____ 2. Blood cells from a person with type B blood will agglutinate with type A antiserum.

_____

_____ 3. Erythropoietin, a hormone that stimulates production of red blood cells, is produced by the kidneys.

_____

_____ 4. Type AB blood contains antibodies to both A and B antigens.

_____

_____ 5. Monocytes are immature neutrophils.

_____

_____ 6. Substances that induce blood clotting are called <u>procoagulants</u>.

_____

_____ 7. The watery fluid that remains after a blood clot has been removed from the blood is <u>plasma</u>.

_____

II. Practical Applications

Study each discussion. Then write the appropriate word or phrase in the space provided.

➤ Group A

1. A young girl named AL fell off her bike, sustaining a deep gash to her leg that bled copiously from a severed vessel. In describing this type of bleeding, the doctor in the emergency clinic used the word _____.
2. While the physician attended to the wound, the technician drew blood for typing and other studies. AL's blood did not agglutinate with either anti-A or anti-B serum. Her blood was classified as group _____.
3. Young AL required a blood transfusion. The only type of blood she could receive is

   _____.
4. Further testing of AL's blood revealed that it lacked the Rh factor. She was, therefore, said to be _____.
5. If AL were to be given a transfusion of Rh-positive blood, she might become sensitized to the Rh protein. In that event, her blood would produce counteracting substances called

   _____.

➤ Group B

1. Mr. KK, age 72, had an injury riding his motorized scooter down a steep hill. He suffered only minor scrapes, but he came to the hospital because his scrapes did not stop bleeding. The process by which blood loss is prevented or minimized is called _____.
2. The physician discovered that Mr. KK was the great-great-great grandson of Queen Victoria. Like many of her offspring, Mr. KK suffers from hemophilia. Hemophilia results from a deficiency in a substance that regulates blood clotting. These twelve substances, which are designated by Roman numerals, are called _____.
3. Mr. KK must be treated with a rich source of clotting factors. The doctor gets a bag of frozen plasma, which has a white powdery substance at the bottom of the bag. The substance is called

   _____.
4. Mr. KK also mentions that he has been very tired and pale lately. His cook recently retired, and he has been surviving on dill pickles and crackers. The physician suspects a deficiency in an element required to synthesize hemoglobin. This element is called _____.
5. The physician orders a test to determine the proportion of red blood cells in his blood. The result of this test is called the _____.

➤ **Group C**

1. Ms. J, an elite cyclist, has come to the hospital complaining of a pounding headache. The physician, Dr. L., takes a sample of her blood, and notices that it is very thick. He decides to count her red blood cells, but the automatic cell counter is not functioning. Dr. L calls for a technician to perform a visual count using the microscope and a special slide called a(n) _____.

2. The technician comes back with a result of 7.5 million cells per μL. This count is abnormally high. Dr. L is immediately suspicious. He asks Ms. J if she consumes any performance-enhancing drugs. Ms. J admits that she has been taking a hormone to increase blood cell synthesis. This hormone is called _____.

3. Dr. L tells Ms. J that she is at risk for blood clot formation. He tells her to stop taking the hormone and to take aspirin for a few days to inhibit blood clotting. Drugs that inhibit clotting are called _____.

III. Short Essays

1. What kind of information can be obtained from blood chemistry tests?

_____

_____

_____

2. Briefly describe the final events in blood clot formation, naming the substances involved in each step.

_____

_____

_____

_____

3. Name one reason to transfuse an individual with:
   a. whole blood

   _____

   b. platelets

   _____

   c. plasma

   _____

   d. plasma protein

   _____

Conceptual Thinking

1. A dehydrated individual will have an elevated hematocrit. Explain why.

_____

_____

_____

2. A man named JA has a history of frequent fevers. His skin is pale and his heart rate rapid. The doctor suspects that he has cancer. His white blood cell count was revealed to be 25,000 per μL of blood.
   a. Is this white blood cell count normal? What is the normal range?

   _____

   b. JA also has a hematocrit of 30%. Is this value normal? What is the normal range?

   _____

   _____

   c. Consider the different functions of blood. Discuss some functions that might be impaired in JA's case.

   _____

   _____

   _____

3. Mr. R needs a blood transfusion. He has type AB blood. The doctor is considering a transfusion using A blood.
   a. Which antigens are present on his blood cells?

   _____

   b. Which antibodies will be present in his blood?

   _____

   c. Which antigens will be present on donor blood cells?

   _____

   d. Is this blood transfusion safe? Why or why not?

   _____

Expanding Your Horizons

The amount of oxygen carried by the blood is an important determinant of athletic prowess. Some elite athletes are always looking for ways to increase the oxygen in their blood. If you follow competitive cycling, you are probably familiar with the hormone erythropoietin (EPO). EPO came to the public's attention during the 1998 Tour de France, when it was found that EPO use is common among elite athletes. Learn about this and other methods that athletes have used to legally or illegally gain an advantage over their competitors. EPO is discussed in an article in *Scientific American*, and you can do a website search for "EPO sport." Information on other methods can be found by doing a website search for "blood doping."

Resources

1. Zorpette G. The athlete's body: the chemical games. *Scientific American* Presents: Building the Elite Athlete 2000;11:16–23.

The Heart

Overview

The ceaseless beat of the heart day and night throughout one's entire lifetime is such an obvious key to the presence of life that it is no surprise that this organ has been the subject of wonderment and poetry. When the heart stops pumping, life ceases. The cells must have oxygen, and it is the heart's pumping action that propels oxygenated blood to them.

In size, the heart is roughly the size of one's fist. It is located between the lungs, more than half to the left of the midline, with the **apex** (point) directed toward the left. Below is the **diaphragm,** the dome-shaped muscle that separates the thoracic cavity from the abdominopelvic cavity.

The heart consists of two sides separated by septa. The septa keep blood that is higher in oxygen entirely separate from blood that is lower in oxygen. The two sides pump in unison, the right side pumping blood to the lungs to be oxygenated, and the left side pumping blood to all other parts of the body.

Each side of the heart is divided into two parts or **chambers.** The upper chamber, or **atrium,** on each side is the receiving chamber for blood returning to the heart. The lower chamber, or **ventricle,** is the strong pumping chamber. Because the ventricles pump more forcefully, their walls are thicker than the walls of the atria. **Valves** between the chambers keep the blood flowing forward as the heart pumps. The muscle of the heart wall, the **myocardium,** has special features to enhance its pumping efficiency. The coronary circulation supplies blood directly to the myocardium.

The heartbeat originates within the heart at the **sinoatrial (SA) node,** often called the pacemaker. Electrical impulses from the pacemaker spread through special conducting fibers in the wall of the heart to induce contractions, first of the two atria and then of the two ventricles. After contraction, the heart relaxes and fills with blood. The relaxation phase is called **diastole,** and the contraction phase is called **systole.** Together, these two phases make up one **cardiac cycle.**

The heart rate is influenced by the nervous system and other circulating factors, such as hormones and drugs.

Addressing the Learning Outcomes

1. Describe the three layers of the heart wall (see exercises for outcome 2).

2. Describe the structure of the pericardium and cite its functions.

EXERCISE 13-1: Layers of the Heart Wall and Pericardium (Text Fig. 13-2)

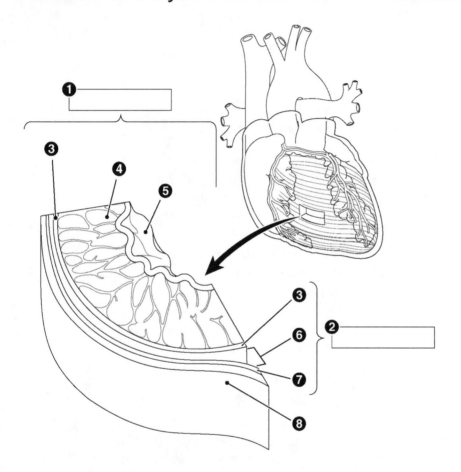

INSTRUCTIONS

1. Write the terms "heart wall" and "serous pericardium" in the corresponding boxes.
2. Write the names of the different structures on the numbered lines in different colors. Use black for structure 6, because it will not be colored.
3. Color the structures 3–8 on the diagram (except structure 6) with the corresponding colors.

3. _____   6. _____

4. _____   7. _____

5. _____   8. _____

EXERCISE 13-2.

INSTRUCTIONS

Write the appropriate term in each blank.

base   apex   endocardium   fibrous pericardium
myocardium   serous pericardium   epicardium

1. The pointed, inferior portion of the heart   _____
2. The membrane consisting of a visceral and a parietal layer   _____
3. A layer of epithelial cells in contact with blood within the heart   _____
4. The heart layer containing intercalated disks   _____
5. The outermost layer of the sac enclosing the heart   _____

3. Compare the functions of the right and left sides of the heart.

EXERCISE 13-3: The Heart Is a Double Pump (Text Fig. 13-4)

INSTRUCTIONS

1. Label the indicated parts.
2. Color the oxygenated blood red and the deoxygenated blood blue.
3. Use arrows to show the direction of blood flow.

1. _____
2. _____
3. _____
4. _____
5. _____
6. _____
7. _____
8. _____
9. _____
10. _____
11. _____
12. _____
13. _____
14. _____

4. Name the four chambers of the heart and compare their functions (see exercises for Outcome 5).

5. Name the valves at the entrance and exit of each ventricle and cite the function of the valves.

EXERCISE 13-4: The Heart and Great Vessels (Text Fig. 13-5)

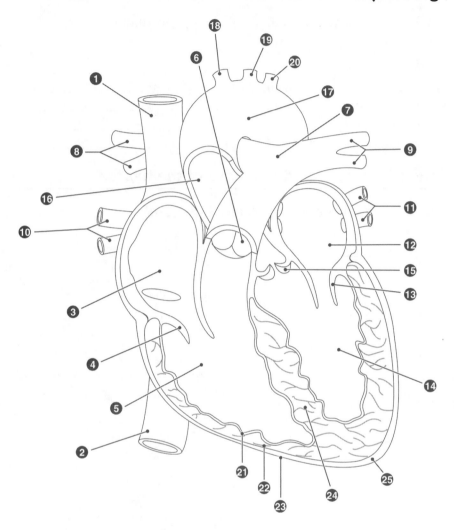

INSTRUCTIONS

1. Label the indicated parts.
2. Color the oxygenated blood red and the deoxygenated blood blue.
3. Use arrows to show the direction of blood flow.

1. _____	10. _____	18. _____
2. _____	11. _____	19. _____
3. _____	12. _____	20. _____
4. _____	13. _____	21. _____
5. _____	14. _____	22. _____
6. _____	15. _____	23. _____
7. _____	16. _____	24. _____
8. _____	17. _____	25. _____
9. _____		

EXERCISE 13-5.

INSTRUCTIONS

Write the appropriate term in each blank.

ventricle   atrium   atrioventricular valve   pulmonary valve
aortic valve   interatrial septum   interventricular septum

1. A lower chamber of the heart   _____
2. The valve that prevents blood from returning to the right ventricle   _____
3. An upper chamber of the heart   _____
4. The valve that prevents blood from returning to the left ventricle   _____
5. The partition that separates the two upper chambers of the heart   _____
6. One of two valves dividing the upper and lower chambers   _____

6. Briefly describe blood circulation through the myocardium.

EXERCISE 13-6.

INSTRUCTIONS

Fill in the blanks.

1. The blood vessels that supply the heart constitute the _____ circulation.
2. The main arteries supplying blood to the heart muscle branch off from the aorta just superior to the _____ valve.
3. Blood from capillaries in the heart muscle eventually enters a dilated vein called the _____.
4. Blood from the heart muscle eventually drains into the _____ atrium.

7. Briefly describe the cardiac cycle.

EXERCISE 13-7.

Do each of the following events occur in diastole (D), atrial systole (A), or ventricular systole (V)?

1. The ventricles are contracting. _____
2. The atria are contracting. _____
3. Blood is entering the aorta. _____
4. Neither the ventricles nor the atria are contracting. _____
5. The atrioventricular valves are closed. _____

EXERCISE 13-8.

INSTRUCTIONS

Write the appropriate term in each blank.

diastole   atrial systole   ventricular systole   cardiac output   stroke volume

1. The amount of blood ejected from a ventricle with each beat   _____
2. The stage of the cardiac cycle that directly follows the resting period   _____
3. The stage of the cardiac cycle which precedes the resting period   _____
4. The volume of blood pumped by each ventricle in 1 minute   _____
5. The resting period of the cardiac cycle   _____

8. Name and locate the components of the heart's conduction system.

EXERCISE 13-9: The Conduction System of the Heart (Text Fig. 13-11)

INSTRUCTIONS

1. Label the indicated parts.
2. Highlight the structures that conduct electrical impulses in yellow. Draw arrows to indicate the direction of impulse conduction.

1. _____
2. _____
3. _____
4. _____
5. _____
6. _____
7. _____
8. _____
9. _____
10. _____
11. _____
12. _____
13. _____
14. _____

EXERCISE 13-10.

INSTRUCTIONS

Write the appropriate term in each blank.

bundle of His   Purkinje fibers   sinus rhythm
sinoatrial node   atrioventricular node

1. The group of conduction fibers found in the ventricle walls   _____
2. The mass of conduction tissue located in the septum at the bottom of the right atrium   _____
3. A normal heart beat, originating from the normal heart pacemaker   _____
4. The group of conduction fibers carrying impulses from the AV node   _____
5. The name of the normal heart pacemaker, located in the upper wall of the right atrium   _____

9. Explain the effects of the autonomic nervous system on the heart rate.

EXERCISE 13-11.

Do each of the following characteristics refer to the parasympathetic nervous system (P) or the sympathetic nervous system (S)?

1. Regulates heart activity via the vagus nerve   _____
2. Uses ganglia located close to the spinal cord   _____
3. Decreases the heart rate   _____
4. Increases the force of each contraction   _____
5. Increases the heart rate   _____

10. List and define several terms that describe variations in heart rates.

EXERCISE 13-12.

INSTRUCTIONS

Write the appropriate term in each blank.

bradycardia   tachycardia   sinus arrhythmia   extrasystole

1. A beat that comes before the normal beat   _____
2. A normal variation in heart rate caused by changes in breathing rate _____
3. A heart rate of less than 60 beats per minute   _____
4. A heart rate of greater than 100 beats per minute   _____

11. Explain what produces the two main heart sounds.

EXERCISE 13-13.

INSTRUCTIONS

Fill in the blanks.

1. The "lub" sound is caused by the closure of the _____ valves.
2. The "dub" sound is caused by the closure of the _____ valves.

12. Briefly describe four methods for studying the heart.

EXERCISE 13-14.

INSTRUCTIONS

Write the appropriate term in each blank.

stethoscope   echocardiography   catheterization
electrocardiography

1. Technique that uses ultrasound to study the heart as it beats   _____
2. Technique that measures the electrical activity of the heart   _____
3. Instrument used to detect heart murmurs by their sound   _____
4. A procedure for measuring pressures within the heart chambers   _____

13. Show how word parts are used to build words related to the heart.

EXERCISE 13-15.

INSTRUCTIONS

Complete the following table by writing the correct word part or meaning in the space provided. Write a word that contains each word part in the Example column.

Word Part	Meaning	Example
1. _____	chest	_____
2. sin/o	_____	_____
3. cardi/o	_____	_____
4. _____	lung	_____
5. _____	slow	_____
6. _____	rapid	_____

Making the Connections

The following flow chart deals with the passage of blood through the heart. Beginning with the right atrium, outline the structures a blood cell would pass through in the correct order by filling in the boxes. Use the following terms: left atrium, left ventricle, right ventricle, right AV valve, left AV valve, pulmonary semilunar valve, aortic semilunar valve, superior/inferior vena cava, right lung, left lung, aorta, left pulmonary artery, right pulmonary artery, left pulmonary veins, right pulmonary veins, and body. You can write the names of structures that encounter blood high in oxygen in red and the names of structures that encounter blood low in oxygen in blue.

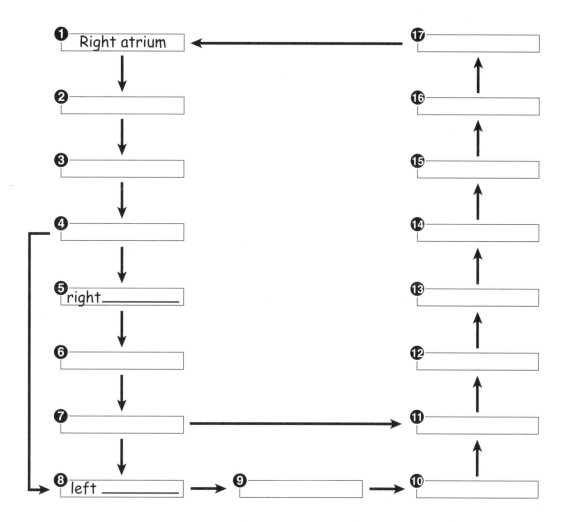

Optional Exercise: Make your own concept map, based on the events of the cardiac cycle. Choose your own terms to incorporate into your map, or use the following list: AV valves open, AV valves closed, blood flow from atria to ventricles, blood flow from ventricles to arteries, atrial diastole, atrial systole, ventricular diastole, and ventricular systole. There will be many links between the different terms.

Testing Your Knowledge

Building Understanding

I. Multiple Choice

Select the best answer and write the letter of your choice in the blank.

1. An average cardiac cycle lasts about
   a. 8 seconds
   b. 5 seconds
   c. 0.8 second
   d. 30 seconds

1. _____

2. The volume of blood pumped by each ventricle in 1 minute is the
   a. stroke volume
   b. cardiac output
   c. heart rate
   d. ejection rate

2. _____

3. Which of the following is NOT a part of the conduction system of the heart?
   a. bundle of His
   b. atrioventricular valve
   c. Purkinje fibers
   d. atrioventricular node

3. _____

4. Activation of the parasympathetic nervous system would
   a. increase heart rate but not myocardial contraction strength
   b. increase heart rate and myocardial contraction strength
   c. decrease heart rate but not myocardial contraction strength
   d. decrease heart rate and myocardial contraction strength

4. _____

5. The vein that carries blood from the coronary circulation back into the right atrium is the
   a. right coronary artery
   b. interatrial septum
   c. pulmonary vein
   d. coronary sinus

5. _____

II. Completion Exercise

Write the word or phrase that correctly completes each sentence.

1. The autonomic nerve that slows the heart beat is the _____.
2. The fibrous sac that surrounds the heart is the _____.
3. One complete cycle of heart contraction and relaxation is called the _____.
4. The fibrous threads connecting the AV valves to muscles in the heart wall are called the

   _____.

5. The right atrioventricular valve is also known as the _____.
6. Normal heart sounds heard while the heart is working are called _____.
7. An abnormally slow heart beat is termed _____.

Understanding Concepts

I. True/False

For each question, write *T* for true or *F* for false in the blank to the left of each number. If a statement is false, correct it by replacing the underlined term and write the correct statement in the blank below the question.

_____ 1. The aorta receives blood directly from the <u>right atrium</u>.

_____

_____ 2. Cardiac output equals heart rate <u>multiplied</u> by stroke volume.

_____

_____ 3. A heart rate of 150 beats/minute is described as <u>tachycardia</u>.

_____

_____ 4. Blood in the heart chambers comes into contact with the <u>epicardium</u>.

_____

_____ 5. The aorta is part of the <u>pulmonary</u> circuit.

_____

_____ 6. Nerve impulses travel down the internodal pathways from the <u>AV node</u>

_____

_____ 7. A heart rhythm originating at the <u>SA node</u> is termed a sinus rhythm.

_____

II. Practical Applications

Study each discussion. Then write the appropriate word or phrase in the space provided.

➤ **Group A**

1. Ms. J, age 82, was participating in a lawn bowling tournament when she suddenly collapsed with chest pain. The paramedics were preparing her for transport to the hospital when they noted a sudden onset of pale skin and unconsciousness. The heart monitor showed a rapid, uncoordinated activity of the lower heart chambers, known as the _____.
2. The paramedics administered an electric shock using an automated defibrillator with the aim of restoring the normal heart rhythm, which is called a(n) _____.
3. In the hospital emergency room, Ms. J was given intravenous medications to dissolve any blood clots in the vessels supplying her heart muscle. Together, these vessels are called the _____.

4. The drugs were not administered in time to prevent damage to the middle layer of the heart wall, which is known as the _____.

5. The electrical activity of Ms. J's heart was analyzed using a(n) _____.

6. The analysis showed that the conduction system was damaged. The electrical impulse generated by her sinoatrial node was not reaching the conducting fibers that pass down the interventricular septum. These fibers are collectively known as the _____.

➤ Group B

1. Baby L has just been born. To her parents' dismay, her skin and mucous membranes are tinged with blue. The obstetrician listens to her heartbeat using an instrument called a(n) _____.

2. The doctor notices an abnormality in the second heart sound (or "dup"), which is largely caused by the closure of the two _____.

3. This abnormal sound probably reflects a structural problem with Baby L's heart and is thus termed a(n) _____.

4. The baby is sent for a test that uses ultrasound waves to examine her heart structure. This technique is known as _____.

III. Short Essays

1. Although the heartbeat originates within the heart itself, it is influenced by factors in the internal environment. Describe some of these factors that can affect the heart.

_____

_____

_____

Conceptual Thinking

1. Atropine is a drug that inhibits activity of the parasympathetic nervous system. Discuss the effects of atropine on the heart. How does the parasympathetic nervous system affect the heart? Which aspects of heart function will be affected and which will be unaffected?

_____

_____

_____

2. Mr. J is undertaking a gentle exercise program, primarily involving walking, to lose weight. His heart rate is 100 beats/minute and his stroke volume is 75 ml. What is his cardiac output, and what does cardiac output mean?

_____

_____

_____

Expanding Your Horizons

How low can you go? You may have heard of the exploits of free divers, who dive to tremendous depths without the aid of SCUBA equipment. The world record for assisted free diving is held by Pipin Ferreras, who dove to 170 m (558 feet) with the aid of a sled. Free diving is not without its dangers. Pipin's wife (Audrey) died during a world record attempt. Free diving is facilitated by the dive reflex, which allows mammals to hold their breath for long periods of time underwater. Immersing one's face in cold water induces bradycardia and diverts blood away from the periphery. How would these modifications increase the ability to free dive? You can learn more about the underlying mechanisms, rationale, and dangers of the dive reflex by performing a website search for "dive reflex." Information is also available in the article listed below.

Resources

1. Hurwitz BE, Furedy JJ. The human dive reflex: an experimental, topographical, and physiological analysis. *Physiol Behav* 1986; 36:287–294.

CHAPTER 14

Blood Vessels and Blood Circulation

Overview

The blood vessels are classified as arteries, veins, or capillaries according to their function. **Arteries** carry blood away from the heart, **veins** return blood to the heart, and **capillaries** are the site of gas, nutrient, and waste exchange between the blood and tissues. Small arteries are called **arterioles**, and small veins are called **venules**. The walls of the arteries are thicker and more elastic than the walls of the veins in order to withstand higher pressure. All vessels are lined with a single layer of simple epithelium called **endothelium**. The smallest vessels, the capillaries, are made only of this single layer of cells. The exchange of fluid between the blood and interstitial spaces is influenced by **blood pressure**, which pushes fluid out of the capillary, and **osmotic pressure**, which draws fluid back in. Blood pressure is determined by the **cardiac output** and the **total peripheral resistance**.

The vessels carry blood through two circuits. The **pulmonary circuit** transports blood between the heart and the lungs for gas exchange. The **systemic circuit** distributes blood high in oxygen to all other body tissues and returns deoxygenated blood to the heart.

The walls of the vessels, especially the small arteries, contain smooth muscle that is under the control of the involuntary nervous system. The diameters of the vessels can be increased (**vasodilation**) or decreased (**vasoconstriction**) by the nervous system in order to alter blood pressure and blood distribution.

Several forces work together to drive blood back to the heart in the venous system. Contraction of skeletal muscles compresses the veins and pushes blood forward, **valves** in the veins keep blood from flowing backward, and changes in pressure that occur during breathing help to drive blood back to the heart. The **pulse rate** and **blood pressure** can provide information about an individual's cardiovascular health.

Addressing the Learning Outcomes

1. Differentiate among the five types of blood vessels with regard to structure and function.

EXERCISE 14-1: Sections of Small Blood Vessels (Text Fig. 14-2)

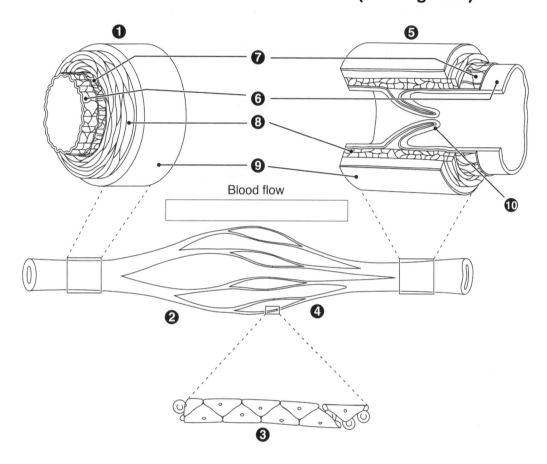

Blood flow

INSTRUCTIONS

1. Write the names of the different vessel types on lines 1 to 5.
2. Write the names of the different vascular layers on the appropriate numbered lines (6 to 10) in different colors. Use black for structure 10, because it will not be colored.
3. Color the structures on the diagram with the corresponding color (except for structures 1, 5, and 10 on the uppermost drawings).
4. Draw an arrow in the box to indicate the direction of blood flow.

1. _____   6. _____

2. _____   7. _____

3. _____   8. _____

4. _____   9. _____

5. _____   10. _____

EXERCISE 14-2.

INSTRUCTIONS

Write the appropriate term in each blank.

artery   capillary   vein   venule   arteriole

1. A small vessel through which exchanges between the blood and
   the cells take place   _____
2. A vessel that receives blood from the capillaries   _____
3. A vessel that branches off the aorta   _____
4. A small vessel that delivers blood to the capillaries   _____
5. A vessel that receives blood from venules and delivers it to the heart _____

2. Compare the pulmonary and systemic circuits relative to location and function.

EXERCISE 14-3.

INSTRUCTIONS

State whether each statement refers to the pulmonary circuit (P) or the systemic circuit (S).

1. The group of vessels that carries nutrients and oxygen to all tissues of the body except the lungs _____
2. The group of vessels that carries blood to and from the lungs for gas exchange _____
3. The group of vessels that includes the aorta _____
4. The group of vessels that delivers blood to the left atrium _____
5. The group of vessels that delivers blood to the right atrium _____
6. The group of vessels that receives blood from the right ventricle _____

3. Name the four sections of the aorta and list the main branches of each section.

EXERCISE 14-4: Aorta and Its Branches (Text Fig. 14-4)

INSTRUCTIONS

1. Write the names of the aortic sections on lines 1 to 4 in different colors, and color the appropriate structures on the diagram. Although the aorta is continuous, lines have been added to the diagram to indicate the boundaries of the different sections.
2. Write the names of the aortic branches on the appropriate lines 5 to 22 in different colors, and color the corresponding artery on the diagram. Use the same color for structures 8 and 9 and for structures 7 and 10. Use black for structure 15, because it will not be colored.

1. _____
2. _____
3. _____
4. _____
5. _____
6. _____
7. _____
8. _____
9. _____
10. _____
11. _____
12. _____
13. _____
14. _____
15. _____
16. _____
17. _____
18. _____
19. _____
20. _____
21. _____
22. _____

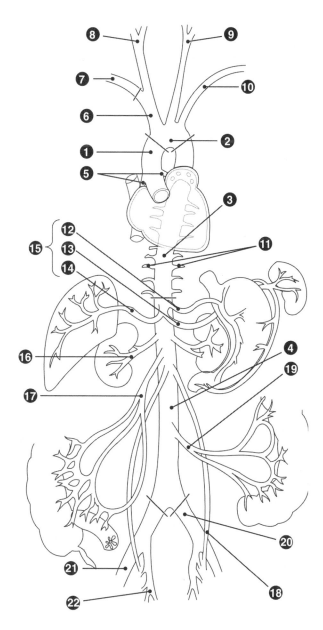

EXERCISE 14-5: Principal Systemic Arteries (Text Fig. 14-5)

INSTRUCTIONS

1. Write the names of the aortic segments and the principal systemic arteries on the appropriate lines in different, preferably darker, colors. Felt tip pens would work well for this exercise. Some structures were also labeled in Exercise 14-4 (for instance, the thoracic aorta); you may want to use the same color scheme for both exercises. Use black for structure 15, because it will not be colored.
2. Outline the arteries on the diagram with the corresponding color. If appropriate, color the left and right versions of each artery (for instance, you can color the right and left anterior tibial arteries). Some arteries change names along their length (for instance, the brachiocephalic artery).

1. _____
2. _____
3. _____
4. _____
5. _____
6. _____
7. _____
8. _____
9. _____
10. _____
11. _____
12. _____
13. _____
14. _____
15. _____
16. _____
17. _____
18. _____
19. _____
20. _____
21. _____
22. _____
23. _____
24. _____
25. _____
26. _____
27. _____
28. _____
29. _____

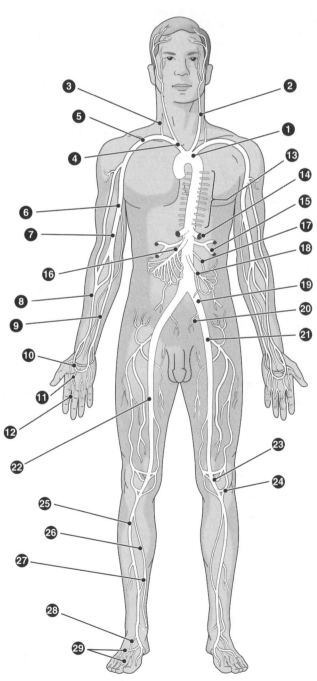

EXERCISE 14-6.

INSTRUCTIONS

Write the appropriate term in each blank.

coronary arteries   carotid arteries   lumbar arteries   common iliac arteries
phrenic arteries   intercostal arteries   ovarian arteries
suprarenal arteries   brachial arteries   renal arteries

1. Paired branches of the abdominal aorta that supply the diaphragm _____
2. The vessels that branch off the ascending aorta and supply the
   heart muscle _____
3. The large, paired branches of the abdominal aorta that supply
   blood to the kidneys _____
4. The vessels formed by final division of the abdominal aorta _____
5. The vessels that supply the head and neck on each side _____
6. The paired arteries that branch into the radial and ulnar arteries _____
7. A group of paired vessels that extend between the ribs _____
8. Paired branches of the abdominal aorta that extend into the
   abdominal wall musculature _____

EXERCISE 14-7.

INSTRUCTIONS

Write the appropriate term in each blank.

ascending aorta   aortic arch   thoracic aorta   abdominal aorta
brachiocephalic artery   celiac trunk   hepatic artery

1. The short artery that branches into the left gastric artery, the
   splenic artery, and the hepatic artery _____
2. A large vessel found within the pericardial sac _____
3. The portion of the aorta supplying the upper extremities, neck,
   and head _____
4. The large vessel that branches into the right subclavian artery and
   the right common carotid artery _____
5. The most inferior portion of the aorta _____
6. The vessel supplying oxygenated blood to the liver _____

4. Define *anastomosis*, cite its function, and give several examples.

EXERCISE 14-8: Principal Systemic Arteries of the Head (Text Fig. 14-5)

INSTRUCTIONS

1. Write the names of cranial arteries on the appropriate lines in different, preferably darker, colors. Felt tip pens would work well for this exercise.
2. Outline the arteries on the diagram with the corresponding color.

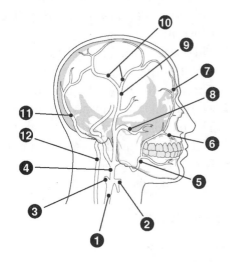

1. _____
2. _____
3. _____
4. _____
5. _____
6. _____
7. _____
8. _____
9. _____
10. _____
11. _____
12. _____

EXERCISE 14-9.

INSTRUCTIONS

Write the appropriate term in each blank.

mesenteric arch	arterial arch	circle of Willis
anastomosis	superficial palmar arch	basilar artery

1. A general term describing communication between two blood vessels _____
2. An anastomosis between vessels supplying the intestines _____
3. An anastomosis under the center of the brain formed by two internal carotid arteries and the basilar artery _____
4. The vessel formed by union of the two vertebral arteries _____
5. A vessel formed by the union of the radial and ulnar arteries _____

5. Compare superficial and deep veins and give examples of each type.

EXERCISE 14-10.

INSTRUCTIONS

For each of the following veins, state whether they are deep (D) or superficial (S).

1. saphenous vein ____   4. femoral vein ____
2. basilic vein ____   5. jugular vein ____
3. brachial vein ____

6. Name the main vessels that drain into the superior and inferior venae cavae.

EXERCISE 14-11: Principal Systemic Veins (Text Fig. 14-8)

INSTRUCTIONS

Label each of the indicated veins. The boundaries between different veins are indicated with perpendicular lines.

1. _____
2. _____
3. _____
4. _____
5. _____
6. _____
7. _____
8. _____
9. _____
10. _____
11. _____
12. _____
13. _____
14. _____
15. _____
16. _____
17. _____
18. _____
19. _____
20. _____
21. _____
22. _____
23. _____
24. _____
25. _____
26. _____

EXERCISE 14-12: Principal Systemic Veins of the Head (Text Fig. 14-8)

INSTRUCTIONS

Label each of the indicated veins.

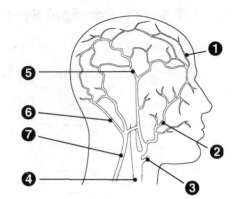

1. _____
2. _____
3. _____
4. _____
5. _____
6. _____
7. _____

EXERCISE 14-13.

INSTRUCTIONS

Write the appropriate term in each blank.

cephalic vein	saphenous vein	jugular vein	gastric vein
femoral vein	lumbar vein	hepatic portal vein	common iliac vein

1. The vein that drains the area supplied by the carotid artery   _____

2. The longest vein   _____

3. A vessel that drains into the subclavian vein   _____

4. A deep vein of the thigh   _____

5. One of four pairs of veins that drain the dorsal part of the trunk   _____

6. A vein that sends blood to hepatic capillaries   _____

7. A vein that drains the stomach and empties into the hepatic portal vein   _____

7. Define *venous sinus* and give several examples of venous sinuses.

EXERCISE 14-14: Cranial Venous Sinuses (Text Fig. 14-9)

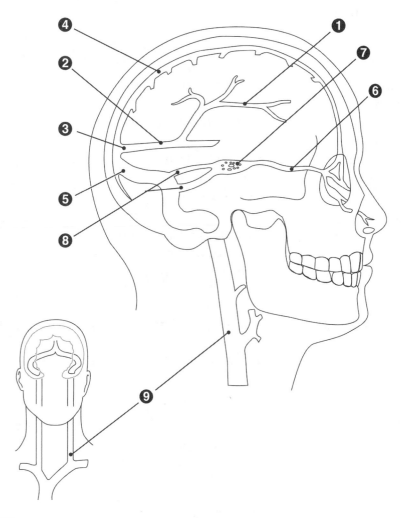

INSTRUCTIONS

1. Label each of the indicated veins and sinuses.
2. Draw arrows to indicate the direction of blood flow through the sinuses into the internal jugular vein.

1. _____
2. _____
3. _____
4. _____
5. _____
6. _____
7. _____
8. _____
9. _____

EXERCISE 14-15.

INSTRUCTIONS

Write the appropriate term in each blank.

coronary sinus   azygos vein   superior vena cava   inferior vena cava
transverse sinus   superior sagittal sinus   median cubital vein   cavernous sinus

1. A vessel that drains blood from the chest wall and empties into the superior vena cava _____
2. The vein that receives blood draining from the head, neck, upper extremities, and chest _____
3. A vein frequently used for removing blood for testing because of its location near the surface at the front of the elbow _____
4. The large vein that drains blood from the parts of the body below the diaphragm _____
5. The channel that drains blood from the ophthalmic vein of the eye
6. The channel that drains into the confluence of sinuses _____
7. The channel that receives blood from most of the veins of the heart wall _____

8. Describe the structure and function of the hepatic portal system.

EXERCISE 14-16: Hepatic Portal Circulation (Text Fig. 14-10)

INSTRUCTIONS

Label each of the indicated parts.

1. _____
2. _____
3. _____
4. _____
5. _____
6. _____
7. _____
8. _____
9. _____
10. _____
11. _____
12. _____
13. _____

9. Explain the forces that affect exchange across the capillary wall.

EXERCISE 14-17.

INSTRUCTIONS

Write the appropriate term in each blank.

diffusion   blood pressure   osmotic pressure

1. A force that pushes water out of the capillary   _____
2. A force that moves substances down their concentration gradients   _____
3. A force that draws water into the capillary   _____

10. Describe the factors that regulate blood flow.

EXERCISE 14-18.

INSTRUCTIONS

Write the appropriate term in each blank.

vasomotor center   vasodilation   vasoconstriction
valve   precapillary sphincter

1. Structure that prevents blood from moving backward in the veins   _____
2. A structure that regulates blood flow into an individual capillary   _____
3. The change in blood vessel diameter caused by smooth muscle
   contraction   _____
4. An increase in blood vessel diameter   _____
5. A region of the medulla oblongata that controls blood vessel
   diameter   _____

11. Define *pulse* and list factors that affect pulse rate.

EXERCISE 14-19.

INSTRUCTIONS

For each of the following situations, will the pulse rate most likely increase (I) or decrease (D)?

1. A newborn baby grows older _____
2. An adult falls asleep _____
3. Thyroid gland secretion increases _____
4. A teenager runs to catch a bus _____
5. A child gets a fever _____

12. List the factors that affect blood pressure.

EXERCISE 14-20.

INSTRUCTIONS

What is the effect of each of the following changes on blood pressure? In the blanks, write *I* for increase or *D* for decrease.

1. Decreased cardiac output _____
2. Increased blood thickness _____
3. Reduced volume of blood ejected from the heart per heartbeat _____
4. Decreased vessel elasticity (from atherosclerosis, for example) _____
5. Uncontrolled bleeding _____
6. Increased heart rate _____
7. Vasoconstriction _____

13. Explain how blood pressure is commonly measured.

EXERCISE 14-21.

INSTRUCTIONS

Write the appropriate term in each blank.

viscosity	systolic pressure	diastolic pressure	stethoscope
hypotension	sphygmomanometer	osmolarity	hypertension

1. Term for the blood pressure reading taken during ventricular relaxation _____
2. An instrument that is used to measure blood pressure _____
3. Term for blood pressure measured during heart muscle contraction _____
4. A term that describes the thickness of a solution _____
5. An abnormal increase in blood pressure _____
6. An abnormal decrease in blood pressure _____

14. Show how word parts are used to build words related to the blood vessels and circulation.

EXERCISE 14-22.

INSTRUCTIONS

Complete the following table by writing the correct word part or meaning in the space provided. Write a word that contains each word part in the Example column.

Word Part	Meaning	Example
1. _____	foot	_____
2. splen/o	_____	_____
3. _____	mouth	_____
4. hepat/o	_____	_____
5. bar/o	_____	_____
6. _____	stomach	_____
7. _____	arm	_____
8. _____	intestine	_____
9. sphygm/o	_____	_____
10. celi/o	_____	_____

Making the Connections

The following concept map deals with the measurement and regulation of blood pressure. Each pair of terms is linked together by a connecting phrase into a sentence. The sentence should be read in the direction of the arrow. Complete the concept map by filling in the appropriate term or phrase. There is one right answer for each term. However, there are many correct answers for the connecting phrases (3, 6, 8, and 11).

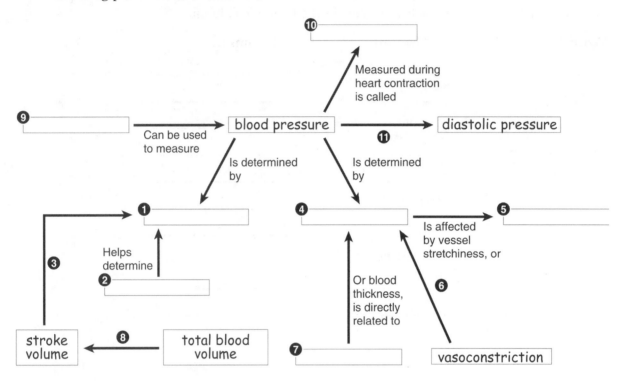

Optional Exercise: Make your own concept map/flow chart, based on the flow of blood from the left ventricle to the foot. It is not necessary to include connecting statements between the terms. You can also make flow charts based on the flow of blood from the leg to the heart, or to and from the arm and/or head. Choose your own terms to incorporate into your map, or use the following list: left ventricle, dorsalis pedis, femoral, anterior tibial, aortic arch, abdominal aorta, descending aorta, ascending aorta, popliteal, common iliac, and external iliac.

Testing Your Knowledge

Building Understanding

I. Multiple Choice

Select the best answer and write the letter of your choice in the blank.

1. Which of the following arteries is unpaired?   1. _____
   a. renal
   b. brachial
   c. brachiocephalic
   d. common carotid

2. The precapillary sphincter is a   2. _____
   a. ring of smooth muscle that regulates blood flow
   b. dilated vein in the liver
   c. tissue flap that prevents blood backflow in veins
   d. valve at the entrance to the iliac artery

3. Which of the following arteries carries blood low in oxygen?   3. _____
   a. pulmonary artery
   b. hepatic portal artery
   c. brachiocephalic artery
   d. superior vena cava

4. The cavernous sinus is found in the   4. _____
   a. lung
   b. liver
   c. heart
   d. head

5. As blood flows through the tissues, a force that draws fluid back into
   the capillaries is   5. _____
   a. blood pressure
   b. osmotic pressure
   c. hypertension
   d. vasoconstriction

6. Which of the following veins is found in the lower extremity?   6. _____
   a. jugular
   b. brachial
   c. basilic
   d. popliteal

7. Which of the following arteries is NOT found in the circle of Willis? 7. _____
   a. anterior cerebral
   b. posterior communicating
   c. vertebral
   d. middle cerebral

8. Which of the following layers is found in arteries AND capillaries?   8. _____
   a. smooth muscle
   b. inner tunic
   c. outer tunic
   d. middle tunic

9. Blood pressure would be increased by
   a. narrowing the blood vessels
   b. reducing the pulse rate
   c. increasing vasodilation
   d. decreasing blood viscosity

9. _____

10. Which of the following is NOT a subdivision of the aorta?
    a. thoracic aorta
    b. descending aorta
    c. pulmonary aorta
    d. abdominal aorta

10. _____

11. The two veins that unite to form the inferior vena cava are the
    a. gastric veins
    b. common iliac veins
    c. jugular veins
    d. mesenteric veins

12. _____

II. Completion Exercise

Write the word or phrase that correctly completes each sentence.

1. One example of a portal system is the system that carries blood from the abdominal organs to the _____.
2. The inner, epithelial layer of blood vessels is called the _____.
3. The aorta and the venae cavae are part of the group, or circuit, of blood vessels that make up the _____.
4. A large channel that drains deoxygenated blood is called a(n) _____.
5. The smallest subdivisions of arteries have thin walls in which there is little connective tissue and relatively more muscle. These vessels are _____.
6. A decrease in a blood vessel's diameter is called _____.
7. The circle of Willis is formed by a union of the internal carotid arteries and the basilar artery. Such a union of vessels is called a(n) _____.

Understanding Concepts

I. True/False

For each question, write *T* for true or *F* for false in the blank to the left of each number. If a statement is false, correct it by replacing the underlined term and write the correct statement in the blank below the question.

_____ 1. The anterior and posterior communicating arteries are part of the anastomosis supplying the <u>brain</u>.

_____

_____ 2. Contraction of the smooth muscle in arterioles would <u>decrease</u> blood pressure.

_____

_____ 3. Increased blood pressure would <u>decrease</u> the amount of fluid leaving the capillaries.

_____

_____ 4. The external iliac artery continues in the thigh as the <u>femoral</u> artery.

_____

_____ 5. The transverse sinuses receive most of the blood leaving the <u>heart</u>.

_____

_____ 6. Sinusoids are found in the <u>liver</u>.

_____

_____ 7. Blood flow into individual capillaries is regulated by <u>precapillary sphincters</u>.

_____

_____ 8. Blood pressure is equal to the <u>pulse rate</u> × peripheral resistance.

_____

II. Practical Applications

Study each discussion. Then write the appropriate word or phrase in the space provided.

➤ Group A

Ms. S, aged 68, was admitted to the hospital suffering from lightheadedness and mental confusion.

1. Physical examination showed a narrowing of the large artery on the side of the neck that carries blood to the brain. This artery is the _____.
2. Small amounts of blood could still reach Ms. S's brain through the two vertebral arteries. These join at the base of the brain to form a single artery called the _____.
3. Despite the impaired blood supply, blood could still assess all parts of Ms. S's brain because blood could pass through the Circle of Willis. This connecting vessel is an example of a(n) _____.
4. Connecting vessels also link the arteries supplying the intestinal tract. These connecting vessels are collectively called the _____.

➤ Group B

1. Ms. L, aged 42, had her blood pressure examined during a routine physical. Her pressure reading was 165/120. Her diastolic pressure is thus _____.
2. The physician was very alarmed by the finding and immediately prescribed a drug to reduce the production of an enzyme produced in the kidneys that causes blood pressure to increase. This enzyme is called _____.
3. Further tests showed evidence of artery disease in several of the larger vessels. One area involved was the first portion of the aorta called the _____.
4. Another vessel that was seriously damaged was the short one that is the first branch of the aortic arch. This artery is called the _____.
5. The damage reflects the accumulation of fatty material in the vessel walls. The lining of the arteries was roughened, which could lead to the fatal formation of a blood clot. The innermost damaged layer of the arteries is known as the _____.

III. Short Essays

1. Explain the purpose of vascular anastomoses.

   _____

   _____

   _____

2. What is the function of the hepatic portal system, and what vessels contribute to this system?

   _____

   _____

   _____

3. List the vessels a drop of blood will encounter traveling from deep within the left thigh to the right atrium.

_____

_____

_____

Conceptual Thinking

1. Mr. B, aged 54, is losing substantial amounts of blood due a bleeding ulcer. What will be the effect on his blood pressure? What are some physiological changes that could be made to correct this effect?

_____

_____

_____

Expanding Your Horizons

Eat, drink, and have happy arteries. Eat more fish. Eat less fish. Drink wine. Do not drink wine. We receive conflicting messages about the effect of different foodstuffs on arterial health. The following two articles discuss some of these claims.

Resources

1. Klatsky AL. Drink to your health? _Sci Am_ 2003; 288:74–81.
2. Covington MB. Omega-3 fatty acids. _Am Fam Physician_ 2004; 70:133–140.

CHAPTER 15

The Lymphatic System and Body Defenses

Overview

Lymph is the watery fluid that flows within the lymphatic system. It originates from the blood plasma and from the tissue fluid that is found in the minute spaces around and between the body cells. The fluid moves from the **lymphatic capillaries** through the **lymphatic vessels** and then to the **right lymphatic duct** and the **thoracic duct**. These large terminal ducts drain into the subclavian veins, adding the lymph to blood that is returning to the heart. Lymphatic capillaries resemble blood capillaries, but they begin blindly, and larger gaps between the cells make them more permeable than blood capillaries. The larger lymphatic vessels are thin-walled and delicate; like some veins, they have valves that prevent backflow of lymph.

The **lymph nodes**, which are the system's filters, are composed of lymphoid tissue. These nodes remove impurities and process **lymphocytes**, cells active in immunity. Chief among them are the cervical nodes in the neck, the axillary nodes in the armpit, the tracheobronchial nodes near the trachea and bronchial tubes, the mesenteric nodes between the peritoneal layers, and the inguinal nodes in the groin.

In addition to the nodes, there are several organs of lymphoid tissue with somewhat different functions. The **tonsils** filter tissue fluid; the **thymus** is essential for development of the immune system during early life. The **spleen** has numerous functions, including destruction of worn out red blood cells, serving as a reservoir for blood, and producing red blood cells before birth.

Another part of the body's protective system is the **reticuloendothelial system,** which consists of cells involved in the destruction of bacteria, cancer cells, and other possibly harmful substances.

The intact **skin** and **mucous membranes** serve as mechanical barriers against bacteria and other harmful microbes, as do certain **reflexes**, such as sneezing and coughing. Body secretions wash away impurities and may kill bacteria as well. By the process of **inflammation**, the body tries to get rid of an irritant or to minimize its harmful effects. **Phagocytes** and **natural killer (NK) cells** act nonspecifically to destroy invaders. **Interferon** can limit viral infections. **Fever** boosts the immune system and inhibits the growth of some organisms.

The ultimate defense against disease is **immunity**, the means by which the body resists or overcomes the effects of a particular disease or other harmful agent. There are two basic types of immunity: **innate** and **adaptive**. **Innate immunity** is inherited; it may exist on the basis of **species**, or **individual** characteristics. **Adaptive immunity** is gained during a person's lifetime. It involves reactions between foreign substances or **antigens** and the white blood cells known as **lymphocytes**. The **T cells** (T lymphocytes) respond to the antigen directly and produce **cell-mediated immunity**. There are different types of T cells involved in immune reactions, some acting to control the response. **Macrophages** participate by presenting the foreign antigen to the T cell. **B cells** (B lymphocytes), when stimulated by an antigen, multiply into **plasma cells**. These cells produce specific **antibodies**, which react with the antigen. Circulating antibodies make up the form of immunity termed **humoral immunity**.

Adaptive immunity may be **natural** (acquired by transfer of maternal antibodies or contact with the disease) or **artificial** (provided by a vaccine or an immune serum). Immunity that involves production of antibodies by the individual is termed **active immunity**; immunity acquired as a result of the transfer of antibodies to an individual from some outside source is described as **passive immunity**.

Addressing the Learning Outcomes

1. List the functions of the lymphatic system.

EXERCISE 15-1.

INSTRUCTIONS

List three functions of the lymphatic system in the blanks below.

1. _____

2. _____

3. _____

EXERCISE 15-2: Lymphatic System in Relation to the Cardiovascular System (Text Fig. 15-1)

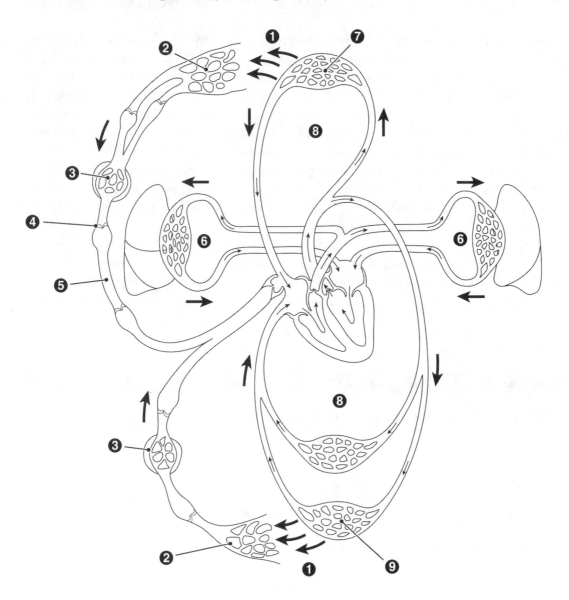

INSTRUCTIONS

1. Label the indicated parts.
2. Color the oxygenated blood red, the deoxygenated blood blue, and the lymph yellow.

1. _____   6. _____

2. _____   7. _____

3. _____   8. _____

4. _____   9. _____

5. _____

2. Explain how lymphatic capillaries differ from blood capillaries.

EXERCISE 15-3.

INSTRUCTIONS

Do the following statements apply to lymphatic capillaries (L), blood capillaries (B), or both (BOTH)? Write the appropriate abbreviation in each blank.

1. The vessel walls are constructed of a single layer of squamous epithelial cells. _____
2. The vessel walls are very permeable, permitting the passage of large proteins. _____
3. The cells in the vessel walls are called endothelial cells. _____
4. The gap between adjacent cells in the vessel wall is very small. _____
5. Lacteals are one example of this type of vessel. _____
6. The vessels form a bridge between two larger vessels. _____
7. The vessel transports erythrocytes. _____

3. Name the two main lymphatic ducts and describe the area drained by each.

EXERCISE 15-4.

INSTRUCTIONS

For each region, state whether its lymph will drain into the right lymphatic duct (R) or the thoracic duct (T).

1. left hand _____
2. right hand _____
3. right breast _____
4. left breast _____
5. left leg _____
6. right leg _____

4. List the major structures of the lymphatic system and give the locations and functions of each.

EXERCISE 15-5: Lymphatic System (Text Fig. 15-4)

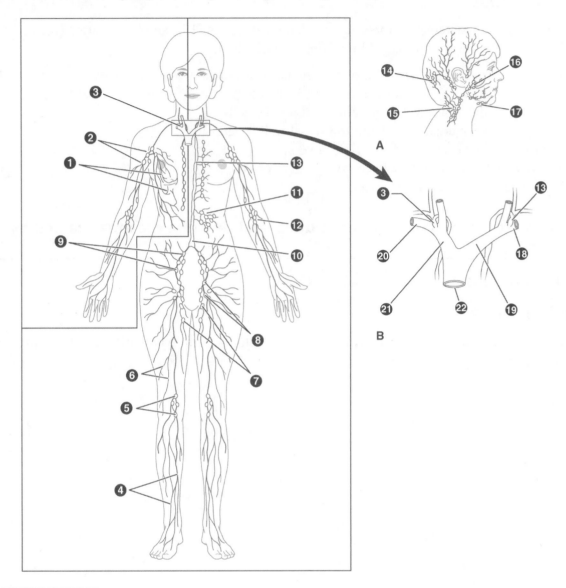

INSTRUCTIONS

Label the indicated parts.

1. _____
2. _____
3. _____
4. _____
5. _____
6. _____
7. _____
8. _____

9. _____
10. _____
11. _____
12. _____
13. _____
14. _____
15. _____
16. _____

17. _____
18. _____
19. _____
20. _____
21. _____
22. _____

EXERCISE 15-6.

INSTRUCTIONS

Write the appropriate term in each blank.

lacteal	superficial	mesothelium	mesenteric nodes
deep	inguinal nodes	axillary nodes	cervical nodes

1. The nodes that filter lymph from the lower extremities and the external genitalia   _____
2. The lymph nodes located in the armpits   _____
3. Term for lymphatic vessels located under the skin   _____
4. The lymph nodes found between the two peritoneal layers   _____
5. A specialized vessel in the small intestine wall that absorbs digested fats   _____
6. The lymph nodes located in the neck that drain certain parts of the head and neck   _____

EXERCISE 15-7.

INSTRUCTIONS

Write the appropriate term in each blank.

lymphatic capillary	right lymphatic duct	chyle	lymph
valve	subclavian vein	thoracic duct	cisterna chyli

1. The temporary storage area formed by an enlargement of the first part of the thoracic duct   _____
2. The fluid formed when tissue fluid passes from the intercellular spaces into the lymphatic vessels   _____
3. The large lymphatic vessel that drains lymph from below the diaphragm and from the left side above the diaphragm   _____
4. The milky-appearing fluid that is a combination of fat globules and lymph   _____
5. Structure that prevents backflow of fluid in lymphatic vessels   _____
6. Blind-ended, thin-walled vessel that absorbs excess tissue fluid and proteins   _____

EXERCISE 15-8: Lymph Node (Text Fig. 15-5)

INSTRUCTIONS

Label the indicated parts.

1. _____
2. _____
3. _____
4. _____
5. _____
6. _____
7. _____
8. _____
9. _____
10. _____
11. _____
12. _____
13. _____

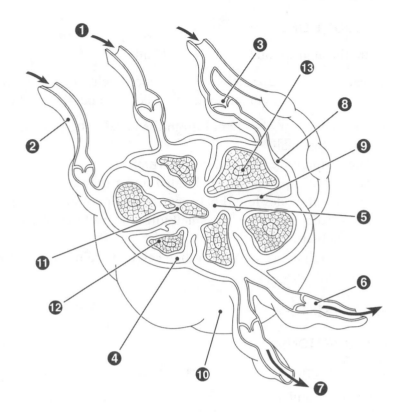

EXERCISE 15-9: Location of Lymphoid Tissue (Text Fig. 15-6)

INSTRUCTIONS

1. Write the names of the different lymphoid organs on the numbered lines in different colors.
2. Color the structures on the diagram with the corresponding colors.

1. _____
2. _____
3. _____
4. _____
5. _____
6. _____
7. _____
8. _____

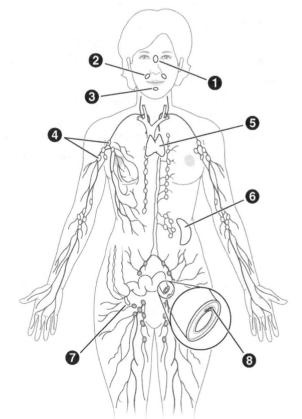

EXERCISE 15-10.

INSTRUCTIONS

Write the appropriate term in each blank.

hilum   germinal center   trabeculae   spleen
palatine tonsil   lingual tonsil   pharyngeal tonsil   thymus

1. An oval lymphoid body located at the side of the soft palate   _____
2. The organ that filters blood and is located in the upper left quadrant (left hypochondriac region) of the abdomen   _____
3. A mass of lymphoid tissue at the back of the tongue   _____
4. The mass of lymphoid tissue located in the pharynx behind the nose and commonly called adenoids   _____
5. The organ in which T cells mature   _____
6. The indented area of a lymph node where efferent lymphatic vessels exit the node   _____

5. Describe the composition and function of the reticuloendothelial system.

Exercise 15-11.

INSTRUCTIONS

Write the appropriate term in each blank.

Peyer patch   MALT   GALT   monocyte
Kupffer cell   reticuloendothelial system   immune system

1. An alternate name for the tissue macrophage system   _____
2. Areas of lymphoid tissue found in mucous membranes   _____
3. Areas of lymphoid tissue specifically found throughout the gastrointestinal system   _____
4. The name given to a macrophage found in the liver   _____
5. An area of lymphoid tissue specifically found in the small intestine wall   _____
6. A large white blood cell circulating in the blood that gives rise to a macrophage   _____

6. Differentiate between nonspecific and specific body defenses and give examples of each.

EXERCISE 15-12.

INSTRUCTIONS

Write the appropriate term in each blank.

nonspecific defenses   specific defenses   natural killer cell
interferon   macrophage   neutrophil

1. A substance that prevents multiplication of viruses   _____
2. A lymphocyte that nonspecifically destroys abnormal cells   _____
3. A general term describing protective responses effective against any pathogen   _____
4. A general term describing immune responses directed against an individual pathogen   _____
5. A granular leukocyte that participates in nonspecific defenses   _____

7. Briefly describe the inflammatory reaction.

EXERCISE 15-13.

INSTRUCTIONS

For each statement, state whether it is true (T) or false (F).

1. Histamine is secreted by the damaged cells themselves. ____
2. Mast cells are similar to macrophages. ____
3. Histamine makes vessels constrict. ____
4. Leukocytes actually leave the blood vessels in order to fight infection in injured tissues. ____
5. The inflammatory exudate does not contain any cells. ____

8. List several types of innate immunity.

EXERCISE 15-14.

INSTRUCTIONS

Which of the following statements applies to species immunity (S) and which statements apply to individual immunity (I)?

1. The type of protection that prevents humans from contracting distemper _____
2. The type of protection that prevents some humans from contracting cold sores _____
3. The type of protection that prevents animals from contracting measles _____

9. Define *antigen* and *antibody* (see Exercise 15-15).

10. Compare T cells and B cells with respect to development and type of activity.

EXERCISE 15-15.

INSTRUCTIONS

Write the appropriate term in each blank.

antigen   antibody   memory cell
plasma cell T_h cell T_{reg} cell T_c cell

1. Any foreign substance introduced into the body that provokes an immune response   _____

2. An antibody-producing cell derived from a B cell   _____

3. A cell that reduces an immune response by inhibiting or destroying activated lymphocytes   _____

4. A cell that matures in the thymus that directly destroys a foreign cell   _____

5. A circulating protein also known as an immunoglobulin   _____

6. A B or T cell that can rapidly activate an immune response when the pathogen is encountered for a second time   _____

11. Explain the role of macrophages in immunity.

EXERCISE 15-16.

INSTRUCTIONS

Write the appropriate term in each blank.

foreign antigen   MHC protein   lysosome   antibody
interleukin   monocyte   neutrophil   T cell receptor

1. Macrophages are derived from this type of cell.   _____

2. The organelle in macrophages that digests a foreign substance   _____

3. The part of a foreign substance that is inserted into a macrophage membrane   _____

4. The self-antigen inserted into the macrophage membrane   _____

5. The part of the helper T cell that binds to a macrophage   _____

6. The substance released by the helper T cell after it is activated by binding to the macrophage   _____

12. Describe some protective effects of an antigen–antibody reaction.

EXERCISE 15-17.

INSTRUCTIONS

List 6 ways by which the antigen–antibody reaction helps the body deal with an infection.

1. _____

2. _____

3. _____

4. _____

5. _____

6. _____

13. Differentiate between natural and artificial adaptive immunity (see Exercise 15-18).

14. Differentiate between active and passive immunity.

EXERCISE 15-18.

INSTRUCTIONS

For each of the following examples, state whether they involve active (ACT) or passive immunity (P), and natural (N) or artificial (ART) immunity.

1. Immunity resulting from exposure to a microbial toxin _____ _____

2. Immunity resulting from the transfer of antibodies from mother to fetus _____ _____

3. Immunity resulting from the HPV vaccination _____ _____

4. Immunity resulting from the administration of antiserum _____ _____

15. Define the terms *vaccine* and *immune serum.*

EXERCISE 15-19.

INSTRUCTIONS

Write the appropriate term in each blank.

toxoid   attenuation   immunization   HPV vaccine
gamma globulin   rubella vaccine   rotavirus vaccine   varicella vaccine

1. The process of reducing the virulence of a pathogen to prepare
   a vaccine   _____
2. A toxin treated with heat or chemicals to reduce its harmfulness so
   that it may be used as a vaccine   _____
3. The fraction of the blood plasma that contains antibodies   _____
4. A process designed to induce an immune response against a particular
   pathogen, resulting in the acquisition of artificial adaptive immunity _____
5. A vaccine that prevents sexually transmitted genital warts   _____
6. A vaccine that prevents chicken pox   _____

16. Show how word parts are used to build words related to the lymphatic system.

EXERCISE 15-20.

INSTRUCTIONS

Complete the following table by writing the correct word part or meaning in the space provided. Write a word that contains each word part in the Example column.

Word Part	Meaning	Example
1. _____	gland	_____
2. lingu/o	_____	_____
3. -oid	_____	_____

Making the Connections

The following concept map deals with the structure and function of the lymphatic system (Map A) and the processes of immunity (Map B). Each pair of terms is linked together by a connecting phrase into a sentence. The sentence should be read in the direction of the arrow. Complete the concept maps by filling in the appropriate term or phrase. There is one right answer for each term. However, there are many correct answers for the connecting phrases.

Map A

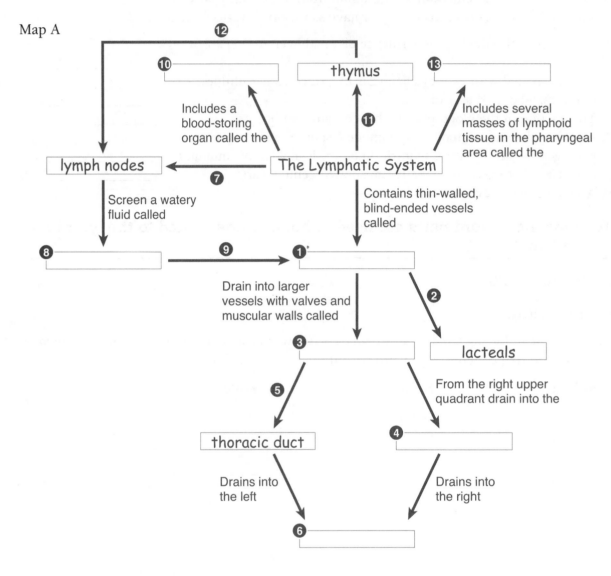

Map B

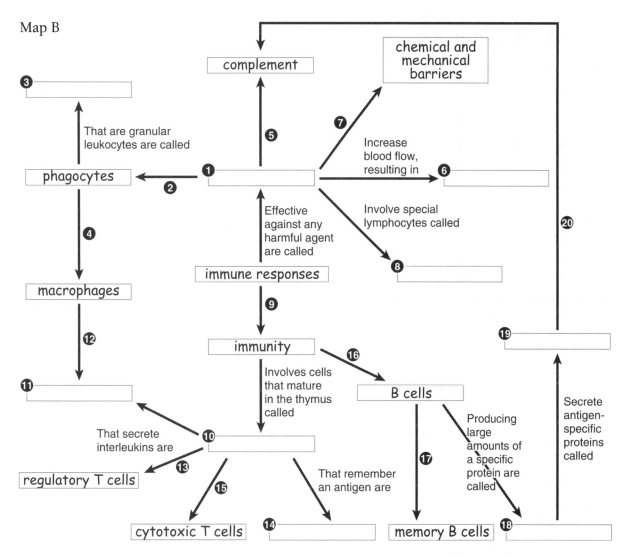

Optional Exercise: Make your own concept map/flow chart, based on the flow of lymph from a body part to the left atrium. It is not necessary to include connecting statements between the terms. For instance, you could map the flow of lymph from the right breast to the right atrium by linking the following terms: superior vena cava, right subclavian vein, right brachiocephalic vein, mammary vessels, axillary nodes, and right lymphatic duct.

Testing Your Knowledge

Building Understanding

I. Multiple Choice

Select the best answer and write the letter of your choice in the blank.

1. Which of the following is NOT a type of cell associated with the reticuloendothelial system?
    a. monocytes
    b. macrophages
    c. dust cells
    d. red blood cells

    1. _____

2. Which of the following is NOT a function of the spleen?
    a. destruction of old red blood cells
    b. blood filtration
    c. blood storage
    d. chyle drainage

    2. _____

3. The mesenteric nodes are found
    a. in the groin region
    b. near the trachea
    c. between the two peritoneal layers
    d. in the armpits

    3. _____

4. An organ that shrinks in size after puberty is the
    a. cisternal chyli
    b. thymus
    c. spleen
    d. liver

    4. _____

5. Unlike blood capillaries, lymphatic capillaries
    a. contain a thin muscular layer
    b. are virtually impermeable to water and solutes
    c. are blind-ended
    d. do not contain any cells

    5. _____

6. The enlarged portion of the thoracic duct is called the
    a. cisterna chyli
    b. right lymphatic duct
    c. hilum
    d. lacteal

    6. _____

7. The type of lymphocyte involved in nonspecific immunity is the
    a. B cell
    b. natural killer cell
    c. memory T cell
    d. cytotoxic T cell

    7. _____

8. Which of the following describes an activity of B cells?
    a. suppression of the immune response
    b. manufacture of antibodies
    c. direct destruction of foreign cells
    d. phagocytosis

    8. _____

9. Which of the following is a specific defense against infection? 9. _____
    a. skin
    b. mucus
    c. antibodies
    d. cilia
10. Cells that combine with foreign antigens and present them to T cells
    are the 10. _____
    a. macrophages
    b. B cells
    c. interferons
    d. viruses
11. Complement proteins 11. _____
    a. promote inflammation
    b. attract phagocytes
    c. destroy cells
    d. all of the above
12. Interleukins are 12. _____
    a. substances in the blood that react with antigens
    b. the antibody fraction of the blood
    c. a group of nonspecific proteins needed for agglutination
    d. substances released from T_h cells that stimulate other leukocytes
13. MHC antigens are 13. _____
    a. bacterial proteins
    b. foreign proteins
    c. one's own proteins
    d. antibodies
14. Which of the following will result in active immunity? 14. _____
    a. vaccination
    b. antiserum administration
    c. breast feeding
    d. none of the above

II. Completion Exercise

Write the word or phrase that correctly completes each sentence.

1. Thymosin is synthesized by the _____ gland.
2. The milky-appearing lymph that drains from the small intestine is called _____.
3. The fluid that moves from tissue spaces into special collecting vessels for return to the blood is called _____.
4. Lymph from the right side of the body above the diaphragm joins the bloodstream when the right lymphatic duct empties into the _____.
5. The lymph nodes surrounding the breathing passageways may become black in individuals living in highly polluted areas. The nodes involved are the _____.
6. Nearly all of the lymph from the arm, shoulder, and breast passes through the lymph node known as the _____.

7. The spleen contains many cells that can engulf harmful bacteria and other foreign cells by a process called _____.

8. Circulating antibodies are responsible for the type of immunity termed _____.

9. Heat, redness, swelling, and pain are considered the classic symptoms of _____.

10. The MMR vaccine protects against rubella, measles, and _____.

11. Antibodies transmitted from a mother's blood to a fetus provide a type of short-term borrowed immunity called _____.

12. The administration of vaccine, on the other hand, stimulates the body to produce a longer lasting type of immunity called _____.

Understanding Concepts

I. True/False

For each question, write *T* for true or *F* for false in the blank to the left of each number. If a statement is false, correct it by replacing the underlined term and write the correct statement in the blank below the question.

_____ 1. Lymph filtered through the mesenteric nodes will drain into the <u>thoracic duct</u>.

_____

_____ 2. An adenoidectomy involves the removal of the <u>lingual tonsils</u>.

_____

_____ 3. Thymosin is produced by the <u>spleen</u>.

_____

_____ 4. Kupffer cells are part of the <u>reticuloendothelial system</u>.

_____

_____ 5. Lacteals are a type of <u>blood capillary</u>.

_____

_____ 6. <u>Complement</u> is a substance that participates in nonspecific body defenses exclusively against viruses.

_____

_____ 7. Cytotoxic T cells participate in <u>humoral</u> immunity.

_____

_____ 8. Any process in which an individual produces his or her own antibodies is called <u>active</u> immunity.

_____

_____ 9. The action of histamine in the inflammatory reaction is an example of a <u>nonspecific</u> defense.

_____

_____ 10. Immunoglobulin is another name for <u>antigen</u>.

_____

_____ 11. <u>Interferons</u> are released by helper T cells in order to stimulate the activity of other leukocytes.

_____

_____ 12. Administration of an antiserum is an example of <u>artificial, passive</u> immunity.

_____

II. *Practical Applications*

Study each discussion. Then write the appropriate word or phrase in the space provided.

➤ **Group A**

1. Ms. L traveled in Asia for 2 years before starting nursing school. During the first week of classes, she noticed swelling in one of her legs. She looked through her pathophysiology text-book to try to identify the cause. She read that excess fluid from tissues drains into small blunt-ended vessels called _____.
2. To her alarm, she discovered that small worms can obstruct these vessels, causing swelling. She rushed to the hospital, where the physician palpated the small lymphoid masses found be-hind her knee. These masses are called the _____.
3. These masses were normal, but the lymphoid tissue masses at the top of the swollen leg were enlarged due to an infected cut in her upper thigh. These lymphoid masses are called the _____.

➤ **Group B**

1. Mr. R stepped on a rusty nail, resulting in a deep puncture wound. When he arrived home 2 hours later, he noticed swelling, heat, and redness in the area surrounding the painful wound. These classic symptoms indicate that a series of defensive processes are occurring called the _____.
2. Many of his symptoms are due to the release of a chemical that dilates blood vessels. This chemical is called _____.
3. Mr. R went to a medical clinic to have his wound treated. The nurse on duty inquired as to the status of Mr. R's immunizations. Another term for immunization is _____.
4. Mr. R had never been immunized against tetanus, so he was injected with a substance to neu-tralize harmful secretions produced by the tetanus bacteria. These harmful secretions are called _____.
5. The injection will produce a short-term form of immunity called _____.

III. *Short Essays*

1. Trace a lymph droplet from the interstitial fluid of the lower leg to the right atrium, based on the structures shown in Figure 15-4.

   _____

   _____

   _____

   _____

2. Discuss the role of macrophages in specific and nonspecific body defenses.

   _____

   _____

   _____

Conceptual Thinking

1. Ms. Y, a healthy 24-year-old woman, is studying for her nursing finals. She has been sitting at her desk for 10 hours straight when she notices that her legs are swollen. Use your knowledge of the lymphatic system to explain the swelling, and suggest how she can prevent it in the future.

   _____

   _____

   _____

2. Baby G was born without a thymus, but was otherwise normal. Speculate as to which aspects of her immune system will be affected by this deficiency, and which aspects will be unaffected.

   _____

   _____

   _____

   _____

   _____

3. Mr. A stepped on a fish while beachcombing in the South Pacific. A spine was embedded in his foot, and he rapidly became dizzy and the foot swelled up alarmingly. Mr. A was told by a local doctor that the fish spine contains an incredibly potent poison, and that he will be dead in 8 hours unless the poison is neutralized.

   A. What would be the best treatment for Mr. A—vaccination with fish toxoid or an injection of an antitoxin? Defend your answer.

   _____

   _____

   _____

   B. What form of immunity will be induced by this treatment?

   _____

   C. Will Mr. A be protected from future encounters with this particular fish poison? Explain why or why not.

   _____

   _____

   _____

Expanding Your Horizons

Have you or one of your friends had the kissing disease? Infectious mononucleosis, or "mono," is an infection of lymphatic cells. It is easily transmitted between individuals living in close contact with one another (not necessarily by kissing) and is thus very common on college campuses. Learn more about this disease by reading articles 1 and 2, below.

A vaccine for AIDS? Although the treatments for AIDS have improved enormously, the disease still results in considerable suffering. The "holy grail" of AIDS research is the development of a vaccine to protect individuals from infection. However, the quest for a vaccine is not an easy one, as discussed in the articles 3 and 4, below.

Resources

1. Cozad J. Infectious mononucleoisis. *Nurse Pract* 1996; 21:14–18.
2. Bailey RE. Diagnosis and treatment of infectious mononucleosis. *Am Fam Physician* 1994; 49:879–888.
3. Baltimore D, Heilman C. HIV vaccines: prospects and challenges. *Sci Am* 1998; 279:98–103.
4. Ezzel C. Hope in a vial. Will there be an AIDS vaccine anytime soon? *Sci Am* 2002; 286:38–45.

UNIT V

Energy: Supply and Use

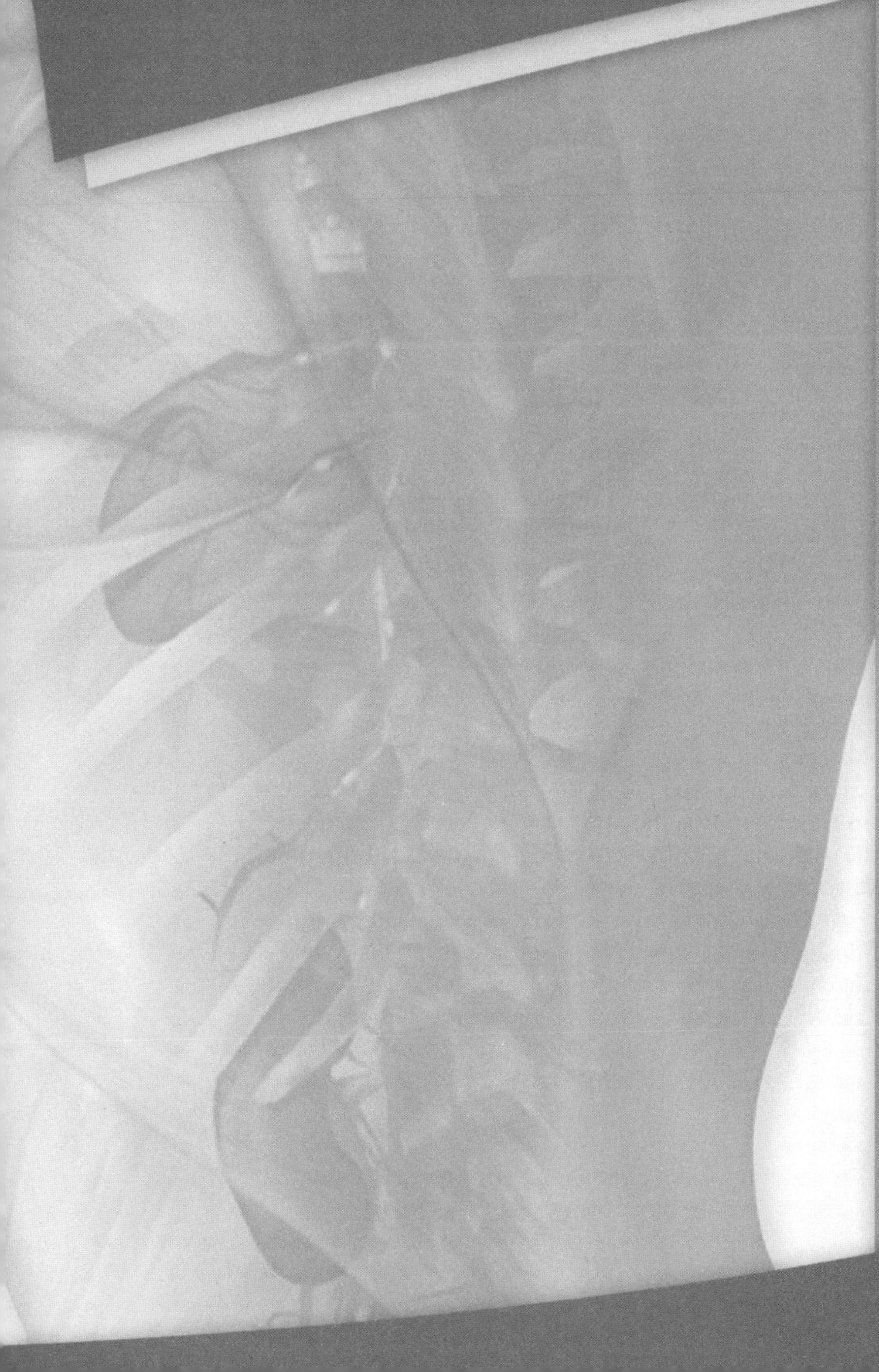

➤ **Chapter 16**

The Respiratory
System

➤ **Chapter 17**

The Digestive
System

➤ **Chapter 18**

Metabolism,
Nutrition, and
Body Temperature

➤ **Chapter 19**

The Urinary
System and Body
Fluids

CHAPTER 16

The Respiratory System

Overview

Oxygen is taken into the body and carbon dioxide is released by means of the organs and passageways of the **respiratory system**. This system contains the **nasal cavities, pharynx, larynx, trachea, bronchi**, and **lungs**.

Oxygen is obtained from the atmosphere and delivered to the cells by the process of **respiration**. The first phase of respiration is **pulmonary ventilation**, which is normally accomplished by breathing. During normal, quiet breathing, air enters the lungs (**inhalation**) because the diaphragm and intercostal muscles contract to expand the thoracic cavity. Air leaves the lungs (**exhalation**) when the muscles relax. Deeper breathing requires additional muscles during both inhalation and exhalation. The other two phases of respiration are: **external gas exchange** between the alveoli of the lungs and bloodstream; and **internal gas exchange** between the blood and tissues. In these exchanges, oxygen is delivered to the cells, and carbon dioxide is transported to the lungs for elimination.

Oxygen is transported to the tissues almost entirely by the **hemoglobin** in red blood cells. Some carbon dioxide is transported in the red blood cells as well, but most is converted into **bicarbonate ions** and **hydrogen ions**. Bicarbonate ions are carried in plasma, and the hydrogen ions (along with hydrogen ions from other sources) increase the acidity of the blood.

Breathing is primarily controlled by the **respiratory control centers** in the medulla and the pons of the brainstem. These centers are influenced by **chemoreceptors** located outside the medulla that respond to changes in the acidity of the cerebrospinal fluid. The acidity reflects the concentration of carbon dioxide.

Addressing the Learning Outcomes

1. Define *respiration* and describe the three phases of respiration.

EXERCISE 16-1.

INSTRUCTIONS

Write the appropriate term in each blank.

external gas exchange   internal gas exchange
cellular respiration   pulmonary ventilation

1. The exchange of air between the atmosphere and the alveoli   _____
2. The exchange of specific gases between the alveoli and the blood   _____
3. The exchange of specific gases between the blood and the cells   _____
4. The process by which cells use oxygen and nutrients to generate energy   _____

2. Name and describe all the structures of the respiratory system.

EXERCISE 16-2: Respiratory System (Text Fig. 16-2)

INSTRUCTIONS

1. Label the indicated parts.
2. Color all of the structures that encounter air green. Color structures containing oxygenated blood red. Color structures containing deoxygenated blood blue.

1. _____
2. _____
3. _____
4. _____
5. _____
6. _____
7. _____
8. _____
9. _____
10. _____
11. _____
12. _____
13. _____
14. _____
15. _____
16. _____
17. _____
18. _____
19. _____
20. _____
21. _____
22. _____
23. _____
24. _____
25. _____
26. _____
27. _____

EXERCISE 16-3: The Larynx (Text Fig. 16-3)

INSTRUCTIONS

1. Write the name of each labeled part on the numbered lines in different colors.
2. Color the different parts on the diagram with the corresponding color.

1. _____
2. _____
3. _____
4. _____
5. _____
6. _____
7. _____

EXERCISE 16-4.

INSTRUCTIONS

Write the appropriate term in each blank.

nares   conchae   pharynx   glottis   epiglottis
larynx   hilum   bronchus   bronchiole   sinus

1. The openings of the nose   _____
2. The three projections arising from the lateral walls of each nasal
   cavity   _____
3. The scientific name for the voice box   _____
4. The leaf-shaped structure that helps to prevent the entrance of
   food into the trachea   _____
5. One of the two branches formed by division of the trachea   _____
6. The notch or depression where the bronchus, blood vessels, and
   nerves enter the lung   _____
7. The area below the nasal cavities that is common to both the
   digestive and respiratory systems   _____
8. A small air-conducting tube containing a smooth muscle layer but
   little or no cartilage   _____

3. Explain the mechanism for pulmonary ventilation.

EXERCISE 16-5: A Spirogram (Text Fig. 16-9)

INSTRUCTIONS

Write the names of the different lung volumes and capacities in the boxes on the diagram.

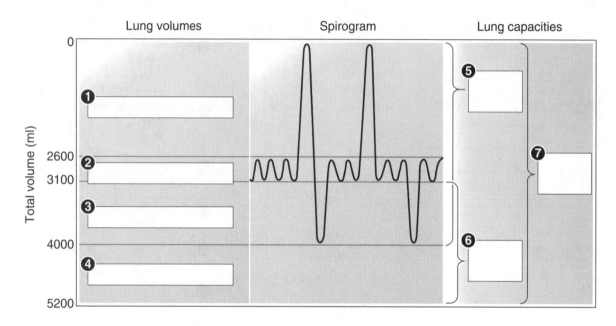

EXERCISE 16-6.

INSTRUCTIONS

Write the appropriate term in each blank.

alveoli	surfactant	pleura	inhalation	tidal volume
exhalation	intercostals	compliance	spirometer	vital capacity

1. The substance in the fluid lining the alveoli that prevents their collapse _____

2. The phase of pulmonary ventilation in which air is expelled from the alveoli _____

3. The phase of pulmonary ventilation in which the diaphragm contracts _____

4. The serous membrane around each lung _____

5. The only respiratory structures involved in external gas exchange _____

6. The amount of air inhaled or exhaled during a relaxed breath _____

7. The ease with which the lungs and thorax can be expanded _____

8. The maximum volume of air that can be exhaled after maximum inspiration _____

EXERCISE 16-7.

INSTRUCTIONS

In the blank following each statement, write T if it is true and F if it is false.

1. Inhalation is the active phase of breathing. _____
2. During quiet breathing, exhalation does not require any muscle contraction. _____
3. The diaphragm rises when it contracts. _____
4. The external intercostal muscles contract during active exhalation. _____
5. The external intercostal muscles contract during a large inhalation. _____
6. The diaphragm relaxes during exhalation. _____

4. List the ways in which oxygen and carbon dioxide are transported in the blood.

EXERCISE 16-8.

INSTRUCTIONS

Write the appropriate term in each blank.

bicarbonate ion	hemoglobin	carbonic anhydrase	carbon dioxide	15%
diffusion	hydrogen ion	oxygen	10%	75%

1. The process by which oxygen moves from the blood into tissues _____
2. The gas converted into bicarbonate in the blood _____
3. An important blood buffer produced from carbon dioxide _____
4. The substance that carries most of the oxygen in the blood _____
5. The gas that is more concentrated in the blood than in metabolically active tissues _____
6. An ion that renders blood more acidic _____
7. The proportion of total blood carbon dioxide dissolved in plasma _____
8. The proportion of total blood carbon dioxide transported in the form of bicarbonate _____
9. The proportion of total blood carbon dioxide carried on plasma proteins _____

5. Describe nervous and chemical controls of respiration.

EXERCISE 16-9.

INSTRUCTIONS

Write the appropriate term in each blank.

hypercapnia   hydrogen ion   bicarbonate ion   phrenic nerve   vagus nerve
brainstem   aortic arch   carbon dioxide   oxygen

1. The location of the central chemoreceptors   _____
2. A rise in the blood carbon dioxide concentration   _____
3. The location of a peripheral chemoreceptor   _____
4. The substance that acts directly on the central chemoreceptors
   to stimulate breathing   _____
5. The gas that stimulates breathing when its concentration increases   _____
6. The nerve that controls the diaphragm   _____

6. Give several examples of altered breathing patterns.

EXERCISE 16-10.

INSTRUCTIONS

For each of the following statements, write HYPO if it refers to hypoventilation and HYPER if it refers to hyperventilation.

1. The breathing pattern that causes hypocapnia   _____
2. The breathing pattern resulting from respiratory obstruction   _____
3. The breathing pattern that causes hypercapnia   _____
4. The breathing pattern that causes acidosis   _____
5. The breathing pattern that sometimes occurs during anxiety attacks   _____

EXERCISE 16-11.

INSTRUCTIONS

Write the appropriate term in each blank.

orthopnea   dyspnea   hyperpnea
hypopnea   tachypnea   apnea

1. Difficult or labored breathing   _____
2. An abnormal increase in the depth and rate of breathing   _____
3. A temporary cessation of breathing   _____
4. Difficult breathing that is relieved by sitting upright   _____
5. An abnormal decrease in the depth and rate of breathing   _____
6. Rapid breathing observed during exercise   _____

EXERCISE 16-12.

INSTRUCTIONS

In the blanks below, list and briefly describe four conditions resulting from inadequate breathing.

1. _____

2. _____

3. _____

4. _____

7. Show how word parts are used to build words related to respiration.

EXERCISE 16-13.

INSTRUCTIONS

Complete the following table by writing the correct word part or meaning in the space provided. Write a word that contains each word part in the Example column.

Word Part	Meaning	Example
1. spir/o-	_____	_____
2. _____	nose	_____
3. -pnea	_____	_____
4. _____	carbon dioxide	_____
5. _____	lung	_____
6. _____	air, gas	_____
7. orth/o-	_____	_____
8. or/o-	_____	_____

Making the Connections

The following concept map deals with the organization of the respiratory system. Each pair of terms is linked together by a connecting phrase into a sentence. The sentence should be read in the direction of the arrow. Complete the concept map by filling in the appropriate term or phrase. There is one right answer for each term. However, there are many correct answers for the connecting phrases.

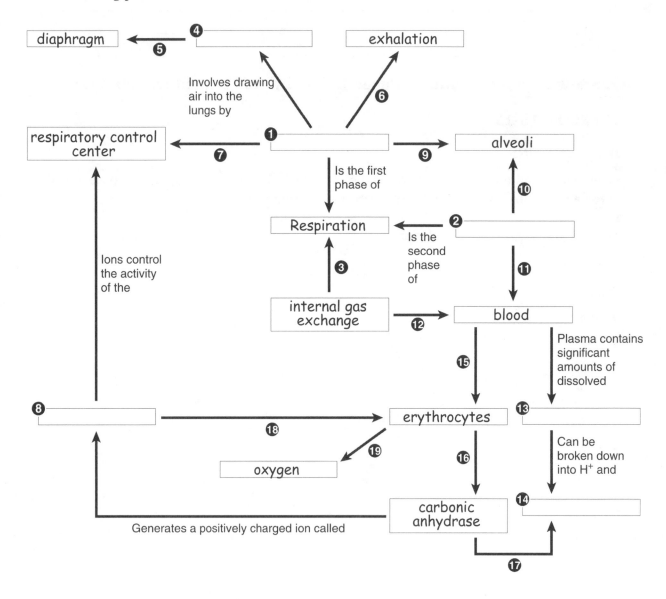

Optional Exercise: Make your own concept map/flow chart based on the structures an oxygen molecule will pass through from the atmosphere to a tissue. Choose your own terms to incorporate into your map, or use the following list: nostrils, atmosphere, nasopharynx, oropharynx, nasal cavities, laryngeal pharynx, trachea, larynx, bronchioles, blood cell, hemoglobin, plasma, tissue, bronchi, and alveoli.

Testing Your Knowledge

Building Understanding

I. Multiple Choice

Select the best answer and write the letter of your choice in the blank.

1. Carbon dioxide will diffuse out of blood during the phase of
   respiration called   1. _____
   a. internal exchange of gases
   b. external exchange of gases
   c. pulmonary ventilation
   d. none of the above
2. Gas exchange occurs in the   2. _____
   a. alveoli
   b. bronchioles
   c. bronchi
   d. all of the above
3. Which of the following terms does NOT apply to the cells that line the
   conducting passages of the respiratory tract?   3. _____
   a. pseudostratified
   b. connective
   c. columnar
   d. ciliated
4. An increase in blood carbon dioxide levels would result in   4. _____
   a. fewer bicarbonate ions in the blood
   b. more hydrogen ions in the blood
   c. more alkaline blood
   d. hypocapnia
5. The substance that reduces surface tension in the alveoli is   5. _____
   a. surfactant
   b. bicarbonate
   c. exudate
   d. effusion
6. The residual volume is   6. _____
   a. the amount of air that is always in the lungs, even after a maximal
      expiration
   b. the total amount of air in the lungs after a maximal inspiration
   c. the amount of air remaining in the lungs after a normal exhalation
   d. the amount of air that can be forced out of the lungs after a normal
      exhalation

II. Completion Exercise

Write the word or phrase that correctly completes each sentence.

1. The space between the vocal cords is called the _____.
2. An abnormal decrease in the depth and rate of respiration is termed _____.
3. A lower than normal level of oxygen in tissues is called _____.
4. Heart disease and other disorders may cause the bluish color of the skin and visible mucous membranes characteristic of a condition called _____.
5. The space between the lungs is called the _____.
6. The type of epithelium that lines the nasal cavity is _____.
7. The term that is used for the pressure of each gas in a mixture of gases is _____.
8. Each heme region of a hemoglobin molecule contains an inorganic element called _____.
9. The nerve that innervates the diaphragm is the _____.

Understanding Concepts

I. True/False

For each question, write *T* for true or *F* for false in the blank to the left of each number. If a statement is false, correct it by replacing the underlined term and write the correct statement in the blank below the question.

_____ 1. Hypercapnia results in greater blood underlined_acidity.

_____

_____ 2. Most underlined_carbon dioxide in the blood is carried bound to hemoglobin.

_____

_____ 3. The wall of an alveolus is made of underlined_stratified squamous epithelium.

_____

_____ 4. During underlined_internal exchange of gases, oxygen moves down its concentration gradient out of blood.

_____

_____ 5. The receptors that detect changes in blood gas concentrations are called underlined_mechanoreceptors.

_____

_____ 6. <u>Inhalation</u> ALWAYS involves muscle contraction.

_____

_____ 7. Hyperventilation results in an <u>increase</u> of carbon dioxide in the blood.

_____

II. Practical Applications

Study each discussion. Then write the appropriate word or phrase in the space provided.

➤ Group A

1. Ms. L's symptoms include shortness of breath, a chronic cough productive of thick mucus, and a "chest cold" of 2 months' duration. She was advised to quit smoking, a major cause of lung irritation. These symptoms were caused in part by the obstruction of groups of alveoli by mucous plugs. Ms. L was told that the mucus is not moving normally out of her airways because the toxins in cigarette smoke paralyze small cell extensions that beat to create an upward current. These extensions are called _____.
2. Ms. L's respiratory function was evaluated by quantifying different lung volumes and capacities using a machine called a(n) _____.
3. Evaluation of Ms. L's respiratory function showed a reduction in the amount of air that could be moved into and out of her lungs. The amount of air that can be expelled by maximum exhalation after maximum inhalation is termed the _____.
4. The other abnormality in Ms. L's evaluation was also characteristic of her disease. There was an increase in the amount of air remaining in her lungs after a normal expiration. This amount is the _____.

➤ Group B

1. Baby L was born at 32 weeks gestation. She is obviously struggling for breath, and her skin is bluish in color. This skin discoloration is called _____.
2. This coloration reflects a lower than normal oxygen level in the blood, technically known as _____.
3. The obstetrician fears that one or both of her lungs are not able to inflate, so baby L is placed on pressurized oxygen to inflate the lung. The physician tells the worried parents that her lungs have not yet matured sufficiently to produce the lung substance that reduces the surface tension in alveoli. This substance is called _____.

III. *Short Essays*

1. Are lungs passive or active players in pulmonary ventilation? Explain.

_____

_____

_____

2. Name some parts of the respiratory tract where gas exchange does NOT occur.

_____

_____

_____

Conceptual Thinking

A. Name the phase of respiration regulated by the respiratory control center.

_____

B. Explain how the respiratory control center can alter this phase of respiration.

_____

_____

_____

C. Name the chemical factor(s) that regulate(s) the activity of the control center.

_____

_____

_____

Expanding Your Horizons

Everyone would agree that oxygen is a very useful molecule. Commercial enterprises, working on the premise that more is better, market water supplemented with extra oxygen. They claim that consumption of hyperoxygenated water increases alertness and exercise performance. Do these claims make sense? Do we obtain oxygen from the lungs or the digestive tract? A logical extension of this premise is that soda pop, supplemented with carbon dioxide, would increase carbon dioxide in the blood and increase the breathing rate! Is this true? You can read about another oxygen gimmick, oxygen bars, on the website of the Food and Drug Administration.

Resources

1. Bren L. Oxygen bars: Is a breath of fresh air worth it? 2002. Available at: http://www.fda.gov/fdac/features/2002/602_air.html.

The Digestive System

Overview

The food we eat is made available to cells throughout the body by the complex processes of **digestion** and **absorption**. These are the functions of the **digestive system**, composed of the **digestive tract** and the **accessory organs**.

The digestive tract, consisting of the **mouth**, **pharynx**, **esophagus**, **stomach**, and small and large **intestines**, forms a continuous passageway in which ingested food is prepared for use by the body and waste products are collected to be expelled from the body. The accessory organs, the **salivary glands**, **liver**, **gallbladder**, and **pancreas**, manufacture and store various enzymes and other substances needed in digestion.

Digestion begins in the mouth with the digestion of starch. It continues in the stomach, where proteins are digested, and is completed in the small intestine. Most absorption of digested food also occurs in the small intestine through small projections of the lining called **villi**. The products of carbohydrate (monosaccharides) and protein (amino acids) digestion are absorbed into capillaries, but the products of fat digestion (glycerol and fatty acids) are absorbed into **lacteals**.

The process of digestion is controlled by both nervous and hormonal mechanisms, which regulate the activity of the digestive organs and the rate at which food moves through the digestive tract.

Addressing the Learning Outcomes

1. Name the three main functions of the digestive system.

EXERCISE 17-1.

INSTRUCTIONS

List the three main functions of the digestive system in the blanks below, in the order in which they occur.

1. _____

2. _____

3. _____

2. Describe the four layers of the digestive tract wall.

EXERCISE 17-2: The Wall of the Small Intestine (Text Fig. 17-1)

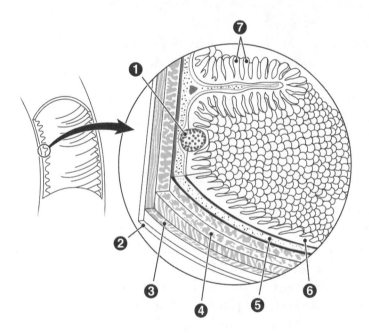

INSTRUCTIONS

1. Write the names of the intestinal layers and associated structures on the appropriate numbered lines in different colors. Use the same color for parts 6 and 7.
2. Color the layers and structures on the diagram with the corresponding color.

1. _____

2. _____

3. _____

4. _____

5. _____

6. _____

7. _____

EXERCISE 17-3.

INSTRUCTIONS

Write the appropriate term in each blank.

digestion   absorption   elimination   mucous membrane   submucosa
serosa   smooth muscle   squamous epithelium   simple columnar epithelium

1. The transfer of nutrients into the bloodstream   _____
2. The visceral peritoneum attached to the surface of a digestive
   organ   _____
3. The layer of connective tissue beneath the mucous membrane in
   the wall of the digestive tract   _____
4. The layer of the digestive tract wall that is responsible for peristalsis   _____
5. The breakdown of food into small particles that can pass through
   intestinal cells   _____
6. The layer of the digestive tract wall that forms villi in the small
   intestine   _____
7. The type of epithelial tissue lining the esophagus   _____
8. The type of epithelial tissue lining the stomach   _____

3. Differentiate between the two layers of the peritoneum.

EXERCISE 17-4: Abdominal Cavity Showing Peritoneum (Text Fig. 17-3)

INSTRUCTIONS

1. Write the names of the abdominal organs on the appropriate numbered lines 1 to 9 in different colors. Use the same color for parts 3 and 4.
2. Color the organs on the diagram with the corresponding color.
3. Label the parts of the peritoneum (lines 10 to 15). Color the greater and lesser peritoneal cavities in contrasting colors.

1. _____

2. _____

3. _____

4. _____

5. _____

6. _____

7. _____

8. _____

9. _____

10. _____

11. _____

12. _____

13. _____

14. _____

15. _____

☐ Greater peritoneal cavity

☐ Lesser peritoneal cavity

EXERCISE 17-5.

INSTRUCTIONS

Write the appropriate term in each blank.

parietal peritoneum   visceral peritoneum   greater peritoneal cavity   lesser peritoneal cavity
mesocolon   greater omentum   lesser omentum

1. The innermost layer of the serous membrane lining the
   abdominopelvic cavity   _____
2. The outer layer of the serous membrane lining the abdominopelvic
   cavity   _____
3. The subdivision of the peritoneum that contains fat and hangs over
   the front of the intestine   _____
4. The subdivision of the peritoneum extending between the stomach
   and liver   _____
5. The subdivision of the peritoneum that extends from the colon to
   the posterior abdominal wall   _____
6. The fluid-filled cavity that extends behind the stomach to the liver
   and the posterior portion of the diaphragm   _____

4. Name and locate the different types of teeth.

EXERCISE 17-6: Digestive System (Text Fig. 17-4)

INSTRUCTIONS

1. Trace the path of food through the digestive tract by labeling parts 1 to 12. You can color all of these structures orange.
2. Write the names of the accessory organs and ducts on the appropriate lines in different colors. Use black for structure 20, because it will not be colored.
3. Color the accessory organs on the diagram with the corresponding colors.

1. _____
2. _____
3. _____
4. _____
5. _____
6. _____
7. _____
8. _____
9. _____
10. _____
11. _____
12. _____
13. _____
14. _____
15. _____
16. _____
17. _____
18. _____
19. _____
20. _____

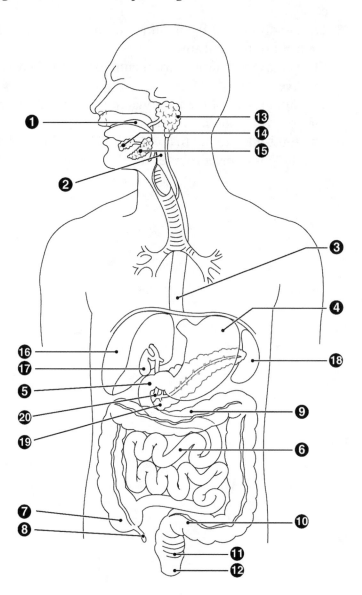

EXERCISE 17-7: The Mouth (Text Fig. 17-5)

INSTRUCTIONS

1. Write the names of the teeth on the appropriate lines 1 to 6 in different colors. Use the same color to label parts 5 and 6.
2. Color all of the teeth with the corresponding colors.
3. Label the other parts of the mouth.

1. _____
2. _____
3. _____
4. _____
5. _____
6. _____
7. _____
8. _____
9. _____
10. _____
11. _____
12. _____
13. _____
14. _____

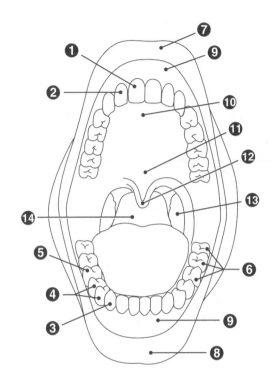

EXERCISE 17-8: Molar (Text Fig. 17-6)

INSTRUCTIONS

1. Write the names of the two divisions of a tooth in the numbered boxes.
2. Write the names of the parts of the tooth and gums on the appropriate numbered lines in different colors. Use the same color for parts 3 and 4 and for 6 and 7. Use a dark color for structure 8, because it will be outlined.
3. Label the other parts of the mouth.

1. _____
2. _____
3. _____
4. _____
5. _____
6. _____
7. _____
8. _____
9. _____
10. _____

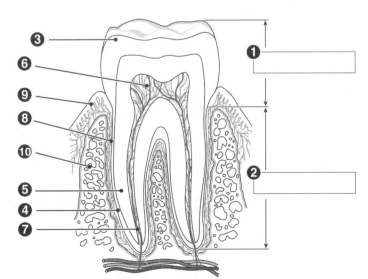

EXERCISE 17-9.

INSTRUCTIONS

Write the appropriate term in each blank.

deglutition   mastication   dentin   gingiva
deciduous   cuspids   incisors

1. Term that describes the baby teeth, based on the fact that they are lost   _____
2. The process of chewing   _____
3. The act of swallowing   _____
4. The medical term for the gum   _____
5. The eight cutting teeth located in the front part of the oral cavity   _____
6. A calcified substance making up most of the tooth structure   _____

5. Name and describe the functions of the organs of the digestive tract.

EXERCISE 17-10: Longitudinal Section of the Stomach (Text Fig. 17-7)

INSTRUCTIONS

1. Label the parts of the stomach, esophagus, and duodenum (parts 1 to 7).
2. Label the layers of the stomach wall (parts 8 to 11). You can use colors to highlight the different muscular layers.
3. Label the two stomach curvatures (labels 12 and 13).

1. _____
2. _____
3. _____
4. _____
5. _____
6. _____
7. _____
8. _____
9. _____
10. _____
11. _____
12. _____
13. _____

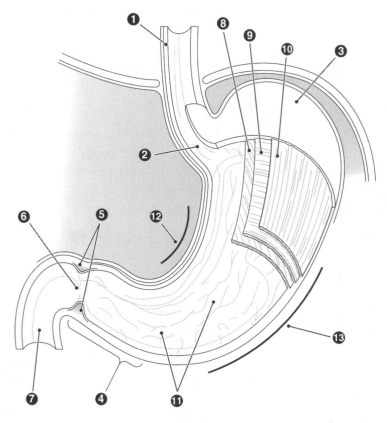

EXERCISE 17-11: The Small and Large Intestines (Text Fig. 17-8)

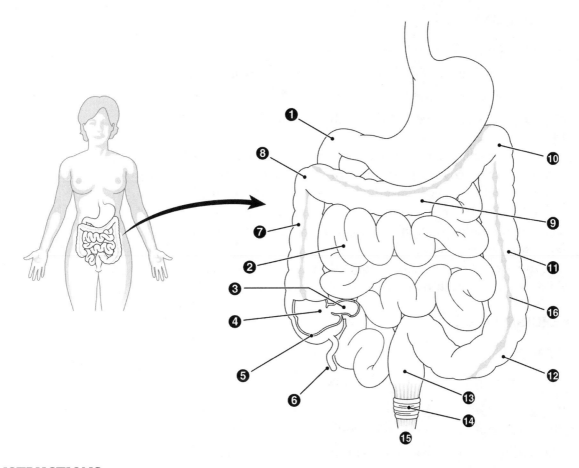

INSTRUCTIONS

Label the indicated parts.

1. _____
2. _____
3. _____
4. _____
5. _____
6. _____
7. _____
8. _____
9. _____
10. _____
11. _____
12. _____
13. _____
14. _____
15. _____
16. _____

EXERCISE 17-12.

INSTRUCTIONS

Write the appropriate term in each blank.

ileum	hard palate	soft palate	epiglottis	pyloric sphincter
LES	rugae	chyme	duodenum	jejunum

1. The valve between the distal end of the stomach and the small intestine _____
2. The structure that guards the entrance into the stomach _____
3. A structure that covers the opening of the larynx during swallowing _____
4. The part of the oral cavity roof that extends to form the uvula _____
5. The final, and longest, section of the small intestine _____
6. The section of the small intestine that receives gastric juices and food from the stomach _____
7. The mixture of gastric juices and food that enters the small intestine _____
8. Folds in the stomach that are absent if the stomach is full _____

EXERCISE 17-13.

INSTRUCTIONS

Write the appropriate term in each blank.

villi	lacteal	teniae coli	cecum	transverse colon
vermiform appendix	sigmoid colon	rectum	ileocecal valve	

1. The part of the large intestine just proximal to the anus _____
2. The small blind tube attached to the first part of the large intestine _____
3. The sphincter that prevents food moving from the large intestine into the small intestine _____
4. Fingerlike extensions of the mucosa in the small intestine _____
5. A blind-ended lymphatic vessel that absorbs fat _____
6. Bands of longitudinal muscle in the large intestine _____
7. The portion of the large intestine that extends across the abdomen _____
8. The most proximal part of the large intestine _____

6. Name and describe the functions of the accessory organs of digestion.

EXERCISE 17-14: Accessory Organs (Text Fig. 17-10)

INSTRUCTIONS

1. Write the names of the labeled parts on the appropriate lines in different colors.
2. Color the structures on the diagram.

1. _____
2. _____
3. _____
4. _____
5. _____
6. _____
7. _____
8. _____
9. _____
10. _____

EXERCISE 17-15.

INSTRUCTIONS

Write the appropriate term in each blank.

parotid glands   submandibular glands   sublingual glands
gallbladder   liver   pancreas

1. The gland that secretes bicarbonate and digestive enzymes _____
2. An organ that stores nutrients and releases them as needed into
   the bloodstream _____
3. The accessory organ that stores bile _____
4. The salivary glands that are inferior and anterior to the ear _____
5. Glands found just under the tongue that secrete into the oral cavity _____

7. Describe how bile functions in digestion (see Exercise 17-16).

8. Name and locate the ducts that carry bile from the liver into the digestive tract.

EXERCISE 17-16.

INSTRUCTIONS

Write the appropriate term in each blank.

| common bile duct | bile | common hepatic duct | cystic duct | pancreatic duct |
| bicarbonate | bilirubin | glycogen | urea | |

1. A substance that emulsifies fat   _____
2. The form in which glucose is stored in the liver   _____
3. A waste product resulting from the destruction of red blood cells   _____
4. A waste product synthesized by the liver as a result of protein metabolism _____
5. The duct connecting the hepatic duct to the gallbladder   _____
6. The duct that delivers bile into the duodenum   _____
7. The duct that carries bile from both lobes of the liver to the common bile duct _____

9. Explain the role of enzymes in digestion and give examples of enzymes.

EXERCISE 17-17.

INSTRUCTIONS

Write the appropriate term in each blank.

| protein | hydrolysis | fat | nuclease | pepsin |
| sodium bicarbonate | lipase | maltose | trypsin | maltase |

1. An enzyme that acts on a particular type of disaccharide   _____
2. A substance (NOT an enzyme) released into the small intestine that neutralizes the acidity in chyme _____
3. A substance that digests DNA   _____
4. A pancreatic enzyme that splits proteins into amino acids   _____
5. An enzyme secreted into the stomach that initiates protein digestion   _____
6. The splitting of food molecules by the addition of water   _____
7. Lipase participates in the digestion of this nutrient   _____

10. Name the digestion products of fats, proteins, and carbohydrates.

EXERCISE 17-18.

INSTRUCTIONS

For each of the following statements, write if they apply to carbohydrates (C), proteins (P), or fats (F).

1. This nutrient type is digested into sugars. ____
2. This nutrient type is digested into amino acids. ____
3. This nutrient type is digested into glycerol and fatty acids. ____
4. This nutrient type is partially digested in the stomach in both children and adults. ____
5. This nutrient type can be broken down into disaccharides. ____

11. Define *absorption*.

EXERCISE 17-19.

INSTRUCTIONS

Write a definition of *absorption* in the space below.

_____

12. Define *villi* and state how villi function in absorption.

EXERCISE 17-20.

INSTRUCTIONS

For each statement, state whether it is true (T) or false (F).

1. Digested carbohydrates are absorbed into lacteals. ____
2. Villi are small extensions of individual intestinal cells. ____
3. Villi are folds in the mucosa, each composed of many cells. ____
4. Digested fats are absorbed into lacteals. ____

13. Explain the use of feedback in regulating digestion and give several examples.

EXERCISE 17-21.

INSTRUCTIONS

Complete the following discussion by choosing one of the terms in brackets after each blank.

Digestion is regulated by a type of feedback that maintains homeostasis and is called (1) _____ [negative, positive] feedback, For instance, (2) _____ [gastrin, secretin] is released from duodenal cells in response to (3) _____ [increased, decreased] acidity in the intestine. This hormone, in turn, stimulates (4) _____ [bile, bicarbonate] release from the pancreas, which neutralizes the change in acidity. Once the intestinal pH returns to normal, the release of this hormone is (5) _____ [increased, decreased].

14. List several hormones involved in regulating digestion.

EXERCISE 17-22.

INSTRUCTIONS

Write the appropriate term in each blank.

leptin   gastrin   gastric-inhibitory peptide
cholecystokinin (CCK)   secretin

1. A hormone released from fat cells that inhibits appetite   _____
2. A duodenal hormone that stimulates insulin release   _____
3. A hormone that stimulates the secretion of gastric juice and increases stomach motility   _____
4. An intestinal hormone that causes the gallbladder to contract, releasing bile   _____

15. Show how word parts are used to build words related to digestion.

EXERCISE 17-23.

INSTRUCTIONS

Complete the following table by writing the correct word part or meaning in the space provided. Write a word that contains each word part in the Example column.

Word Part	Meaning	Example
1. _____	starch	_____
2. mes/o-	_____	_____
3. _____	intestine	_____
4. chole	_____	_____
5. bil/i	_____	_____
6. _____	bladder, sac	_____
7. _____	stomach	_____
8. _____	away from	_____
9. hepat/o	_____	_____
10. lingu/o	_____	_____

Making the Connections

The following concept map deals with the structure and regulation of the gastrointestinal system. Each pair of terms is linked together by a connecting phrase into a sentence. The sentence should be read in the direction of the arrow. Complete the concept map by filling in the appropriate term or phrase. There is one right answer for each term (1, 2, 4, 7, 15, 17, 18). However, there are many correct answers for the connecting phrases. Write the connecting phrases along the arrows if possible. If your phrases are too long, you may want to write them in the margins or on a separate sheet of paper.

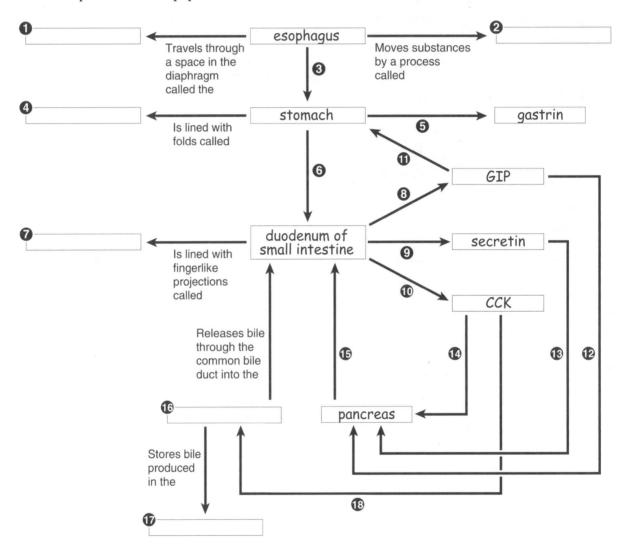

Optional Exercise: Make your own concept map, based on the three processes of digestion and how they apply to proteins, sugars, and fats. Choose your own terms to incorporate into your map, or use the following list: digestion, absorption, elimination, stomach, small intestine, large intestine, fats, carbohydrates, proteins, amylase, lipase, bile, hydrochloric acid, pepsin, trypsin, peptidase, and maltase.

Testing Your Knowledge

Building Understanding

I. Multiple Choice

Select the best answer and write the letter of your choice in the blank.

1. Which teeth would NOT be found in a 20-year-old man?
   a. bicuspid
   b. cuspid
   c. deciduous
   d. incisor

   1. _____

2. Which of the following is the correct order of tissue from the innermost to the outermost layer in the wall of the digestive tract?
   a. submucosa, serous membrane, smooth muscle, mucous membrane
   b. smooth muscle, serous membrane, mucous membrane, submucosa
   c. serous membrane, smooth muscle, submucosa, mucosa
   d. mucous membrane, submucosa, smooth muscle, serous membrane

   2. _____

3. The parotid salivary gland is located
   a. inferior and anterior to the ear
   b. under the tongue
   c. in the cheek
   d. in the oropharynx

   3. _____

4. Which of the following is NOT a portion of the peritoneum?
   a. mesocolon
   b. mesentery
   c. hiatus
   d. greater omentum

   4. _____

5. The active ingredients in gastric juice are
   a. amylase and pepsin
   b. pepsin and hydrochloric acid
   c. maltase and secretin
   d. bile and trypsin

   5. _____

6. Gastric-inhibitory peptide stimulates the release of
   a. gastric juice
   b. insulin
   c. bicarbonate
   d. none of the above

   6. _____

7. In the adult, fats are digested in the
   a. mouth
   b. stomach
   c. small intestine
   d. all of the above

   7. _____

8. Which of the following does NOT occur in the mouth?
   a. mastication
   b. digestion of starch
   c. absorption of nutrients
   d. ingestion

   8. _____

9. Which of the following is an enzyme?　　　　　　　　　　9. _____
   a. bile
   b. gastrin
   c. trypsin
   d. secretin
10. Which of the following is associated with the intestine?　　10. _____
   a. rugae
   b. lacteals
   c. LES
   d. greater curvature

II. Completion Exercise

Write the word or phrase that correctly completes each sentence.

1. The process by which ingested nutrients are broken down into smaller components is called _____.

2. The lower part of the colon bends into an S shape, so this part is called the _____.

3. A temporary storage section for indigestible and unabsorbable waste products of digestion is the _____.

4. The wavelike movement created by alternating muscle contractions is called _____.

5. The ascending and descending colon can be examined using a type of endoscope called a(n) _____.

6. Most of the digestive juices contain substances that cause the chemical breakdown of foods without entering into the reaction themselves. These catalytic agents are _____.

7. The portion of the peritoneum extending between the stomach and liver is called the _____.

8. The process of swallowing is called _____.

9. Teeth are largely composed of a calcified substance called _____.

10. The esophagus passes through the diaphragm at a point called the _____.

11. The hormone that stimulates gallbladder contraction is called _____.

12. Small projecting folds in the plasma membrane of intestinal epithelial cells are called _____.

13. The stomach enzyme involved in protein digestion is called _____.

Understanding Concepts

I. True/False

For each question, write *T* for true or *F* for false in the blank to the left of each number. If a statement is false, correct it by replacing the underlined term and write the correct statement in the blank below the question.

_____ 1. There are <u>32</u> deciduous teeth.

_____

_____ 2. The layer of the peritoneum attached to the liver is the <u>visceral</u> peritoneum.

_____

_____ 3. Ms. Q is deficient in lactase. She will be unable to digest some <u>carbohydrates</u>.

_____

_____ 4. Trypsin is secreted by the <u>gastric glands</u>.

_____

_____ 5. Increased acidity in the chyme could be neutralized by the actions of the hormone <u>gastrin.</u>

_____

_____ 6. Fats are absorbed into <u>capillaries</u> in the intestinal villi.

_____

_____ 7. The middle section of the small intestine is called the <u>jejunum</u>.

_____

_____ 8. Folds in the stomach wall are called <u>villi</u>.

_____

_____ 9. The <u>common bile</u> duct delivers bile from the liver and gallbladder into the duodenum.

_____

_____ 10. Amylase is involved in the digestion of <u>carbohydrates</u>.

_____

_____ 11. The <u>pancreas</u> is responsible for the synthesis of urea.

_____

II. Practical Applications

Study each discussion. Then write the appropriate word or phrase in the space provided.

1. Mr. P, age 42, came to the clinic reporting pain in the "pit of the stomach." He was a tense man who divided his long working hours with coffee and cigarette breaks. When asked about his alcohol consumption, Mr. C mentioned that he drank 3 or 4 beers and 1 glass of wine each night, and significantly more on the weekends. Endoscopy showed inflammation of the innermost layer of the stomach. This layer is called the _____.
2. A damaged area was also found in the most proximal part of the small intestine. This section of the small intestine is called the _____.
3. Mr. P had an ulcer diagnosed and was given a prescription for antibiotics. The antibiotics will eliminate the *H. pylori* bacterium involved in ulcer formation. Mr. P was also given a medication to inhibit the release of the hormone that stimulates gastric juice secretion. This hormone is called _____.
4. The physician had almost completed her physical examination of Mr. P when she felt the edge of his liver about 5 cm (2 in) below the ribs. She also noticed that the whites of his eyes were tinged with yellow. This coloration results from the release of a hepatic secretion into the bloodstream. This secretion, which is needed for the digestion of fat, is called _____.
5. Based on her clinical findings and Mr. P's self-reported alcohol abuse, the physician suspected that Mr. P has cirrhosis, a chronic liver disease. However, further testing revealed that Mr. P's liver function was normal. His jaundice was due to a blockage in the duct that empties bile into the duodenum, the _____.

III. Short Essays

1. Describe some features of the small intestine that increase the surface area for absorption of nutrients.

_____
_____
_____

2. List four differences between the digestion and/or absorption of fats and proteins.

_____
_____
_____

Conceptual Thinking

1. Ms. M is taking a drug that blocks the action of cholecystokinin. Discuss the impact of this drug on digestion.

_____

_____

_____

2. Is bile an enzyme? Explain your answer.

_____

_____

_____

Expanding Your Horizons

A growing number of young women (and even some young men) are "Dying to Be Thin." Due to eating disorders, they starve themselves and/or binge-and-purge, sometimes to death. You can learn more about eating disorders by viewing the PBS Nova program "Dying to Be Thin," which is available through the PBS website (http://shop.wgbh.org). The two journal articles listed below discuss eating disorders from a nurse's perspective.

Resources

1. Clark-Stone S, Joyce H. Understanding eating disorders. *Nurs Times* 2003; 99:20–23.
2. Murphy B, Manning Y. An introduction to anorexia nervosa and bulimia nervosa. *Nurs Stand* 2003; 18:45–52.

CHAPTER 18

Metabolism, Nutrition, and Body Temperature

Overview

The nutrients that reach the cells following digestion and absorption are used to maintain life. All the physical and chemical reactions that occur within the cells make up **metabolism**, which has two phases: a breakdown phase, or **catabolism**, and a building phase, or **anabolism**. Nutrients are oxidized to yield energy for the cells in the form of ATP using catabolic reactions. This process, termed **cellular respiration**, occurs in two steps: the first is **anaerobic** (does not require oxygen) and produces a small amount of energy; the second is **aerobic** (requires oxygen). This second step occurs within the cells' mitochondria. It yields a large amount of the energy contained in the nutrient plus carbon dioxide and water.

By the various metabolic pathways, the breakdown products of food can be built into substances needed by the body. The **essential** amino acids and fatty acids cannot be manufactured internally and must be ingested in food. **Minerals** and **vitamins** are also needed in the diet for health. A balanced diet includes carbohydrates, proteins, and fats consumed in amounts relative to individual activity levels.

The rate at which energy is released from nutrients is termed the **metabolic rate**. It is affected by many factors including age, size, sex, activity, and hormones. Some of the energy in nutrients is released as heat. Heat production is greatly increased during periods of increased muscular or glandular activity. Most heat is lost through the skin, but heat is also dissipated through exhaled air and eliminated waste products (urine and feces). The **hypothalamus** maintains body temperature at approximately 37° C (98.6° F) by altering blood flow through the surface blood vessels and the activity of sweat glands and muscles.

Addressing the Learning Outcomes

1. Differentiate between catabolism and anabolism.

EXERCISE 18-1.

INSTRUCTIONS

Which of the following statements apply to catabolism (C) and which apply to anabolism (A)?

1. The metabolic breakdown of complex compounds   _____
2. The metabolic building of simple compounds into substances
   needed by cells   _____
3. This process usually releases energy   _____

2. Differentiate between the anaerobic and aerobic phases of cellular respiration and give the end products and the relative amount of energy released by each.

EXERCISE 18-2.

INSTRUCTIONS

Which of the following statements apply to the anaerobic phase (AN) and which apply to the aerobic phase (AE) of cellular respiration?

1. This process generates 2 ATP per glucose molecule ____
2. This process generates about 30 ATP per glucose molecule ____
3. The end products are carbon dioxide and water ____
4. The end product is pyruvic acid ____
5. This process can occur in the absence of oxygen ____
6. This process requires oxygen ____
7. This process occurs first ____

3. Define metabolic rate and name several factors that affect the metabolic rate.

EXERCISE 18-3.

INSTRUCTIONS

Write a definition for each term in the blanks provided.

1. metabolism _____

   _____

2. metabolic rate _____

   _____

3. basal metabolism _____

   _____

4. Explain the roles of glucose and glycogen in metabolism (see Exercise 18-4).

5. Compare the energy contents of fats, proteins, and carbohydrates.

EXERCISE 18-4.

INSTRUCTIONS

Write the appropriate term in each blank.

glycolysis   lactic acid   pyruvic acid   glycerol
glycogen   deamination   fat   protein

1. The storage form of glucose   _____
2. A modification of amino acids that occurs before they can be
   oxidized for energy   _____
3. An organic product of glucose catabolism that can be completely
   oxidized within the mitochondria   _____
4. An organic substance produced when a muscle is generating energy
   in the absence of oxygen   _____
5. The nutrient type that generates the most energy per gram   _____
6. A product of fat digestion that can be used for energy   _____
7. The nutrient type that is used to generate energy only in emergencies _____

6. Define *essential amino acid* (see Exercise 18-5).

7. Explain the roles of minerals and vitamins in nutrition and give examples of each.

EXERCISE 18-5.

INSTRUCTIONS

Write the appropriate term in each blank below.

essential amino acids   nonessential amino acids   essential fatty acids   antioxidants
trace elements   vitamins   minerals

1. A class of substances that stabilizes free radicals   _____
2. Minerals required in extremely small amounts   _____
3. Complex organic molecules that are essential for metabolism   _____
4. Protein components that must be taken in as part of the diet   _____
5. Inorganic elements needed for body structure and many body
   functions   _____
6. Protein building blocks that can be manufactured by the body   _____
7. Linoleic acid and linolenic acid are examples of   _____

EXERCISE 18-6.

INSTRUCTIONS

Write the appropriate term in each blank below.

zinc   iodine   iron   potassium   calcium
folate   calciferol   riboflavin   vitamin A   vitamin K

1. The vitamin that prevents dry, scaly skin and night blindness   _____
2. The vitamin needed to prevent anemia, digestive disorders, and
   neural tube defects in the embryo   _____
3. Another name for vitamin D, the vitamin required for normal
   bone formation   _____
4. The mineral component of thyroid hormones   _____
5. A mineral important in blood clotting and muscle contraction   _____
6. The characteristic element in hemoglobin, the oxygen-carrying
   compound in the blood   _____
7. A mineral that promotes carbon dioxide transport and energy
   metabolism   _____
8. A vitamin involved in the synthesis of blood clotting factors that
   can be synthesized by colonic bacteria   _____

8. List the recommended percentages of carbohydrate, fat, and protein in the diet.

EXERCISE 18-7.

INSTRUCTIONS

Match each percentage to the corresponding nutrient type by writing the appropriate letter in each blank.

1. protein ___   a. 55% to 60%
2. fat ____   b. < 30%
3. carbohydrate ____   c. 15% to 20%

9. Distinguish between simple and complex carbohydrates, giving examples of each (see Exercise 18-8).

10. Compare saturated and unsaturated fats.

EXERCISE 18-8.

INSTRUCTIONS

Write the appropriate term in each blank.

trans-fatty acids   unsaturated fats   monosaccharides
saturated fats   polysaccharides   disaccharides

1. Fats that are usually of animal origin and are solid at room
   temperature   _____
2. Fats that are artificially saturated to prevent rancidity   _____
3. Carbohydrates with a low glycemic effect   _____
4. Glucose and fructose are examples of this type of nutrient   _____
5. Plant-derived fats that are usually liquid at room temperature   _____

11. List some adverse effects of alcohol consumption.

EXERCISE 18-9.

INSTRUCTIONS

Write three adverse effects of alcohol consumption in the spaces below.

1. _____
2. _____
3. _____

12. Explain how heat is produced and lost in the body.

EXERCISE 18-10.

INSTRUCTIONS

Write the appropriate term in each blank.

convection   evaporation   conduction   radiation

1. The direct transfer of heat to the surrounding air   _____
2. Heat loss resulting from the conversion of a liquid, such as
   perspiration, to a vapor   _____
3. Heat loss resulting from moving air   _____
4. Heat that travels from its source as heat waves   _____

13. Describe the role of the hypothalamus in regulating body temperature.

EXERCISE 18-11.

INSTRUCTIONS

Which of the following body changes would the hypothalamus induce when the body is cold (C), and which would it induce when the body is excessively hot (H)?

1. Constriction of the skin's blood vessels _____
2. Increased sweat gland activity _____
3. Dilation of the skin's blood vessels _____
4. Increased skeletal muscle contraction (shivering) _____

14. Show how word parts are used to build words related to metabolism, nutrition, and body temperature.

EXERCISE 18-12.

INSTRUCTIONS

Complete the following table by writing the correct word part or meaning in the space provided. Write a word that contains each word part in the Example column.

Word Part	Meaning	Example
1. -lysis	_____	_____
2. _____	sugar, sweet	_____

Making the Connections

The following concept map deals with nutrition and metabolism. Each pair of terms is linked together by a connecting phrase into a sentence. The sentence should be read in the direction of the arrow. Complete the concept map by filling in the appropriate term or phrase. There is one right answer for each term (1 to 3, 8). However, there are many correct answers for the connecting phrases. Write the connecting phrases along the arrows if possible. If your phrases are too long, you may want to write them in the margins or on a separate sheet of paper.

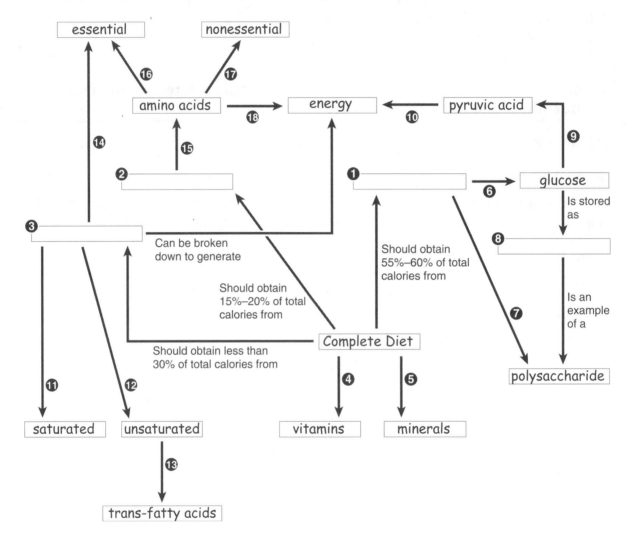

Optional Exercise: Make your own concept map, based on the regulation of body temperature. Choose your own terms to incorporate into your map, or use the following list: body temperature, hypothalamus, sweating, shivering, dilation, constriction, skin, respiratory system, radiation, convection, conduction, evaporation.

Testing Your Knowledge

Building Understanding

I. Multiple Choice

Select the best answer and write the letter of your choice in the blank.

1. The brain region involved in temperature regulation is the
    a. hypothalamus
    b. cerebral cortex
    c. hippocampus
    d. thalamus

    1. _____

2. A complete protein contains
    a. all the amino acids
    b. all the essential fatty acids
    c. a variety of minerals
    d. all the essential amino acids

    2. _____

3. Deamination is
    a. an anabolic reaction
    b. the conversion of proteins into amino acids
    c. the conversion of glucose into glycogen
    d. the removal of a nitrogen group from an amino acid

    3. _____

4. The end product of the anaerobic phase of glucose metabolism is
    a. glycogen
    b. pyruvic acid
    c. folic acid
    d. tocopherol

    4. _____

5. Trace elements in the diet are
    a. sugars with a high glycemic effect
    b. vitamins needed in very small amounts
    c. minerals needed in large quantity
    d. minerals needed in extremely small amounts

    5. _____

6. Profuse sweating increases heat lost by the process of
    a. radiation
    b. evaporation
    c. convection
    d. none of the above

    6. _____

7. Unsaturated fats
    a. are generally healthier than saturated fats
    b. can be converted into trans fats
    c. contain double bonds between the carbon atoms
    d. all of the above

    7. _____

8. Which of the following is an example of an anabolic reaction?
    a. glycerol and fatty acids are used to form a fat
    b. starches and glycogen are converted into glucose
    c. a short peptide is converted into arginine and cysteine
    d. glucose is completely oxidized to carbon dioxide and water

    8. _____

II. Completion Exercise

Write the word or phrase that correctly completes each sentence.

1. The unit used to measure energy is the _____.
2. The amount of energy needed to accomplish necessary cell functions at rest is termed the _____.
3. Shivering to generate additional body heat results from increased activity of the _____.
4. Organic substances needed in small amounts in the diet are the _____.
5. The most important heat-regulating center is a section of the brain called the _____.
6. The series of catabolic reactions that results in the complete breakdown of nutrients is called _____.
7. Heat that is moved away from the skin by the wind is lost by the process of _____.
8. Glycolysis occurs in the part of the cell called the _____.
9. Fatty acids that must be consumed in the diet are called _____.

Understanding Concepts

I. True/False

For each question, write *T* for true or *F* for false in the blank to the left of each number. If a statement is false, correct it by replacing the underlined term and write the correct statement in the blank below the question.

_____ 1. A body temperature of 35° C is abnormally underlined.

_____

_____ 2. Grapeseed oil is liquid at room temperature. This oil is most likely a saturated fat.

_____

_____ 3. The conversion of glycogen into glucose is an example of a catabolic reaction.

_____

_____ 4. Most heat loss in the body occurs through the skin.

_____

_____ 5. The element nitrogen is found in all sugars.

_____

_____ 6. Mr. B is training for an upcoming road race by doing sprints. His leg muscles are working anaerobically. The <u>pyruvic acid</u> accumulating in his muscles may be responsible for the fatigue he is experiencing.

_____

_____ 7. The rate at which energy is released from nutrients in Mr. B's cells during his sprints is called his <u>basal metabolism</u>.

_____

_____ 8. Pernicious anemia is caused by a deficiency in vitamin <u>B₁₂</u>.

_____

_____ 9. Linoleic acid is an example of an <u>essential amino acid</u>.

_____

_____ 10. Copper and calcium are examples of <u>vitamins</u>.

_____

II. Practical Applications

Ms. S is researching penguin behavior at a remote location in Antarctica. She will be camping on the ice for 2 months. Study each discussion. Then write the appropriate word or phrase in the space provided.

1. Ms. S is spending her first night on the ice. She is careful to wear many layers of clothing to avoid a dangerous drop in body temperature. The extra clothing will reduce the direct transfer of heat from Ms. S's body to the surrounding air by the process of _____.
2. She is out for a moonlight walk to greet the penguins when she surprises an elephant seal stalking a penguin. Frightened, she sprints back to her tent. Her muscles are generating ATP by an oxygen-independent pathway. Each glucose molecule is generating a small number of ATP molecules, or to be exact _____.
3. The next morning, Ms. S is suffering from soreness in her leg muscles. She attributes the soreness to the accumulation of a byproduct of anaerobic metabolism called _____.
4. This byproduct must be converted into another substance before it can be completely oxidized. This substance is called _____.
5. After 2 weeks on the ice, Ms. S is out of fresh fruits and vegetables, and the penguins have stolen her multivitamin supplements. She has been reading accounts of early explorers with scurvy and fears she will experience the same fate. Scurvy is caused by a deficiency of _____.
6. Ms. S's diet is now reduced to luncheon meat and crackers. The crackers are still tasty because they contain significant amounts of artificially hydrogenated fats, known as _____.
7. She looks forward to eating her normal diet when she returns home, which is rich in fruits, vegetables, and complex carbohydrates, also known as _____.

8. Ms. S hikes to a distant penguin colony on her final day on the ice. She is dressed very warmly, and the sun is very bright. After several hours of hiking, Ms. S is sweating profusely, so she removes some clothing to cool off. Some excess heat will be lost through the evaporation of sweat. The wind will also increase heat loss by the process called _____.

III. Short Essays

1. Is alcohol a nutrient? Defend your answer.

   _____

   _____

   _____

2. A glucose molecule has been transported into a muscle cell. This cell has ample supplies of oxygen. Discuss the steps involved in using this glucose to produce energy. For each step, describe its location and oxygen requirements and name the substances produced.

   _____

   _____

   _____

   _____

   _____

Conceptual Thinking

1. Your friend wants to lose some weight. She is following a diet that contains 20% carbohydrates, 40% fat, and 40% protein. Why is this diet designed to limit fat deposition? You may have to review the actions of pancreatic hormones (see Chapter 11) to answer this question.

   _____

   _____

   _____

Expanding Your Horizons

How does your diet measure up? Go to http://www.mypyramid.gov to find out. By clicking on "MyPyramid Plan," you can get personalized dietary recommendations based on your age, gender, height, weight, and activity level. Some nongovernmental agencies, such as the Harvard School of Public Health, have criticized the government's efforts and proposed a different pyramid, the Healthy Eating Pyramid. You can read about their critique at http://www.hsph.harvard.edu/nutritionsource/pyramids.html/.

CHAPTER 19

The Urinary System and Body Fluids

Overview

The urinary system comprises two **kidneys**, two **ureters**, one **urinary bladder**, and one **urethra**. This system is thought of as the body's main excretory mechanism; it is, in fact, often called the **excretory system**. The kidney, however, performs other essential functions; it aids in maintaining water and electrolyte balance and in regulating the acid–base balance (pH) of body fluids. The kidneys also secrete a hormone that stimulates red blood cell production and an enzyme that increases blood pressure.

The functional unit of the kidney is the **nephron**. It is the nephron that produces **urine** from substances filtered out of the blood through a cluster of capillaries, the **glomerulus**. The processes involved in urine formation in addition to filtration are tubular reabsorption, tubular secretion, and concentration of urine. Oxygenated blood is brought to the kidney by the **renal artery**. The arterial system branches through the kidney until the smallest subdivision, the **afferent arteriole**, carries blood into the glomerulus. Blood leaves the glomerulus by means of the **efferent arteriole** and eventually leaves the kidney by means of the **renal vein**. Before blood enters the venous network of the kidney, exchanges occur between the filtrate and the blood through the **peritubular capillaries** that surround each nephron.

The majority (50% to 70%) of a person's body weight is **water**. This water is a solvent, a transport medium, and a participant in metabolic reactions. A variety of substances are dissolved in this water, including electrolytes, nutrients, gases, enzymes, hormones, and waste products. Body fluids are distributed in two main compartments: (a) The **intracellular fluid** compartment within the cells, and (b) The **extracellular fluid** compartment located outside the cells. The latter category includes blood plasma, interstitial fluid, lymph, and fluids in special compartments, such as the humors of the eye, cerebrospinal fluid, serous fluids, and synovial fluids.

Water balance is maintained by matching fluid intake with fluid output. Fluid intake is stimulated by the thirst center in the **hypothalamus,** but humans voluntarily control their fluid intake and may consume excess or insufficient fluids. Normally, the amount of fluid taken in with food and beverages equals the amount of fluid lost through the skin and the respiratory, digestive, and urinary tracts.

The composition of intracellular and extracellular fluids is an important factor in homeostasis. These fluids must have the proper levels of electrolytes and must be kept at a constant pH. The kidneys are the main regulators of body fluids. Other factors that aid in regulation include hormones, buffers, and respiration. The normal pH of body fluids is a slightly alkaline 7.4.

Addressing the Learning Outcomes

1. List the systems that eliminate waste and name the substances eliminated by each.

EXERCISE 19-1.

INSTRUCTIONS

For each substance, determine the system or systems that eliminate it and write the appropriate letter(s) in the blank (U for urinary, D for digestive, R for respiratory, and I for integumentary). There may be more than one answer for each substance.

1. carbon dioxide _____
2. bile _____
3. water _____
4. salts _____
5. food residue _____
6. nitrogenous wastes _____

2. Describe the parts of the urinary system and give the functions of each.

EXERCISE 19-2: Male Urinary System (Text Fig. 19-1)

INSTRUCTIONS

1. Write the names of the arteries on the appropriate numbered lines in red, and color the arteries (except for the small box) on the diagram.
2. Write the names of the veins on the appropriate numbered lines in blue, and color the veins (except for the small box) on the diagram.
3. Write the names of the remaining structures on the appropriate numbered lines in different colors, and color the structures on the diagram.
4. Put arrows in the small boxes to indicate the direction of blood/urine movement.

1. _____
2. _____
3. _____
4. _____
5. _____
6. _____
7. _____
8. _____
9. _____
10. _____
11. _____
12. _____
13. _____
14. _____
15. _____
16. _____
17. _____
18. _____

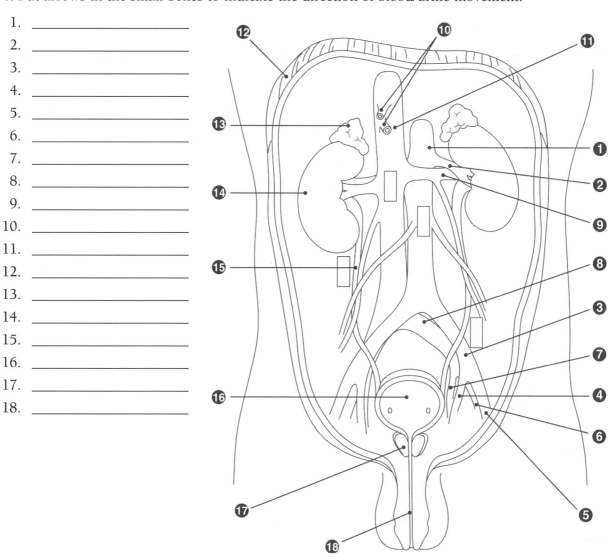

EXERCISE 19-3: Longitudinal Section through the Kidney (Text Figs. 19-2 and 19-3)

INSTRUCTIONS

1. Write the names of the blood vessels on lines 1 and 2 (vessel 1 drains from the abdominal aorta and vessel 2 drains into the inferior vena cava). Use red for the artery and blue for the vein.
2. Color the artery and arterioles on the diagram red and the veins and venules blue.
3. Write the names of the remaining structures on the appropriate numbered lines in different colors, and color the structures on the diagram. Use the same, dark color for structures 3 and 4. Use the same color for structures 6 and 7. Use yellow for structures 8 to 10.

1. _____
2. _____
3. _____
4. _____
5. _____
6. _____
7. _____
8. _____
9. _____
10. _____

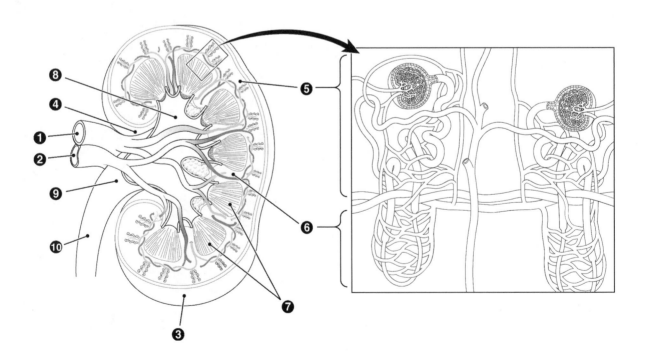

EXERCISE 19-4.

INSTRUCTIONS

Write the appropriate term in each blank.

ureter	urinary bladder	urethra	renal capsule	renal cortex
retroperitoneal space	nephron	renal pelvis	adipose capsule	renal medulla

1. A funnel-shaped basin that collects urine from collecting ducts   _____
2. The tube that carries urine from the bladder to the outside   _____
3. The area behind the peritoneum that contains the ureters and
   the kidneys   _____
4. A microscopic functional unit of the kidney   _____
5. A tube connecting a kidney with the bladder   _____
6. The crescent of fat that helps to support the kidney   _____
7. The inner region of the kidney   _____
8. The outer region of the kidney   _____

3. List the activities of the kidneys in maintaining homeostasis.

EXERCISE 19-5.

INSTRUCTIONS

In the spaces below, list five body parameters that the kidney helps to maintain within tight limits.

1. _____
2. _____
3. _____
4. _____
5. _____

4. Trace the path of a drop of blood as it flows through the kidney (see Exercise 19-6).

5. Describe a nephron.

EXERCISE 19-6: A Nephron and Its Blood Supply (Text Fig. 19-4)

INSTRUCTIONS

1. Follow the passage of blood by labeling structures 1 to 6. Use different shades of red for the arteries/arterioles, purple for the capillaries, and blue for the venules/veins. Lines indicate the boundaries between different vessels.
2. Follow the passage of filtrate through the nephron by labeling structures 7 to 13. Use different colors (perhaps shades of yellow and orange) for the different structures. Lines indicate the boundaries between the different nephron parts.
3. Write the names of the remaining structures on the appropriate numbered lines in different colors, and color the structures on the diagram.

1. _____
2. _____
3. _____
4. _____
5. _____
6. _____
7. _____
8. _____
9. _____
10. _____
11. _____
12. _____
13. _____

EXERCISE 19-7.

INSTRUCTIONS

Write the appropriate term in each blank.

afferent arteriole   proximal convoluted tubule   peritubular capillaries   nephron loop
glomerulus   glomerular capsule   efferent arteriole   renal artery
collecting duct   renal vein

1. A hollow bulb at the proximal end of the nephron   _____
2. The blood vessels connecting the afferent and efferent arterioles   _____
3. The portion of the nephron receiving filtrate from the glomerular
   capsule   _____
4. The vessel that branches to form the glomerulus   _____
5. The vessel that drains the kidney   _____
6. The blood vessels that exchange substances with the nephron   _____
7. A tube that receives urine from the distal convoluted tubule   _____
8. The portion of the nephron that dips into the medulla   _____

6. Name the four processes involved in urine formation and describe the action of each.

EXERCISE 19-8: Filtration Process (Text Fig. 19-6)

INSTRUCTIONS

1. Write the names of the different structures on the appropriate numbered lines in different colors, and color the structures on the diagram. Use different shades of red for structures 1 to 3 and yellow for part 7. Do not color over the symbols. Some structures have appeared on earlier diagrams. You may want to use the same color scheme.
2. Color the symbols beside "soluble molecules," "proteins," and "blood cells" in different, dark colors and color the corresponding symbols on the diagram.

1. _____

2. _____

3. _____

4. _____

5. _____

6. _____

7. _____

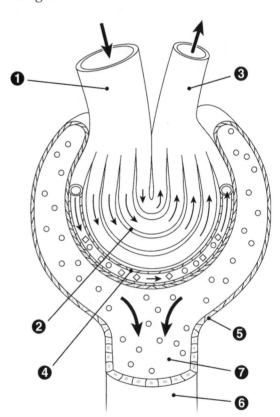

○ Soluble molecules
◇ Proteins
○ Blood cells

EXERCISE 19-9: Summary of Urine Formation (Text Fig. 19-8)

INSTRUCTIONS

1. Label the structures and fluids by writing the appropriate terms on lines 5 to 11.
2. Write the name of the hormone that controls water reabsorption in the distal tubule and collecting duct on line 12.
3. In boxes 1 to 4, summarize the process that is occurring.

5. _____

6. _____

7. _____

8. _____

9. _____

10. _____

11. _____

12. _____

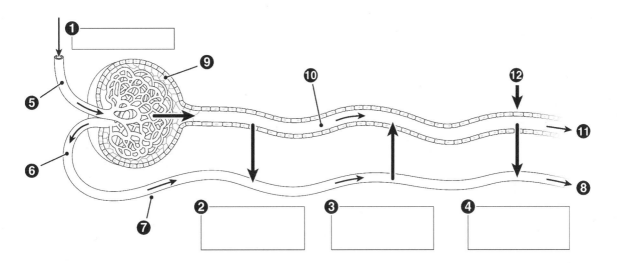

7. Identify the role of antidiuretic hormone (ADH) in urine formation.

EXERCISE 19-10.

INSTRUCTIONS

Which of the following processes is promoted by ADH? Write the correct answer here. _____

A. filtration in the glomerulus
B. establishment of the interstitial fluid concentration gradient
C. water reabsorption from the collecting duct back into the blood
D. water reabsorption from the descending nephron loop back into the blood

8. Describe the components and functions of the juxtaglomerular (JG) apparatus.

EXERCISE 19-11: Structure of the Juxtaglomerular (JG) Apparatus (Text Fig. 19-9)

INSTRUCTIONS

Write the names of the different structures on the appropriate numbered lines in different colors, and color the structures on the diagram. Use different shades of red for structures 1 to 3. Use a dark color to outline the box surrounding structure 8. Some structures have appeared on earlier diagrams. You may want to use the same color scheme.

1. _____
2. _____
3. _____
4. _____
5. _____
6. _____
7. _____
8. _____

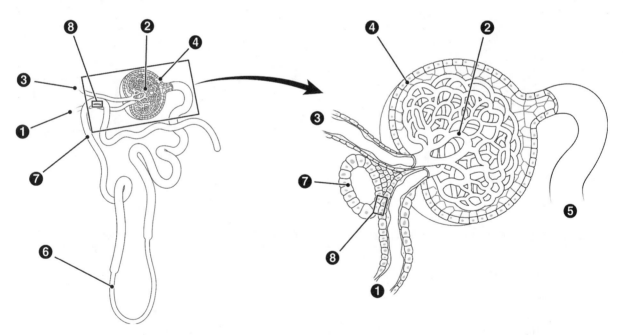

EXERCISE 19-12.

INSTRUCTIONS

Write the appropriate term in each blank.

renin   juxtaglomerular apparatus   urea   EPO   angiotensin
filtration   tubular reabsorption   tubular secretion   antidiuretic hormone   aldosterone

1. An enzyme produced by the kidney   _____
2. The hormone that increases sodium reabsorption in the DCT   _____
3. The process that returns useful substances in the filtrate to the
   bloodstream   _____
4. The process by which substances leave the glomerulus and enter
   the glomerular capsule   _____
5. The structure in the kidney that produces renin   _____
6. The hormone produced in the kidney that stimulates erythrocyte
   production by the bone marrow   _____
7. The process by which the renal tubule actively moves substances
   from the blood into the nephron to be excreted   _____
8. The hormone that increases the permeability of the DCT and
   collecting duct to water   _____

9. Describe the process of micturition.
_____

EXERCISE 19-13: Interior of the Male Urinary Bladder (Text Fig. 19-10)

INSTRUCTIONS

Label the indicated parts.

1. _____
2. _____
3. _____
4. _____
5. _____
6. _____
7. _____
8. _____
9. _____

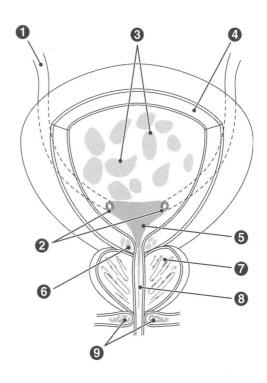

EXERCISE 19-14.

INSTRUCTIONS

In the blank following each statement, write T if the statement is true and F if it is false.

1. The internal urethral sphincter is formed of skeletal muscle. ____
2. The external urethral sphincter is formed by the pelvic floor muscles. ____
3. When the bladder fills with liquid, stretch receptors are activated. ____
4. When the bladder fills with liquid, muscles in the bladder wall contract. ____
5. Urination will occur when the external urethral sphincter is contracted. ____

10. Name three normal constituents of urine.

EXERCISE 19-15.

INSTRUCTIONS

List three normal constituents of urine in the spaces below.

1. _____
2. _____
3. _____

11. Compare intracellular and extracellular fluids (see Exercises 19-15 and 19-18).

12. List four types of extracellular fluids.

EXERCISE 19-16: Main Fluid Compartments (Text Fig. 19-11)

INSTRUCTIONS

Label the different fluid compartments.

1. _____
2. _____
3. _____
4. _____

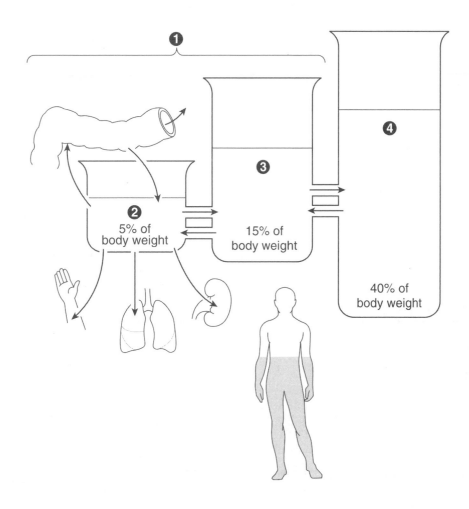

13. Name the systems that are involved in water balance.

EXERCISE 19-17: Daily Gain and Loss of Water (Text Fig. 19-12)

INSTRUCTIONS

Write the names of the different sources of water gain and loss on the appropriate numbered lines in different colors. Color the diagram with the appropriate colors.

1. _____
2. _____
3. _____
4. _____
5. _____
6. _____
7. _____

Water gain
2500 mL/day

❶ 200 mL

❷ 700 mL

❸ 1600 mL

Water loss
2500 mL/day

❹ 200 mL

❺ 300 mL

❻ 500 mL

❼ 1500 mL

14. Explain how thirst is regulated.

EXERCISE 19-18.

INSTRUCTIONS

Write the appropriate term in each blank.

hypothalamus   brainstem   interstitial   intracellular   extracellular
water   blood plasma   body fluid concentration   body fluid volume

1. The substance that makes up about 4% of a person's body weight   _____
2. The substance that makes up 50% to 70% of a person's body weight   _____
3. The part of the brain that controls the sense of thirst   _____
4. Term that specifically describes fluids in the microscopic spaces
   between cells   _____
5. The thirst center is stimulated when this is increased   _____
6. The thirst center is stimulated when this is decreased   _____
7. Term that describes the fluid within the body cells   _____

15. Define *electrolytes* and describe some of their functions.

EXERCISE 19-19.

INSTRUCTIONS

Write the appropriate term in each blank.

cation   anion   potassium   phosphate
electrolyte   sodium   calcium   chloride

1. A general term describing any positively charged ion   _____
2. A general term describing any negatively charged ion   _____
3. A component of stomach acid   _____
4. The most abundant cation inside cells   _____
5. A compound that forms ions in solution   _____
6. A cation involved in bone formation   _____
7. The most abundant cation in the fluid surrounding cells   _____

16. Describe the role of hormones in electrolyte balance.

EXERCISE 19-20.

INSTRUCTIONS

Write the appropriate term in each blank.

parathyroid hormone   aldosterone   antidiuretic hormone
atrial natriuretic peptide   calcitonin

1. A hormone secreted from the posterior pituitary that causes the
   kidney to reabsorb water   _____
2. A hormone that is secreted when blood pressure rises too high   _____
3. The adrenal hormone that promotes the reabsorption of sodium   _____
4. A hormone that causes the kidney to reabsorb calcium   _____
5. A hormone that promotes calcium deposition in bones   _____

17. Describe three methods for regulating the pH of body fluids.

EXERCISE 19-21.

INSTRUCTIONS

Write the appropriate term in each blank.

buffer   hydrogen ion   kidney   lungs   carbon dioxide

1. Any substance that aids in maintaining a constant pH   _____
2. Substance that directly determines the acidity or alkalinity of a fluid   _____
3. The organ that regulates pH balance by altering urine acidity   _____
4. The organ that regulates pH balance by altering carbon dioxide
   retention   _____

18. Show how word parts are used to build words related to the urinary system and body fluids.

EXERCISE 19-22.

INSTRUCTIONS

Complete the following table by writing the correct word part or meaning in the space provided. Write a word that contains each word part in the Example column.

Word Part	Meaning	Example
1. _____	night	_____
2. intra-	_____	_____
3. _____	partial, half	_____
4. osmo-	_____	_____
5. nephr/o-	_____	_____
6. _____	many	_____
7. _____	backward, behind	_____
8. _____	next to	_____
9. ren/o	_____	_____
10. extra-	_____	_____

Making the Connections

The following concept maps deal with the organization of the kidney (Map A) and the distribution of body fluids (Map B). Each pair of terms is linked together by a connecting phrase into a sentence. The sentence should be read in the direction of the arrow. Complete the concept map by filling in the appropriate term or phrase. There is one right answer for each term. However, there are many correct answers for the connecting phrases. Three phrases in Map A (13 and 15 and 16) involve 3 terms. For each of these phrases, build a single sentence linking the three terms together. For instance, use terms 4 and 8 and filtration to build phrase 13; term 12, peritubular capillaries, and secretion to build phrase 15; and term 9, reabsorption, and peritubular capillaries to build phrase 16. Write the phrase beside the number (if space permits) or on a separate piece of paper.

Map A

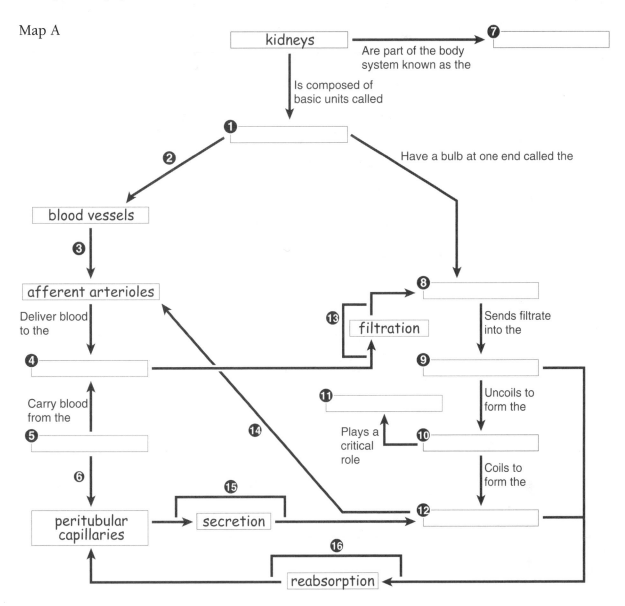

Map B

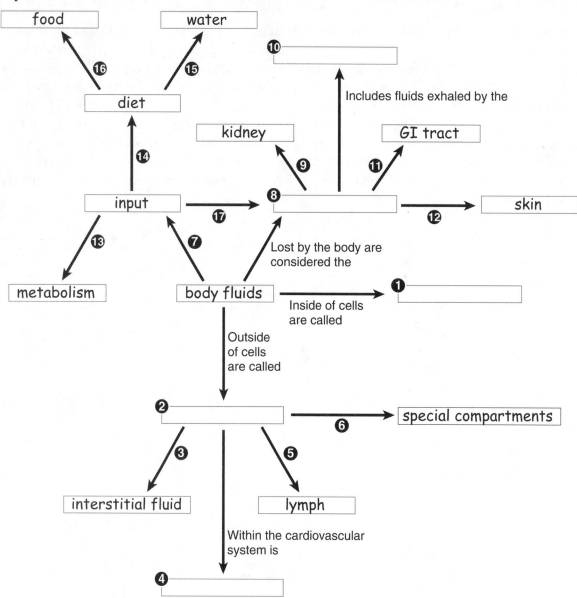

food

water

10

Includes fluids exhaled by the

diet

16

15

kidney

GI tract

14

9

11

input

8

skin

17

12

13

7

Lost by the body are
considered the

metabolism

body fluids

1

Inside of cells
are called

Outside
of cells
are called

2

special compartments

6

3

5

interstitial fluid

lymph

Within the cardiovascular
system is

4

Testing Your Knowledge

Building Understanding

I. Multiple Choice

Select the best answer and write the letter of your choice in the blank.

1. Select the correct order of urine flow from its source to the outside of the body.
   a. urethra, bladder, kidney, ureter
   b. bladder, kidney, urethra, ureter
   c. kidney, ureter, bladder, urethra
   d. kidney, urethra, bladder, ureter

   1. _____

2. Select the correct order of filtrate flow through the nephron
   a. nephron loop, distal convoluted tubule, proximal convoluted tubule, collecting duct
   b. glomerular capsule, proximal convoluted tubule, nephron loop, distal convoluted tubule
   c. proximal convoluted tubule, distal convoluted tubule, nephron loop, glomerular capsule
   d. glomerular capsule, distal convoluted tubule, proximal convoluted tubule, collecting duct

   2. _____

3. The enzyme renin raises blood pressure by activating
   a. urea
   b. glomerular filtration
   c. angiotensin
   d. erythropoietin

   3. _____

4. The juxtaglomerular apparatus consists of cells in the
   a. proximal convoluted tubule and efferent arteriole
   b. renal artery and afferent arteriole
   c. collecting tubules and renal vein
   d. distal convoluted tubule and afferent arteriole

   4. _____

5. Which of the following is NOT a function of the kidneys?
   a. red blood cell destruction
   b. blood pressure regulation
   c. elimination of nitrogenous wastes
   d. modification of body fluid composition

   5. _____

6. The movement of a substance from the distal convoluted tubule to the peritubular capillaries occurs by the process of
   a. secretion
   b. filtration
   c. reabsorption
   d. excretion

   6. _____

7. Urine does NOT usually contain
   a. sodium
   b. hydrogen
   c. casts
   d. urea

   7. _____

8. The process of expelling urine is called   8. _____
   a. reabsorption
   b. micturition
   c. dehydration
   d. defecation
9. Aldosterone is produced by the   9. _____
   a. hypothalamus
   b. pituitary
   c. kidney
   d. adrenal cortex
10. Antidiuretic hormone   10. _____
    a. increases salt excretion by the kidney
    b. inhibits thirst
    c. decreases urine production
    d. increases calcium reabsorption by the kidney
11. Normal bone formation requires   11. _____
    a. calcium
    b. phosphate
    c. neither calcium nor phosphate
    d. both calcium and phosphate
12. Which of the following is NOT a buffer?   12. _____
    a. hemoglobin
    b. bicarbonate
    c. oxygen
    d. phosphate
13. Which of the following fluids is NOT in the extracellular compartment? 13. _____
    a. cytoplasm
    b. cerebrospinal fluid
    c. lymph
    d. interstitial fluid

II. Completion Exercise

Write the word or phrase that correctly completes each sentence.

1. When the bladder is empty, its lining is thrown into the folds known as _____.

2. The vessel that brings blood to the glomerulus is the _____.

3. The most distal portion of the nephron is the _____.

4. Fluid passes from capillaries into the glomerular capsule of the nephron by the process of _____.

5. A negatively charged electrolyte is called a(n) _____.

6. The receptors that detect an increase in body fluid concentration are called _____.

7. The electrolyte that plays the largest role in maintaining body fluid volume is _____.

8. Water balance is partly regulated by a thirst center located in a region of the brain called the _____.

9. The hormone that decreases blood volume is _____.

Understanding Concepts

I. True/False

For each question, write *T* for true or *F* for false in the blank to the left of each number. If a statement is false, correct it by replacing the underlined term and write the correct statement in the blank below the question.

_____ 1. The movement of hydrogen ions from the peritubular capillaries into the distal convoluted tubule is an example of tubular secretion.

_____

_____ 2. Urine with a specific gravity of 0.05 is more concentrated than urine with a specific gravity of 0.04.

_____

_____ 3. Aldosterone tends to decrease the amount of urine produced.

_____

_____ 4. Adults can control the internal urethral sphincter.

_____

_____ 5. The triangular-shaped region in the floor of the bladder is called the renal pelvis.

_____

_____ 6. Most water loss occurs through the actions of the digestive system.

_____

_____ 7. The exhalation of carbon dioxide makes the blood more <u>acidic</u>.

_____

_____ 8. The fluids found in joint capsules and in the eyeball are examples of <u>extracellular</u> fluids.

_____

_____ 9. The organ that excretes the largest amount of water per day is the <u>skin</u>.

_____

II. Practical Applications

Study each discussion. Then write the appropriate word or phrase in the space provided.

➤ Group A

1. Ms. S, age 26, was teaching English in rural India. She developed severe diarrhea, probably as a result of a questionable pakora from a road-side stand. On admission to a hospital, she was found to be severely dehydrated. Ms. S's blood will contain high levels of a hormone synthesized by the hypothalamus called _____.

2. The physician's first concern was to increase Ms. S's plasma volume. Her fluid deficit was addressed by administering a 0.9% sodium chloride solution. This solution contains the same concentration of solutes as Ms. S's cells and is thus termed _____.

3. Next, the physician addressed Ms. S's acid–base balance. The pH of a blood sample was tested. The laboratory technician was looking for a pH value outside the normal range. The normal range pH of blood is _____.

4. Ms. S's blood pH was found to be abnormal, and sodium bicarbonate was added to her IV. Bicarbonate is an example of a substance that helps maintain a constant pH. These substances are known as _____.

➤ Group B

1. Young S, age 1, was brought to the hospital with an enlarged abdomen. His blood pressure was abnormally high, suggesting that S may suffer from hypertension. This disorder can result from abnormally high levels of renin. Renin is produced by a specialized region of the kidney called the _____.

2. S was administered a medication that blocks the activation of the renin substrate. Renin activates a substance called _____.

3. Further testing showed that S was suffering from the irreversible loss of the small units of the kidney that produce urine. These units are the _____.

4. S's enlarged abdomen is due to the accumulation of fluid outside cells. Body fluids that are not intracellular are termed _____.

5. S was also quite lethargic, due to a deficiency in red blood cells. This deficiency probably reflects the fact that the kidney synthesizes a hormone called _____.

III. *Short Essays*

1. Compare and contrast the processes of filtration and secretion. Name at least one similarity and two differences.

   _____

   _____

   _____

   _____

   _____

2. Explain why breath holding will increase blood acidity, and how the kidney would respond to repeated eposides of breath holding.

   _____

   _____

   _____

Conceptual Thinking

1. Ms. W has just eaten a large bag of salty popcorn. Her blood is now too salty and must be diluted. Is it possible for the kidney to increase water reabsorption without increasing salt absorption? Explain.

   _____

   _____

   _____

2. Mr. R is taking penicillin to cure a throat infection. He must take the drug frequently, because the kidney clears penicillin very efficiently. That is, all of the penicillin that enters the renal artery leaves the kidney in the urine. However, only some penicillin molecules will be filtered into the glomerular capsule. How can the kidney excrete all of the penicillin it receives?

   _____

   _____

   _____

3. Ms. J is stranded on a desert island with limited water supplies. A. How will the volume and concentration of her body fluids change? B. How will her hypothalamus and pituitary gland respond to these changes? C. What will be the net effect of these responses?

   _____

   _____

   _____

Expanding Your Horizons

"Space. The final frontier." The classic statement from the show *Star Trek* remains valid in terms of human physiology. The effects of prolonged weightlessness and space travel on the human body remain an area of hot research. One effect of weightlessness is a dramatic redistribution of body fluids. You can read all about this and other effects of space travel in *Scientific American*.

Resources

1. White RJ. Weightlessness and the human body. *Sci Am* 1998; 279:58–63.

UNIT VI

Perpetuation of Life

➤ **Chapter 20**

The Male
and Female
Reproductive
Systems

➤ **Chapter 21**

Development
and Heredity

The Male and Female Reproductive Systems

Overview

Reproduction is the process by which life continues. Human reproduction is **sexual,** that is, it requires the union of two different **germ cells** or **gametes.** (Some simple forms of life can reproduce without a partner in the process of **asexual** reproduction.) These germ cells, the **spermatozoon** in males and the **ovum** in females, are formed by **meiosis,** a type of cell division in which the chromosome number is reduced to one half. When fertilization occurs and the gametes combine, the original chromosome number is restored.

The reproductive glands or **gonads** manufacture the gametes and also produce hormones. These activities are continuous in the male but cyclic in the female. The male gonad is the **testis.** The remainder of the male reproductive tract consists of passageways for storage and transport of spermatozoa; the male organ of copulation, the **penis;** and several glands that contribute to the production of **semen.**

The female gonad is the **ovary.** The ovum released each month at the time of **ovulation** travels through the **oviducts** to the **uterus,** where the egg, if fertilized, develops. If no fertilization occurs, the ovum, along with the built-up lining of the uterus, is eliminated through the **vagina** as the **menstrual flow.**

Reproduction is under the control of hormones from the **anterior pituitary,** which in turn is controlled by the **hypothalamus** of the brain. These organs respond to **feedback** mechanisms, which maintain proper hormone levels.

Aging causes changes in both the male and female reproductive systems. A gradual decrease in male hormone production begins as early as age 20 and continues throughout life. In the female, a more sudden decrease in activity occurs between ages 45 and 55 and ends in **menopause,** the cessation of menstruation and the childbearing years.

Addressing the Learning Outcomes

Note that the learning outcomes address male and female reproductive physiology together, while the textbook covers them in separate sections. Use these exercises to compare the anatomy and physiology of the male and the female.

1. Name the male and female gonads and describe the function of each. (Note that the female gonad is shown in Exercise 20-6.)

EXERCISE 20-1: Structure of the Testis (Text Fig. 20-2)

INSTRUCTIONS

Label the indicated parts. (Hint: The vein is more branched than the artery.)

1. _____
2. _____
3. _____
4. _____
5. _____
6. _____
7. _____
8. _____
9. _____
10. _____
11. _____
12. _____

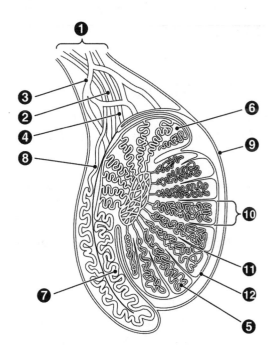

EXERCISE 20-2.

INSTRUCTIONS

Write the appropriate term in each blank.

interstitial cell   sustentacular cell   spermatozoon
seminiferous tubule   ovarian follicle   ovum

1. A cell that nourishes and protects developing spermatozoa   _____
2. A cell that secretes testosterone   _____
3. The germ cell of the male   _____
4. The germ cell of the female   _____
5. The cluster of cells that surrounds the female germ cell   _____

2. State the purpose of meiosis.

EXERCISE 20-3.

INSTRUCTIONS

In the blank following each statement, write T if the statement is true and F if it is false.

1. Meiosis only occurs in germ cells. _____
2. After meiosis occurs, the cells will have the same number of chromosomes as the parent cell.

   _____

3. List the accessory organs of the male and female reproductive tracts and cite the function of each.

EXERCISE 20-4: Male Reproductive System (Text Fig. 20-1)

INSTRUCTIONS

1. On the diagram on the next page, write the names of the structures that are not part of the reproductive system on the appropriate lines 1 to 6 in different colors. Use the same color for structures 1 and 2 and for structures 4 and 5. Color the structures on the diagram.
2. Write the names of the parts of the male reproductive system on the appropriate lines 7 to 20 in different colors. Use the same color for structures 10 and 11. Color the structures on the diagram.

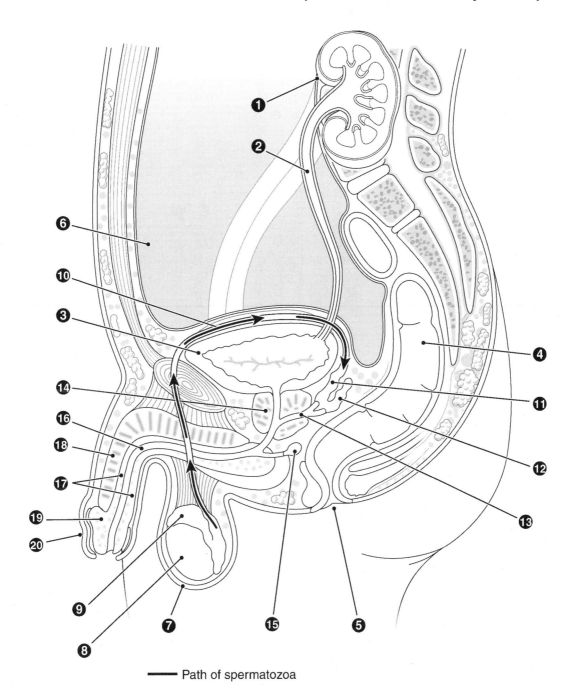

Path of spermatozoa

1. _____   11. _____
2. _____   12. _____
3. _____   13. _____
4. _____   14. _____
5. _____   15. _____
6. _____   16. _____
7. _____   17. _____
8. _____   18. _____
9. _____   19. _____
10. _____   20. _____

EXERCISE 20-5: Cross-section of the Penis (Text Fig. 20-5)

INSTRUCTIONS

1. Write the names of the parts on the appropriate lines in different colors. (Hint: the nerve is solid and the veins have larger lumens than the artery.)
2. Color the structures on the diagram.

1. _____

2. _____

3. _____

4. _____

5. _____

6. _____

7. _____

8. _____

9. _____

10. _____

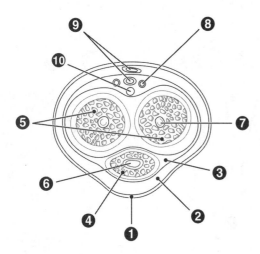

EXERCISE 20-6: Female Reproductive System (Text Fig. 20-6)

INSTRUCTIONS

1. Write the names of the parts on the appropriate lines in different colors. Use the same color for parts 8 and 9, for parts 10 to 13, and for parts 14 and 15.
2. Color the structures on the diagram.

1. _____
2. _____
3. _____
4. _____
5. _____
6. _____
7. _____
8. _____

9. _____
10. _____
11. _____
12. _____
13. _____
14. _____
15. _____
16. _____

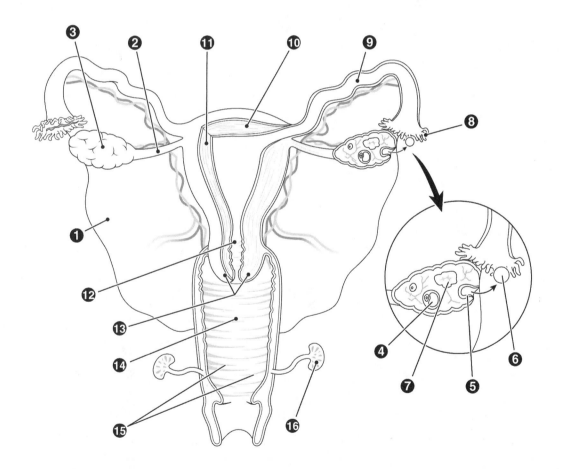

EXERCISE 20-7: Female Reproductive System (Sagittal Section) (Text Fig. 20-9)

INSTRUCTIONS

1. Write the names of the structures that are not part of the reproductive system on the appropriate lines 1 to 8 in different colors. Use the same color for structures 1 and 2, for structures 3 and 4, and for structures 5 and 6. Color the structures on the diagram.
2. Write the names of the parts of the female reproductive system and supporting ligaments on the appropriate lines 9 to 19 in different colors. Use the same color for structures 15 and 16. Color the structures on the diagram.

1. _____
2. _____
3. _____
4. _____
5. _____
6. _____
7. _____
8. _____
9. _____
10. _____

11. _____
12. _____
13. _____
14. _____
15. _____
16. _____
17. _____
18. _____
19. _____

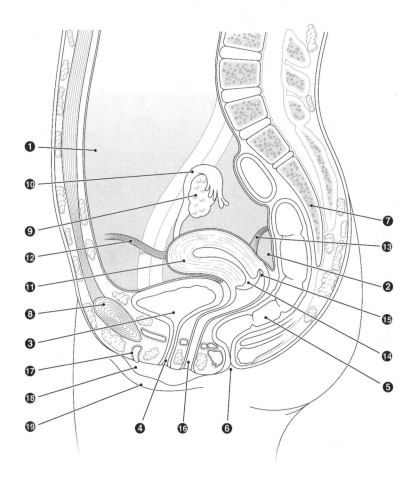

EXERCISE 20-8: External Parts of the Female Reproductive System (Text Fig. 20-10)

INSTRUCTIONS

Label the indicated parts.

1. _____
2. _____
3. _____
4. _____
5. _____
6. _____
7. _____
8. _____
9. _____

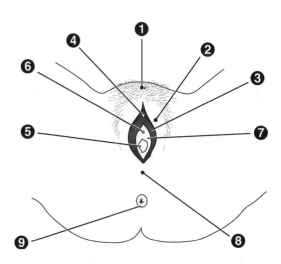

EXERCISE 20-9.

INSTRUCTIONS

Write the appropriate term in each blank.

epididymis   vas deferens   seminal vesicle   prostate gland   ejaculatory duct
fimbriae   oviduct   bulbourethral gland   greater vestibular gland

1. One of the two glands that secrete a thick, yellow, alkaline secretion   _____
2. The gland that secretes a thin, alkaline secretion and that can contract to aid in ejaculation   _____
3. The coiled tube in which spermatozoa are stored as they mature and become motile   _____
4. The tube that transports the female germ cells   _____
5. Fringelike extensions that sweep the ovum into the uterine tube   _____
6. A gland in the female reproductive tract that secretes into the vagina   _____
7. A duct in the male that empties into the urethra   _____
8. A gland located inferior to the prostate that secretes mucus during sexual stimulation   _____

EXERCISE 20-10.

INSTRUCTIONS

Write the appropriate term in each blank.

cervix   myometrium   fundus   vestibule
endometrium   fornix   hymen   perineum

1. The Bartholin glands secrete into this area   _____
2. The vaginal region around the cervix   _____
3. The specialized tissue that lines the uterus   _____
4. The small, rounded part of the uterus located above the openings of the oviducts   _____
5. A fold of membrane found at the opening of the vagina   _____
6. The necklike part of the uterus that dips into the upper vagina   _____
7. The muscular wall of the uterus   _____

4. Describe the composition and function of semen.

EXERCISE 20-11.

INSTRUCTIONS

In the spaces below, list 5 functions of semen.

1. _____
2. _____
3. _____
4. _____
5. _____

5. Draw and label a spermatozoon.

EXERCISE 20-12: Diagram of a Human Spermatozoon (Text Fig. 20-4)

INSTRUCTIONS

1. Write the names of the parts on the appropriate lines in different colors. Use black for structures 1 to 3, because they will not be colored.
2. Color the structures on the diagram.

1. _____
2. _____
3. _____
4. _____
5. _____
6. _____
7. _____

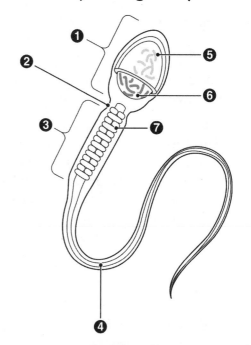

6. List in the correct order the hormones produced during the menstrual cycle and cite the source of each.

EXERCISE 20-13: The Menstrual Cycle (Text Fig. 20-11)

INSTRUCTIONS

1. Identify the hormone responsible for each of the numbered lines in graph A, and write the hormone names on the appropriate lines in different colors. Trace over the lines in the graph with the appropriate color.
2. Write the names of the phases of the ovarian cycle (part B) and the uterine cycle (part C) on the appropriate lines.

1. _____
2. _____
3. _____
4. _____
5. _____
6. _____
7. _____
8. _____
9. _____
10. _____

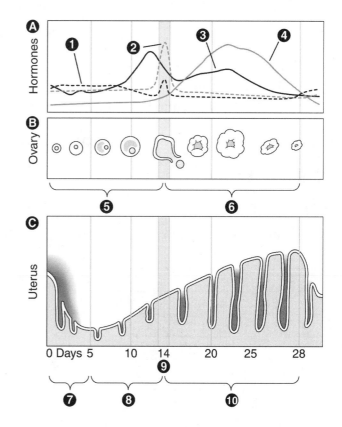

7. Describe the functions of the main male and female sex hormones.

EXERCISE 20-14.

INSTRUCTIONS

Write the appropriate term in each blank.

luteinizing hormone   follicle stimulating hormone   testosterone   estrogen
corpus luteum   ovulation   menstruation   progesterone

1. A hormone that is produced only during the luteal phase of the menstrual cycle   _____
2. An ovarian hormone that is produced during the follicular and luteal phases of the menstrual cycle   _____
3. A hormone produced by the testicular interstitial cells   _____
4. Discharge of an ovum from the surface of the ovary   _____
5. The hormone that stimulates Sertoli cells   _____
6. The structure formed by the ruptured follicle after ovulation   _____
7. The phase of the menstrual cycle when the endometrium is degenerating   _____

8. Explain how negative feedback regulates reproductive function in both males and females.

EXERCISE 20-15.

INSTRUCTIONS

For each statement, choose the correct term from the two in brackets.

1. Testosterone _____ [stimulates, inhibits] the production of FSH and LH.
2. Just before ovulation, high estrogen levels _____ [stimulate, inhibit] the production of LH.
3. During the rest of the menstrual cycle, estrogen and/or progesterone _____ [stimulate, inhibit] the production of FSH and LH.

9. Describe the changes that occur during and after menopause.

EXERCISE 20-16.

INSTRUCTIONS

Write 5 different changes that may be associated with menopause in the spaces below.

1. _____
2. _____
3. _____
4. _____
5. _____

10. Cite the main methods of birth control in use.

EXERCISE 20-17.

INSTRUCTIONS

Write the appropriate term in each blank.

IUD	birth control patch	birth control ring	tubal ligation
male condom	diaphragm	vasectomy	

1. A method used to administer estrogen and progesterone through the skin _____
2. A device implanted into the uterus that prevents fertilization and implantation _____
3. A rubber cap fitted over the cervix _____
4. The birth control method that is also highly effective against sexually transmitted infections _____
5. A method used to administer birth control hormones internally _____
6. A surgical method of birth control in females _____

11. Show how word parts are used to build words related to the reproductive systems.

EXERCISE 20-18.

INSTRUCTIONS

Complete the following table by writing the correct word part or meaning in the space provided. Write a word that contains each word part in the Example column.

Word Part	Meaning	Example
1. _____	extreme end	_____
2. semin/o-	_____	_____
3. _____	egg	_____
4. metr/o	_____	_____
5. test/o	_____	_____
6. _____	around	_____
7. fer	_____	_____
8. rect/o	_____	_____

Making the Connections

The following concept map deals with the organization of the reproductive system. Each pair of terms is linked together by a connecting phrase into a sentence. The sentence should be read in the direction of the arrow. Complete the concept map by filling in the appropriate term or phrase. There is one right answer for each term (1, 2, 4, 14). However, there are many correct answers for the connecting phrases.

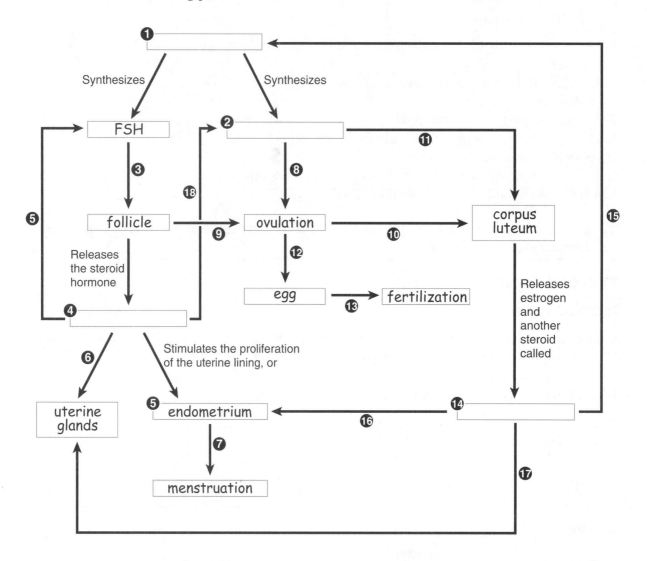

Optional Exercise: Make your own concept map, based on male reproductive anatomy and physiology. Choose your own terms to incorporate into your map, or use the following list: spermatozoon, testosterone, testis, FSH, LH, interstitial cell, epididymis, vas deferens, seminiferous tubule, Sertoli cell, prostate gland, bulbourethral gland, and penis.

Testing Your Knowledge

Building Understanding

I. Multiple Choice

Select the best answer and write the letter of your choice in the blank.

1. The corpus luteum secretes
   a. testosterone
   b. progesterone
   c. FSH
   d. LH

   1. _____

2. Which of the following is NOT part of the uterus?
   a. cervix
   b. fimbriae
   c. endometrium
   d. corpus

   2. _____

3. Spermatozoa develop in the walls of the
   a. prostate gland
   b. penis
   c. seminal vesicles
   d. seminiferous tubules

   3. _____

4. The glans penis is formed from the
   a. corpus spongiosum
   b. corpus cavernosum
   c. pubic symphysis
   d. vas deferens

   4. _____

5. The ovum develops within the
   a. corpus luteum
   b. ovarian follicle
   c. interstitial cells
   d. Sertoli cells

   5. _____

6. Which of the following glands is found in the female?
   a. greater vestibular glands
   b. bulbourethral glands
   c. Cowper glands
   d. prostate gland

   6. _____

7. Semen does NOT contain
   a. seminal fluid
   b. a high concentration of hydrogen ions
   c. sugar
   d. sperm

   7. _____

II. Completion Exercise

Write the word or phrase that correctly completes each sentence.

1. The enzyme-containing cap on the head of a spermatozoon is called the _____.
2. The hormone that promotes development of spermatozoa in the male and development of ova in the female is _____.
3. The process of cell division that reduces the chromosome number by half is _____.
4. The testes are contained in an external sac called the _____.
5. The main male sex hormone is _____.
6. The pelvic floor in both males and females is called the _____.
7. The hormone that stimulates ovulation is _____.
8. In the male, the tube that carries urine away from the bladder also carries sperm cells. This tube is the _____.
9. The surgical removal of the foreskin of the penis is called _____.

Understanding Concepts
I. True/False

For each question, write *T* for true or *F* for false in the blank to the left of each number. If a statement is false, correct it by replacing the underlined term and write the correct statement in the blank below the question.

_____ 1. The urethra is contained in the corpus spongiosum of the penis.

_____

_____ 2. When estrogen and progesterone levels are high, luteinizing hormone secretion is inhibited.

_____

_____ 3. Gametes are produced by the process of mitosis.

_____

_____ 4. Progesterone levels are highest during the follicular phase of the menstrual cycle.

_____

_____ 5. Progesterone is the first ovarian hormone produced in the menstrual cycle.

_____

_____ 6. A deficiency in luteinizing hormone would result in testosterone deficiency.

_____

II. Practical Applications

Study each discussion. Then write the appropriate word or phrase in the space provided.

➤ Group A

1. Ms. J, age 22, reported painful menstrual cramps and excessive menstrual flow. Menstruation is the shedding of the uterine layer called the _____.
2. The physician suggested anti-inflammatory medication, but Ms. J had previously tried medication to no avail. An alternate approach was tried, in which the passageway between the vagina and uterus was artificially dilated. The part of the uterus containing this passageway is the _____.
3. It was also suggested that Ms. J take contraceptive pills. These pills contain two ovarian steroids, progesterone and _____.
4. These hormones prevent ovulation by inhibiting the secretion of a pituitary hormone called _____.

➤ Group B

1. Mr. and Ms. S, both age 35, had been trying to conceive for 2 years with no success. Analysis of Mr. S's semen revealed a low concentration of the male gametes, known as _____.
2. Blood tests were performed, revealing a deficiency in the pituitary hormone that acts on sustentacular cells. This hormone is called _____.
3. Conversely, testosterone production was normal. The cells that produce testosterone are called _____.
4. Mr. S's hormone deficiency was successfully treated, and Mr. and Ms. S became the proud parents of triplets. Mr. S went to the clinic soon after the birth, and the duct extending from the epididymis to the ejaculatory duct was cut to prevent further conceptions. This duct is called the _____.

III. Short Essays

1. Discuss changes occurring in the ovary and in the uterus during the follicular phase of the menstrual cycle.

_____

_____

_____

2. Compare and contrast the male and female gametes. Discuss their structure and their production.

_____

_____

_____

Conceptual Thinking

1. Mr. S is taking synthetic testosterone in order to improve his wrestling performance. To his alarm, he notices that his testicles are shrinking. Explain why this is happening.

_____

_____

_____

2. Compare and contrast the role of FSH in the regulation of the male and female gonad.

_____

_____

_____

Expanding Your Horizons

Have you heard of kamikaze sperm? Based on studies in animals, some animal behavior researchers have hypothesized that semen contains a population of spermatozoa that is capable of destroying spermatozoa from a competing male. A "sperm team" contains blockers, which are misshapen spermatozoa with multiple tails and/or heads. Other sperm, the kamikaze spermatozoa, seek out and destroy spermatozoa from other males. A very small population of egg-getting spermatozoa attempts to fertilize the ovum. Although some aspects of this hypothesis have been challenged, the presence of sperm subpopulations is now well established. You can read more about the kamikaze sperm hypothesis in the following scientific articles.

Resources

1. Baker RR, Bellis MA. Elaboration of the Kamikaze sperm hypothesis: a reply to Harcourt. _Anim Behav_ 1989; 37:865–867.
2. Moore HD, Martin M, Birkhead TR. No evidence for killer sperm or other selective interactions between human spermatozoa in ejaculates of different males in vitro. _Proc R Soc Lond B Biol Sci_ 1999; 266:2343–2350.

CHAPTER 21 Development and Heredity

Overview

Pregnancy begins with fertilization of an ovum by a spermatozoon to form a **zygote**. Over the next 38 weeks of **gestation**, the offspring develops first as an **embryo** and then as a **fetus**. During this period, it is nourished and maintained by the **placenta**, formed from tissues of both the mother and the embryo. The placenta secretes a number of hormones, including progesterone, estrogen, human chorionic gonadotropin, human placental lactogen, and relaxin. These hormones induce changes in the uterus and breasts to support the pregnancy and prepare for childbirth and milk production.

Childbirth or **parturition** occurs in four stages, beginning with contractions of the uterus and dilation of the cervix. Subsequent stages include delivery of the infant, delivery of the afterbirth, and control of bleeding. Milk production, or **lactation**, is stimulated by the hormones prolactin and oxytocin. Milk removal from the breasts stimulates further production.

The scientific study of heredity has advanced with amazing speed in the past 50 years. Nevertheless, many mysteries remain. Gregor Mendel was the first person known to have carried out formal experiments in genetics. He identified independent units of heredity, which he called factors and which we now call **genes**.

The chromosomes in the nucleus of each cell are composed of a complex molecule, **DNA**. This material makes up the many thousands of genes that determine a person's traits and are passed on to offspring at the time of fertilization. Genes direct the formation of **enzymes**, which in turn make possible all the chemical reactions of metabolism. Defective genes, produced by **mutation**, may disrupt normal enzyme activity and result in hereditary disorders such as sickle cell anemia, albinism, and phenylketonuria. Some human traits are determined by a single pair of genes (one gene from each parent), but most are controlled by multiple pairs of genes acting together.

Genes may be classified as **dominant** or **recessive**. If one parent contributes a dominant gene, then any offspring who receives that gene will show the trait (e.g., Huntington disease). Traits carried by recessive genes may remain hidden for generations and be revealed only if they are contributed by both parents (e.g., blue eyes).

Addressing the Learning Outcomes

1. Describe fertilization and the early development of the fertilized egg.

EXERCISE 21-1.

INSTRUCTIONS

Write the appropriate term in each blank.

gestation   zygote   embryo   implantation   fetus   ovum

1. The fertilized egg   _____
2. The developing offspring from the third month until birth   _____
3. The entire period of development in the uterus   _____
4. Attachment of the fertilized egg to the lining of the uterus   _____
5. The developing offspring from implantation until the third month   _____

2. Describe the structure and function of the placenta (also see Exercise 21-3).

EXERCISE 21-2.

INSTRUCTIONS

Write the appropriate term in each blank.

placenta   venous sinuses   placental villi   umbilical cord
human placental lactogen   human chorionic gonadotropin   relaxin

1. The hormone that loosens the pubic symphysis and softens the cervix for parturition   _____
2. A hormone that prepares the breasts for lactation and alters maternal metabolism   _____
3. A placental hormone that stimulates progesterone synthesis and is detected by pregnancy tests   _____
4. The structure that serves as the organ for nutrition, respiration, and excretion for the fetus   _____
5. The portion of the placenta containing fetal capillaries   _____
6. Channels in the placenta containing maternal blood   _____

3. Describe how fetal circulation differs from adult circulation.

EXERCISE 21-3: Fetal Circulation (Text Fig. 21-2)

INSTRUCTIONS

1. On the diagram on the next page, label the parts of the fetal circulation and placenta. (Hint: you can differentiate between the uterine arterioles and uterine venules by following the path of the vessels into the umbilical arteries and vein.)
2. Color the boxes in the legend using the following color scheme: color the oxygen-rich blood box red, the oxygen-poor blood box blue, and the mixed blood box purple.
3. As much as possible, color the blood vessels on the diagram with the appropriate color, based on the oxygen content of the blood.

1. _____
2. _____
3. _____
4. _____
5. _____
6. _____
7. _____
8. _____
9. _____
10. _____

☐ Oxygen-rich blood
☐ Oxygen-poor blood
☐ Mixed blood

11. _____
12. _____
13. _____
14. _____
15. _____
16. _____
17. _____
18. _____

4. Briefly describe changes that occur in the fetus and the mother during pregnancy.

EXERCISE 21-4: Midsagittal Section of a Pregnant Uterus (Text Fig. 21-5)

INSTRUCTIONS

Write the name of each labeled part on the numbered lines.

1. _____   8. _____

2. _____   9. _____

3. _____   10. _____

4. _____   11. _____

5. _____   12. _____

6. _____   13. _____

7. _____   14. _____

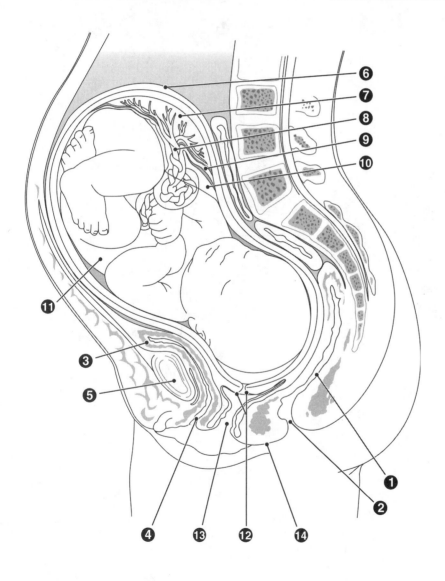

EXERCISE 21-5.

INSTRUCTIONS

Write the appropriate term in each blank.

vernix caseosa   ultrasonography   amniotic sac
ductus arteriosus   foramen ovale   ductus venosus

1. The structure that surrounds the developing offspring and serves
   as a protective cushion   _____
2. A small vessel joining the pulmonary artery to the descending aorta   _____
3. A small hole in the fetal atrial septum   _____
4. The cheeselike material that protects the skin of the fetus   _____
5. A technique commonly used to monitor fetal development   _____

5. Briefly describe the four stages of labor.

EXERCISE 21-6.

INSTRUCTIONS

Write the appropriate term in each blank.

oxytocin   prostaglandin   cortisol   first stage   second stage   third stage   fourth stage

1. A fetal hormone that inhibits maternal progesterone secretion and
   stimulates uterine contractions   _____
2. The hormone that can initiate labor and stimulate milk ejection   _____
3. A substance produced by the myometrium that stimulates uterine
   contractions   _____
4. The stage of labor that begins when the cervix is completely dilated   _____
5. The stage of labor that ends with the expulsion of the afterbirth   _____
6. The stage of labor in which both the baby and the afterbirth have
   been expelled   _____
7. The stage of labor during which the cervix dilates   _____

6. Compare fraternal and identical twins.

EXERCISE 21-7.

INSTRUCTIONS

Write "F" in the blank following statements applying to fraternal twins and "I" in the blank following statements applying to identical twins.

1. Twins formed from a single zygote _____
2. Twins formed from the fertilization of two ova by two spermatozoa _____
3. Twins that may be of the same sex or different sexes _____
4. Twins that are genetically identical _____
5. Twins that always have their own placenta _____

7. Cite the advantages of breastfeeding.

EXERCISE 21-8: Section of the Breast (Text Fig. 21-7)

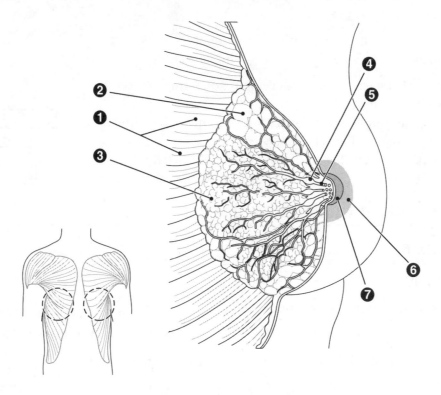

INSTRUCTIONS

Write the name of each labeled part on the numbered lines.

1. _____
2. _____
3. _____
4. _____
5. _____
6. _____
7. _____

EXERCISE 21-9.

INSTRUCTIONS

Briefly summarize four advantages of breastfeeding in the spaces below.

1. _____
2. _____
3. _____
4. _____

8. Briefly describe the mechanism of gene function.

EXERCISE 21-10.

INSTRUCTIONS

In the blank following each statement, write "T" if the statement is true and "F" if it is false.

1. Genes are segments of proteins. ____
2. Genes contain the blueprints to make proteins. ____
3. Genes are composed of DNA. ____
4. Genes code for specific traits. ____
5. Humans have 46 autosomes. ____
6. Humans have 46 chromosomes. ____

9. Explain the difference between dominant and recessive genes.

EXERCISE 21-11.

INSTRUCTIONS

Write the appropriate term in each blank.

heterozygous   homozygous   autosome   sex chromosome
recessive   dominant   allele

1. One member of a gene pair that controls a specific trait   _____
2. Term describing a gene that expresses its effect only if homozygous   _____
3. A gene pair consisting of two dominant or two recessive alleles   _____
4. Any chromosome except the X and Y chromosomes   _____
5. Term describing a gene pair composed of two different alleles   _____
6. Term describing a gene that expresses its effect if homozygous or heterozygous   _____

10. Compare phenotype and genotype and give examples of each.

EXERCISE 21-12.

INSTRUCTIONS

In the blank following each statement, write "P" if the statement applies to *phenotype* and "G" if it applies to *genotype.*

1. The genetic makeup of an individual ____
2. The characteristics that can be observed and/or measured ____
3. Eye color ____
4. Homozygous dominant ____
5. Blood type ____
6. Heterozygous ____

11. Describe what is meant by a carrier of a genetic trait.

EXERCISE 21-13.

INSTRUCTIONS

Circle the correct answer.

A carrier is:

A. an individual heterozygous for a recessive trait.
B. an individual heterozygous for a dominant trait.
C. an individual that shows the symptoms of a disease.
D. an individual homozygous for either a dominant or a recessive trait.

12. Define *meiosis* and explain its function in reproduction.

EXERCISE 21-14.

INSTRUCTIONS

In the blank following each statement, write "T" if the statement is true and "F" if it is false.

1. Following meiosis, each reproductive cell contains 46 chromosomes. _____
2. Following meiosis, each reproductive cell contains 23 chromosomes. _____
3. Some reproductive cells contain all of the maternal chromosomes, while other reproductive cells contain all of the paternal chromosomes. _____
4. Each reproductive cell contains a mix of maternal and paternal chromosomes. _____

13. Explain how sex is determined in humans.

EXERCISE 21-15.

INSTRUCTIONS

For each of the following examples, state if the genotype would result in a female phenotype (F) or a male phenotype (M), assuming that development proceeds normally.

1. Union between an X sperm and a X ovum _____
2. Union between an Y sperm and an X ovum _____

14. Describe what is meant by the term sex-linked and list several sex-linked traits.

EXERCISE 21-16.

INSTRUCTIONS

In the blank following each statement, write "S" if the statement refers to sex-linked traits or "A" if it applies to autosomal (non–sex-linked) traits.

1. A trait carried on the Y chromosome ____
2. A trait carried on the X chromosome ____
3. A trait carried on chromosomes other than the X or Y chromosomes ____
4. A trait for which males or females can be carriers ____
5. A trait for which only females can be carriers ____

15. List several factors that may influence the expression of a gene.

EXERCISE 21-17.

INSTRUCTIONS

In the spaces below, list three factors that influence gene expression.

1. _____
2. _____
3. _____

16. Define *mutation*.

EXERCISE 21-18.

INSTRUCTIONS

In the spaces below, define *mutation* and *mutagen*. In your definition of mutation, describe some different types of mutations.

1. mutation: _____

_____

2. mutagen: _____

_____

17. Show how word parts are used to build words related to development and heredity.

EXERCISE 21-19.

INSTRUCTIONS

Complete the following table by writing the correct word part or meaning in the space provided. Write a word that contains each word part in the Example column.

Word Part	Meaning	Example
1. _____	color	_____
2. zyg/o	_____	_____
3. _____	labor	_____
4. ox/y	_____	_____
5. chori/o	_____	_____
6. _____	body	_____
7. phen/o	_____	_____
8. _____	self	_____
9. _____	other, different	_____
10. homo-	_____	_____

Making the Connections

The following concept maps deal with different aspects of development (Map A) and heredity (Map B). Each pair of terms is linked together by a connecting phrase into a sentence. The sentence should be read in the direction of the arrow. Complete the concept map by filling in the appropriate term or phrase. There is one right answer for each term. However, there are many correct answers for the connecting phrases.

Map A

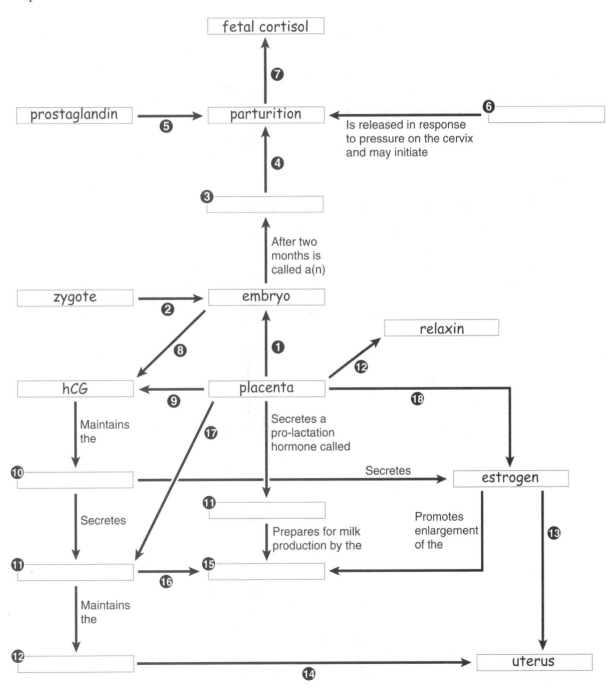

Map B

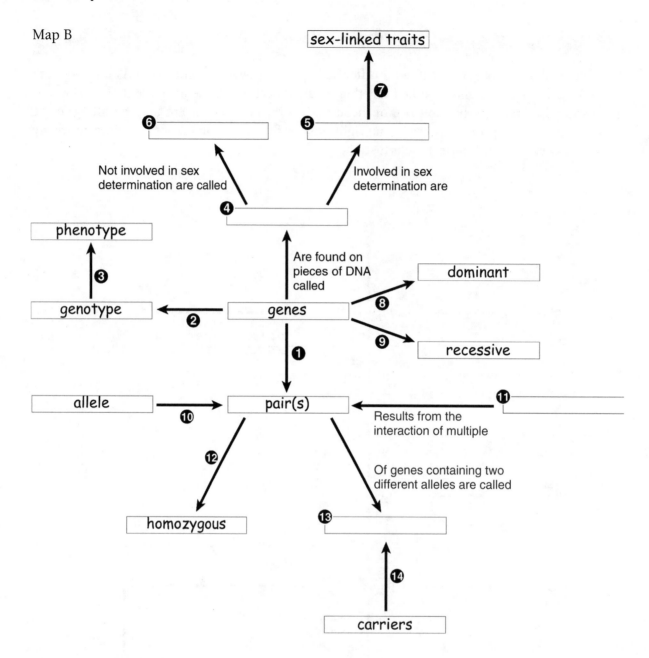

sex-linked traits

❻ [   ]   ❺ [   ]

Not involved in sex
determination are called   Involved in sex
determination are

❹ [   ]

phenotype

❸   Are found on
pieces of DNA
called   dominant

genotype   ◀ ❷   genes   ❽

❾

recessive

❶

allele   ➡ ❿   pair(s)   ◀ ⓫ [   ]

Results from the
interaction of multiple

⓬   Of genes containing two
different alleles are called

homozygous   ⓭ [   ]

⓮

carriers

Testing Your Knowledge

Building Understanding

I. Multiple Choice

Select the best answer and write the letter of your choice in the blank.

1. Contractions of the myometrium are stimulated by
   a. progesterone
   b. estrogen
   c. prolactin
   d. prostaglandin

   1. _____

2. The fetal circulation is designed to bypass the
   a. lungs
   b. placenta
   c. spleen
   d. brain

   2. _____

3. The second stage of labor includes
   a. the onset of contractions
   b. expulsion of the afterbirth
   c. passage of the fetus through the vagina
   d. expulsion of the placenta

   3. _____

4. The term *viable* is used to describe a fetus that is
   a. spontaneously aborted
   b. developing outside the uterus
   c. capable of living outside the uterus
   d. stillborn

   4. _____

5. Maternal blood is found in the
   a. umbilical cord
   b. placental villi
   c. venous sinuses of the placenta
   d. all of the above

   5. _____

6. Two parents with normal pigmentation can give birth to a child with albinism. Albinism is NOT a
   a. recessive disease
   b. dominant trait
   c. congenital disorder
   d. genetic disorder

   6. _____

7. Gender in humans is determined by
   a. the number of X chromosomes
   b. the sex chromosome carried by the ovum
   c. the number of autosomes
   d. the sex chromosome carried by the spermatozoon

   7. _____

8. Traits that are determined by more than one more gene pair are termed
   a. sex-linked
   b. recessive
   c. multifactorial
   d. dominant

   8. _____

II. Completion Exercise

Write the word or phrase that correctly completes each sentence.

1. A surgical cut and repair of the perineum to prevent tearing is called a(n) _____.

2. By the end of the first month of embryonic life, the beginnings of the extremities may be seen. These are four small swellings called _____.

3. The mammary glands of the female provide nourishment for the newborn through the secretion of milk; this is a process called _____.

4. The stage of labor during which the afterbirth is expelled from the uterus is the _____.

5. Twins that develop from the same fertilized egg are called _____.

6. The normal site of fertilization is the _____.

7. The clear liquid that flows from the uterus when the mother's "water breaks" is technically called _____.

8. The larger sex chromosome is called the _____.

9. A change in a gene or chromosome is called a(n) _____.

10. The number of autosomes in the human genome is _____.

11. The process of cell division that halves the chromosome number is called _____.

12. An agent that induces a change in chromosome structure is called a(n) _____.

Understanding Concepts

I. True/False

For each question, write *T* for true or *F* for false in the blank to the left of each number. If a statement is false, correct it by replacing the underlined term and write the correct statement in the blank below the question.

_____ 1. Ms. J is 7 weeks pregnant. Her uterus contains an embryo.

_____

_____ 2. The baby is delivered during the fourth stage of labor.

_____

_____ 3. Fraternal twins are genetically distinct.

_____

_____ 4. Blood is carried from the placenta to the fetus in the umbilical vein.

_____

_____ 5. Oxytocin secreted from the fetal adrenal gland may help induce labor.

_____

_____ 6. Sex-linked traits appear almost exclusively in <u>males</u>.

_____

_____ 7. The sex of the offspring is determined by the sex chromosome carried in the <u>spermatozoon</u>.

_____

_____ 8. Carriers for a particular gene are always <u>homozygous</u> for the gene.

_____

_____ 9. A recessive trait is expressed in individuals <u>heterozygous</u> for the recessive gene.

_____

II. Practical Applications

Study each discussion. Then write the appropriate word or phrase in the space provided.

➤ Group A

1. Mr. and Ms. L had been trying to conceive for 2 years. Finally, Ms. L realized her period was late and purchased a pregnancy detection kit. These kits test for the presence of a hormone produced exclusively by embryonic tissues that helps maintain the corpus luteum. This hormone is called _____.
2. The pregnancy test was positive. Based on the date of her last menstrual period, Ms. L was determined to be 6 weeks pregnant. The gestational age of Ms. L's new offspring at this time would be _____.
3. During a prenatal appointment 14 weeks later, Ms. L was able to see her future offspring using a technique for visualizing soft tissues without the use of x-rays. This technique is called _____.
4. The operation went smoothly, and baby L was born. Ms. L immediately began to breastfeed her infant. The first secretion from her breasts was not milk, but rather _____.

➤ Group B

1. Mr. and Ms. J have consulted a genetic counselor. Ms. J is 8-weeks pregnant, and cystic fibrosis runs in both of their families. Cystic fibrosis is a disease in which an individual may carry the disease gene but not have cystic fibrosis. A term to describe this type of trait is _____.
2. Mr. and Ms. J were screened for the presence of the cystic fibrosis gene. It was determined that both Mr. and Ms. J have the gene, even though they do not have cystic fibrosis. For the cystic fibrosis trait, they are both considered to be _____.
3. Ms. J wanted to know if her baby would have cystic fibrosis. Amniocentesis revealed that the fetus carried _____.
4. The analysis revealed the presence of two XX chromosomes. The gender of the baby is therefore _____.

➤ Group C

1. Mr. and Ms. B have a child with three copies of chromosome 21. This abnormality, like any change in DNA, is known as a(n) _____.
2. Chromosome 21 is one of 22 pairs of chromosomes known as _____.
3. The remainder of the child's chromosomes are normal. The total number of chromosomes in the child's cells is _____.
4. The chromosome abnormality arose during the production of gametes. The form of cell division that occurs exclusively in germ cell precursors is called _____.

III. Short Essays

1. Compare and contrast human placental lactogen (hPL) and human chorionic gonadotropin (hCG). Discuss the synthesis and action of each hormone.

   _____

   _____

   _____

2. Describe the site of synthesis and actions of the hormones involved in lactation and preparing the breasts for lactation.

   _____

   _____

   _____

3. Some traits in a population show a range instead of two clearly alternate forms. List some of these traits, and explain what causes this variety.

   _____

   _____

   _____

Conceptual Thinking

1. Trace the path of a blood cell from the placenta to the fetal heart and back to the placenta. Assume that this blood cell passes through the foramen ovale.

   _____

   _____

   _____

2. Ms. J has suffered from repeated miscarriages. Blood tests reveal a deficiency in progesterone. Could this deficiency be implicated in Ms. J's miscarriages?

   _____

   _____

   _____

3. Are identical twins identical individuals? Defend your answer, using the terms "genotype" and "phenotype."

   _____

   _____

   _____

Expanding Your Horizons

Have you ever wondered why animals can give birth alone, but humans require all sorts of technological equipment? Women rarely give birth alone, even in societies with few technological advances. The difficulties of human birth reflect some of our evolutionary adaptations. For instance, walking upright requires the pelvis to be backward, and the large human brain size results in large fetal skulls. You can read more about "The Evolution of Birth" in *Scientific American* article.

The movie *Gattaca* (1997) describes a futuristic world in which genetic screening and engineering are the norm. Everyone has a genetic description (including lifespan) available to potential mates, and virtually everyone (except the hero) is genetically engineered. Genetic screening determines one's future on Gattaca, and genetic engineering has essentially abolished independent thought and creativity. Science fiction aside, genetic screening and engineering may soon become a technological reality in our society. What are the implications of genetic screening and engineering? Will a poor genetic outlook affect health insurance coverage and job prospects? Will society genetically engineer away creativity? The articles listed below can provide you with more information about the use and abuse of genetic testing.

Resources

1. Rosenberg KR, Trevathan WR. *Sci Am* 2001; 285:72–77.
2. Hodge JG, Jr. Ethical issues concerning genetic testing and screening in public health. *Am J Med Genet* 2004; 125C:66–70.
3. Sermon K, Van Steirteghem A, Liebaers I. Preimplantation genetic diagnosis. *Lancet* 2004; 363:1633–1641.